IntranetWare/NetWare 4.11 Administration, Troubleshooting, and TCP/IP

Mike Mutasem Awwad, CNE

Prentice Hall
Upper Saddle River, New Jersey   Columbus, Ohio

Library of Congress Cataloging-in-Publication Data

Awwad, Mike Mutasem.
    IntranetWare/NetWare 4.11: administration, troubleshooting, and TCP/IP /
  Mike Mutasem Awwad.
        p.   cm.
    ISBN 0-13-927138-4
    1.   Novell IntranetWare. 2. NetWare (Computer file) 3. Intranets (Computer networks)
I. Title.
    TK5105.8.8N65A98 2000
    005.4'4769—dc21   99-17221
                                                                                CIP

Editor: Charles Stewart
Production Editor: Rachel Besen
Production Manager: Deidra Schwartz
Cover Designer: Alice Shikina
Director of Marketing: Ben Leonard

This book was set in Times Roman by Mike Awwad and Bret Workman and was printed and bound by
R.R. Donnelley & Sons. The cover was printed by Phoenix Color.

©2000 by Prentice-Hall, Inc.
Pearson Education
Upper Saddle River, New Jersey 07458

Printed in the United States of America

10 9 8 7 6 5 4 3 2

ISBN: 0-13-927138-4

Prentice-Hall International (UK) Limited, *London*
Prentice-Hall of Australia Pty. Limited, *Sydney*
Prentice-Hall of Canada, Inc., *Toronto*
Prentice-Hall Hispanoamericana, S. A., *Mexico*
Prentice-Hall of India Private Limited, *New Dehli*
Prentice-Hall of Japan, Inc., *Tokyo*
Prentice-Hall (Singapore) Pte. Ltd., *Singapore*
Editora Prentice-Hall do Brasil, Ltda., *Rio de Janeiro*

PREFACE

This book is designed to teach the essentials of data communication (Networking Technologies), NetWare 4.11 administration, and TCP/IP. It is an excellent resource for students thinking of getting their certificate as a CNA (Certified NetWare Administrator) or CNE (Certified NetWare Engineer). It is written with the intention of helping students develop some practical hands-on experience, speeding up the learning process and improving retention of the concepts learned. And so students should have the fundamental skills required to operate minicomputer systems in order to fully utilize the text. This book is also designed to provide insight on various Novell networking components; this valuable information can be an aid to decision making, and should lead to more effective choices of networking equipment.

This text is intended to develop the essential skills needed to operate, troubleshoot, and administer a NetWare 4.11 network. Emphasis is placed on the practical hands-on experience a student needs to become a professional network technician or administrator. Prior knowledge of computer or electronics theory, therefore, is required.

The material is divided into 10 chapters. Chapter 1 introduces students to the basic fundamentals of data communication (Networking Technologies); this chapter discusses the concepts of data communication through the OSI model. Chapters 2 through 7 teach students how to develop, design, and administer a NetWare 4.11 network. Chapter 8 covers all the necessary knowledge to install, upgrade and configure a NetWare 4.11 network. Chapter 9 covers all the essential skills a LAN technician needs to troubleshoot a NetWare or non-NetWare network. Chapter 10 covers the fundamental concepts of TCP/IP; how to implement it, troubleshoot it, and administer it on a NetWare 4.11 network.

This book can be used as a first-semester manual to introduce computer-networking fundamentals or as a reference manual for NetWare 4.11 certification. I believe that I have provided an adequate amount of theory to explain the topics and allow for further exploration if a student so desires. On the other hand, I would be happy to hear from any readers about how to improve this text.

I would like to thank Cindy Zughbi and Jack R. Harper for their time spent editing and proofreading part of the material in this text. I would also like to thank my colleagues here at DeVry for their invaluable technical input.

Mike Mutasem Awwad
DeVry Institute
630 US Highway One
North Brunswick, New Jersey 08902-3362
E-mail: MAwwad@admin.nj.devry.edu

This book is dedicated to my wife, son (Adam), parents, brothers and sisters for their love and support

CONTENTS

1

Networking Technologies

This chapter summarizes the concepts of computer networks, their services and their protocols. Most of the material in this chapter prepares you to pass the Networking Technologies test needed to become a CNE (Certified NetWare Engineer). This chapter will cover Network Basics, Network Services, and the seven layers of the OSI model and the most famous protocol suites. You really do not need to remember all the information in this chapter to become a good network administrator, but much of this information is required to pass the networking technologies exam that Novell and Microsoft offer.

1.1   NETWORK BASICS

A network is a group of devices that are connected together to allow them to communicate and to share files, printers, and other resources. Almost every company that has at least ten or more employees has some sort of workstations or clients connected to a server to form a network. A server on a network is a special computer that has resources used by clients and acts as the host for the other computers (workstations). The difference between a server and a workstation is that a server runs special software called a Network Operating System (NOS). The NOS is what makes a computer a server. The NOS provides you with two things. One of these things is resource sharing with security and managing users, such as creating, removing or providing privileges to users. The NOS ties all the PCs and peripherals in the network together and coordinates the functions of all PCs and peripherals in a network. Finally, it provides security for and access to all databases and peripherals in a network. The NOS setup consists of two major multitasking operations—preemptive and non-preemptive. In preemptive multitasking, the NOS can take control of the processor without the task's cooperation, while in non-preemptive multitasking (cooperation), the task itself decides when to give up the processor. No other program can run until the non-preemptive program gives up control of the processor.

On the other hand, a workstation is a computer that connects, requests data from, and exchanges information with a server. Often a workstation is referred to as a client. In fact, any peripheral that request data from or exchanges data with a server is called a client. The client software performs several tasks:

- It processes the forwarding of requests.

- It intercepts incoming requests.

- It determines if the incoming requests should be left alone to continue on the local PC or redirected out of the network to another server or peripheral.

- It designates share drives in other PCs.

A peripheral is any device, other than a computer, connected in a network or to any other computer. Every client, including the server, must connect to a network through a device called a Network Interface Card (NIC). The NIC is an interface card located inside a PC to make it interface with the rest of the network. Below is a list of tasks an NIC card performs:

- It prepares the data from the PC to be placed on the network cable.

- It sends the data to another PC.

- It controls the flow of data between the PC and the cabling system.

- It contains firmware programs that implement the logical link control and access media control functions (data link layer).

- It is responsible for making sure that data are transmitted serially. On the network cable data must travel in a single bit stream. This is called serial communication, which means that one bit follows another (like cars on a one-lane highway). Data can go one way at a time, either send or receive.

- It translates the PC's digital signals to electrical and optical signals for the network cable (transceiver).

- The network address on the NIC (regulated by the IEEE committee) is used for moving data from PC to PC. It also signals the PC requesting data for receiving. Finally the address is required for receiving the data from memory into the card memory (buffer). This address is called the MAC (Media Access Control) address.

- The card enables you to select an Interrupt Request (IRQ) number, (commonly IRQ 5 is free), and a base I/O port address. The I/O port is where information flows between the PC's hardware and its CPU. The port appears to the CPU as an address. In addition, you need to select a base memory address on the card to identify a location in RAM as a buffer area. Finally, you need to select what type of transceiver you will use (i.e. 10 Base2, 10 BaseT, or external).The card may come in different architectures, such as ISA 8 bits, EISA 16 or 32 bits, Micro-Channel 16 or 32 bits, or PCI 32 or 64 bits. Data may be transmitted faster, depending on its architecture.

- The card may come in different connectors, such as a BNC connector (round, thinnet), AUI connector (15 pins, like a joystick port, thicknet), or RJ-45 (like a telephone plug, 10 BaseT).

- The speeds of the data coming in and going out of the card are determined by the card's DMA, buffering RAM, and the onboard microprocessor. DMA (Direct Memory Access) is an onboard chip responsible for moving data directly from the network card to the PC memory. The computers always share the card's memory and vice versa. When the card takes temporary control of the PC's bus in EISA and Micro-Channel Architectures, it is called mastering.

Computer networks are generalized into three different computing categories: centralized computing, distributed computing, and collaborative computing. Centralized computing is generally known as mainframes. A mainframe is a big computer that handles all the data storage and processing. It uses dumb terminals for input/output devices. Although data is not really shared, it is still called a network because of the connection of the dumb terminals to the mainframe. Centralized computing was the sole type of network before the evolution of personal computers in the 1980's. With the evolution of personal computers, the distributed computing concept came into play. Distributed computing is a model that involves intelligent computers called clients. In a distributed computing model, a client has the power to process its own task and to exchange data and services with other computers. Collaborative computing (sometimes called cooperative computing), on the other hand, is an extension of the distributed computing model. In a collaborative computing environment, clients have internal processing power yet can still exchange data and services. The difference between collaborative and distributed computing is that collaborative computing allows multiple clients to perform tasks in order to maximize processing power.

Another way of categorizing networks is by their size. We can categorize a network according to its size in three different areas: Local Area Network (LAN), Metropolitan Area Network (MAN), and Wide Area Network (WAN). A LAN network is a network that usually covers a small area (i.e. a single building). In fact, any two PCs connected together will make up a LAN network. Typically in a LAN network, computers are connected to each other with a cable. A MAN network usually covers a metropolitan area and is a little bigger than a LAN, but smaller than a WAN. Different types of transmission media are required to connect PCs in a MAN network. Typically in a MAN network, computers are connected to each other with a transmission media such as cables, radio frequencies, or fiber optic cabling. The WAN network is the biggest of the three categories. A WAN network can cover a multi-city or even a multi-nation area. There are two types of WAN networks: enterprise networks and global networks. In an enterprise network, all of the clients are connected for a single organization or company, while in a global network, all of the clients are connected for multiple organizations that span the world. The Internet is an excellent example of a global network.

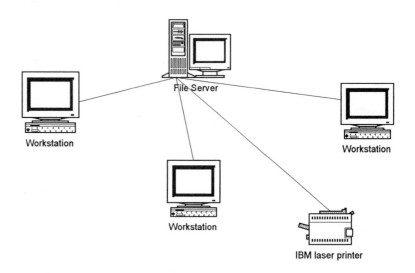

Figure 1.1 A typical LAN network.

1.2 NETWORK SERVICES

For a network to work properly, it needs certain components such as network services, transmission media, and protocols. The reason we connect computers together in the first place is for them to share services. A computer on a network that provides services, such as a file server, is called a service provider. A computer that requests services is called a service requester. The service provider and all service requesters must be connected together in some sort of transmission media to enable them to share services. A transmission media is the physical cables or wireless technology that allows clients to communicate with one another. On the other hand, network protocols are the rules or guidelines of communications that allow computers and other peripherals to communicate with one another. We will discuss only network services in this section. Network transmission media and network protocol suites are discussed later in this chapter.

The five most common network services are file, print, message, application, and database services. File services are services that allow a user to transfer files, store and move files, back up files, and update synchronization of a file. In a network environment, you do not have to save your file on a disk to move it from one computer to another. Rather, you can save it on a network drive where any client (with security in place) can share and use that file. You can even exchange files with a server if you want to. File transfer services give you the ability to move or store big files on the network rather than on a workstation. A network can provide you with three types of storage categories. On-line storage gives you the ability to store data on a local hard drive, whereas off-line storage provides a means of storing data on a removable media such as a tape drive or an optical disk. Finally, near-line storage is when a machine such as a jukebox or a tape carrousel automatically retrieves and mounts the tape or a disk. File services also provide you the opportunity to back up your files and use file update synchronization to ensure that each user has the latest version of a specific file.

The second most common network service is print services. A network gives clients the opportunity to share printers, place printers where they are convenient with respect to all workstations, and allow clients to share network fax services. The network uses what is called a print queue to store print jobs before they are sent to a printer. Using a print queue, a network administrator can prioritize, move, or purge any print job from a print queue before that job is sent to the printer.

The third most common network services are message services. While file services transfer data in a file form, message services allow you to transfer data in any other form such as graphics, video, and audio. There are four types of message services: electronic mail, workgroup applications, object-oriented applications, and directory services. Now you can transfer messages on a network using electronic mail (e-mail). E-mail can transmit a text, audio, video, resources and services on a network.

The fourth most common network services are application as well as graphics. Workgroup applications, on the other hand, are used to produce more efficient ways to process a task among multiple users. You can handle a large amount of tasks by using object-oriented applications message services. Object-oriented applications are programs made up of small applications called objects. Finally, a directory service is a directory or a database that contains all the information about the services. An application service on a network allows you to have a server dedicated to provide only application services. That is why a Windows NT server is an excellent application server. NetWare provides server applications by using NetWare Loadable Modules (NLMs) to support third-party applications.

The fifth most common network services are database services. Most database systems run under client/server base systems. Client/server base system implies that the server handles the intensive part of the task performance. With database services, you can distribute a huge database into portions to maximize network efficiency. NetWare 4.11 uses NDS (NetWare Directory Services) as its primary database management.

In 1977 the International Standards Organization (ISO) was formed to develop standards on a wide range of topics. The United States' representative of ISO is the American National Standards Institute (ANSI). ISO is most famous for its development of the Open System Interconnection (OSI) reference model. This model is designed to give developers a set of rules or guidelines to follow, and it organizes network communications into seven different layers: Layer1- Physical, layer 2- Data Link, layer 3- Network, layer 4- Transport, Layer 5- Session, Layer 6- Presentation, and layer 7- Application. To help you remember the names and order (from layer 7 to layer 1) of the seven layers use the phrase " **All People Seem To Need Data Processing**". Even though a description of each layer will be provided in the following sections, let's first take a look at a brief summary of how data are being sent within the OSI model, and what are the responsibilities protocols have in that model.

The functions of each layer in the OSI model communicate and work with the functions of the layers immediately above and below that layer. In addition, layers are separated from each other by a boundary called an interface. The purpose of each layer is to provide service to the next higher layer. Data are passed from one layer to another in the form of broken data called packets. If data were to be sent in large units, then the network would be tied up. Packets are therefore used to reduce traffic and error in transmission. The packets consist of six components—source address, data, destination address, instructions for the network components on how to pass the data along, information that tells the receiving PC how to connect the packet to other packets and reassemble the complete data, and error-free checking.

You can also think of a packet as consisting of three parts—headers, data (contains CRC), and a trailer protocol.

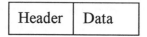

The headers and CRC are attached or removed at each layer as they move within the OSI model. The headers are used to send an alert signal to indicate that a packet is being sent. In addition, a header consists of source, address, destination address, and clock information. Data is the actual useful data, which can be in the range of 0.5 KB to 4 KB. The CRC is used to ensure the data integrity as it travels through the transmission media. The transport layer is where the original block of data gets divided into packets. In addition, sequencing information and address information are placed with the data as headers to guide the receiving PC in reassembling the data from the packet.

Again, network protocols are rules of behavior, which means that they are sets for procedures in performing each task before sending the data from one PC. Keep in mind that there are many protocols out there, and that some work at various OSI layers. Here are some facts about protocols and what they are responsible for:

1) The receiving PC uses protocols to break outgoing data into small sections (packets), add addressing information, and prepare the data for actual transmission.

2) The receiving PC uses protocols to take incoming data packets off the cable, strip the addressing information, copy the data packets to a buffer for reassembly, and then pass the reassembled data to the application.

3) Several protocols may work together (protocol stack) in an OSI model:

   a) Application layer—The protocols initiate the request or accept the requests.
   b) Presentation layer—The protocols add, format, display, and encrypt information into the packet.
   c) Session layer—The protocols control the flow of information and send the packets on their way.
   d) Transport layer—The protocols add error-free handling information.
   e) Network layer—The protocols add sequences and address information.
   f) Data link layer—The protocols add error-check information (CRC) and prepare the data for the physical layer.
   g) Physical layer—The protocols packet and send the data as bit streams.

4) All protocols must be bound. For example, if TCP/IP is bound as the first protocol, then TCP/IP will be used to attempt to make a network connection. If this network connection fails the PC will transparently attempt to make a connection using the next protocol in the binding order.

5) There are three basic types of protocols:

   a) Application protocols—These types of protocols work in the upper three layers of the OSI model. They can be application-to-application or data exchange protocols. Examples are SMTP or FTP.
   b) Transport protocols—These types of protocols work at the transport layer. They provide for communication session, between PCs and ensure that the data are able to move reliably. Examples are TCP, SPX, and NetBEUI (NetBIOS Extended User Interface, not routable).
   c) Network protocols—These types of protocols work at the lower three layers of the OSI model. They provide the link services and handle addressing, routing information, error checking, and retransmission requests. Examples are IP, IPX, Nwlink and NetBEUI.

1.3 PHYSICAL LAYER

The first layer of the OSI model is the physical layer. It deals with issues such as he electrical specifications of cabling, how data is accessed from a cable, and how the network interface cards connect the cabling. It transmits the unstructured raw bit stream (0 or 1) over a physical medium (cable). At this layer, data are referred to as bits. A repeater is a typical device that operates at the physical layer. In this layer, we will discuss data signals, network structures, transmission devices, and transmission media.

1.3.1 Data Signals

Most data signals come in two forms: analog or digital. Analog signals are continuous electromagnetic varying signals. An example of an analog signal is a radio wave carrying music, or a voice being carried over a telephone line. In a WAN network it could be a dial-up line via public switched telephone network (PSTN), or a dedicated line, which is more reliable, faster, and expensive. Analog signals have three important characteristics: amplitude, frequency, and phase. Amplitude is the measure of the strength of a signal and is determined by the height of the signal's peaks. Frequency is measured in hertz with one hertz being equal to a waveform that completes one cycle in one second. One cycle means that the waveform will start to repeat itself after the first cycle is completed. Phase is the measured difference of time between two different waveforms. For example, if signal one started at 0 degrees and signal two at 90 degrees later, signal two would be out of phase from signal one by 90 degrees.

Digital signals are signals that are discrete. They have specific values of either a high or a low voltage, and nothing in between. For example, in WAN networks digital signals are used in Digital Data Services (DDS). DDS provides point-to-point synchronous communication at 2.4, 4.8, 9.6, or 56 Kbps. DDS can be made into a guaranteed full-duplex bandwidth by setting up a permanent link from each end point. It is 99% error free and does not require a modem.

Furthermore, in a WAN network, digital signals can be transmitted on a T1, T3, or a switched 56 line. A T1 line is point-to-point transmission and uses two wire pairs (1 pair to send, 1 pair to receive). It is a full-duplex signal that transmits at 1.544 Mbps. It uses multiplexing, which involves signals from different sources that are collected into a component called a multiplexer, and then fed into one cable at the speed of 8,000 times a second. Each channel can transmit at 64 Kbps (DS-0) or at 1.544 Mbps (DS-1). T3 line can transmit at 6 Mbps to 45 Mbps. Conversely, a switch 56 line can transmit at 56 Kbps, but it can only be used on demand and requires a CSU/DSU to dial up another switched 56 sites. Because computers use only high and low voltages, digital signals are used. High and low voltages are represented by values of 1s and 0s, where 1 represents a high voltage and 0 represents a low voltage. Data that have values of 1s and 0s are called binary.

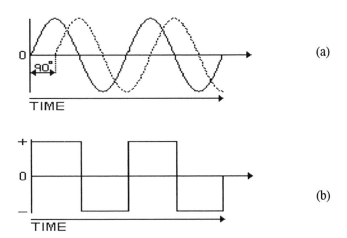

Figure 1.2 (a) Two analog signals with a 90-degree phase shift; (b) digital signal.

To transfer data, either an analog or digital signal must somehow transmit both analog and digital data. Digital signals can carry (transmit) analog or digital data from one place to another. Analog signals can also carry (transmit) analog or digital data from one place to another. The technique that enables an analog signal to carry digital data is called modulation. There are three types of analog modulation: amplitude modulation (AM), frequency modulation (FM), and phase modulation (PM). We can use these three analog types of modulation to encode (place) digital data on analog signals.

Amplitude-Shift Keying (ASK) is an analog modulation technique used when the amplitude of an analog signal is varied between two distinct values. Frequency-Shift Keying (FSK) is another analog modulation technique used when two different frequencies are used to represent digital data. Phase-Shift Keying (PSK), on the other hand, is an analog modulation technique that varies the phase of the signal to represent digital data.

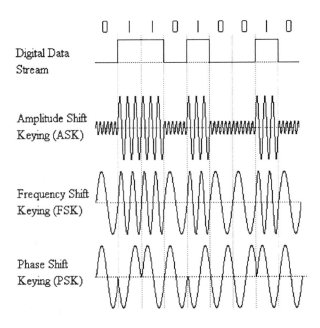

Figure 1.3 ASK, FSK, and PSK modulation waveforms.

Digital data are also encoded on digital signals. Almost all LANs transmit digital data via digital signals. There are several techniques used to encode digital data on a digital signal. What follows are some digital encoding techniques.

Unipolar encoding is a technique used when only one voltage is used with the reference voltage zero. Voltage in unipolar encoding can be either positive or negative. The polar encoding technique uses both positive and negative voltages, while the bipolar encoding technique uses three distinct voltage values, usually positive, negative and zero. In the return to zero encoding (RZ) technique, the signal voltage is always zero for a portion of each bit to guarantee a voltage transition for each bit. RZ, therefore, is called self-clocking. In the non-return to zero encoding (NRZ) technique, if a transition occurs at the beginning of a bit, a one is represented; otherwise, a zero is represented. Since NRZ does not guarantee a signal transition for each bit, it is not self-clocking. The biphase encoding technique requires at least one voltage transition per bit; therefore, the bits are self-clocking. There are two types of biphase encoding techniques: Manchester encoding and differential Manchester encoding. Manchester encoding technique uses a mid-bit transition to encode data. For example, the middle of negative to positive transition could indicate a one, whereas positive to negative transition could indicate a zero. Ethernet LANs make use of Manchester encoding. Finally, differential Manchester encoding technique uses the mid-bit transition to provide clocking. Data are encoded in a voltage transition at the start of the bit. Token ring LANs make use of differential Manchester encoding.

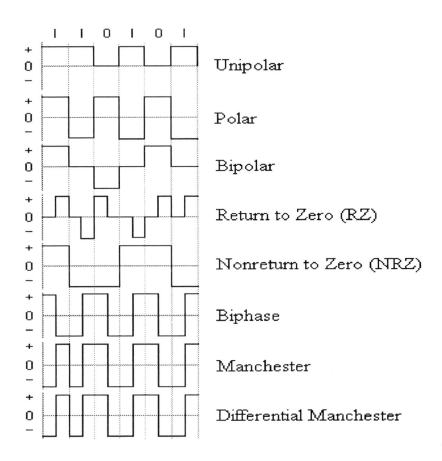

Figure 1.4 Examples of digital encoding.

Most analog and digital signals are transmitted through a bounded transmission media (cables). The capacity of a transmission media is referred to as the bandwidth. Bandwidth can be divided into channels to transmit more than one signal on a bounded transmission media. There are two types of transmission media bandwidth: baseband and broadband. Baseband transmission uses the entire media bandwidth to transmit digital signals on a single channel, with digital signaling over a single frequency. A digital signal uses the entire bandwidth of the cable (one channel). It is bidirectional, and uses a repeater to regenerate the signal. Most LANs use baseband to transmit their signals.

Broadband transmission, on the other hand, divides the media bandwidth into channels to support multiple, simultaneous signals over a single transmission medium. It is an analog signal, and it uses a wide range of frequencies. Broadband is also unidirectional. To solve this problem, it either uses a mid-split broadband, which divides the bandwidth into two channels with different frequencies, or uses two physical cables, one for sending, and the other for receiving. It uses amplifiers to regenerate the signal.

Multiplexing is a technique used to allow both baseband and broadband media to use multiple data channels. There are three methods of multiplexing: frequency-division, time-division, and statistical-time-division multiplexing. Frequency-division multiplexing (FDM) is a technique that uses different frequencies to add multiple data channels onto a broadband medium. Time-division multiplexing (TDM) is a technique that divides a channel into time slots. Each device communicates in its own allocated time slot. Statistical-time division multiplexing (StatTDM) is a technique that allocates time slots.

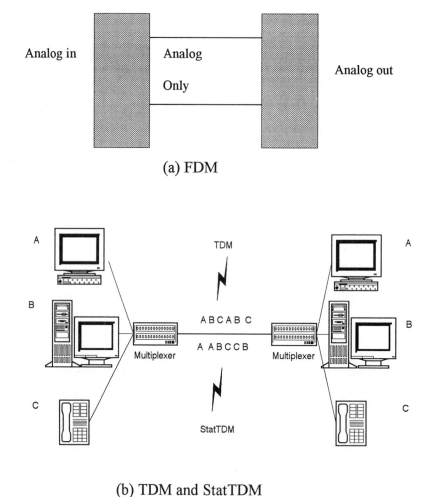

(b) TDM and StatTDM

Figure 1.5 Different methods of multiplexing.

1.3.2 Transmission Media

Signals must be transmitted through a transmission media. Transmission media come in two different classes: bounded and unbounded. Bounded media is a media that carries data in a physical pathway (i.e. cable). Unbounded media is a media that carries data through space (i.e. microwaves). Before we look at the four types of bounded media, UTP, STP, COAX, and fiber optic cables, we need to look at the consideration for cable:

1) Installation logistics—How easy is it to install and work with the cable.

2) Shielding—The noisier the area, the more shielding it requires, thus increasing the cost.

3) Crosstalk—Remember that power line generators, motors, relays, etc. may crosstalk with the cable. Security is crucial.

4) Transmission speed—Always measured in Mbps.

5) Attenuation—This is one of the reasons for specifications that recommend certain length limits on different types of cabling.

6) Cost—Of course this is also an important factor.

Unshielded Twisted Pair (UTP) is a cable that has two wires twisted together to reduce Electromagnetic Interference (EMI). It consists of two insulated strands of copper wire twisted around each other. The twisting cancels out electrical noise from adjacent pairs and from other sources, such as motors, relays, and transformers. UTP can be category 3, which means the cable has a four-twist-pair with three twists per foot. This makes it capable of transmitting up to 10 Mbps. If it is category 5, then it transmits up to 100 Mbps. UTP is the least expensive in cost (because cables might already be installed). On the other hand, UTP is very sensitive to EMI, has a very low bandwidth, and is sensitive to crosstalk. UTP can be used in token ring, Ethernet ,or ARCnet networks.

Shielded Twisted Pair (STP) is a UTP cable with a braided shield placed around the twisted pair of wires to reduce EMI. Although EMI sensitivity in STP cable is low, the cable cost is a lot more expensive than that of a UTP. Even though the bandwidth is bigger than that of a UTP cable, STP cable is used only by IBM Token-Ring and Apple's LocalTalk networks. STP cable has a copper braid jacket, which is a higher quality, more protective jacket than UTP has. STP also uses a foil wrap between the wire pairs and internal twisting of the pairs. It is less susceptible to electrical interference, and thus a higher bandwidth is transmitted over a long distance. Both UTP and STP can travel up to 100 meters and they both need connection hardware, such as RJ45, which is similar to the RJ11, which is a telephone connector. Below are the five categories that UTP and STP use:

Category	Used For	Speed
1	Voice	< 4 Mbps
2	Voice	4 Mbps
3	Data	10 Mbps
4	Data	16 Mbps
5	Data	100 Mbps

A coaxial cable (COAX) is a cable that contains two conductors with a COmmon AXis. COAX is relatively inexpensive compared to a fiber optic cable. It is solid copper surrounded by insulation (a braided metal shielding). It can be dual shielded- where one layer is foil insulation and another layer is a braided metal shielding- or it can be quad shielded, where two layers are foil insulation and two layers are braided metal shielding. COAX is used for environments that are subject to higher interference. The shielding protects the transmitted data by absorbing stray electronics signal called noise. The insulating layers protect the core from electrical noise and crosstalk signals that overflow from an adjacent wire. The conducting core and the wire mesh must always be separated from each other (or have insulation in between them); otherwise, the cable will experience a short or noise.

COAX cables come in two types—thin (thinnet) 10Base2 or thick (thicknet) 10Base5. The thinnet cable can transmit data up to 180 meters without any attenuation. It uses RG-58 family cables with a 50-ohm impedance. It can use RG-58 A/U cable, which is a stranded wire core, or use RG 58 /U cable, which is a solid copper wire. The thicknet wire is a standard Ethernet cable, which has a thicker copper core. A thicknet cable can transmit data up to 500 meters with minimal attenuation. This type of cable is often used as a backbone cable. A transceiver is used to connect thinnet COAX to the larger thicknet COAX. There are two types of grade associated with COAX cables—polyvinyl cable (PVC) or plenum. If a PVC cable is burnt, it will give off a poisonous gas. Plenum cable, on the other hand, is fire resistant, and produces only a small amount of smoke.

The advantage of a COAX cable is that it has very low EMI sensitivity and a high bandwidth, but the disadvantage is that the cost is much more expensive than UTP or STP cables. Below is a summary list of COAX cable types and their descriptions:

Cable Type	Description
RG-58 /U	Solid copper core, uses 50-ohm impedance.
RG-58 A/U	Stranded wire core, uses thinnet and 50-ohm impedance.
RG-59	Cable TV uses 75-ohm impedance.
RG-6	Larger in diameter and rated with higher frequencies than RG-59, can be used for broadcast transmission as well.
RG-62	Used for ARCNet network. It uses 93-ohm impedance.

Fiber optic cables are cables that transmit data through a thin glass or plastic fiber using light waves. They can carry digital data at 4 Gbps. Fiber optic cable is the safest way to transmit data, because no electrical impulses are carried with the signal. It has a very high speed and can carry a large amount of information. Fiber optic cable has an extremely thin cylinder of glass, called the core, which is surrounded by a concentric layer of glass called cladding. Each glass strand passes signals in only one direction, and so a fiber optic cable consists of two strands in separate jackets. Fiber optic cables are not subject to any electrical interference and are extremely fast. Thus the signal cannot be tapped easily. Signals can travel up to hundreds of kilometers without significant attenuation. The advantages of a fiber optic cable are that it has a very high bandwidth and no sensitivity to EMI. The disadvantage is that it is the most expensive type of bounded media. Below is a list of factors for each of the four types of cables:

Factor	UTP	STP	COAX	Fiber Optics
Cost	Lowest	Moderate	Moderate	Highest
Capacity	1 to 100 Mbps. Typically 10 Mbps	1 to 155 Mbps. Typically 16 Mbps	Typically 10 Mbps	Up to 2 Gbps. Typically 100 Mbps.
Attenuation	High, in the range of a hundred meters	High, in the range of a hundred meters	Low, in the range of a few km	Lowest, in the range of tens of km
EMI	Most sensitive to EMI and eavesdropping	Less sensitive than UTP, but sensitive to EMI and eavesdropping	Same as STP	Not affected by EMI or eavesdropping

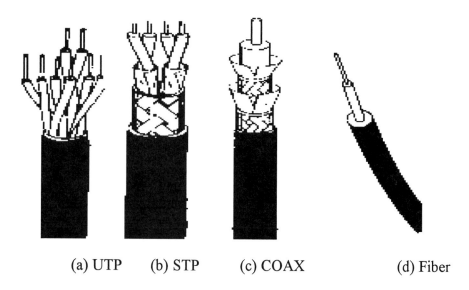

(a) UTP   (b) STP   (c) COAX   (d) Fiber

Figure 1.6 Different types of cables.

If you have an extended local area network, you might need multipoint wireless connectivity, which is a wireless bridge that links two buildings without using cables. In addition, if the buildings are 25 or more miles apart, then a spread-spectrum radio transmission can be used. This will eliminate the need for a T1 line or a microwave connection. A T1 line transmission carries data and voice at the rate of 1.544 Mbps.

If you have a mobile computing network, you might have to use a telephone line to transmit and receive data and voice. The telephone line transmission rate range is approximately 110 Kbps to 56 Kbps. In addition to telephone line, you might want to use a cellular network, which is faster, but suffers from sub-seconds delays.

For a wireless communication (unbounded media) the transceiver (access point) broadcasts and receives signals to and from the surrounding computers. It uses a small wall-mounted transceiver to the wired network, and it establishes radio contact with portable networked devices. Now let us look at four types of unbounded media: radio, microwaves, laser, and infrared. Radio waves are electromagnetic waves in the frequency range of kilohertz to low giga hertz. Some radio waves have broad beams and high EMI sensitivity. A PC tunes to narrow-band (single frequency) radio waves (like radio broadcasting). It can transmit up to 5000 square meters, but cannot transmit through steel or load bearing walls. It can transmit data at 4.8 Mbps. Spread-spectrum radio waves are waves that broadcast over a range of frequencies. These frequencies are divided into channels or hops. They can transmit data up to 250 Kbps.

Microwaves are electromagnetic waves that fall near light waves in frequency. Microwaves have to transmit by a "line of sight" and cannot transmit around the world. Microwaves make use of terrestrial relay stations to transmit data for a few miles. If a microwave signal needs to be transmitted over a longer distance, the satellite communication link that is orbiting the earth will be used. Microwaves have moderate EMI sensitivity and a narrow or broad beam.

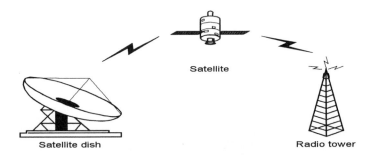

Figure 1.7 Microwave communication.

Laser is a light beam operating at one frequency. The waves of a laser are synchronized, and are transmitted in one direction. It is the most ideal type of unbounded media, because it has no EMI sensitivity due to a very narrow beam. Infrared transmission transmits several narrow beams at once from one station to another. It can transmit up to 1 Mbps as long as the distance is within 10 feet. It does not have a strong ambient light. Infrared line-of-sight transmission must be clear, while scattered infrared transmission limits the transmission to 4 Mbps at 3 feet, because the signals bouncing off walls and ceilings attenuate the signal. In a reflective infrared transmission, optical signals are transmitted toward a common location, where they are redirected to the appropriate PC. A broadband optical telepoint infrared transmission can handle the high quality requirements of multimedia, which in turn can provide broadband services such as bounded media. This technology is used mostly in television and wireless networks.

1.3.3 Transmission Devices

There are two types of transmission devices: communication devices and interconnection devices. Communication devices include modems, codecs, and MUXs. Interconnection devices include repeaters, hubs, bridges, routers, and gateways.

One of the most popular communication transmission devices is the modem. A modem is a hardware device that lets you connect two computers using standard phone lines. First, the sending computer's modem **mo**dulates the computer's digital signals into analog signals that can pass over the phone lines. Then the receiving computer's modem **dem**odulates the analog signal back into the digital signal that computers understand. There are two types of modems- internal and external. Internal modems are based on a board, which can be plugged into any of the expansion slots in a PC. External modems are plugged into the RS232 port or the COM port of a PC with a RS232 cable. The speed of a modem is measured in baud- the speed of the oscillation of the sound wave on which a bit of data is carried over the telephone wire. The bps (bits per second) can be greater than the baud rate due to encoded data, so that each modulation of sound can carry more than one bit of data over the telephone line. There are two types of modem communications—synchronous and asynchronous:

1) Synchronous communication modems rely on a timing scheme coordinated between two devices to separate groups of bits and transmit them in blocks known as frames. If an error occurs, it will then retransmit it. Some synchronous protocols perform certain tasks that asynchronous protocols do not perform. These tasks include formatting data into blocks, adding control information to the data, and checking the information to provide error control. The primary protocols in synchronous communication are the Synchronous Data Link Control (SDLC), High-level Data Link Control (HDLC), and binary synchronous communication protocol. Synchronous communication modems use two types of modems— public dial up network lines and leased lines. The public dial up network lines are bisynchronous lines that manually dial up a connection. The leased

(dedicated) lines are a full time connection that does not go through a series of switches. The speed of a leased line ranges between approximately 56 Kbps and 45 Mbps.

2) Asynchronous communication modems use common telephone lines. They do not have any clocking devices and are not synchronized. Their speed can be up to 56 Kbps (as of today). Asynchronous communication uses a parity bit, which is used in an error checking and correction scheme called parity checking. Asynchronous communication modems are rated by their signaling (channel speed) and throughput. Signaling is the measurement of how fast the bits are encoded onto the communication channel, while throughput is the amount of useful information going across the channel.

Often you will encounter the terms DTE (Data Terminal Equipment) and DCE (Data Communication Equipment). A modem is a type of a DCE that interfaces with a DTE. On the other hand, a codec (COder/DECoder) is a hardware device that converts analog data for transmission on a digital medium. A codec actually functions as a mirror image of a modem. A multiplexer (MUX) is a hardware device that allows multiple simultaneous signals to share a single transmission medium.

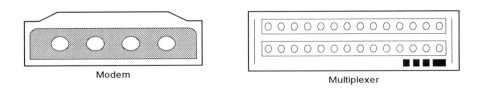

Figure 1.8 A modem and a multiplexer.

Interconnection devices are devices that connect computers or networks together.
A repeater is an interconnection device that operates at the physical layer. Its main purpose is to amplify or reshape a signal to extend the range of the network. Repeaters do not translate or filter anything. Both segments on a repeater must use the same access method (i.e. CSMA/CD). Repeaters can take an Ethernet packet from a thinnet COAX and pass it onto a fiber optic segment.
A hub, sometimes called a concentrator, is a device that connects workstations to a central point (hub). It is a special kind of repeater and/or bridge designed to

facilitate a star topology. There are three types of hubs: passive, active, and intelligent. A passive hub splits the signal and only route traffic to all nodes. Active hubs perform similarly to passive hubs, but they regenerate, amplify, and retransmit signals. Intelligent hubs perform similarly to passive and active hubs, but they route traffic only to the branch of the receiving node and perform some network management. You can think of bridges and routers as intelligent hubs.

A bridge is an intelligent device used to connect two separate network segments. A bridge uses the physical addresses of the source and destination to separate and keep traffic to a minimum on each segment of the network. A bridge has all the features of a repeater. It works at the MAC (Media Access Control) sub layer. As traffic passes through bridges, information about the PC's addresses is stored in the bridge's RAM. This RAM builds a bridging table based on the source addresses. If a bridge knows the location of the destination node, it forwards the packet to it. If it does not know the destination, it forwards the packet to all the segments. A bridge regenerates the data at the packet level, and packets can travel by more than one route. Since a bridge has access to the physical address, it operates at the data link layer.

A router is a device that makes use of the logical address of the network. A router can minimize traffic by connecting two networks together and keeping each network segment's traffic on its own side of the network. A router determines the best path for sending data, and it filters broadcast traffic to the local segment. A router filters and isolates traffic, connects network segments together, and passes information only if the network address is known. The routing table in the router contains all the known network addresses, how to connect to other networks, all the possible paths between those routers, costs of sending data over those paths, and the media access control layer addresses, as well as the network addresses (logical addresses). A router can choose the best path available. It decides the path the data packet will follow by determining the number of hops between the internetwork segments.

There are two types of routers—dynamic and static. Dynamic routers are automatic discovery routers, while static routers are manually configured to set up a routing table to specify each route. A router not only recognizes an address, as a bridge does, but also recognizes the type of protocol. In addition, a router can identify addresses of other routers, and determines which packet to forward to which router. Examples of routable protocols are DECnet, IP, IPX, OSI, XNS, and DDP (Apple). Examples of non-routable protocols are LAT and NetBEUI. TCP/IP is supported by the protocol called OSPF, which is a link-state routing algorithm. IPX is supported by the protocol called NLSP, which is a link-state algorithm. In addition, IPX and TCP/IP are supported by the protocol called RIP, which uses a distance-vector algorithm to determine the routes. Since the router makes use of the logical address, it operates at the network layer.

Brouters are bridges and routers combined in one device. Remember that a bridge does not support routable protocols. A brouter can operate at either the data link or the network layer.

Gateways are devices that connect two completely different types of network together. A gateway re-packages and converts data from one environment to another, so that one environment can understand the other environment's data. Gateways link two systems that do not have the same protocols, data formatting structure, languages, and architecture. Gateways operate at the transport layer and at higher layers of the OSI model.

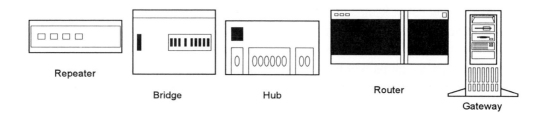

Figure 1.9 Different types of interconnection devices.

1.3.4 Network Structures

Network structures are often referred to as network physical topologies. The physical topology of a network is the layout of the cabling, or how computers are connected in a network. There are two types of physical topologies: point-to-point and multipoint. A point-to-point (PTP) physical topology is the connection of two nodes directly together.

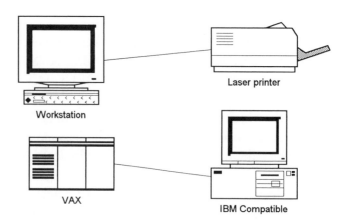

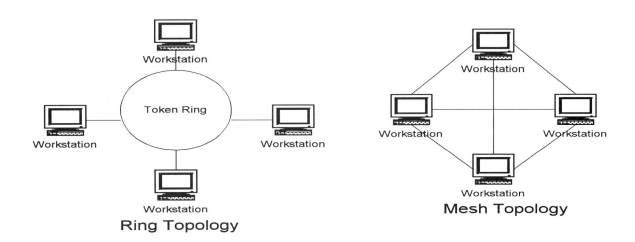

Figure 1.12 A ring and a mesh topology.

Table 1.1 shows a summary of the advantages and disadvantages of multipoint topologies:

TOPOLOGY	ADVANTAGES	DISADVANTAGES
BUS	1) Cable is cheap 2) Media is easy to work with 3) Simple, reliable 4) Easy to expand	1) Slow in heavy traffic 2) Problems are hard to isolate 3) Cable break can affect the network
STAR	1) Easy to expand and modify 2) Centralized monitoring and management 3) One node failure does not affect the network	1) If the centralized point goes down, the whole network goes down 2) Slow unless switched
RING	1) Equal access to all PCs 2) Even performance despite many users	1) One PC going down affects the network 2) Problems are hard to isolate 3) Hardware is expensive
MESH	Signal can always find a path despite node failures	Cost from many networking devices
HYBRID	Workgroup efficiency and traffic	Cannot be placed with other topologies without hardware changes

Table 1.1 Advantages and disadvantages of multipoint topologies.

Although physical topologies have the same names as logical topologies, logical topologies describe the way data are traveling on the network. There are two types of logical topology associated with networks—ring and bus. It is possible to have different physical and logical topologies in the same network. In a ring logical topology the data are passed from one node to the next. With a bus logical topology, the data are passed to all the nodes on the network at once, and data will always be available to all nodes on the network.

1.4   DATA LINK AND NETWORK LAYERS

The data link layer is capable of reading the source and destination physical address contained in a packet. Based on this information, the data link layer can determine for what node the packet is destined. It sends data frames from the network layer to the physical layer. At the receiving end, it packages the raw bits of data from the physical layer into data frames, and it provides the error-free transfer of these frames. The data link layer sends a frame, and waits for an acknowledgment from the recipient. At this layer, data are referred to as frames. A bridge is a typical device that operates at the data link layer. The data link layer is broken into two sub layers: LLC (Logical Link Control) and MAC (Media Access Control).

1.4.1 Logical Link Control (LLC) Sublayer

The main job of the LLC sublayer is to provide services to the network layer. It provides three distinct services: frame synchronization, error checking and flow control. The frame synchronization identifies the boundaries of a frame, while the error checking tests for the integrity of a frame, using the technique of CRC (Cyclic Redundancy Check) testing. The flow control at the LLC layer examines how much data is coming in by using two methods- stop and wait or sliding window. In stop and wait method, the sender must wait for an acknowledgment before continuing to send frames. In the sliding window method, the receiver sets the size of the window. The sender can then send the number of frames according to the size of the window without having to stop and wait. The sliding window method is full duplex.

1.4.2 Media Access Control (MAC) Sublayer

The MAC sublayer's main responsibility is to control which devices can transmit and when they can transmit. The MAC sublayer is subdivided into two sections—media access methods and addressing. The media access method, are subdivided into three types: contention, token passing, and polling. On a contention network, any device can transmit data whenever it needs. Since devices can transmit data at any time, data collisions will occur frequently. To avoid data collisions, a specific protocol was developed. The Carrier Sense Multiple Access with Collision Detection (CSMA/CD) was developed to avoid data collision on a network having contention as its media access method. CSMA/CD works by "listening" to the cable for traffic while transmitting information. If collision occurs, data will be retransmitted. CSMA/CD is the access protocol used in Ethernet and IEEE 802.3. CSMA/CD is not effective beyond 2,500 meters. AppleTalk networks use the CSMA/CA (Carrier Sense Multiple Access with Collision Avoidance) protocol as its main access mechanism. The advantages of contention are that it is a very simple access method, and that it provides high data throughput at low traffic. The disadvantage of contention is that it is probabilistic and not deterministic. In addition, at high traffic levels, data collisions occur more frequently, resulting in poor performance. On a token passing network, a token is passed to one device at a time in an orderly manner (that is why token ring network is considered to be deterministic rather than probabilistic), and only devices that have the token may transmit data. The advantage of token passing is that it offers high throughput at high traffic.. The disadvantage of a token passing are that its protocols for managing the network are complicated, and that devices using token passing are much more expensive. The token passing method is used with networks such as IEEE 802.4 (token bus topology), IEEE 802.5 (token ring topology), ARCnet, and TokenTalk for Apple's Macintosh.

RESTRICTIONS	VALUE/DESCRIPTION
Network	ARCnet
Physical topology	Star or bus
Logical topology	Bus
Access control method	Token passing
Cables	COAX (common), UTP or Fiber
Data speed	2.5 Mbps, broadband
Maximum distance between nodes	2,000 feet (610 meters), star topology
Maximum distance between two farthest nodes	20,000 feet, star topology
Maximum distance between node and a passive hub	100 feet, star topology
Maximum distance between node and an active hub	2,000 feet, star topology
Maximum distance between passive hub and an active hub	100 feet, star topology
Maximum distance between two active hubs	2,000 feet, star topology
Using 93-ohm RG-62 A/U	610 meters maximum, in a star topology will be 305 meters maximum in a bus topology
Using RJ-11, RJ-45 UTP	244 meters maximum on a star or a bus topology

Table 1.2 Restrictions on the ARCnet network.

RESTRICTIONS	VALUE/DESCRIPTION
Network	Ethernet 10Base2
Physical topology	Bus
Logical topology	Bus
Access control method	Contention-CSMA/CD
Cables	Thin COAX
Data speed	10 Mbps, baseband
Minimum distance between workstations	½ meter (1 ½ feet)
Maximum segment length	185 meters (607 feet)
Maximum network length	925 meters (3,035 feet)
Maximum node separations	5 segments/4 repeaters
Maximum nodes per segment	30
Maximum populated segments per LAN	3
Connectors	BNC barrel, BNC T-connectors, or BNC terminators
5-4-3 rule applies	5 cable segments are connected with 4 repeaters, but only 3 segments can have stations attached

Table 1.3 Restrictions on the Ethernet 10Base2 network.

RESTRICTIONS	VALUE/DESCRIPTION
Network	Ethernet 10Base5
Physical topology	Bus
Logical topology	Bus
Access control method	Contention-CSMA/CD
Cables	Thick COAX
Data speed	10 Mbps, baseband
Minimum distance between transceivers	2 ½ meters (8 feet)
Maximum transceiver cable length	50 meters (164 feet)
Maximum segment length	500 meters (1,640 feet)
Maximum network length	2,500 meters (3,035 feet)
Maximum node separations	5 segments/4 repeaters
Maximum taps per segment	100
Maximum populated segments per LAN	3
Connectors	DIX , AUI, N-series connectors or terminators
5-4-3 rule applies	5 cable segments are connected with 4 repeaters, but only 3 segments can have stations attached

Table 1.4 Restrictions on the Ethernet 10Base5 network.

RESTRICTIONS	VALUE/DESCRIPTION
Network	Ethernet 10Base-T
Physical topology	Star
Logical topology	Star
Access control method	Contention-CSMA/CD
Cables	UTP with RJ-45 connectors, STP, category 3,4,5
Data speed	10 Mbps, baseband
Maximum distance between workstation and hub	100 meters (328 feet)
Maximum nodes per segment	512
Maximum node separations	5 segments/4 repeaters
Maximum hubs in sequence	4
Maximum populated segments per LAN	3

Table 1.5 Restrictions on the Ethernet 10Base-T network

In addition to the above networks, there are other Ethernet networks in use today. These include 10BaseFL, 100VG-AnyLAN, and 10BaseX. 10BaseFL networks operate at 10Mbps (baseband), use fiber optic cable, and have a maximum segment length of 2000 meters. In the network 100VG-AnyLAN, (VG stands for Voice Grade) data transmitted at 100 Mbps, and is connected with category 5 UTP, STP cables or, a fiber optic cable. It uses polling as its access control method, and can support both Ethernet and token ring packets. It has a star topology with child hubs that act as computers to their parent hubs. In a 100BaseT hub, links cannot exceed 250 meters. 100BaseX is a fast Ethernet that uses a UTP category 5 cable. It uses CSMA/CD as its access control method. 100BaseT4 networks use 4-pair category 5 UTP or STP cable. 100BaseTX networks use 2-pair category UTP or STP. 100BaseFX networks use 2-strand fiber optic cable.

In a token ring network frame, the media access control field indicates whether the frame is a token or a data frame. When the first token ring PC comes online, the network generates a token. Only one PC, which has the token, can send data over the network. After it finishes sending data, the PC removes the frame from the ring and transmits a new token back on the ring. In a token ring network, each PC acts as a unidirectional repeater.

RESTRICTIONS	VALUE/DESCRIPTION
Network	Token ring
Physical topology	Star
Logical topology	Ring
Access control method	Token passing

Cables	UTP or STP with UDC connector
Data speed	4 or 16 Mbps, baseband
Maximum number of MAUs (Multi-Access Units) that can connect to each other	12 using STP
Maximum number of nodes	72 using UTP
Maximum number of nodes	96 using STP
Maximum patch cable distance connecting all MAUs	400 feet
Maximum patch cable distance between two MAUs	150 feet
Maximum distance between MAU and a node	150 feet
MAU to PC for IBM type 1 cable	101 meters
MAU to PC for IBM type 3 cable	150 meters
MAU to PC for UTP cable	45 meters
MAU to PC for STP	100 meters

Table 1.6 Restrictions on the token ring network.

RESTRICTIONS	VALUE/DESCRIPTION/MATERIAL NEEDED
Network	FDDI
Physical topology	Ring or star
Logical topology	Ring
Access control method	Token passing
Cables	Fiber
Data speed	100 Mbps
Maximum number of nodes in a ring topology	500
Maximum total cable length in a ring topology	100,000 meters

Table 1.7 Restriction on the FDDI network

In addition, AppleTalk has two types of network called LocalTalk and AppleTalk. LocalTalk networks use CSMA/CA for their access control method. A device attached in a LocalTalk network assigns itself an address randomly. The device then broadcasts the address to see if is being used. If not, the device will use it the next time it goes online. A LocalTalk can operate with a star or a bus topology, use STP cables, and can have a maximum of 32 devices attached. Appleshare network is a file server running on an AppleTalk network. It is divided into two zones: EtherTalk, which allows protocols run on an Ethernet COAX cable, and TokenTalk, which allows Macintosh to connect to a token ring network.

The other section of the MAC sub layer is addressing. The physical address, sometimes referred to as the MAC address, is the hardware address that is assigned by a vendor. It is hard coded into the NIC card. The hardware address is the responsibility of the data link layer, whereas, the network number is the responsibility of the network layer. You can think of the hardware address as a home on a street and the network address as the street address where the home is located. A bridge on a network uses the physical address to direct data to the right device, resulting in diminished traffic.

The network layer of the OSI model examines the network layer address and directs data to the appropriate networks. It addresses, manages, and translates logical addresses to physical addresses, and it determines the route from the source to the destination PC. It uses packet switching and routing, and it controls the congestion of data. If the network card on the router cannot transmit data in big chunks, the network layer on the router will compensate by breaking the data into smaller units. I

Information passed by the network layer is referred to as packets or datagrams. A router is a typical device that operates at the network layer. The network layer is broken into three categories: internetworking routing and network control.

1.4.3 Internetworking

Internetworking refers to data flow between multiple independent networks. Internetworking is subdivided into three areas: network path, addressing, and switching. Network path refers to the logical flow of data and is sometimes referred to as the logical topology of a network. There are two types of logical topologies—ring and bus. In a ring logical topology, data are passed from one node to the next. Each node on the network functions as a repeater. As you can see from table 1.4, a token ring network has a physical star topology, but the data inside the network flow in a ring fashion (logical ring). In a bus logical topology, data is transmitted to all the nodes on the network. Note in table 1.3 that a 10BASE-T network has a star physical topology with a bus logical topology.

The second area of internetworking is addressing. The MAC address is a physical address used to transmit frames to and from a specific workstation within a single LAN segment. This addressing is handled with a bridge device at the data link layer. If information has to cross LAN segments, a logical as well as a physical address must be used. The logical network address, which is a combination of network external and physical addresses, is needed to identify nodes on separate networks. Routers are devices that can interpret logical addresses and route data to the appropriate network segment.

The third area of internetworking is switching. Switching techniques are used to route messages through internetworks. There are three different types of switching: circuit, message and packet. Circuit switching is a dedicated circuit that provides a physical connection between the sender and the receiver. It is maintained for as long as data are being transferred. Message switching uses source and destination addresses to transfer data. A message is transmitted from one device to the next. Every time a device receives the message, it is stored until the next device is ready to receive it. This process is repeated until the message reaches its destination. This is why message switching is sometimes referred to as store and forward. E-mail is an excellent example of message switching, because e-mail messages are forwarded form one server to another until they reach the receiver.

Packet switching uses both circuit and message switching to avoid the disadvantages of both. In packet switching, information is broken into small pieces called packets. Each packet contains a header with source, destination, and intermediate node address information. The difference between packet switching and message switching is that packet switching limits the length of a packet. Since packets are much smaller than messages, packets can be stored and forwarded from memory, resulting in a much faster and more efficient way of transferring data. Packet switching uses a virtual circuit—a logical connection between the sending computer and the receiving computer. Data paths for the individual packets depend on the best route at any given instant.

There are two types of packet switching—datagram and virtual-circuit. In datagram packet switching, each packet is treated as if it were a whole message rather than a piece of something larger. Virtual circuit switching establishes a logical connection between the sender and the receiver devices. All packets in virtual-circuit switching will flow in this logical path.

1.4.4 Routing

There are two types of routing in a network—route discovery and route selection. Route discovery is the process of finding all possible routes through the internetwork. Route discovery then builds a routing table to store that information. There are two methods of route discovery—distance-vector and link-state. In distance-vector routing, each router on the network periodically broadcasts the information in the routing table. The other routers then update their routing tables with the broadcast information they receive. NetWare 4.11 uses the concept of distance-vector routing. In link-state routing, routers broadcast their complete routing tables only at startup, and at many fewer time intervals, to minimize network traffic.

Route selection is the process of answering the question, "What is the best way to get there." There are two types of route-selections—dynamic and static. Dynamic route selection uses the cost information in routing tables to find the best way through the network. Cost information (sometimes measured as hops) indicates the different paths the network has used to transfer data from one place to another. The router has the capability to select new paths "on the fly" as it transmits data. In static route selection, the data are designated in advance. They are not selected from routing tables or programmed by an administrator.

1.4.5 Network Control

At the network layer, there are three different types of network controls to provide connection services. These types are network layer flow control, network layer error control, and packet sequence layer control. Network layer flow control is often referred to as congestion control because its principal aim is to avoid congestion on the network by controlling the amount of data sent over a given route. In network layer error control, routers the cyclic redundancy check (CRC) algorithms to detect errors. In packet sequence control, packets are reordered so they can be passed off to upper layers. The network layer also supports different types of packets such as IPX/SPX and TCP/IP.

1.5 TRANSPORT, SESSION, PRESENTATION, AND APPLICATION LAYERS

1.5.1 Transport Layer

The transport layer ensures data are sent and received properly over the network. At this layer, acknowledgments are generated from the receiving station to confirm that a packet was received. At the upper four layers of the OSI model, a gateway is the typical device that operates, and data are referred to as a message. The transport layer is broken into two sections: service addressing, and transport control. There are two types of service addressing. The first is connection identifiers (connection IDs), which are sometimes called sockets or ports. The connection IDs keep track of the dialog and what channel the dialog is delivered on. The second type of service addressing is transaction identifiers (transaction IDs). Transaction IDs are responsible for keeping track of individual requests. They are more flexible than connection IDs, but are a lot harder to track.

The second section of the transport layer is transport control. Transport control is divided into three areas: segmentation, error checking and, end-to-end flow control. The transport layer segmentation groups network layer datagrams into segments for delivery to upper layer services. It also breaks the upper layer service messages into smaller segments for delivery to the network layer. The second area of transport control is error checking. Error checking is the main function of the transport layer. It is responsible for finding out if the message has arrived at its destination or not. Three reliability features are used to ensure that segments arrive at the correct destination. First, the transport layer allows only one virtual circuit per session. Second, it continually monitors the connection ID's segment number. Finally, it uses the network layer time-outs to drop packets that have been passed around the network for too long. The final area of the transport layer is end-to-end control. End-to-end flow control is responsible for completing the communication between the receiver and sender.

1.5.2 Session Layer

The session layer of the OSI model establishes and terminates connections between nodes on the network. After a connection has been established, the session layer manages what occurs between the two nodes and directs problems from the upper layers. Three main tasks are performed at the session layer. First, the session layer is responsible for verifying the password. Then, as at the transport layer, the session layer sends acknowledgments after data are sent successfully. Finally, the session layer assigns the connection ID to be used throughout the session. The session layer is broken into three different sections: connection establishment, data transfer and connection release. Connection establishment is where the verification of the LOGIN name and password is performed. It also establishes a connection ID, agrees on services required, and how long those services would take. Connection establishment also initializes who should start the dialog by coordinating the sequence numbering and the acknowledgment scheme.

The data transfer section of the session layer is responsible for the direction the data can travel through the medium. Data at the session layer may be transferred in three different ways: simplex, half duplex, and full duplex. Simplex communication is when the information in a communication channel flows in one direction only at all times. An example is a radio or TV station. Duplex refers to two-way communication between two systems. Half duplex is when data can be sent in only one direction at a time. Full duplex is when data can be sent in both directions at the same time.

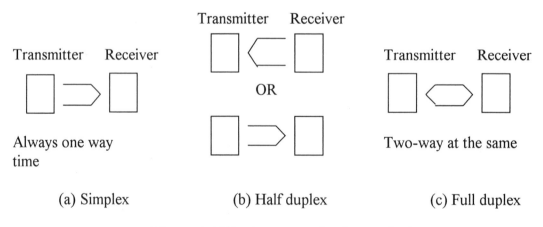

(a) Simplex   (b) Half duplex   (c) Full duplex

Figure 1.13 Basic communication methods

The connection release section of the session layer is mainly responsible for ending a dialog. The most common kind of connection release happens when a user types LOGOUT at a workstation.

1.5.3 Presentation Layer

The presentation layer is responsible for translating data into a format the sending and receiving stations can read. In addition to translation, the presentation layer also manages services such as data compression and encryption. The presentation layer is broken into two sections—translation and encryption. Translation is the main task that is performed by the presentation layer. This term refers to the process by which two computers speaking different languages open up a dialog. Data translation can be performed in four different approaches, namely, bit order, byte order, character code, and file syntax translation. Encryption is a method of scrambling data, and data encryption is the secondary task performed at the presentation layer.

1.5.4 Application Layer

The application layer provides the communication interface between the computer and the user. Examples of functions performed by the application layer are electronic mail, network management, and transfers. The application layer is broken into two sections-service advertisement and service availability. Service advertisement is services that are available on the network. Examples of service advertisement are file, print, message, application, and database services. Service availability is broken down into three concepts; OS call interception, remote operation, and collaborative computing. OS call interception is used when the local operating system is completely unaware of the network, and remote operation is when there are servers unaware of clients on the network. Collaborative computing is when both the server and the client are aware of each other and work together.

1.6 PROTOCOL SUITES

In this section we will cover the most widely used protocol suites, as well as miscellaneous protocols and standards used throughout the world. A protocol suite is a group of protocols that work together. We will cover NetWare protocols, Internet protocols, AppleTalk protocols, DNA protocols, SNA protocols, and miscellaneous protocols. Each protocol corresponds to a layer in the OSI model.

1.6.1 NetWare Protocols

The most famous NetWare protocols are MLID, IPX, NLSP, RIP, SPX, NCP, and SAP. Novell developed NetWare protocols in the early 1980s. Xerox, Inc. designed them at their research center called the Xerox Network System (XNS).

MLID (Multiple Link Interface Drivers) operates at the MAC sub layer of the data link layer of the OSI model. It is mainly concerned with medium access methods. MLID is a standard for network drivers. It is sometimes referred to as a LAN or network driver. IPX (Internetwork Packet Exchange) operates at the network layer of the OSI model. It is a connectionless protocol, and it deals with the addressing, route selection, and connection services. NLSP (Network Link Services Protocol) operates at the network layer of the OSI model. It uses the link-state discovery method to build routing tables based upon IS-IS (Intermediate System - Intermediate system). RIP (Routing Information Protocol) operates at the network layer of the OSI model. It is the main routing protocol for NetWare. It uses the distance-vector routing discovery method to determine the hop count.

SPX (Sequenced Packet Exchange) operates at the transport layer of the OSI model. It is a connection-oriented protocol that provides reliability to IPX through connection IDs. NCP (NetWare Core Protocol) operates at the fourth layer of the OSI model. NCP at the transport layer is used for connection services. It uses segment sequencing, error control, and end-to-end flow control. NCP at the session layer handles administration for data transfer, while at the presentation layer it handles the translation of character code and file syntax. NCP at the application layer handles service use and provides an operating system redirector. Finally, the protocol SAP (Service Advertising Protocol) operates at the session and application layers of the OSI model. SAP at the session layer is responsible for file transfer, and at the application layer it is responsible for active service advertisement.

1.6.2 Internet Protocols

The most used Internet protocols are IP, ARP, ICMP, OSPF, TCP, UDP, DNS, FTP, TELNET, SMTP, and NFS. The Internet protocols are often referred to as TCP/IP. As in NetWare protocols, Internet protocols do not include the physical and data link layers of the OSI model. TCP/IP protocols are so flexible that they can run over Ethernet, token ring, token bus, HDLC, and X.25 systems- with minor configuration adjustments.

Let us begin with the IP protocol. IP (Internet Protocol) operates at the network layer of the OSI model. It is responsible for addressing, switching purposes, and route selection services. ARP (Address Resolution Protocol) operates at the network layer of the OSI model. ARP is used to map nodes to IP addresses. ICMP (Internet Control Message Protocol) operates at the network layer of the OSI model. ICMP works with IP to augment error handling and control procedures. OSPF (Open Shortest Path First) operates at the network layer of the OSI model. OSPF is a link-state routing protocol that provides load balancing and routing based on class of service.

TCP (Transport Control Protocol) operates at the transport layer of the OSI model. TCP is concerned with addressing services at the network layer. It is full duplex, provides reliability, and is connection-oriented. UDP (User Datagram Protocol) operates at the transport layer of the OSI model. UDP is a connectionless protocol that transports datagrams without acknowledging their arrival. DNS (Domain

Name System) operates at the transport layer. DNS is a distributed database that provides name-to-address mappings to client applications.

FTP (File Transfer Protocol) operates at the session, presentation, and application layers of the OSI model. FTP at the session layer allows you to transfer files from one host to another, and it is responsible for connection establishment and connection release. At the presentation layer, FTP is responsible for translation. At the application layer, FTP is responsible for file services and collaborative service use. Telne*t* operates at the session, presentation, and application layers of the OSI model. It enables a computer to emulate a terminal for connection to a host-based application. At the session layer, Telnet is responsible for dialog control. It is full duplex and handles connection establishment, message transfer, and connection release. At the presentation layer, Telnet is responsible for translation using byte order and character code. At the application layer, Telnet is responsible for service use and remote operation. SMTP (Simple Mail Transfer Protocol) operates at the application layer of the OSI model. SMTP is responsible for routing e-mail messages. Finally, NFS (Network File System) operates at the application layer of the OSI model. NFS is responsible for file services and remote operation service use.

1.6.3 AppleTalk Protocols

AppleTalk is the main operating system for Apple Macintosh computer systems. AppleTalk is broken into two phases. Phase 1 does not provide support for internetworks. It supports only 254 node connections per network. Phase 2 allow internetworking and it can support up to 16 million nodes per network. The most famous AppleTalk protocols are LocalTalk, EtherTalk, TokenTalk, AARP, DDP, RTMP, NBP, ATP, ADSP, ASP, PAP, ZIP, AFP, and Appleshare.

LocalTalk (LLAP- LocalTalk Link Access Protocol) operates at the physical and data link layers of the OSI model. LocalTalk handles all the properties of the physical and data link layer of the OSI model. EtherTalk (ELAP) operates at the physical and data link layers of the OSI model. EtherTalk uses Ethernet protocols at the physical and data link layers of the OSI model. TokenTalk (TLAP) operates at the physical and data link layers of the OSI model. TokenTalk uses Token ring protocols at the physical and data link layers of the OS model. AARP (AppleTalk Address Resolution Protocol) operates at the data link layer of the OSI model. It is responsible for mapping AppleTalk addresses to Ethernet and Token ring. DDP (Datagram Delivery Protocol) operates at the network layer of the OSI model. DDP is responsible for providing connectionless and datagram services. RTMP (Routing Table Maintenance Protocol) operates at the network layer of the OSI model. RTMP is a distance-vector routing protocol similar to RIP.

NBP (Name Building Protocol) operates at the transport layer of the OSI model. It is responsible for matching a logical device name with its associated address. ATP (AppleTalk Transaction Protocol) operates at the transport layer. ATP is responsible for acknowledging connectionless transaction using transaction IDs.

ADSP (AppleTalk Data Stream Protocol) operates at the session layer of the OSI model. It is responsible for establishing and releasing connections. ASP (AppleTalk Session Protocol) operates at the session layer of the OSI model. It is responsible for establishing, maintaining, and releasing a connection. PAP (Printer Access Protocol) operates at the session layer. It is responsible for printing and initiating service requesters and service providers. ZIP (Zone Information Protocol) operates at the session layer of the OSI model. It is responsible for organizing devices into logical groups of zones to reduce the complexity of internetworks. AFP (AppleTalk Filing Protocol) operates at the session and presentation layers of the OSI model. At both layers, AFP is responsible for facilitating file sharing and translation of file system commands. It also enhances security by establishing connection through encryption of the login information. Appleshare operates at the application layer of the OSI model. It provides file server, print server, and Appleshare PC services.

1.6.4 DNA Protocols

DNA (Digital Network Architecture) protocols are proprietary standards designed by Digital Equipment Corporation (DEC) for managing terminal-host networks. DNA in recent years came up with DNS phase V protocols to support the OSI model. The most famous DNA protocols are DDCMP, HDLC, CLNS, CONS, NSP, ISO 8327, ANS.1 with BER, FTAM, DAP, NVTS, Mailbus X.400, and Naming Service X.500. DDCMP (Digital Data Communication Message Protocol) operates at the physical and LLC layers of the OSI model. DDCMP can be half or full duplex. It is connection-oriented and it uses commands and acknowledgments for error control. HDLC (High-Level Data Link Control) operates at the data link layer of the OSI model. HDLC can support synchronous and asynchronous transmission. CLNS (Connectionless Network System) operates at the network layer of the OSI model. CLNS is a connectionless protocol that can support the protocols ISO 8473, ISO 9542, and ISO 10589. CONS (Connection Oriented Network Service) operate at the network layer of the OSI model. CONS is a connection-oriented protocol that can support the protocols ISO 8208 and ISO 8878. CONS and CLNS both provide link-state route discovery and dynamic route selection.

NSP (Network Services Protocol) operates at the transport layer of the OSI model. NSP is connection-oriented, and full duplex, and it uses guaranteed rate or sliding window for flow control method. ISO 8073 (Connection-Oriented Transport Protocol Specification) operates at the session layer of the OSI model. ISO 8327 is half duplex, and it is responsible for negotiating connections and connection release. ASN.*1* with BER (Abstract Syntax Notation One with Basic Encoding Rules) operates at the presentation layer of the OSI model. ASN.1 with BER is responsible for explaining the syntax rules for data exchange between different systems. FTAM (File Transfer Access and Management) operates at the application layer of the OSI model. FTAM is a generic file transfer, access, and management protocol. DAP (Data Access

Protocol) operates at the application layer of the OSI model. DAP has the ability to transfer files. NVTS (Network Virtual Terminal Service) operates at the presentation and application layers of the OSI model. At both layers, NVTS is responsible for virtual terminal access hosts. Mailbus and X.400 Message Handling System (MHS) operates at the application layer of the OSI model. Mailbus and X.400 are responsible for e-mail services. Novell uses X.400 (MHS) for their message handling services (e-mail). Naming Services and X.500 Directory operates at the transport and application layers of the OSI model. Naming Services and X.500 are responsible for address-name resolution.

1.6.5 SNA Protocols

SNA (System Network Architecture) protocols are proprietary standards designed by IBM for use in mainframes, communication controllers, and terminals. Recently SNA enhanced the protocols with LU (Logic Unit) 6.2 and PU (Physical Unit) 2.1. Logical Units (LUs) are the end points of network communication and include terminals, printers, and programs that communicate by using SNA. Physical Units (PUs) provide physical connection on the network, and they consist of a combination of hardware, firmware and software. The most famous SNA protocols are SDLC, NCP, APPN, VTAM, CICS, IMS, APPC, DDM, SNADS, and DIA. SDLC (Synchronous Data Link Control) operates at the data link layer of the OSI model. SDLC uses the polling method to support multi-point topologies. NCP (Network Control Program) operates at the data link layer of the OSI model. NCP is responsible for controlling resources that are attached to the communication controllers. APPN (Advanced Peer-to-Peer Networking) operates at the network and transport layers. At both layers, APPN is responsible for peer-to-peer networking between multiple physical units. VTAM (Virtual Telecommunication Access Method) operates at the transport layer of the OSI model. VTAM is responsible for controlling data communication and data flow. CICS (Customer Information Control System) operates at the session layer of the OSI model. CISC is half duplex, and it is responsible for building transactions and processing application. IMS (Information Management System) operates at the session layer of the OSI model. It is also a transaction-processing programming environment similar to CICS. APPC (Advanced Program-to-Program Communication) operates at the transport and session layers of the OSI model. At both layers, APPC allows peer-to-peer communication between logical units. DDM (Distributed Data Management) operates at the application layer of the OSI model. DDM is responsible for transparent remote access to files. SNADS (SNA Distributed Services) operates at the application layer of the OSI model. SNADS is responsible for controlling the distribution of messages and documents. DIA (Document Interchange Architecture) operates at the application layer of the OSI model. It is responsible for defining a standard for exchanging documents between dissimilar systems.

1.6.6 Miscellaneous Protocols

This section will primarily cover miscellaneous protocols used in LAN and WAN networks. The IEEE (Institute of Electrical and Electronics Engineers) is responsible for the 802 series standards. The 802 series standards are important in the world of LAN networks, since they define Ethernet and token ring networks. The following table (Table 1.7) defines the IEEE series, the standard it defines, and the layer of the OSI model it corresponds to.

IEEE	STANDARD	OSI MODEL
802.1	Overall	Physical to transport
802.2	LLC	Logic control layer
802.3	Ethernet-CSMA/CD	Physical and data link
802.4	Token bus-Token passing	Physical and data link
802.5	Token ring-Token passing	Physical and data link
802.6	MAN network	Physical and data link
802.7	Broadband technology	"Under development", physical and data link
802.8	FDDI-token passing	Physical and data link
802.9	Integrated voice & data (ISDN)	LLC
802.10	LAN Security	Network to session
802.11	Wireless LANs	"Under development", physical and data link
802.12	100VG-AnyLAN	"Under development", physical and data link

Table 1.7 IEEE 802 series

Other miscellaneous protocols include SLIP, PPP, FDDI, X.25, Frame relay, ISDN, SONET, ATM, and SMDS.

SLIP (Serial Line Internet Protocol) and PPP (Point-to-Point Protocol) are used with dial-up connection to the Internet. PPP is an improved version of SLIP.

FDDI (Fiber Distributed Data Interface) is a LAN or a MAN standard that can be physically connected in a ring or a star. It uses a token passing media access method similar to IEEE 802.5. It is a 100 Mbps token ring network that uses fiber optic cables. Its maximum ring length is 100 km and 500 PCs. It is different from the IEEE 802.5 standard. FDDI can transmit as many frames as it can produce within a predetermined time before letting the token go. Furthermore, more than 1 computer can transmit at the same time with an FDDI network. The computer detects a fault and then sends a "beacon" to its upstream neighbor, and so on, until it reaches the computer that originally sent the beacon. The original computer then receives its own beacon back and assumes that the problem is fixed; then it regenerates the token.

The CCITT (Telephone Consultative Committee International Telegraph and) developed the X.25 protocol. X.25 is a WAN standard protocol that uses packet switching technology. It uses switches, circuits, and routes as available to provide the best routing to any particular time. It also uses telephone lines, which are slow, and has error checking. Finally, the X.25 protocol requires a DTC/DCE interface, and it can be a synchronous packer-mode host, as in a Public Data Network (PDN over a dedicated leased-line circuit, or some other device).

Frame relay is similar to X.25 protocol. It makes use of packet switching technology with virtual circuits. Frame relay is a fast packet variable-length, and digital technology. In addition, it requires a frame-relay capable router or a bridge. It is a point-to-point technology, and uses PVC to transmit at the data link layer over a leased digital line.

ISDN (Integrated Services Digital Networks) provides transmission of voice, video, and data over digital telephone lines. It uses 3 data channels—2 for 64 Kbps, and 1 for 16 Kbps. The 64 Kbps channels are known as B channels and carry voice, data, or images. The 16 Kbps channels are known as the D channels which carry signaling and link management data. The basic rate = 2B + D. Finally, ISDN is a dial-up service- not dedicated, and not bandwidth on demand.

SONET (Synchronous Optical Network) is a physical layer protocol generally used by WAN networks. It is a synchronous optical network that uses fiber optic cables. It works with frequencies larger than 1 Gbps.

ATM (Asynchronous Transfer Mode) is a data link layer mostly used for WANs. It uses cell-switching technology. A cell is a 53-byte packet. It is a fixed-sized packet over broadband and baseband LANs or WANs. It can be transmitted at 155 Mbps, 622 Mbps or more. It is a broadband cell relay method that transmits data in 53-byte cells (each with 48 bytes of application information) rather than in variable-length frames. You can transmit up to 1.2 Gbps or more. An ATM requires hardware, such as routers or bridges, that is compatible with ATM. ATMs also require switches (multiple hubs; router-like devices). The transmission rate of ATM depends on what media are being used:

Media	Rate
FDDI	100 Mbps
Fiber channel	155 Mbps
OC3 SONET	155 Mbps
T3	45 Mbps

SMDS (Switched Megabit Data Service) is similar to ATM. It also uses cell switching, but it can be mapped into the data link and network layers of the OSI model. It is a multi-mega bit data service that can transmit at 1 Mbps to 34 Mbps.

Questions

1. What is the purpose of the OSI model?
2. List all the layers of the OSI model, and name the data in each layer.
3. Describe the function of each layer of the OSI mode.
4. Where do the following devices operate in the OSI model? Describe the function of each.

   Gateway, Repeater, Bridge, Router

5. What is the transmission media for a 10BaseT?
6. What are the possible physical topologies and media access control methods for the following networks?

   FDDI, 10Base5, Token Ring, 10BaseT, 10Base2

7. What is the name of the node that ensures the integrity of the token as it travels along the channel?
8. Describe the following:

   a) Centralized computing
   b) Distributed computing
   c) Collaborative computing
   d) Network models
   e) MAN (Metropolitan Area Network)
   f) Network services
   g) File update synchronization
   h) Application servers
   i) Configuration management
   j) Fault management
   k) Performance management
   l) Security management
   m) Account management
   n) Fiber optic cable
   o) COAX cable
   p) Active hub

9. What are the advantages of having a bounded media?
10. What is the capacity of a UTP?
11. Which bounded media has the worst attenuation and EMI?

12. What type of cable would you use to connect 100 PCs on one floor of a building?
13. Name three components of the physical layer.
14. Name all of the communication devices and interconnectivity devices.
15. Name all the most popular multi-point physical topologies and name the two main components required in a physical topology.
16. List all the advantages and disadvantages of the most popular multi point physical topologies.
17. What does beaconing mean?
18. Which digital encoding strategy uses the Manchester coding scheme? Which uses the differential Manchester scheme?
19. Describe the following:

    a) Asynchronous transmission
    b) Synchronous transmission
    c) TDM
    d) StatTDM
    e) FDM

20. Name the five functions of the data link layer.
21. Describe the following:

    a) Packet switching
    b) Message switching
    c) Circuit switching
    d) Path congestion
    e) Connection identifier
    f) Transaction identifier
    g) Simplex transfer method
    h) Duplex transfer method
    i) Half-duplex transfer method
    j) OS call interception

22. Name three reliability features used at the transport layer.
23. Name two tasks performed at the session layer.
24. At what layer do the following protocols operate?

    a) FTAM
    b) FTP
    c) AARP
    d) ATP
    e) IPX
    f) NCP

g) SPX
h) TCP

25. Define all 12 IEEE 802 series standards. How does each compare to the OSI model?
26. Name an emerging broadband ISDN standard that uses cell relay technology to perform network layer activities.

2

Introduction to IntranetWare/NetWare 4.11

In this chapter, you will learn the responsibilities of an IntranetWare administrator, user interfaces, and how to create multiple users using UIMPORT. In addition, you will learn how to implement a client installation in a DOS and Windows environment. A quick overview of NDS, user objects, and login security will also be introduced.

2.1 INTRANETWARE/NETWARE 4.11 BASICS

The main purpose of having a network is to provide clients access to network resources and services. A network resource could be a disk volume or a network printer for example. A network service is a system or a method of providing a resource. In the latest version of NetWare (NetWare 4.11, sometimes called IntranetWare), the service provider (server) provides a vast range of network services. As an example, multiple clients may access network services from the server simultaneously. Remember that a network administrator's main responsibility is to manage all the network services provided by the server. Now let us discuss the six fundamental network services that NetWare 4 provides.

1. NDS—This stands for NetWare Directory Services. It oversees the whole network operation from logging in to multiprotocol routing. It is the most fundamental type of network service after network communications. It maintains a database of information on all of the network resources. Users are authenticated (logged in and verified) by the network itself through NDS. NDS replaces the Bindery used in earlier versions of NetWare. It processes a client's request for a network resource in the following ways:

- A client requests a resource.

- The NetWare server responds.

- NDS locates the object in the directory.

- The resource location is identified.

- NDS checks the client for validity.

- NDS connects the client with the resource.

2. Security services— With IntranetWare Novell provides the NetWare Enhanced Security (NES) which is designed to meet class C-2 compliance. Class C-2 is the minimum-security specification for high-security corporate and government networks. NetWare security regulates access to network resources. The network user account and NDS user objects are the most fundamental type of network security.

3. File services—The IntranetWare file system can now support extended name spaces and can hold 8,000,000 files per volume. It is used to store shared data files and applications and allows clients to share disk drives on the file server. The file system is enhanced when clients use the new 32-bit IntranetWare client architecture. The new 32-bit client architecture delivers a higher level of performance.

4. Print services—Printing in IntranetWare allows clients to print to a shared printer attached to the network. The network printer may be attached to a print server, file server, workstation, or network cable.

5. SMS—This stands for Storage Management Services. It enables data to be stored and retrieved by using a variety of front-end applications. SBACKUP is the SMS background engine for IntranetWare. It is used for backing up or restoring server or workstation data. SBACKUP consists of SBACKUP.NLM and other TSA NLMs.

6. MHS—This stands for Message Handling Services. It provides a background engine for storing and forwarding IntranetWare messages. In addition, it has the starter e-mail application FirstMail.

A network can connect multiple computers and peripherals to share resources with one another. These resources could be any of the following: file storage and printing, connectivity and interoffice communication, central and distributed management, backup, data protection and security, and access to remote hosts or other networks. The most basic hardware components of a network are workstations, servers, network boards, communication media, and peripheral devices.

Workstation—This is the most common type of client on a network. It requests resources and services from a server. It may also process and manage its own applications and data files. A workstation could be a personal computer, an Apple

MAC machine, a UNIX machine, an OS/2 machine, a printer, or another server, but in most cases it is a standalone PC. Its synonyms are user, station, client, and end node.

Server—This is a computer that provides network resources and services through the use of the NetWare operating system to clients.

Network boards—This is an interface card, and it is sometimes called a NIC (Network Interface Card). Every server and workstation must have a NIC installed. The NICs in the server and workstation are connected through a communication medium.

Communication media— This is the media that links all the network devices together. Examples of communication media are coaxial cable, fiber optic cable, microwave signals, etc.

Peripheral devices—These are devices that connect to a workstation, server, or a cable. Examples of peripheral devices are printers, disk drives, modems, etc.

Novell Inc. has designed the NetWare network computer operating system to connect, manage, and maintain a computer network and its services. Most NetWare components run on the file server while others run only on the client side. IntranetWare can support many workstation operating systems including DOS, MS Windows 3.x, MS Windows 95, OS/2, Macintosh, and UNIX. All of these workstation operating systems and environments can access NetWare network resources. However, DOS, MS Windows 3.x, MS Windows 95 and OS/2 operating systems and environments also have utilities to administer the network.

2.2 THE INTRANETWARE ADMINISTRATOR AND CLIENT SUPPORT

A network administrator is responsible for many tasks that include setting up, organizing, managing, tuning, protecting, backing up, and documenting the network. These tasks can all be performed using IntranetWare software.

• Setting up—The network administrator must be familiar with IntranetWare to be able to set up a server and workstations, network hardware and software, and storage of data and applications, as well as to set up workstations to connect automatically to the network.

• Organizing—The network administrator should know how to organize and configure all the network resources.

• Managing—The network administrator must be able to implement and maintain a security system and a network-printing environment.

- Tuning—The network administrator must have the knowledge to tune the server to its optimum performance.

- Protecting—The network administrator must guarantee data integrity and protection.

- Backing up—The network administrator must be able to back up and retrieve data.

- Documenting—The network administrator must document the entire network hardware configuration, system configuration, applications, and licensing information.

Remember, IntranetWare provides communication, file, and print services to DOS, MS Windows, OS/2, Macintosh, and UNIX. In this book we will be mostly concerned with DOS and MS Windows client support of IntranetWare. To administer the network, DOS clients can support the protocols IPX, TCP/IP and many others. To have a DOS and Windows client running on your computer, you must run the file INSTALL.EXE. In order to support long name and extended attributes for OS/2 or Macintosh clients, the network administrator must install OS/2 and Macintosh name space on the NetWare volumes.

You can attach a client in a 32-bit or a 16-bit environment. The 32-bit environment provides 32 bits of graphical access to IntranetWare servers. This allows Windows 95, Windows 3.x, and DOS workstations to connect to NetWare 4.11 servers. Through Windows IntranetWare provides you with graphical logins and you can access network resources using Windows 95 Network Neighborhood and the Windows Explorer. Client 32 is the newest and most powerful workstation connectivity. The 16-bit environment provides DOS access to an IntranetWare server through ODI drivers, VLMs, and NET.CFG.

In the 16-bit environment, ODI (Open Data-Link Interface) increases the functionality of the network by supporting multiple network protocols and drivers through a single NIC or cabling system. In addition, ODI allows devices with different communication protocols to coexist on the same network. The main advantages of using ODI are:

- You can communicate simultaneously with a mixture of workstations, servers, and mainframes.

- You can communicate through a network board written to ODI specifications.

- Fewer hardware components need to be supported.

- Easy configuration using NET.CFG.

IntranetWare will set up DOS workstations as DOS ODI workstations by default. Do not forget that DOS can provide file storage to disks, screen display access, printer access, and communication or modem access. You must load the following four files on the workstation in the order listed below. Remember that you can always load these files in AUTOEXEC.BAT to have them load automatically.

Layer	Program	Description
Link support layer	LSL.COM	This is a protocol used to route data from a different protocol between the LAN driver and the communication protocol.
MLID and LAN Driver	NE2000.COM	NE2000 is an example of a LAN driver. MLID stands for Multiple Link Interface Drivers. MLIDs are LAN drivers that support ODI. The LAN driver is a program that connects the software and the hardware of the network together. A LAN driver also provides communications between the LSL layer and MLID layer.
Communication protocol	IPXODI.COM	This program manages communication between stations by sending and receiving data. Once data is received it will pass it to the DOS requester or to another network.
NetWare DOS requester	VLM.EXE	VLM stands for Virtual Loadable Module. VLM.EXE, which enables the DOS requester is the program that actually does the work on the workstation. VLM.EXE is the VLM manager. It works with DOS to handle file and print requests. VLMs are programs that perform related functions. The DOS requester is the "middle man" between the local software and the network services. It lies between DOS and NetWare. All logins and logouts are stored in the DOS requester and it deletes them when the user disconnects from the network. The DOS requester can perform tasks such as file and print redirection, connection maintenance, and packet (data) handling. The DOS requester is designed to let us load or unload VLMs whenever we want. It also reduces workstation overhead by using only the needed components.

The above four files must be loaded in the order in which they are listed above, i.e., LSL.COM, NE2000.COM, IPXODI.COM, then VLM.EXE. However, a DOS workstation will establish connection with the network using the above four programs in the following order: NE2000.COM, LSL.COM, IPXODI.COM and VLM.EXE.

VLM.EXE, the VLM manager which can support DOS 3.1 and above, is responsible for handling requests from applications and routing them to the proper VLM. It also manages communications between modules and controls memory services, allocation, and management. You have to run VLM.EXE to enable the DOS requester. VLM.EXE will load a series of VLM files by default and will go into the extended memory by default. If the extended memory is not available, it will then select the expanded memory. If neither the extended nor the expanded memory is available, then VLM.EXE will default to the conventional memory. You can load VLMs using VLM.EXE by loading them from the current directory, loading them as specified in NET.CFG if the "USE DEFAULT = OFF:" setting is used, or loading the ones listed in the directory, or file_spec, if "VLM /C = file_spec" is used.

You must add the command VLM = vlm_name in the DOS requester section of the NET.CFG file to specify the VLM load sequence. The following are the VLM.EXE commands that are used to load the DOS requester:

Command	Description
VLM/?	Displays the help screen.
VLM	Loads the VLMs in the current directory or as specified in the NET.CFG file.
VLM U	Unloads the VLM.EXE program from memory.
VLM /PS=server_name	During load, this attaches the server name requested to ensure that all users do not try to attach to the same server.
VLM /PT=tree_name	During load, this attaches the tree name requested to ensure that all users do not try to attach to the same tree.
VLM /C=file_spec	Loads the VLMs that are found or listed in the file file_spec.
VLM /mx	Loads VLMs in the extended memory.
VLM /me	Loads VLMs in the expanded memory.
VLM /mc	Loads VLMs in the conventional memory.
VLM /D	Displays the VLM.EXE file diagnostic or status information.
VLM /V0	Displays copy right and critical errors.
VLM /V1	Displays warning messages.
VLM /V2	Displays loaded VLM module names.
VLM /V3	Displays the configuration file parameters in the NET.CFG file.
VLM /V4	Displays diagnostic messages.

In a 32-bit environment it is Client 32 that makes the most powerful workstation. Here are some advantages of connecting a Client 32 using Windows 95:

- Windows 95 is a true 32-bit operating system.

- NIOS, the core Client 32 file, runs as a virtual device driver (VXD) rather than as an executable file.

- Windows 95 loads Client 32 automatically, therefore it does not need a STARTUP.BAT file.

- The configuration settings are saved in the Registry of Windows 95, therefore Client 32 does not need the NET.CFG file.

- Client 32 supports long filenames.

- Using the "Batch Install", you can upgrade Windows 3.1 to Windows 95 and Client 32 in one process.

When you install Client 32, a directory named C:\NOVELL\CLIENT32 is created on drive C. All the files for Client 32 are placed in this directory and changes are made to the Windows 95 Registry. When Windows 95 boots up the following files are executed in order.

1. NIOS.VXD—This is the core Client 32 component. It is executed as a virtual device driver (VXD).

2. LSLC32.NLM—This is the link support layer for protocol switchboarding.

3. MLID—This is the multiple link interface driver. It is a type of a LAN driver (NIC), i.e., NE2000.com.

4. CMSM.NLM—This is a C-based version of the Media Support Module in the ODI architecture.

5. ETHERTSM.NLM—This is a Client 32 that uses Topology Support Modules (TSMs). It provides Ethernet topology support for the NIC driver.

6. CLIENT 32.NLM—This provides all the Client 32 services.

2.3 CLIENT INSTALLATION AND CONFIGURATION

Before we begin the installation of a Client 32 workstation using Windows 95, the following hardware is needed:

- An 80386 microprocessor or higher.

- A minimum of 6 MB of RAM for Windows 95, and a minimum of 5 MB for Windows 3.1 and DOS.

- A network board that supports a 32-bit LAN driver.

- Physical connection to a network with an operating system (Windows 95) installed locally.

Client 32 workstation installation for Windows 95 is a simple task. Just perform the following steps and you'll be on your way to connecting a Client 32 workstation.

1. Run the file SETUP.EXE from the directory SYS:\PUBLIC\WIN95\IBM_ENU or from the CD-ROM directory D:\PRODUCTS\WIN95\IBM_ENU.

2. After the license agreement, select start to begin. SETUP will automatically install and configure your Client 32 workstation with default properties.

3. When SETUP is complete, click on customize to make changes to properties like Preferred Server, Preferred Tree, Name Context, Login Scripts, and NIC Settings.

You can also install a Client 32 workstation for Windows 3.1, but you will have to configure the CONFIG.SYS, AUTOEXEC.BAT, and NET.CFG files. If you want to install Client 16, you also must configure the CONFIG.SYS, AUTOEXEC.BAT, and NET.CFG files. In IntranetWare the DOS requester on the workstation is what makes the client communicate with the server. When you install a Client 16 workstation the NetWare DOS requester file is copied into the directory C:\NWCLIENT and then the CONFIG.SYS and AUTOEXEC.BAT files are modified so the workstation can boot up automatically. Again, the three files that need to be modified when configuring a Client 16 workstation are CONFIG.SYS, AUTOEXEC.BAT, and NET.CFG.

- CONFIG.SYS—The command LASTDRIVE = Z must be placed at the end of the CONFIG.SYS file so that when the NetWare DOS requester reads all the hardware configuration it can make all the letters between the last known drive and the letter declared in the LASTDRIVE command available for mapping network drives.

- AUTOEXEC.BAT—The command @CALL C:\NWCLIENT\STARTNET.BAT must be placed in AUTOEXEC.BAT. STARTNET.BAT is a workstation startup file that loads the DOS client software in the order shown below:

Content Of STARTNET.BAT	Description
SET NWLANGUAGE = ENGLISH	Provides internationalization.
C:\NWCLIENT\LSL.COM	Loads the link support layer.
C:\NWCLIENT\3C5X9.COM	Loads the LAN driver 3C5X9.
C:\NWCLIENT\IPXODI.COM	Loads the protocol file.

C:\NWCLIENT\VLM.EXE   Loads the VLM manager to enable the DOS requester.

You must also place in AUTOEXEC.BAT the command F:, which sets up the first network drive pointer, and the line LOGIN user_name, which enables user_name to log in automatically. A typical AUTOEXEC.BAT file should look like this:

```
PATH=C:\NWCLIENT
@CALL STARTNET.BAT
F:
LOGIN user_name
```

Since all of the required commands are in STARTNET.BAT, we can execute them automatically from the AUTOEXEC.BAT file without running STARTNET.BAT. In this case AUTOEXEC.BAT may look like the following:

```
C:
CD \NWCLIENT
SET NWLANGUAGE = ENGLISH
LSL.COM
3C5X9.COM
IPXODI.COM
VLM.EXE
F:
LOGIN  user_name
```

You must unload the DOS client software in reverse order to avoid corruption. You can use the following commands to unload the client software from memory.

```
VLM.EXE /U
IPXODI.COM /U
3C5X9.COM /U
LSL.COM /U
```

Before we discuss NET.CFG, remember that if you are installing Client 16 on Windows 3.1, INSTALL.EXE will modify the files SYSTEM.INI, WIN.INI, and PROGMAN.INI. Also remember that if the installation is not successful we may copy .BNW files over the .INI files to restore Windows.

- NET.CFG—The NET.CFG file on the workstation is used to modify the operating parameters of the DOS requester or IPX. You can use any DOS text editor to create the NET.CFG file. The NET.CFG file provides information to the network startup files. There are three major section headings you should be concerned with in a NET.CFG file. In other words, the NET.CFG file stores configuration information such as frame types, protocols used, and preferred server names.

a) Link Driver driver_name—This heading declares the name and setting of the LAN driver that is in the workstation

b) Link Support—This heading sets the receive buffers, memory pool buffers, maximum number of boards and stacks used, etc. The link support layer is usually included when there is more than one protocol running.

c) NetWare DOS requester—This heading sets the user environment and loads VLMs.

NET.CFG is a standard ASCII text file that acts as a central location where other programs such as LSL.COM and VLM.EXE can read any configuration options that you have set. When configuring your NET.CFG file you must follow the syntax and convention rules listed below:

a) Section headings are placed flush against the left margin.

b) Configuration options for each section are indented with one tab directly beneath the appropriate heading; there should be no space after the section heading.

c) A single space should be left between sections.

d) Each comment line to be inserted in the NET.CFG file should be preceded by a semicolon (;) or a pound sign (#).

e) All numbers must be written in decimal notation except where noted.

f) End each line with a hard return.

The following is a sample of a NET.CFG file with a line-by line description:

Command	Description
LINK DRIVER *3C5X9*	Declares the 3C5X9 ODI driver for the NIC.
INT 10	Declares an interrupt of 10.
PORT 300	Declares a port address of 300 hex.
FRAME Ethernet_802.3	Declares frame type. Both the server and the workstation must have the same frame type.

PROTOCOL IPXODI	Configures to use IPXODI.COM protocol.
NetWare DOS REQUESTER	
FIRST NETWORK DRIVE = F	Declares F as the first network drive.
PREFERRED SERVER = FS_1	Sets FS_1 as the default server.
NAME CONTEXT = "OU=AC.O=EN"	Sets the current context. Notice that you must use the distinguished name, so no leading period is allowed.
CONNECTION = 50	Sets the maximum amount of connections to 50.
USE DEFAULTS = OFF	To override the default VLMs that VLM.EXE loads.
VLM = SECURITY.VLM	Loads the VLM SECURITY.VLM file.

If you have a large number of users, you should always create or customize the NET.CFG file during the DOS client installation by editing the NET.CFG parameters in the INSTALL.CFG file before executing the NetWare Client installation program. Initially the information in the NET.CFG file is based on the information in the INSTALL.CFG file. If you use INSTALL.CFG, then the client installation program will place the customized NET.CFG from INSTALL.CFG on each workstation.

2.4 LOGGING IN

Logging into the network using Client 32 is a very easy task. The GUI (Graphical User Interface) of the Windows 3.1 or the Windows 95 login utility provides simple name and password boxes in the Login page. The other three pages are the Connection page, which is used to specify an NDS tree, server, and/or login context; the Script page, which is used to allow a user to override a container and a profile script with a text file; finally, the Variable page is used to customize the login script variables.

Before any user can log onto the network, he/she must be connected. IntranetWare provides three different login utilities for Windows and DOS users: LOGINW95.EXE is a Windows 95 GUI login utility and can be found in the directory C:\NOVELL\CLIENT32. LOGINW31.EXE is a Windows 3.1 GUI login utility and also can be found in the directory C:\NOVELL\CLIENT32. The LOGIN.EXE is not a GUI login utility. It is for DOS users only and can be found in the directory SYS: LOGIN.

If you are running Client 16 NetWare DOS, you can include the DOS client commands to log on to the network in three different ways: the AUTOEXEC.BAT file, the STARTNET.BAT file, or by commands entered from the DOS prompt. Here is a list of DOS client commands that may be helpful during logging into and logging out of the network.

Command	Description
LOGIN .ADMIN.NET	Logs in as the user .ADMIN.NET.
ENTER YOUR PASSWORD	After typing the login name you must type in a password.
DIR	List the contents of the current drive or directory you are in.
NVER	Finds out what NetWare version you are using.
NDIR /?	Gets help on the NDIR command.
NDIR /DO	Lists the directories only in the current drive or directory.
NDIR /FO	Lists the files only in the current drive or directory.
NLIST /?	Gets help on NLIST command.
NLIST SERVER	Lists all the servers available.
NLIST USER	Lists all the user objects.
NLIST USER /A	Lists all the active or logged in users.
CX	Displays the current context.
CX /?	Gets help on the CX command.
CX /T	Lists the NDS tree at or below the current context.
CX /T /A	Lists all the objects at or below the current context.
CX /T /A /R	Lists all the objects at or below the [Root].
CX /R	Changes the current context to the [Root].
LOGOUT	Logs the user out of the network.

That's all it really takes to log in and connect to a network. Now it is time to discuss the fundamentals of NDS, user objects, and login security.

2.5 NDS FUNDAMENTALS

NDS (NetWare Directory Services) is a directory (sometimes referred to as a naming service) provided by IntranetWare to maintain a database of network resources. Each component in the NDS is called an object. An object is a unit of information about a specific resource. Since an object is similar to a row of information in a database, it must contain a property and a value. A property is the information given about an object. A value of an object is the actual data within the property. NDS uses the properties to record information about the object. Some objects may have similar properties but others may not. Properties may contain a lot of information about a specific object. Some of this information is critical to the network. For example, if you want to create an object, you must specify the object name. The object name is considered to be a vital property of the object. For a user object, Login Name and Last Name are the two critical properties. Their values may be JSMITH for Login Name and SMITH for Last Name. For a printer object, Name and Net_Address are the two critical properties. Their values may be P_HP4_ENG for Name and A3D0FC8 for Net_Address. NDS objects come in three different types: [Root], container objects, or leaf objects.

- [Root]—The [Root] object defines the top of the NDS structure. It may contain other objects such as country, organization or alias objects only. Only one [Root] object must be assigned to each directory and it is created during installation. No one can delete, rename, or move the [Root] object.

- Container objects—The container objects could be visualized as a directory in a DOS operating system. They are logical organizers. They may also be considered as natural groups. Container objects are used to organize or group NDS objects together. There are three different types of container objects:

  a) Country—A country container object is an object used to organize the NDS objects within a country. It must have a valid two-character country abbreviation. A country object is optional and it must be placed only under the [Root] object. It can consist of organization and alias objects only.

  b) Organization—An organization container object is used to define an organization, a department, or a company. Every directory must have at least one organization object. It is the first level where leaf objects can be placed. An organization object may contain organization units or leaf objects.

  c) Organization unit—An organization unit container object is used to represent a division, a team leader, or a company within an organization. It is at least one level below an organization object. An organization unit may contain other organization units or leaf objects.

- Leaf objects—The leaf objects could be visualized as files in a DOS operating system. Leaf objects are the objects that actually represent a network resource. Let us look at some of the 24 network resources or leaf objects IntranetWare supports.

User Leaf Objects:

Leaf Object		Description
	User	Represents a person who uses the network.
	Group	Groups users to grant them the same rights (group) on the network.
	Profile	Groups users to assign them the same (profile) login scripts on the network.
	Organizational Role	Defines a position within the organization to grant rights to network.
	User Template	Creates multiple user objects.

Printer Leaf Objects:

Leaf Object		Description
	Printer	Represents a physical printer device attached to a WAN.
	Printer Queue	Represents a printer queue on a WAN.
	Print Server	Represents a print server.

The printers, print queue, print server, and all user objects should be placed in the same container.

Server Leaf Objects:

Leaf Object		Description
	NetWare Server	Represents any NetWare server physically connected on the network.
	Directory Map	Points to a physical directory in the file system.
	Volume	Points to a physical volume on the WAN.

Messaging Leaf Objects:

Leaf Object		Description
	Messaging Server	Represents a messaging server residing on the server.
	Message Routing Group	Represents a group of messaging servers that send e-mail to each other.
	Distribution List	Represents a list of e-mail recipients.
	External Entity	Represents a non-NDS object for e-mail purposes.

Miscellaneous Leaf Objects:

Leaf Object		Description
	Computer	Other than a server, this represents a PC, a router, or a notebook on the network.

56

Application   Manages applications as application objects.

 Alias   Points to a real NDS object.

The main purpose of the NDS is to model a network after a common human ideal or paradigm and to make a network easier to use. IntranetWare organizes all of its objects under one hierarchical tree. This tree is composed of the [ROOT] and container objects. The NDS tree is very similar to a DOS file system structure. The top of the tree is called the [Root] like the root directory in DOS. Container objects are like directories, which are placed under the [Root] or other containers. Leaf objects are similar to files, which are placed inside containers. A parent container is a container object that contains other objects. The difference between NDS structure and the DOS file system is that NDS places restrictions on where objects can be placed in the directory tree container and what objects can be placed within a container.

The main advantage of having NDS is that it is a global database. This means that NDS can provide a central access to and manage network information, resources, and services. Another advantage of implementing NDS is that it can be considered as a standard management structure. It provides a standard method of managing, viewing, and accessing all network information, resources, and services. A third advantage is that NDS can also be considered as a logical organization structure. It logically organizes network resources independent from the physical layout of the network. Finally, it is best to implement NDS structure because NDS provides dynamic mappings. NDS can dynamically map any object and the referred physical resource together.

A system administrator should always organize and plan the directory tree structure based on a logical, and not physical organization of shared network resources. This is the best way to organize the directory tree because the directory tree structure affects how we use and manage network resources like NDS planning, resource access, and resource group and user environment automation. All objects that share network resources must be placed in a common container. You can plan the directory tree structure based on organization structure, geographic location, administrative responsibilities, or any combination of these three. To organize the directory tree, you must study the workgroups within the organization, study the resource allocation within the organization, and all the information that flows within the organization. The results of designing a directory tree correctly can simplify network administration and maintenance, minimize the impact of users, reduce the need for training, allow users to access network resources easily, provide network NDS fault tolerance, and eliminate any unnecessary network traffic.

2.6 NDS NAMING CONVENTIONS

Every resource on the network must have a unique name in the directory tree. NDS naming is important for two reasons. One, when a user logs in, IntranetWare needs to identify the exact location of the user in the NDS tree in order to authenticate the user during login. Second, NDS naming exactly identifies the type and location of IntranetWare resources such as file servers, files, printers, and login scripts. NDS does not search the entire tree to find an object: it uses the exact object name to access the network resources correctly. Below are the syntax and rules for identifying, or naming, a NDS object correctly.

- Common name—(syntax: CN=John) Common name is sometimes referred to as a relative distinguished name. It is a leaf object name and is always shown next to the leaf object in the directory.

- Context—(syntax: OU=CIS.O=TECH) Context is the position of an object in the directory tree structure. It is a list of container objects leading from the parent container to the one immediately above the object [Root]. When a user requests a particular resource, he/she must identify the object's context so that NDS can find it. Two objects that are in the same directory tree may have the same common name, but different contexts as shown in figure 2.1.

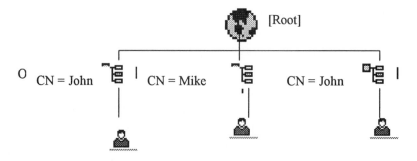

Figure 2.1 Understanding context.

- Current context—(syntax: OU=CIS.O=TECH) Current context can be thought of as the current position of the login NDS user in the directory. The current context identifies where you are in the NDS tree at any given time. For example, from figure 2.1, let's assume that John resides in OU=EET.O=TECH but can be at O=TECH or OU=CIS.O=TECH any time he desires. This is made possible by tree walking. Tree walking allows the user to navigate anywhere in the NDS tree structure. John current context determines the utilities he uses and resources he can access. Current context is a logical pointer in the NetWare DOS requester, or 32-bit Client, that identifies the default NDS container for the workstation. Current context states the location of where you are at a given time, not where you reside. Since the current context is the same as the context of an object, you can refer to an object current name by its common name. Hence, the current context of a user should be set inside the container that holds the resources the user most commonly uses. A user current context can be set in one of the following three ways:

1) During login—Use NAME CONTEXT statement in NET.CFG.

2) In the login script—Use the word CONTEXT.

3) Anytime—Use the CX command.

- Distinguished name—(syntax: .CN=John.OU=CIS.O=TECH) The distinguished name is the combination of the common name and context of an object. The distinguished name is the complete NDS path. From figure 2.1, John's distinguished name is .CN=John.OU=CIS.O=TECH. Remember the following rules when using distinguished names: A distinguished name must start with a leading period, objects are always separated by a period, no trailing periods are allowed, and no two objects can have the same distinguished name.

- Relative distinguished name—(syntax: CN=John.OU=CIS.) The relative distinguished name of an object lists the path of objects leading from the object to the current context. The rules when using relative distinguished names are: no leading periods are allowed; objects are separated by a period; and no two objects may have the same relative distinguished name. Every trailing period in the relative distinguished name informs NDS to remove one level, or one object name from the left side of the current context. NDS always builds the distinguished name from the relative distinguished name by appending the current context to the relative distinguished name. For example, if we have the user Mike at some time in OU = CIS then:

Mike's current context =   .OU=CIS.O=TECH
and his relative distinguished name =   CN=Mike.OU=TCM
and his distinguished name is =   .CN=Mike.OU=TCM.O=TECH

As shown above, the relative distinguished name also identifies an object exactly.

- Typeful name—(syntax: CN=P_HP5.OU=CIS.O=TECH) A typeful name can be either a distinguished name or a relative distinguished name. It uses the following attributes to identify the container and leaf objects used in the object name

  > CN—Common Name (Used for all leaf objects)
  > O—Organization
  > OU—Organization Unit
  > C—Country

- Typeless name—(syntax: .Mike.TCM.TECH) A typeless name is a typeful name without the attributes. NDS will figure out the attribute type for each object. You can use both typeful and typeless names to log on to the network. For example, from figure 2.1, let's assume Mike wants to log on to the network. He can do it the following four ways:

  Typeful name (Distinguished name) =   LOGIN .CN=Mike.OU=TCM.O=TECH
  Typeful name (Relative distinguished name) =   LOGIN CN=Mike.OU=TCM.O=TECH
  Typeless name (Distinguished name) =   LOGIN .Mike.TCM.TECH
  Typeless name (Relative distinguished name) = LOGIN Mike.TCM.TECH

The location of an object in the directory can affect how the object is accessed and managed. There is no need to know which server provides a particular resource. Any IntranetWare server can provide the client resource requested by just providing the correct object name and using its distinguished name or relative distinguished name.

You must establish and document the naming standard for the NDS directory objects before creating any objects. Consistent object naming schemes will provide the administrator with a guideline for managing objects within a directory. In addition, they give administrators an efficient model to meet their needs, reduce redundant planning, and help users to identify resources quickly to maximize their productivity. Always keep the NDS object names short and descriptive. This will make the NDS objects easy to remember and identify. It also makes the NDS objects easier for users to search. Below is a list of objects and examples of names:

Object Type	Sample	Description
User	JSMITH	In this case, the user's name is John Smith. This name is composed of the user's first initial, middle initial (if he or she has one), and up to 6 letters of the users' last name.
Group	Gp_CIS	Uses the prefix Gp for group as a prefix.
Printer	P_HP5_LPT1	Uses the prefix P for printer as a prefix.
Print server	PS_FS2_A	Uses the prefix PS for print server as a prefix.
Print queue	Q_HP5_LPT1	Uses the prefix Q for print queue as a prefix.

| File server | FS1_EET | Uses the prefix FS for print server as a prefix. |

2.7 USING THE NDS DIRECTORY AND LOGIN SECURITY

All IntranetWare servers on the same network using the same directory will have information on all the resources of the network. The NDS directory provides a single point of accessing and managing most of the network resources. We can view or browse the NDS directory structure using three utilities: CX, NETADMIN (NetWare Administrator for DOS), or NWADMIN (NetWare Administrator for Windows).

The CX command allows the administrator to change a workstation's current context or to view information about any resource's object context. The CX command is very similar to the DOS CD command. If you forget where you reside in the directory tree the CX command can help. Below is a list of CX commands with optional switches.

Command	Description
CX	Lets you view the workstation's current context
CX /?	Lets you view on-line help
CX .	Changes from current context to parent container
CX /VER	Lets you view version information
CX /R	Changes the current context to the [Root]
CX /T	Lets you view directory structure below the current directory
CX /A/T	Lets you view all objects in the directory tree structure below the current context
CX /R/A/T	Changes the current context to the [Root] and lets you view all objects in the directory tree
CX /C	Scrolls continuously through output
CX /CONT	Lets you view containers below the current context
CX .OU=CIS.O=TECH	Changes your current context to the CIS container of TECH

A user object is a person who is using the network. Every network user should have a unique user object to differentiate them from other users. The user object should contain information about the user, and the networking environment of that specific user, to regulate that user's access to the network and its services. For example, a user must be in the Printer Queue Users list in order to use a network printer. As an administrator, you can use NETADMIN or NWADMIN to create NDS user objects. The administrator must provide property values like login name, last name, and home directory when creating a user object. Usually you should place all the users' home directories in a directory called USERS and name a user's home directory by his/her login name.

The ADMIN user object is created automatically when IntranetWare is installed for the first time. It is the only default user object. The ADMIN object has all the rights all the way to the [ROOT] of the directory tree. Remember this: the ADMIN object in IntranetWare can be deleted, modified, or have its security access revoked. Therefore, make sure that you have backup user objects with all rights to the [ROOT] of the directory tree. Never revoke the supervisory right of an ADMIN object or its equivalent to a container.

NETADMIN (NetWare Administrator) is a DOS text menu. This utility does not need MS Windows to be executed. It is often used to test user login security and login scripts. The functions of NETADMIN are limited to the following:

- You can use NETADMIN to create and manage NDS objects in the directory tree only.

- You may not delete, create, or modify any NDS printing objects using NETADMIN.

- You can load and unload NETADMIN a lot faster than NWADMIN (which requires MS Windows to be loaded first).

Remember, NWADMIN allows you to manage NDS, the file system, and all the printing services provided by IntranetWare.

IntranetWare provides five different security levels on the network. The five security levels are login security, file system security, server security, network printing security, and NDS security. In this section we will discuss login security only. Login security is the security that regulates the user's initial access to the network. The user object, the central accessing item used to access the network, contains the properties about the user's working environment and login security. Login security makes decisions on who can or can not log on to the network, whether or not a user should have a password, when a user can log on to the network, how often the user may change his/her password, or what specific workstation the user can log in from. Login security controls the user's initial access to the network and continuously verifies the user's identity on the network. Users should always log out from the network before leaving a workstation. Unattended logged in workstations cause critical security breaches.

Login security is divided into three categories:

1) Account restrictions—You can set the following restrictions on a user object:

   a) You can enable or disable his/her user account.
   b) You can set an expiration date on the account.
   c) You can set the maximum number of concurrent connections.
   d) You can set password restrictions.
   e) You can set time restrictions.

f) You can set network address restrictions.

g) You can set an intruder lockout status for unlocking the account.

h) You can set an account balance.

i) You can set disk or volume space restrictions.

2) Authentication—Authentication is the process that enables the user to log on to an IntranetWare 4.11 network using a single login. It is a procedure used to verify and validate a request from a client in the background. When a user makes a login request, the network returns a unique user code. It creates a unique identification code by combining the user code, password, workstation network address, and time to authenticate the user request. The authentication process guarantees that a message from a client contains no false information and has not been corrupted or tampered with.

3) Intruder detection—Every user object has properties that track the user's number of incorrect login attempts, account reset time, time until reset, and network address. Intruder detection is used to limit the number of times a user can try to log in using an invalid password. If a user passes the limited number of attempts to enter an invalid password, then the network address of the "intruder" is recorded and the account will be locked for a period of time.

2.8 EXAMPLES OF HOW TO CREATE OBJECTS AND MANAGE NDS

Example 1:   How to load and invoke NWADMIN95:

Step 1: Make a shortcut icon for NWADMIN95. NWADMIN95.EXE is located in the directory F:\PUBLIC\WIN95\NWADMIN95.EXE.

Step 2: Double-click on the NWADMIN95 icon. See figure 2.2.

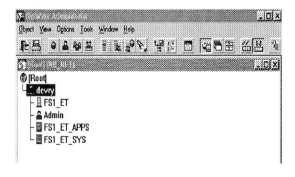

Figure 2.2 NWADMIN95.

Example 2:   How to create an organizational object under the [Root]:

Step 1: Click once on the [Root] object.
Step 2: Click once on "Object" from the title bar.
Step 3: Click once on "Create".
Step 4: Double-click on the "Organization" object. See figure 2.3.
Step 5: Enter a valid name for the organization.

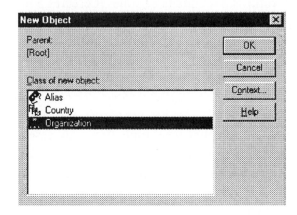

Figure 2.3 New object "Organization".

Example 3:   How to create a user object under an organizational object:

Step 1: Click once on an organizational object.
Step 2: Click once on "Object" from the title bar.
Step 3: Click once on "Create".
Step 4: Double-click on the "user" object.
Step 5: Enter the login name and last name for the user, and make sure to mark the "Create User Home Directory" box.
Step 6: Set up the path for the user home directory by clicking on the "Browse" button on the right, and, in the Directory Context frame on the right, double-clicking on the volume where the USERS directory is located.
Step 7: Double-click on the directory USERS from the left frame. See figure 2.4.

Step 8: Click on "Create".

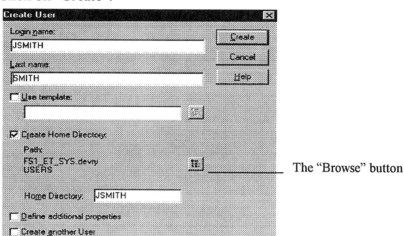

The "Browse" button

Figure 2.4 New user under an organizational object.

Example 4:   How to create a user template under a container object:

Step 1: Click once on an organization object.

Step 2: Click once on "Object" from the title bar.

Step 3: Click on "Create".

Step 4: Choose the "Template" option.

Step 5: Name it User_Template.

Step 6: Click next to the box that says "User template or user".

Step 7: Click the "Browse" button to add all the users that need to be in the User_Template, then click on "Create". See figure 2.5.

Step 8: After the User_Template is placed under the "organization", double-click on it or right-click the mouse button on the User_Template object, then choose "Details".

Step 9: Under Details, you can set a common environment for all the users. For example, click on the "Environment" button to set up the users home directory. Click on the "Login Restriction" button to limit the number of concurrent user connections. Click on the "Password Restrictions" button to set a minimum password length, or click on the "Login Time Restrictions" button to allow users to log in only at a certain time of the day. See figure 2.6.

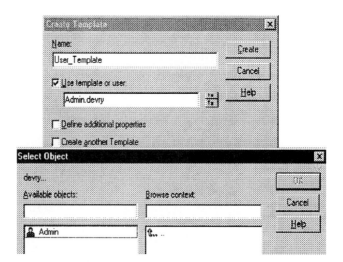

Figure 2.5 How to create a User_Template.

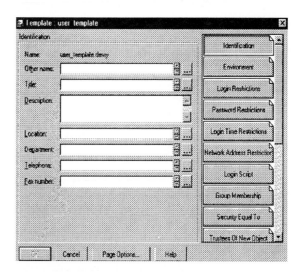

Figure 2.6 Details option on User_Template.

Example 5:   How to create a backup network administrator:

Step 1: Click on the [Root] object.
Step 2: Click once on "Object" from the title bar.
Step 3: Choose the "Trustee of this object…" option.
Step 4: Click on the "Add Trustee" button. Set the directory. context by double-clicking on an organization object in the right frame. Pick a user object from the left frame.
Step 5: Make sure to mark all object rights and property rights. See figure 2.7.
Step 6: Click on "OK".

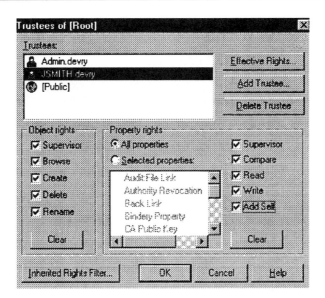

Figure 2.7 Creating a backup network administrator.

Example 6:   How to create a backup container administrator:

Step 1: Click on a container object.
Step 2: Repeat steps 1 to 6 from example 5.

Example 7:   How to create organization unit objects:

Step 1: Click on an organization object.
Step 2: Click once on "Object" from the title bar.
Step 3: Click on "Create".
Step 4: Choose the "Organization Unit" option.
Step 5: Enter an organization unit name.
Step 6: Mark the box that says "Create another
         Organization Unit".See figure 2.8.
Step 7: Click on "Create" again.
Step 8: Enter an additional organization unit name.
Step 9: Click on "Create".

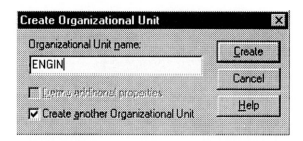

Figure 2.8 Creating an organization unit.

Example 8:   How to create a user under an organization unit object

      Step 1: Click on an organization unit object.
      Step 2: Click once on "Object" from the title bar.
      Step 3: Click on "Create".
      Step 4: Choose the "User" option.
      Step 5: Enter the user Login name and last name.
      Step 6: Click on "Create".

Example 9:   How to move users from one organization unit to another:

      Step 1: Double-click on the source organization unit to
           expand the subtree.
      Step 2: Double-click on the target organization unit to
           expand the subtree.
      Step 3: Click once on a user in the source organization unit.
      Step 4: Click once on "Object" from the title bar.
      Step 5: Choose the "move..." option. Indicate the target organization
           unit by clicking on the "Browse". button on the right. See figure
           2.9.
      Step 6: After the target organization has been picked. Click on "OK".

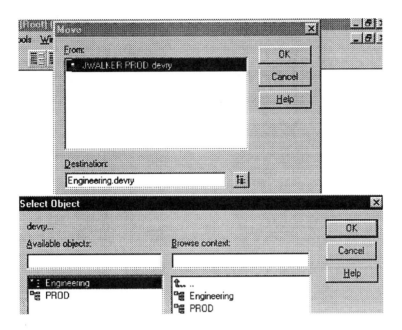

Figure 2.9 How to move users from one container to another.

2.9 CREATING USER OBJECTS USING UIMPORT

You may use the IntranetWare UIMPORT utility to create multiple users automatically. You can do this by storing a large number of user records in a database or a spreadsheet program, then exporting this data into a delimited ASCII data file. You may use the UIMPORT utility to add or create user objects in the NDS database. You can also use the UIMPORT utility to update the user properties in the NDS database when the records are changed in the database. Finally, UIMPORT is useful when you need to delete user objects when their network accounts are no longer needed. The UIMPORT utility requires two parameters as shown below:

UIMPORT Control_Filename Data_Filename

Control_Filename is the control file name and Data_Filename is the ASCII data file name. You must first export the user data from the database program to a delimited ASCII data file. Then, you can use any text editor to create an import control file. In a control file, you can specify the control parameters or how records in the data file are imported into the NDS. In addition you can use the control file to define field definitions or determine which fields, or NDS properties, the data will be placed in. Below is a list of UIMPORT control parameters and their descriptions:

Control Parameter	Description
Quote = "	Specifies the delimiter used in the import data file.
Separator =,	Specifies the field separator used in the data file.
Import Mode = B	Creates and updates user objects.
Import Mode = C	Creates user objects only.
Import Mode = U	Updates data for existing objects only.
Import Mode = R	Removes user objects.
Name Context = "Current_Context"	Declares a context to place the user objects. You must use a distinguished name for context. The current context is the default.
User Template = N	Does not use the template properties with user objects.
User Template = Y	Uses the template properties with user objects.
Create Home Directory = N	Does not create a home directory for user objects.
Create Home Directory = Y	Creates a home directory for user objects.
Home Directory Path = "Path"	Does not include a volume name in the "Path".
Home Directory Volume = "Volume"	Uses a distinguished name for the volume name object.
Delete Mailbox Dirs = N	Does not delete the mailbox directories.
Delete Mailbox Dirs = Y	Deletes the mailbox directories.
Replace Value = N	Allows you to overwrite or add data to a single property.
Replace Value = Y	Allows you to overwrite or add data to multiple properties.
Delete Property =	Allows you to delete property values of a user object.
Delete Property = #del	Allows you to delete property values by placing a #del in the corresponding fields in the data file.
Maximum Directories Retries = 7	Informs UIMPORT how many times it should try to get a new created user object ID for creating home and mailbox directories.

You may include any of the above control parameters in the data file as long as you precede them with the character "!". Below are examples of the field definitions used in the control file:

Field definition	Description
Name	The user's login name is required.
Given Name	The user's given name.
Last name	The user's last name. It is required to create a user object.

70

Full Name	The user's full name.
Skip	Ignore this field.

The import control and fields section headings in the import control file must be left justified. In addition, the entries under each of the headings must be preceded by one space as shown in the following example:

Command	Description
Import Control	Specifies the control parameters or how the information in the data file will be imported into the NDS database.
Quote =	Specifies that no delimiter is to be used in the import data file.
Separator ='	Specifies that a comma is being used in the data file.
Import Mode = C	Specifies creating users only.
Name Context = .ENGIN.ACME	Places the user objects in the container .ENGIN.ACME.
User Template = Y	Applies the user template for user objects.
Create Home Directories = Y	Creates user home directories.
Home Directory Path = "users"	Specifies that "users" is the parent of the home directories.
Home Directory Volume = ". FS1.ACME"	Specifies that .FS1.ACME is the volume object where the home directories should be stored.
Fields	These define the field definitions, i.e, determine which fields, or NDS properties, the data will be placed in.
Name	This field requires the user's login name for the user's object property.
Given Name	Specifies the user's given name.
Last Name	This field requires the user's last name for the user's object property.
Skip	Ignore this field.

Below is an example of the UIMPORT data file:

```
JSmith, John, Smith,
JWwalker, Jim, Walker,
MMiller, Mike, Miller
```

Questions

1) What are the steps you should follow when using NWADMIN to create two users with a home directory in SYS: \USERS?
2) What are the steps you should follow when using NWADMIN to create a user template under a container object?
3) List some essential components that are needed in an IntranetWare/NetWare 4.11 network?
4) What is the next step in NetWare after loading DOS and LSL?
5) What is the most common drive used for the first network drive?
6) Describe NDS.
7) Name three basic types of NDS objects.
8) Where is NWADMIN stored?
9) What is the advantage of a shallow NDS directory?
10) Name three basic network services.
11) Name four procedures that are usually performed by a network administrator.
12) What are the three files that automate network connection and the login process?
13) If a DOS workstation has three floppy drives, two hard drives, a CD-ROM drive, and a LASTDRIVE = X statement in its CONFIG.SYS file, how many network drives will the DOS requester make available?
14) What is the loading order of the files in the STARTNET.BAT file to connect a DOS workstation to an IntranetWare network?
15) Describe the DOS requester.
16) What is the name of the file used to configure a DOS workstation's network software?
17) Describe three benefits of NDS.
18) Describe the [Root] in relation to NDS objects.
19) What two types of NDS objects can an organization object contain?
20) In which two containers can all leaf objects exist?
21) Name three leaf objects.
22) Which two naming schemes can exactly identify an object in the directory tree?
23) What is the name shown next to a leaf object in a directory tree called?
24) What is your current position in a directory tree called?
25) Describe the relative distinguished name of an object.
26) What statement must you add to the file NET.CFG to make sure that all users who log in from a specific workstation are in the same context?
27) Name three shortcuts that can be used to access or manage resources in other containers.

28) Name three utilities that may be used to view or browse the NDS directory tree structure.
29) Name three things the NLIST command can display.
30) What is the command used to display all objects in the entire directory tree, regardless of your context?
31) What is the command used to change your current context to your parent container?
32) What are the four unique identifications NDS uses when a user logs in?

3

IntranetWare File System

In this chapter, you will learn how to manage an IntranetWare file system using file system management utilities. You will get familiar with how to set up a NetWare file system security by implementing directory and file rights and attribute security.

3.1 INTRODUCTION TO THE INTRANETWARE FILE SYSTEM

IntranetWare operating systems provide a file storage service for all users on the network as a default service. File storage allows all users on the network to share stored applications and files. The benefit of using a file system is that shared storage can reduce disk space requirement, provide private or unshared storage area, and improve access to file resources. In addition, a file system can provide excellent data security and a central management and backup utility. The file system in NetWare starts with the server, then the disk volume, and then the directories and subdirectories under the disk volume. Figure 3.1 shows a skeletal IntranetWare directory structure of a server file system that consists of two volumes.

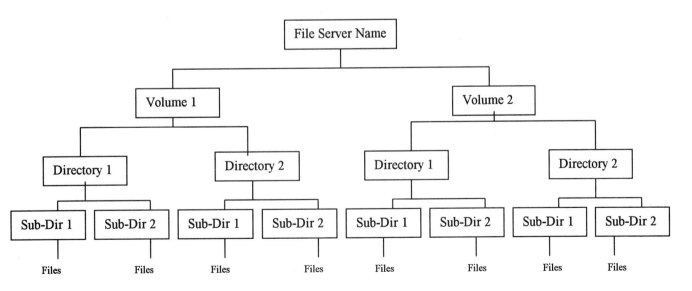

Figure 3.1 The IntranetWare directory structure.

The file system must be organized by using the IntranetWare directory tree structure. In order for IntranetWare to locate a file or a directory, path name must consists of the file server name, disk volume name, directory name, and subdirectory name. The file server name must be declared before any disk volume name is declared. The first level where we may create directories, equivalent to the root directory in DOS, is called a volume. Let's look at the four components of IntranetWare file system.

- Volumes—This is the physical amount of storage on a hard disk and is a logical grouping of physical hard disk storage. It can be a CD-ROM or other storage peripherals. It is the highest level in the NetWare directory structure, similar to DOS root directory. NetWare 4.11 server can support up to 64 volumes. These volumes may each be divided logically on a single hard disk, be a single volume per hard disk, or be a single volume spanning multiple hard disks (a maximum of 32 disks). Volumes are created during server installation. Each physical volume has a volume object in the directory tree. The volume object, which is created at installation time, has two critical properties to identify the actual physical volume. The two properties are the NetWare server name and the physical volume name. Every volume must be mounted so that a user can use the volume object to provide access to the file system. Mounting a volume means that the volume becomes visible to the operating system and that the FAT (File Allocation Table) and DET (Directory Entry Table) are loaded into memory.

- Directories—A directory is a labeled area under a volume. They may contain both files and other directories, and are used to organize a file system.

- Subdirectories—These are directories that reside inside other directories.

- Files—Files are applications or text documents that are stored under a directory or a subdirectory.

There is a general format way of declaring a directory path name. The format must follow the following convention, server_name\volume_name: directory\subdirectory. server_name must be in the length of 2 to 47 characters. It cannot begin with a period ".". It cannot contain the characters * ? \ or /, and must be unique. You must use the character \ or / after the server_name to separate it from the volume_name. A volume_name must be between 2 to 15 characters long. You cannot add spaces, periods, backslashes, or any special graphical symbols when declaring a volume_name. In addition, no two volumes on the same server should have the same volume_name, and at least one volume_name must be declared as SYS. You can use the backslash "\" or forward slash "/" after the colon ":" to separate the volume from the directory. A directory must be between 1 to 8 characters long. You cannot add spaces, periods, backslashes or any special graphical symbols when naming a directory. A directory extension must not exceed 3 characters and no two directories should have the same name. You can use the backslash "\" or forward slash "/" to separate the directory from the subdirectory. To ease maintenance and backup, you should never create directories too deep and you should always keep applications and data separate. A subdirectory follows the same naming conventions as those for a directory. The disk space and file server RAM limit how many of these you can create.

When you install a file server, a volume called SYS must be declared. After the SYS volume has been created, the eight directories listed below are created in it by default:

- SYS: LOGIN—The LOGIN directory contains important files like LOGIN.EXE, CX.EXE, NLIST.EXE, MAP.EXE, and SLIST.EXE. When the user attaches to the file server, he/she is given access to the LOGIN directory be default.

- SYS: MAIL—The mail directory can be used for any purpose, but most importantly, it is used to store individual login script and printer configuration files. Every user has a numeric subdirectory in the MAIL directory to store the login script and print configuration files.

- SYS: PUBLIC—The PUBLIC directory contains the entire body of network commands and utilities that are generally available to all users.

- SYS: SYSTEM—The SYSTEM directory contains important system files such as .NLMs, .LANs, AUTOEXEC.NCF, and SERVER.EXE. Only the system administrator (the ADMIN) can access the SYSTEM directory.

- SYS: ETC—The ETC directory contains an Internet database to help configure the server for TCP/IP protocols.

- SYS: DELETED.SAV—The DELETED.SAV directory is a directory that contains files that have been deleted, but not purged from the volume. Each volume will have a DELETED.SAV directory. DELETED.SAV is a hidden directory.

- SYS: QUEUES—The QUEUES directory is for queue directories if the print queue is installed on the SYS volume. You should never place print queues on the SYS volume unless it is absolutely necessary.

- SYS: DOC—The DOC directory contains NetWare manuals in electronic form like IntranetWare's electronic documentation.

Each of the main system-created directories has a NLS subdirectory. The NLS (NetWare Language Support) is the IntranetWare translator. It is a directory that contains messages and help files for multilingual IntranetWare utilities. If multiple languages have been installed on the server, then each language will have its own subdirectory under the NLS directory.

In addition to the default directories, the network administrator should create additional directories to meet the needs of users on the network, such as DOS directories, home directories, application directories, configuration file directories, and shared application directories.

- DOS directories—The DOS directories are optional, but they can be created to ensure that the users on the network can access needed DOS files and have the proper exit from a network application. The DOS directory should be created under the PUBLIC directory for each DOS version available on the workstation, for example, directory "V6.00" for DOS version 6.0 and "V6.22" for DOS version 6.22.

- Home directories—Every user on the network should have a home directory. The home directory of a user should always be named after his/her login name. In addition, the users should have all the rights to their home directories. All users' home directories should be in a parent directory called USERS under a volume called DATA.

- Application directories—Every application that needs to be installed on the server should be stored in a directory called APPS in the DATA volume. This method will make it easier to establish security assignments for the applications. Store only application files in the APPS directory. Any files created by the user should be stored in their home directory.

- Configuration file directory—After considering where the configuration file should be stored and what rights the user should have, the configuration file directory should be created and placed under the user home directory or under the application directory. The configuration file directory is a directory that is used by many of the applications to allow the user to make changes to applications without affecting other application users.

- Shared data directories—Shared data directories should be created to make it easier for users to share and distribute information across the network.

In addition to setting rules and guidelines for directories, planning and following the guidelines for IntranetWare volumes should also be done. Volumes are a basic component of the NetWare file system and their use must be carefully planned before you create any directories. Here are some rules and guidelines you should follow when planning for IntranetWare volumes:

- SYS volume—Every IntranetWare file server must have a volume called SYS. Remember that the SYS volume is like any other volume: it is created when the installation of the server is done. Make sure to set the size of the SYS volume large enough to hold all the NetWare utilities, on-line documentation, and any other NetWare files needed.

- Applications volume—An Applications volume should be created for any application and data files that need to be installed on the server.

- Name space volume—You should create a separate volume to support MAC or OS/2 name space.

- Heavy performance—If the performance of your server is more important to you than fault tolerance, then you should span one volume over many disks.

- Heavy system fault tolerance (SFT)—If fault tolerance for your server is more important than the performance, then you should create one volume per disk.

- Balancing performance and SFT—To balance the SFT and performance, you can span each volume over many disks, then duplex each disk.

3.2 DRIVE POINTER MANAGEMENT

All the IntranetWare commands and utilities access the IntranetWare file system using the volume names. On the other hand, DOS applications can only access volumes on the server using the volume name drive pointer and not using the volume name. A drive pointer is a letter that designates where files are or can be stored. The DOS and IntranetWare pointers are designed to move faster in a directory structure. You can set a local physical drive device to a drive pointer using the DOS BIOS and you can use the IntranetWare MAP utility to assign drive pointers to logical devices.

As you know, in DOS, drive letters point to physical devices. In IntranetWare, drive letters point to logical directories instead of physical drives. IntranetWare uses drive mapping as pointers to areas on the file server's disk drives. You can use drive mappings to reduce the amount of work necessary to run an application or to locate files by changing directories. At a workstation, you can have up to 26 letters to assign to drive pointers. Depending on the DOS version you have on your workstation, certain letters are used to point to a physical local drive. For example, DOS 3.3 uses the letters A through E by default for its local physical drives while DOS 6.22 uses letters A through C by default for its local physical drives. In IntranetWare, the statement LASTDRIVE = Z must be placed in CONFIG.SYS file on the workstation to ensure the drives D through Z will be available for use as pointers with the network. Although DOS allows us to move to any physical device by just typing the assigned letter followed by a colon and then moving among directories using the CD command, it is easier to user IntranetWare drive pointers to do the same. There are two types of IntranetWare drive pointers, Network drive pointers and search drive pointers. You can have up to 26 network drive pointers. They are used for data directories to move faster among directories by just typing the assigned letter followed by a colon. The search drive pointers can have up to 16 letters assigned to them. They are used to execute files immediately. The IntranetWare search drive numbers start from S1 to S16. They correspond to network drive letters in reverse order. You can access any executable file in the search drives from anywhere. Remember that the network drive pointers and search drive pointers cannot exceed the total number of the remaining letters.

IntranetWare uses three types of drive mapping: local (DOS) drive mapping, IntranetWare network drive mapping, and IntranetWare search drive mapping. Some default drive mappings are assigned automatically when a user boots his/her machine.

Drive Pointer Type	Default Letters Assigned	Description
DOS drive pointers	A to C by default Range from A to Z (max of 26)	
Network drive pointers	F by default	The letter F is mapped by default to the directory
	Range from A to Z (max of 26)	SYS:LOGIN of the user.
Search drive pointers	Z and Y by default	The letter Z is mapped as a search drive to the directory
	Range from Z to K (max of 16)	SYS: PUBLIC and the letter Y is mapped to the directory SYS: PUBLIC\%OS VERSION.

Mapping is the technique of setting logical pointers to physical directory locations. There are two ways to map network drive pointers.

MAP DRIVE: =SERVER_NAME/VOLUME_NAME: \DIRECTORY
or
MAP *#: =SERVER_NAME/VOLUME_NAME: \DIRECTORY

When using the syntax above:

1) Replace DRIVE with the drive letter you want to assign, such as G, H, I, etc.

2) Replace the # with a number to identify the first, second, third, etc., available network drives. If you use this method, the "*" character must precede the number.

3) Replace SERVER_NAME with the file server to which you are mapping. This parameter is not required when mapping a drive to your default file server. If the SERVER_NAME is left out, then the VOLUME_NAME should not be preceded by a "/" or "\".

4) Replace VOLUME_NAME with the name of the volume on which the directory resides.

5) Replace DIRECTORY with the name of the directory to which you are mapping.

As an example, let us assume that you have the following current mappings.

DRIVE H: =FS_1/SYS: \DATA
DRIVE K: =FS_1/SYS: \LAB

If you were to type

MAP F: =SYS: \PUBLIC

Then your drive mappings would change to

DRIVE F: =FS_1/SYS: \PUBLIC
DRIVE H: =FS_1/SYS: \DATA
DRIVE K: =FS_1/SYS: \LAB

What if you did not know that the first drive mapped was G: and you wanted to make sure that the first available drive was mapped to the PUBLIC directory? You can achieve this by replacing the specified drive pointer F: in the previous example with "*1". Therefore, typing MAP *1: =SYS: \PUBLIC would achieve the same effect. Keep the following point in mind: the "*#" method overwrites a drive mapping currently in the position the command is mapping to. For example, if there was already a drive mapping for F: to the PUBLIC directory, typing MAP *1: =SYS\APPS would change the drive mapping of F: =from PUBLIC to APPS.

Search drive mappings are similar to the settings in the DOS PATH statement. Once the search drive is created, you can access files no matter to what your default drive is set. When search drives are created, drive letters are allocated in the reverse order of the alphabet, starting at Z: and working backward. If a command is entered, IntranetWare will execute the command based on the following search order. It will search the workstation RAM, then search the current directory, then finally, it searches the search drives that are declared. There are two ways to map and create search drive pointers:

MAP DRIVE: =SERVER_NAME/VOLUME_NAME: \DIRECTORY
or
MAP INS DRIVE: =SERVER_NAME/VOLUME_NAME: \DIRECTORY

When using the syntax above:

1) Replace DRIVE with the search drive's number, such as S1, S2, S3, etc.

2) Replace SERVER_NAME with the file server to which you are mapping. This parameter is not required when mapping a drive to your default file server. If the SERVER_NAME is left out, then the VOLUME_NAME should not be preceded by a "/" or "\".

3) Replace VOLUME_NAME with the name of the volume on which the directory resides.

4) Replace DIRECTORY with the name of the directory to which you are mapping.

The difference between the two commands listed above is how the mapping affects the rest of your search drives and the DOS PATH settings. When you use MAP INS, IntranetWare inserts the mapping into the desired path location. When you just use the MAP command, IntranetWare overwrites the path assignment stored in the position. As an example let us assume that your current search drives are set as follows:

SEARCH1: = Z: FS_1\SYS: \PUBLIC
SEARCH2: = Y: FS_1\SYS: \LOGIN

If you were to type the command MAP INS S1: = SYS: \MAIL, your search drive settings would be adjusted as follows:

SEARCH1: = X: FS_1\SYS: \MAIL
SEARCH2: = Z: FS_1\SYS: \PUBLIC
SEARCH1: = X: FS_1\SYS: \MAIL

On the other hand, if you type the command MAP S1: = SYS: \MAIL, your search drive settings will be adjusted as follows:

SEARCH1: = X: FS_1\SYS: \MAIL
SEARCH2: = Y: FS_1\SYS: \LOGIN

All the commands shown above can also use a feature called mapping to the root. Mapping to the root is when you create a false root directory in your drive mapping. For example, if you mapped the F: drive to the directory USERS\JSMITH, the user would have the DOS prompt "F:\USERS\JSMITH>" if he or she made the F: drive the default. With this prompt, the user could use the CD DOS command to switch to USERS or another directory. When mapped to the root, the user's F: drive prompt would appear as: F:\>. To map a drive to the ROOT, insert the command ROOT directly after the word MAP in your mapping statement. Following are MAP statements to assign network drive pointers and search drive pointers:

MAP Command	Example	Description
MAP	MAP	Lists the current drive mappings of a user.
MAP drive: = Dir_path	MAP H: =SYS: \ PUBLIC	Maps the H: to the PUBLIC directory.
MAP *1: = Dir_path	MAP *1: =SYS: \LOGIN	Maps the first available default drive to the LOGIN directory.
MAP N Dir_path	MAP N SYS: \MAIL	Maps the next available drive to the mail directory. You will not know which drive pointer you are getting with this command, so stay away from it.
MAP P phy_vol_name	MAP P APPS	Maps the current drive to the physical volume APPS.
MAP R drive: = Dir_path	MAP R K: =SYS: \ PUBLIC	Maps and makes the K: to the PUBLIC directory a pseudo root.
MAP C drive:	MAP C X:	Changes the network drive X: to a search drive.
MAP Sx: =Dir_path	MAP S1: =SYS: \PUBLIC	Maps the PUBLIC directory as search drive. It overwrites the first search drive settings. Try to keep away from this type of statement.
MAP INS Sx: =Dir_path	MAP INS S1: =SYS: \PUBLIC	Inserts and maps the PUBLIC directory as a search drive. It does not overwrite the first search drive settings.
MAP R INS Sx: =Dir_path	MAP R INS S1: = SYS: \PUBLIC	Inserts, maps, and makes the PUBLIC directory a root directory and a search drive. It does not overwrite the first search drive settings.
MAP ROOT drive: =Dir_path	MAP ROOT H: = SYS: \MAIL	Maps the MAIL directory to the pseudo root, H:
MAP drive: =drive:	MAP H: =J:	Maps J: to H:

MAP DISPLAY ON/OFF	MAP DISPLAY ON	Displays the drive mappings as they are mapped. This command is used in the login script.
MAP DEL drive:	MAP DEL G:	Deletes the network drive G:. You cannot delete the current drive letter.

3.3 INTRANETWARE FILE SYSTEM MANAGEMENT

The network file system is the most important type of service on the network. A network administrator is responsible for managing the file system. To manage the file system, you must be able to navigate through the IntranetWare volume and directory structure with ease. This is done using the DOS CD command, application programs, the IntranetWare MAP command, and the IntranetWare FILER and NWADMIN utilities. Remember this: If you use the DOS CD command to change directories while in a IntranetWare drive pointer, the current IntranetWare drive pointer will be mapped to the new directory. The IntranetWare file system contains several file management utilities that are designed to work in a network environment.

- FILER—FILER is a text-based menu utility for IntranetWare that is used to manage directories and files, display volume information, and salvage and purge deleted files.

- NWADMIN—NWADMIN (NetWare Administrator) which runs under Windows can be used to perform the same file management tasks as FILER. In addition, it is an NDS-based tool that can be used to create, delete, rename, copy, and move directories or files.

- FLAG—The FLAG command allows you to view, modify, or change directory and file attributes. You can use the FLAG command to set a file or a directory to be purged upon deletion.

- NCOPY—The NCOPY command allows you to copy files from one location to another. NCOPY is faster for copying files between network directories. You can use the NCOPY command to copy a directory's structure or files.

- NLIST—The NLIST command is an NDS utility that is used to display information about NDS objects and/or properties.

- NDIR—The NDIR command is used to view names and detailed information about files and directories.

- RENDIR—The RENDIR command allows you to rename a directory. The directory content, attributes, and rights do not change.

- SETPASS—The SETPASS command allows you to change your password. The user will be prompted for both his/her old and new passwords.

- SYSTIME—The SYSTIME command allows you to display the current workstation time. In addition, it synchronizes the workstation time with the file server time.

- SEND—The SEND command allows you to send a message up to 40 characters long to any user or group on the network.

- PURGE—The PURGE command allows you to permanently remove files that were deleted.

You can use NWADMIN or FILER to do many file system management tasks such as viewing directory or file information, modifying directory or file information, and creating or deleting directories or files. In addition, these utilities can move a directory structure of files, rename a directory, salvage deleted files, purge deleted files, and set a file or a directory to purged out upon deletion. If you need help or want to know how to use any of the above commands, just type the command followed by the switch "/?". This will give you detailed information on how to use the optional switches with each command. In addition to IntranetWare file system utilities, we can use DOS commands or Windows File Manager to help us manage the IntranetWare file system. These DOS commands are COPY, XCOPY, PROMPT, DIR, CD or CHDIR, MD or MKDIR, RD or RMDIR, DEL, COPY CON, and TYPE. It is important to understand that you should always use IntranetWare utilities to copy files from one location to another. IntranetWare copy utilities provide you the following benefits:

- An entire directory or file structure can be copied.

- IntranetWare volume names may be used for copying files.

- Notification is given to the user if the extended file information cannot be copied.

- Verification is given if the copy was accurate.

- IntranetWare extended file information can be copied.

Be aware that IntranetWare stores deleted files in the same directory in which they were deleted. If the directory is deleted, then the deleted files will be stored in a directory called DELETED.SAV. In DOS, removing the directory in which files were deleted will prevent you from retrieving those files. In IntranetWare, you can salvage deleted files anytime until they are purged out. Purging out the directory using the command PURGE will permanently delete all the deleted files that were saved for retrieval. You can purge deleted files in five different ways:

- As a user with a supervisory right on the files.

- Having the files in a directory that is marked for purging immediately upon deletion.

- Marking files for purging immediately upon deletion.

- Deliberately purging files, if they are your own files.

- Letting IntranetWare purge files on a First-In-First-Out (FIFO) basis when it runs out of disk space on the volume.

In order to salvage a file, a user must have the read and file scan rights to the file and the create right to the directory where the file resides. Let us now discuss the two important command line utilities used to view file system information.

1) NLIST—NLIST is a command line utility used to list information about the NDS volume objects. The NLIST command works like the CX command, but with more details given. You can use the NLIST command to list NDS objects without logging in. NDS stores the object class, current context, volume name, host server name, and the physical volume name of a volume in the directory. Below is a list of NLIST commands that you can execute to view information about NDS volume objects:

Command	Description
NLIST /?	Lets you view the help on the NLIST command.
NLIST server	Lets you view all the server objects and related information found.
NLIST volume	Lets you view all the volume objects and related information found.
NLIST volume /N	Lets you view only the names of all the volumes found.
NLIST volume /D	Lets you view detailed information on all the volume objects found.
NLIST user	Lets you view all the user objects and related information found.

NLIST group	Lets you view all the group objects and related information found.
NLIST queue	Lets you view all the print queue objects and related information found.

2) NDIR—NDIR is a command line utility used to list information about volumes, directories, and files. It works like the DOS DIR command, and you can use NDIR to search information in various ways including by owner and by dates. For example, the command NDIR SYS: *WP* /S will search for any file that has WP in it. You will notice when using the NDIR command that the pattern matching method used in IntranetWare allows you to use the wild card character "*" before and after a pattern, such as "*WP*", to search for the pattern anywhere in either the filename or extension. You can use the NDIR command to track the amount of disk space used by the user, check the date of network files and when they were last accessed, and search for any specific file. When using the command NDIR, you may direct the list to a file or a printer. In addition, when using NDIR with an option the forward slash "/" character must precede the first element of the option list. Below is a list of NDIR commands that you can execute to view information about NDS volumes, directories, and files:

General Options:

Command	Description
NDIR /?	Lets you view the help on the NDI command.
NDIR / DO	Lets you view the directory name, IRF, effective rights, creation date, owner name, and subdirectories. This command will not list when the directories were last accessed.
NDIR /DO /R	Lets you view all the attributes, IRF, effective rights, and others.
NDIR /DO /SUB	Lets you view all levels of subdirectories.
NDIR /S	Lets you view subdirectories.
NDIR /FO	Lets you view the file's name, IRF, effective rights, creation date, and owner name. This command will not list when the file was last accessed.
NDIR /VOL	Lets you view the name and storage space used by a volume.
NDIR /SPA	Lets you view volume and directory space limitation and usage.
NDIR /FI	Lets you view where a file can be found in a search drive.
NDIR /V	Lets you view the version information.
NDIR /C	Lets you view information continuously.

Restriction Options:

Command	Description
NDIR /UP	Lets you view files by the last date accessed, on or before update or modified date.
NDIR /UP NOT value	Lets you view files by the last date accessed, on or before update or modified date, but does not include value.

NDIR /AC	Lets you view files by last date accessed, on, or before accessed date.
NDIR /AC NOT value	Lets you view files by last date accessed, on, or before accessed date, but does not include value.
NDIR /AR	Lets you view files by last date accessed, on, or before archived date.
NDIR /AR NOT value	Lets you view files by last date accessed, on, or before archived date, but does not include value.
NDIR /CR	Lets you view files by last date accessed, on, or before created or copied date.
NDIR /CR NOT value	Lets you view files by last date accessed, on, or before created or copied date, but does not include value.
NDIR /SI	Lets you view files by equal, less than or greater than file size.
NDIR /SI NOT value	Lets you view files by equal, less than or greater than file size, but does not include value.
NDIR /OW	Lets you view files by owner of files.
NDIR /OW NOT value	Lets you view files by owner of files, but does not include value.
NDIR /NAM	Lets you view files in name space.
NDIR /NAM NOT value	Lets you view files in name space, but does not include value.
NDIR /UP EQ value	Lets you view files by the last date accessed, on, or before update or modified date equal to value.
NDIR /AC EQ value	Lets you view files by last date accessed, on, or before accessed date equal to value.
NDIR /AR EQ value	Lets you view files by last date accessed, on, or before archived date equal to value.
NDIR /CR EQ value	Lets you view files by last date accessed, on, or before created or copied date equal to value.
NDIR /SI EQ value	Lets you view files by equal, less than, or greater than file size equal to value.
NDIR /OW EQ value	Lets you view files by owner of files equal to value.
NDIR /NAM EQ value	Lets you view files in name space equal to value.
NDIR /UP GR value or NDIR /UP AFT value	Lets you view files by the last date accessed, on or before update or modified date greater than or after the value.
NDIR /AC GR value or NDIR /AC AFT value	Lets you view files by last date accessed, on, or before accessed date greater than or after the value.
NDIR /AR GR value or NDIR /AR AFT value	Lets you view files by last date accessed, on, or before archived date greater than or after the value.
NDIR /CR GR value or NDIR /CR AFT value	Lets you view files by last date accessed, on, or before created or copied date greater than or after the value.
NDIR /SI GR value or NDIR /SI AFT value	Lets you view files by equal, less than, or greater than file size greater than or after the value.

NDIR /OW GR value
or
NDIR /OW AFT value   Lets you view files by owner of files greater than or after the value.

NDIR /NAM GR value
or
NDIR /NAM AFT value   Lets you view files in name space greater than or after the value.

NDIR /UP LE value
or
NDIR /UP BEF value   Lets you view files by the last date accessed, on, or before update or modified date less than or before the value.

NDIR /AC LE value
or
NDIR /AC BEF value   Lets you view files by last date accessed, on, or before accessed date less than or before the value.

NDIR /AR LE value
or
NDIR /AR BEF value   Lets you view files by last date accessed, on, or before archived date less than or before the value.

NDIR /CR LE value
or
NDIR /CR BEF value   Lets you view files by last date accessed, on, or before created or copied date less than or before the value.

NDIR /SI LE value
or
NDIR /SI BEF value   Lets you view files by equal or less than file size or before the value.

NDIR /OW LE value
or
NDIR /OW BEF value   Lets you view files by owner of files less than or before the value.
NDIR /NAME LE value
or
NDIR /NAM BEF value   Lets you view files in name space less than or before the value.

Sort Options:

Command	Description
NDIR /SORT UP	Sorts by the last update or modified date in an ascending order.
NDIR /SORT AC	Sorts by last accessed date in an ascending order.
NDIR /SORT AR	Sorts by last archived date in an ascending order.
NDIR /SORT CR	Sorts by last created or copied date in an ascending order.
NDIR /SORT SI	Sorts by file size in an ascending order.
NDIR /SORT OW	Sorts by owner in ascending order.
NDIR /SORT UN	Sorts in no specific order.
NDIR /REV SORT UP	Sorts by the last update or modified date in a descending order.
NDIR /REV SORT AC	Sorts by last accessed date in a descending order.
NDIR /REV SORT AR	Sorts by last archived date in a descending order.
NDIR /REV SORT CR	Sorts by last created or copied date in a descending order.
NDIR /REV SORT SI	Sorts by file size in a descending order.

NDIR /REV SORT OW   Sorts by owner in a descending order.
NDIR /REV SORT UN   Sorts in no specific order.

Display Format Options:

Command	Description
NDIR /D	Lets you view detailed information about a file.
NDIR /DA	Lets you view all the date information about a file.
NDIR /R	Lets you view all the IRF, rights, and attributes.
NDIR /COMP	Lets you view information about a compressed file.
NDIR /L	Lets you view information about MAC, OS/2, and NFS long names.
NDIR /MAC	Lets you view up to 31 characters of a MAC file and subdirectories.

Attributes Options:

Command	Description
NDIR /SY	Lets you view files that are flagged system.
NDIR /NOT SY	Lets you view files that are not flagged system.
NDIR /H	Lets you view files that are flagged hidden.
NDIR /NOT H	Lets you view files that are not flagged hidden.
NDIR /Rw	Lets you view files that are flagged read/write.
NDIR /NOT Rw	Lets you view files that are not flagged read /write.
NDIR /Ro	Lets you view files that are flagged read only.
NDIR /NOT Ro	Lets you view files that are not flagged read only.
NDIR /Sh	Lets you view files that are flagged shareable.
NDIR /NOT Sh	Lets you view files that are not flagged shareable.
NDIR /X	Lets you view files that are flagged execute-only.
NDIR /NOT X	Lets you view files that are not flagged execute-only.
NDIR /Di	Lets you view files that are flagged delete-inhibit.
NDIR /NOT Di	Lets you view files that are not flagged delete-inhibit.
NDIR /Ri	Lets you view files that are flagged rename-inhibit.
NDIR /NOT Ri	Lets you view files that are not flagged rename-inhibit.
NDIR /Ci	Lets you view files that are flagged copy-inhibit.
NDIR /NOT Ci	Lets you view files that are not flagged copy-inhibit.
NDIR /Co	Lets you view files that are flagged file compressed.
NDIR /NOT Co	Lets you view files that are not flagged file compressed.
NDIR /Ic	Lets you view files that are flagged immediate compressed.
NDIR /NOT Ic	Lets you view files that are not flagged immediate compressed.
NDIR /Dc	Lets you view files that are flagged do not compress.
NDIR /NOT Dc	Lets you view files that are not flagged do not compress.
NDIR /Cc	Lets you view files that are flagged can not compress.
NDIR /NOT Cc	Lets you view files that are not flagged can not compress.
NDIR /M	Lets you view files that are flagged file migrated.
NDIR /NOT M	Lets you view files that are not flagged file migrated.
NDIR /Dm	Lets you view files that are flagged do not migrate.
NDIR /NOT Dm	Lets you view files that are not flagged do not migrate.
NDIR /Ds	Lets you view files that are flagged do not suballocate.

NDIR /NOT Ds	Lets you view files that are not flagged do not suballocate.
NDIR /A	Lets you view files that are flagged modified.
NDIR /NOT A	Lets you view files that are not flagged modified.
NDIR /P	Lets you view files that are flagged purge.
NDIR /NOT P	Lets you view files that are not flagged purge.
NDIR /I	Lets you view files that are flagged index.
NDIR /NOT I	Lets you view files that are not flagged index.
NDIR /T	Lets you view files that are flagged transactional.
NDIR /NOT T	Lets you view files that are not flagged transactional.

Here are some examples of how to use the NDIR commands:

Command	Description
NDIR *.* /OW EQ JOHN	This command will list all files owned by the user JOHN.
NDIR *.* /OW NOT EQ JOHN	This command will list all files except the ones owned by the user JOHN.
NDIR *.* /UP GR 11/01/96	This command will list all files after the date 11/01/96.
NDIR *.* /UP NOT GR 11/01/96	This command will list all files before the date 11/01/96. You could have used the command NDIR *.* /UP LE 11/01/96 and gotten the same result.
NDIR *.* /OW LE 0	This command will list all files with no specific owner.

You can limit the volume space usage by limiting the directory space that is used for files and their subdirectories. In addition, you can limit the volume space by setting a volume restriction on a user to use one volume only or you can use the calculated user volume space from the owner property of files. A user becomes the owner of the files created by the user for the first time. You can redistribute the volume space usage by changing that owner of files. You can use several utilities to manage volume space. For example, you can use the NDIR command to locate a file by its access date, owner, and size. You can use the NWADMIN and FILER utilities to restrict volume space usage by directory or change file ownership. You can use the NWADMIN, NETADMIN, and FILER utilities and the NDIR command to view data migration statistics, volume compression statistics, and volume space statistics and usage. You can use the NWADMIN and FILER utilities and the FLAG commands to set migration attributes on directories and files, and to set compression attributes on directories and files. Finally, you can use the NWADMIN and NETADMIN utilities to restrict volume space usage by a user.

IntranetWare can effectively increase disk space by 63% by enabling file compression on volumes. You can only enable file compression on a volume during or after IntranetWare installation. Once enabled, only recreating the volume can disable the file compression on a volume. For IntranetWare to manage file compression internally, you can flag files or directories to be compressed after the files have not been used for a period of time, immediately compress a file that has been flagged immediate compress, or immediately compress a file if the parent directory was flagged immediate compress. Files are immediately compressed when they have not been accessed for a specific amount of time after compression. A file is decompressed once the user accesses the file again.

IntranetWare offers three ways to migrate data to storage media such as on-line storage media (i.e., hard drive), near-line storage media (i.e., CD-ROM, optical drives), and off-line storage media (i.e., tape drives). Data migration allows you to move inactive data on a volume to a near-line storage area, such as an optical drive. The optical drive is sometimes referred to as a jukebox. This will free valuable disk space for often-used files while still providing near on-line access to the less frequently used files. The data migration is always transparent to the user and the files will still appear to be stored on the volume.

3.4 MANAGING FILE SYSTEM SECURITY

File system security occurs within the file server. It controls who can access the file system and how. Since the server contains the volumes that contain directories and files, file security ends once it gets to the server. There is no transition into the NDS security structure. You can use the file system security to grant directory and file rights to trustees, modify the directory and file inherited rights filter (IRF) , and modify directory and file attributes. File system security and NDS security are two different types of security. NDS has ten access rights broken down into two groups, object and property. The file system uses eight access rights. Rights do not flow from NDS into the file system except in one special case. A supervisor object grants rights to the server object, which grants the trustee supervisor file rights to the [ROOT] of all the server's volumes. The supervisor NDS rights can be blocked by the IRF. The supervisor file system right, on the other hand, cannot be blocked by the IRF. Even though they are independent of each other, both file system security and NDS security use similar systems of trustees, rights, inheritance, IRFs, and effective rights. Here are some terms and concepts that we'll be discussing throughout the file system security assignments:

- Resource—Directories or files.

- Account—The basic resource access identifier.

- Trustee—This is an account's right to a resource. In order to have privileges, you must be made a trustee of the directory or the file. You can also give an individual or a group trustee rights.

- Rights—These establish the type of access an account can have to a resource.

- Attribute—A type of condition assigned to a resource.

- IRF—It stand for Inherited Rights Filter. It blocks rights granted at a higher directory level and effectively limits the amount of rights any user can have at that level. Once in place, the IRF flows down the directory structure, affecting all subdirectory levels below. Assigning new trustee assignments to files and directories can overwrite the IRF. All the rights can be blocked using IRF except the supervisory [S] right, which means all rights granted. This prevents a user, such as a workgroup manager, from being blocked out of a directory structure that he/she manages. You can use the utility FILER or NWADMIN to remove rights from a directory or a file .

- Effective rights—These are the rights a user is granted specifically (explicit rights) plus any rights that a user inherited through their group membership (implicit rights) minus any rights that were revoked using IRF.

The eight rights that can be granted to a directory or a file spell the word W(O)RMFACES, with the letter (O) being implied. Below is a list of the eight rights and the file system tasks that can be performed with these rights:

Symbol	Right	File System Task
W	Write	You can open and make changes to the content of a file or a directory.
R	Read	You can open files, read their contents, or run programs in the directory.
M	Modify	You can rename a file or a directory or change the attributes of a file or a directory.
F	File Scan	You can list and see subdirectories or filenames, and search a directory for files.
A	Access Control	You can change the IRF, change trustee assignment, modify a directory's disk space restriction, or grant any right to a user except the supervisory [S] right.
C	Create	You can create a new directory, or create and write to a file.
E	Erase	You can delete a file or a directory, its files, and subdirectories.
S	Supervisory	You have all the above rights to a file or a directory, its files, and subdirectories.

Here are some examples of what rights are needed to perform a task:

File system task	Rights required
Salvage deleted files	[R] and [F] to the files and [C] to the directory
NCOPY files to a directory	[W] [C] and [F]
NCOPY files from a directory	[R] and [F]
DOS copy to a directory	[C]
DOS copy from a directory	[R]
Execute a .EXE file	[R] and [F]
Open and write to an existing file	[W] [C] [E] and [M]
Open and read a file	[R]
Create and write to a file	[C]

Make a new directory	[C]
Search for filename or a directory	[R]
Delete a file or an empty directory	[E]
Rename a file or a directory	[M]
Change a file or a directory attribute	[M]
Modify a directory disk space assignment	[A]
Grant any right, except the [S] right	[A]
Change trustee assignment	[A]
Change the IRF assignment	[A]

Remember, by default all users are granted the right to search the root of a directory (but cannot see any of its subdirectories), if they are granted any right of the eight rights. In addition, IntranetWare automatically assigns all the rights to a user home directory when the NDS object with a home directory is created for the first time. The supervisor, or the bindery services user object, the creator of the file server object, or any object that has an NDS supervisor object right on the server object is assigned the supervisor [S] right.

IntranetWare allows us to manage directories and files by assigning rights to a directory or a file. Effective rights are the rights that a user can or cannot have to a directory or a file. IntranetWare implements effective rights by assigning a trustee to the trustee list of a directory or a file or by modifying the default IRF of a directory or a file. Every directory and file has a trustee list. This list specifies who can access the file system. Therefore, a trustee is an object that has been assigned to the trustee list of a directory or a file. You can assign a user or a group to the trustee list, but the object must be a trustee before any access rights to a directory or a file are given. You can give or inherit rights when any of the following objects is made a trustee and granted rights in the trustee list:

- User—This is an NDS leaf object that represents a network user. It stores all the information about a specific user.

- Group—This is an NDS object that represents a group of users on the network. This object stores and maintains a list of members on the network. Members are users from different containers within the directory tree.

- Organizational role—This is an NDS leaf object that defines a role or a position within an organization. You can use the organizational role to specify a position that can be filled by different people. An organization role object maintains an occupant list. When a user is added to the occupant list, the organizational role object will be listed in that user's security equal to property. All of the occupants are granted rights from the organizational role object.

- Parent containers—This is an NDS object that is used to assign the same rights to multiple users. All the users in the container or its subdirectories will have the same directory or file rights if the container object is made a trustee list of a directory or a file.

- [Public] trustee—Anything that is connected to the network will be granted rights to the [Public] directory .

- Security equivalence—You can assign a user to have the same security equivalence as another user to give the user the same access rights granted to the user or groups in its security equivalence list. Be aware that security equivalence will be revoked if the original user object is deleted, and that security equivalence cannot be passed on from one user to another. Therefore, you should assign security equivalence only on a temporary basis.

Here is an example of how to add a user object called JSMITH a trustee list of the directory SYS: PUBLIC:

Step 1: Double-click on the organization object that contains the SYS volume object.

Step 2: Double-click on the SYS volume object, then click once on the directory SYS: PUBLIC.

Step 3: Click the "Object" from the tile menu bar, then choose "Details..." from the drop-down menu.

Step 4: Click on the "Trustee of this Directory" button on the right, then click on the "Add Trustee" button.

Step 5: On the right frame, double-click on the UP arrow till you find the object JSMITH.

Step 6: On the left frame, double-click on the object JSMITH.

Step 7: Mark the "Read" and "File Scan" rights under the title access rights. See figure 3.2.

Step 8: Click on the "OK" button.

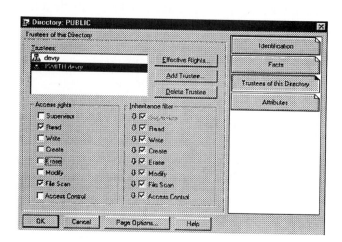

Figure 3.2 Adding an object to the trustee list of the directory SYS: PUBLIC.

Once trustee rights are granted to a trustee of a directory, all files and subdirectories within and below the directory will inherit all the rights granted. You can block the inherited rights by making a new trustee assignment at a lower level in the file system structure or modifying the default IRF to block the flow to the lower levels in the file system. The new trustee assignment to the same object eliminates the need for IRF modification. The IRF of a directory or a file does not and can never block rights that are granted to a trustee of the same directory or a file. Be aware that if you make the same user or group account as the trustee of a directory or a file, the trustee rights granted to the user or group account will overwrite any rights that would have been inherited from the same user or group account from the directory above.

Every directory and file has an IRF (Inherited Rights Filter). The IRF method is the most common method used to block inheritance for multiple users. It has the same eight possible rights as in the trustee assignment. IntranetWare automatically assigns a full IRF to a directory or a file upon creation. You can remove any right (except the supervisory [S]) from the default IRF to block the unwanted rights inherited from the trustee assignments made above a directory or a file. Be aware that you cannot restrict the supervisory trustee right at a lower level of the directory structure. Once the supervisory trustee right is assigned to a user over a directory or a file, the user will have all the rights in the entire directory structure below it. Here is an example of how to modify the IRF of a file system directory called (SYS: SHARED):

Step 1: Double-click on the organization object that contains the SYS volume object.
Step 2: Double-click on the SYS volume object.
Step 3: Click once on the directory SYS: SHARED.
Step 4: Click the "Object" from the title menu bar.
Step 5: Choose "Details..." from the drop-down menu.

Step 6: Click on the "Trustee of this Directory" button on the right.

Step 7: Mark the inheritance filter. You can mark any of the rights or not mark any of the rights (blocking them, in effect). Figure 3.3 shows that the [M], [A], and [F] rights are blocked. Also notice that the [S] right is grayed out, meaning it cannot be unchecked (blocked).

Step 8: Click on the "OK" button.

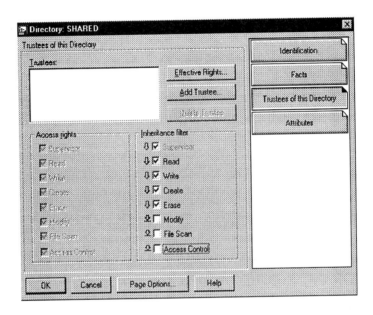

Figure 3.3 Modifying the IRF.

The rights the user can have to a directory or a file are called effective rights. The effective rights of a user to a directory or a file are a combination of:

1. The trustee assignment to any NDS object that the user object belongs to.

2. The trustee assignment to the user object.

3. The security equivalence of the user object.

4. The rights inherited from the directory above minus the rights revoked by the IRF.

If the trustee rights and the security equivalence are not explicitly assigned to a user, then the effective rights of a user on a directory or a file are a combination of:

1. The trustee assignment to the group account to which the user belongs.

2. The rights inherited from the directory above minus the rights revoked by the IRF.

If there are no inherited rights, the effective rights of a user on a directory or a file are the same as the trustee rights explicitly assigned to the user account or the combination of:

1. The trustee assignment to the group account to which the user belongs.

2. The trustee assignment to the user account.

3. The security equivalence of the user account.

When in doubt about rights, give minimum rights and add more as the need arises. It is better to miss assigned rights by limiting the user privileges. Let us look at the following example:

Suppose that we have a LAB directory in the APPS volume. In addition, the LAB directory has a subdirectory called DATA. If a user called JSMITH has all the rights except the supervisory [S] rights:

FS_1\APPS: \LAB   [MFA]
|
DATA

a)   What are JSMITH's effective rights to the DATA subdirectory?

b)   The PROD group has the rights [WR F C] on the directory DATA. If JSMITH belongs to the group called PROD, what are JSMITH's effective rights to the subdirectory DATA?

c)   What rights must be revoked on the DATA subdirectory if we want JSMITH to only execute .EXE files in the DATA directory?

Answers:

a)   Since rights flow down in a directory structure, JSMITH's effective rights to the DATA subdirectory are [MFA E].

b)
Individual rights from the above directory	[MFA]
+	
PROD group rights	[WR F C]
Resulting effective rights are	[WRMFAC]

c)   Only the rights [R] and [F] are needed to execute .EXE files. You can do the [R] and [F] rights on the subdirectory DATA in two ways:

     1)   Assign a new trustee rights [R] and [F] to the subdirectory DATA, or

2) Use IRF to revoke the rights [W M AC]. If you use this method, then the calculation of the effective rights at the DATA subdirectory is as follows:

Individual rights from the above directory   [MFA]

        +

PROD group rights   [WR F C]

        –

IRF   [W M AC]

Resulting effective rights are   [R   F   ]

You can design the file system security by planning the rights on a top-down basis using the concept of rights inheritance, or plan trustee assignments based on the concept of group rights. If you are designing your file system security rights using the top-down concept of inheritance rights, you must follow the following plan:

1) Design the top-down directory structure from less access to greater access.

2) Plan the rights starting from the root directory and work downward.

3) Avoid granting rights high in the directory tree.

4) Grant only the rights needed at any level.

5) Use IRF to block unwanted inherited rights.

If you are designing your file system security rights using trustee assignments based on the concept of group rights, you must adhere to the following plan:

1) Grant trustee assignments to the group accounts to which the user belongs.

2) Grant trustee assignments to the individual user account.

3) Assign security equivalence to the individual user account.

You should always plan the trustee assignments from the largest group to the smallest. Since the user also inherits the rights from the groups to which it belongs, you may simplify user access to the network by creating the group accounts first, assigning trustees to access the resources second, and then assigning the user accounts to the group accounts. Remember that you should always use group accounts to reflect the business organization and use user accounts to reflect the individual in each department or work group.

As a system administrator, to implement the file system security, you must be able to assign trustees and grant rights to trustees, modify the default IRF, and view the effective rights. Anybody that needs to modify the trustee assignments or IRF of a file or a directory must have the access control [A] right to the file or directory. You can always use the NWADMIN and FILER utilities to assign trustees, grant rights, or set attributes. In addition, you can use the NETADMIN utility to assign trustee and grant rights on volumes only. You can use the command line RIGHTS to view or modify the effective rights on a file or a directory. Or you can use the command line WHOAMI to view the current user's security equivalence, view the groups to which the user belongs, view the user's effective rights, and view the workgroup manager information.

Another type of file system security is attribute security. Attributes are special properties assigned to any directory or a file. You can assign attributes to directories or files to prevent users from performing tasks that the effective rights allow. Often, attribute security has the final say-so on whether or not a task can be performed even when a user or the group he/she belongs to has rights to a file or a directory. Attribute security overrides other trustee rights that have been granted to users and groups through trustee rights assignments. Attributes are assigned to files or directories to define their access mode. To be able to modify or assign attributes, a user must have the modify [M] right. Again the assigned attributes supersede the effective rights of a directory or a file. Here is a list of the file system rights hierarchy with the highest priority first:

- File attributes

- Directory attributes

- File trustee rights

- Directory trustee rights

Below is a list of available attributes and their descriptions:

Symbol	Attribute Name	Description
A	Archived Needed	Used on files only. It is assigned automatically to any file modified after the last backup.
C or CI	Copy Inhibit	Used on files only. It affects the Macintosh users by overriding their [R] and [F] rights to prevent them from copying files.
D or DI	Delete Inhibit	Used on files or directories. It overrides the erase [E] rights to prevent users from deleting a directory or a file.
X	Execute Only	Used on files only. It prevents backing up or copying a file. Only the supervisor equivalent can set this attribute.

		Once it is set, it cannot be removed. It can only be erased. It is assigned only to program files, such as .EXE or .COM files.
H	Hidden	Used on files or directories. It hides files or directories from the DOS DIR command scan to prevent a file from being deleted or copied. On the other hand, if a user has the file scan right [F], he/she will be able to scan the files or directories using the NDIR command.
P	Purge	Used on files or directories. It purges all files or directories upon deletion. You will not be able to salvage any of the deleted files or directories.
RO	Read Only	Used on files only. It used to only read a file. IntranetWare automatically assigns the attributes DI and RI to any file that is flagged RO.
RW	Write Only	Used on files only. RW attribute is automatically flagged when a file is created. It is used to be able to modify a file.
R or RI	Read Inhibit	Used on files or directories. It is used to prevent users from renaming a file or a directory. It overrides the modify [M] right.
S or Sh	Shareable	Used on files only. It is usually used with the flag RO. It is used to allow a file to be accessed by more than one user at the same time.
T	Transactional	Used on files only. It marks the files as being tracked by the Transactional Tracking System (TTS) to prevent it from data corruption. All of the database files should be flagged with the transactional attribute.
Sy	System	Used on files or directories. It is assigned for system file and directories. It hides the files or directories from the DOS DIR command scan to prevent a file from being deleted or copied. On the other hand, if a user has the file scan right [F], he/she will be able scan the files or directories using the NDIR command.
I	Indexed	Used on files only. It enables the turbo FAT to allow files to be accessed quickly. It is automatically assigned to files bigger than 64 FAT entries.
Co	Compressed	Used on files only. It is used to compress files after an interval of time.
Ic	Immediate Compress	Used on files and directories. It is used to immediately compress a file or a directory.
Dc	Don't Compress	Used on files and directories. It is used to never compress a file or a directory.
Cc	Can't Compress	Used on files only. It is used to never compress a file.
M	Migrate	Used on files only. It is used to allow a file to be migrated.
Dm	Don't Migrate	Used on directories only. It is used to never allow a directory to be migrated.
Ds	Don't Suballocate	Used on files only. It is used to never suballocate a file.
N	Normal	Used on files and directories. It is used to clear all the flags set on a file or a directory. It also assigns the RW attribute to a file.

ALL	ALL	Used on files only. It is used to set all the attributes on a file.
SUB	Subdirectory	Used on files only. It is used to make changes to file attributes in a directory and its subdirectory.

Even though you can use the command FLAG to set an attribute to a file or a directory, let us see how to use NWADMIN to set the attributes DI and RI to the directory SYS: \SHARED:

Step 1: Double-click on the organization object that contains the SYS volume object.
Step 2: Double-click on the SYS volume object.
Step 3: Click once on the directory SYS: SHARED.
Step 4: Click the "Object" from the title menu bar.
Step 5: Choose "Details..." from the drop-down menu.
Step 6: Click on the "Attribute" button on the right.
Step 7: Mark the attributes "Delete Inhibit" and " Rename Inhibit". See figure 3.4.
Step 8: Click on the "OK" button.

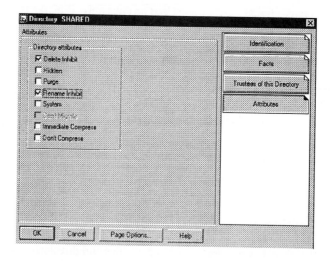

Figure 3.4 How to set attributes on the directory SYS: SHARED.

Now that you have learned how to secure files and directories, it is time to learn how to set up a user environment. Chapter 4 will discuss how to set up a user environment to allow users to have easy access to essential network services and resources.

Questions

1) What are the basic components of an IntranetWare file system, created during server installation?
2) Give a brief description about IntranetWare volumes.
3) Describe what drive pointers are.
4) Give reasons why IntranetWare copy utilities are superior to the DOS COPY command.
5) Where can you use LOGIN <username> to automate the login process?
6) What do the following commands do?

   a) NDIR
   b) NDIR /FO /SORT CR
   c) NDIR *.JOE /FO /OW EQ JOE /REV SORT SI
   d) NDIR /DO /FO
   e) NDIR *.EXE /FO /SUB
   f) NDIR /DO /S
   g) RIGHTS /D

7) Where does the system store AUTOEXEC.NCF and NWADMIN?
8) What is the name of the directory used to store files deleted from an IntranetWare volume?
9) Name two utilities that can be used to recover a file from an IntranetWare volume.
10) When is it a good idea to create one volume per disk when planning the IntranetWare file system?
11) Name four tasks that can be performed to manage space on an IntranetWare volume.
12) In what two ways can you limit volume space usage?
13) How much disk space increase can you expect by using IntranetWare's file compression system?
14) When home directories are created along with the user object, what default rights are given to the user?
15) Where should you assign rights to if access to a directory or a file is unique to a user?
16) What are the rights needed to:

   a) copy files to a directory?
   b) see files and directories?
   c) execute an .EXE file?
   d) create and write to a file?
   e) open and write an existing file?

    f)   modify a closed file?

    g)   salvage a file deleted from an IntranetWare volume?

    h)   change attributes or name a file or directory?

17) Which attribute prevents a file from being renamed?

18) What does the following mapping do?

    MAP S1: = SYS: PUBLIC

    MAP S2: = SYS: WORD

    MAP INS S2: = APPS: \DATA

4

User Environment and IntranetWare Printing

In this chapter, you will learn how to automate the network user environment to let users have easy access to essential network services and resources. You can automate the user environment by configuring the user workstation's CONFIG.SYS, AUTOEXEC.BAT, and NET.CFG files. In addition, you can design a login script and set up a customize menu to automate application execution. Finally, you will learn how to set up and manage network printing.

4.1 LOGIN SCRIPTS

We have already learned how to configure the CONFIG.SYS file to set up a DOS working environment, automate the workstation connection using AUTOEXEC.BAT, and set up the initial network environment using the NET.CFG file. It is time now to learn how to set an initial working environment for each user and provide access to the network resources needed by each user using login scripts. A *login script* is a set of instructions the system follows and executes during the login process. It customizes the system for users by setting up default and search drive mappings, displaying system messages, setting up environmental variables, attaching users to other servers, and running other startup functions when a user first logs into the network.

To set up a user login script, one must consider the needs of the users, the knowledge levels of all the users, the needs and types of the workgroups, access requirements to the network resources, and the size and complexity of the network. IntranetWare provides four types of login scripts, and when a user logs into the network they are executed in the order shown below:

- Container—A container login script of the immediate parent container of the user object will be executed first. If it does not exist, then no container login script is executed. You may want to set up a container login script to meet the general environment of users in an organization or an organization unit object. Only a supervisor (ADMIN) or a supervisor equivalent can create a container login script. You can use a container login script to do the following:

    a) Activate menus or applications used by all user objects in the container.

b) Connect to a network printer used by all user objects in the container.

c) Set up search drive mappings to SYS PUBLIC.

d) Set up search drive mappings to application directories.

e) Set up network drive mappings to the home directory of each user.

f) Use IF statements to provide resources based on time, group membership, or other criteria.

g) Send messages to all user objects in the container.

- Profile—A profile login script is executed after the container login script if the user object has been specified to be part of the profile property. The profile login script is a property of a profile object. Each user object contains a profile property. You are allowed only one profile login script per user and the profile property specifies which profile login script will be executed. You may want to set up a profile login script to meet the general environment of users in different organizations or organization unit objects. Only a supervisor (ADMIN) or a supervisor equivalent can create a profile login script. You can use a profile login script to do the following:

  a) Send messages to all user objects with the same profile property.

  b) Connect all user objects with the same profile property to a network printer.

  c) Set up common search drive mappings for all user objects with the same profile property.

  d) Set up common network drive mappings for all user objects with the same profile property.

- User—A user login script is the last login script that is executed. It sets a special environment for a specific user. A supervisor, supervisor equivalent, workgroup manager, or a user account manager can create a user login script. If a user is allowed to change his/her password, then the individual user can create and edit his/her own login script. You can use a profile login script to do the following:

  a) Connect to a network printer unique to the user.

    b) Activate a menu or applications unique to the user.

    c) Set up network drive mappings unique to the user.

- Default—A default login script sets the initial login environment after server installation. It is hard coded into the file LOGIN.EXE. It cannot be modified. It assigns the first available drive to the user's home directory (only if it is located at SYS: PUBLIC), and to the DOS directory on the file server. If ADMIN logs in, then the default login script will set the first available drive to SYS: SYSTEM. The default login script will execute for any user who does not have a user login script. You can disable the default login script by placing the command NO_DEFAULT in the container or profile login script. The default login script contains the following two drive mappings and command:

Login script command	Description
MAP S1:= SYS: PUBLIC	A search drive mapping to the PUBLIC directory to allow a user to have access to the IntranetWare client utilities.
MAP S2:= SYS: PUBLIC\%MACHINE\%OS\%OS_VERSION	A search drive mapping to the DOS directory that allows a user to have access to the DOS utilities.
COMSPEC = S2: COMMAND.COM	A DOS directory to reload the proper COMMAND.COM to the workstation

When you are planning to design login scripts on the network, you should always use a container login script to provide access to network resources. Use a profile login script for the needs of a specific group or for the needs of a specific user.

    You can set up the current context of a user before or during login. To set up the current context before login, you must add the statement NAME CONTEXT = "distinguished_ name path" to the NET.CFG file. This is a workstation-specific task. The NetWare DOS requester will set the current context specified in the NAME CONTEXT statement when it loads the workstation files. To set up the current context during login, you must add the statement CONTEXT "distinguished name path" in any login script. This is also a workstation-specific task. IntranetWare will set the current context to the context specified in the CONTEXT statement in the login script.

    Login scripts consist of certain commands and identifiers that can only be used in a login script. In addition, all of the commands used in login scripts must have a specific syntax and structure. The maximum number of characters a line can have is 150, although 78 is recommended for readability. The commands are not case sensitive but the identifiers are. Blank lines in the login script have no effect on the execution. Below is a list of login script commands and their descriptions:

Login Script Command	Description
REMARK, REM, "*", ";"	Any line in the login script that begins with REMARK, REM, or the characters "*" and ";" will be ignored by IntranetWare and will be interpreted as a comment. This login script command must be left justified. Comments will not be shown on the screen during execution of the login script.
WRITE	This is used to display text messages on the screen during execution. The text message must be enclosed with quotation marks.
MAP	This command is used to set logical pointers (NetWare drive pointers) to physical directories. It supplies a path to data and program files. In addition, default and search drives may also be mapped using the MAP command.
CONTEXT	This command is used to set the current context to a "distinguished name path". Remember that there is no leading period in a "distinguished name path". This command is similar to the CX utility. It changes the workstation's current NDS during login script execution.
BREAK	If this command is "BREAK ON", then it allows the user to stop the login process by pressing the keys <CTRL> <C> or <CTRL> <BREAK>. The default is "BREAK OFF".
COMPSPEC	COMPSPEC specifies the location of the command processor COMMAND.COM to be reloaded in case it is overwritten.
DISPLAY	This displays the content of a specified text file on the screen.
FDISPLAY	This filters out the control characters of a specified text file, then it displays its content on the screen.
SET	SET is used to set DOS environmental variables. Its value must be enclosed with double quotes.
DRIVE	DRIVE specifies the drive to be set as the default drive at the termination of the login script. Remember, you cannot move to a drive in a login script using a drive pointer.
EXIT	This command terminates the execution of the login script and allows the execution of any .COM, .EXE, or .BAT files. The login script following it will not be executed.
#EXTERNAL FILE_NAME	This allows you to leave the login script, execute the EXTERNAL FILE_NAME, and come back to the login script. The EXTERNAL FILE_NAME can be an IntranetWare command or utility, or a .BAT, .EXE, or .COM DOS file. If you run a DOS application this way, it will take about 70 KB to 100 KB extra from the workstation memory. This happens because some TSR external programs are loaded to memory upon execution and are never returned to the workstation disk upon completion.
SWAP	SWAP is used to force 70 KB to 100 KB out of memory into a local or a network disk . You need to identify the path with the SWAP command.

#COMMAND /C FILE_NAME	This command allows you to leave the login script, execute the FILE_NAME and come back to the login script. The FILE_NAME can be an internal DOS command, or a .BAT, .EXE, or .COM DOS file. No extra workstation memory is required if this method is applied.
FIRE PHASORS	This command is used to make a sound alarm or noise maker sound to draw attention to the listing on the screen.
IF...THEN...ELSE	This command sequence sets a conditional criteria that must be met in order for the statement to execute. The maximum nesting clause is 10.
INCLUDE	INCLUDE is used to include a sub-program, which is a text file that contains login statements. You may execute a container login script by specifying the container name.
GOTO	GOTO is used to execute a portion of the login script out of regular sequence
LASTLOGINTIME	This is used to display the last time the user logged in
NO_DEFAULT	This command is used to skip the execution of the default login script even without a login script. Remember, the execution sequence of the login scripts is as follows: the container script, if it is present; the profile script, if it is present; and a user script, if it is present. If a user login script is not present, then the default login script will execute.
PASSWORD_EXPIRES	This is used to warn a user that his/her password is about to expire
PAUSE	PAUSE stops the screen from scrolling, displays the message "Strike a key when ready..." on the screen, and waits for the user to press a key to continue

In addition to the login script commands, you can also use the login script identifier variables for more flexibility and efficiency. The identifiers must be written in upper-case letters and must be preceded with a percent sign "%" to have them replace the actual condition during execution. They are useful in statements, such as WRITE and IF...THEN...ELSE, or in commands for which you can specify a path name. There are two ways of displaying the identifiers in a WRITE statement. You can precede the identifier variable with a semicolon (;), or you can enclose the identifier inside quotation marks. If you enclose it in quotation marks, the identifier variable must be written in upper-case letters and be preceded by a percent sign, "%". Below is a list of identifier variables that you can use in a login script:

Category	Identifier Variable	Description
Time	AM_PM	Displays AM or PM.
	HOUR	Displays hour of the day (1 to 12).
	HOUR24	Displays hour of the day in military time (1 to 24).
	MINUTE	Displays minutes (00 to 59).
	SECOND	Displays seconds (00 to 59).
	GREETING_TIME	Displays a greeting (morning, afternoon, or evening).

Date	DAY	Displays day numbers 01 to 31.
	DAY_OF_WEEK	Displays day of the week (Monday, Tuesday, etc.).
	NDAY_OF_WEEK	Displays weekday numbers 1 to 7, where 1 = Sunday.
	MONTH	Displays month numbers 01 to 12.
	MONTH_NAME	Displays the month name (January, February, March, etc.).
	YEAR	Displays all four digits of the year (e.g., 1998).
	SHORT_YEAR	Displays the last two digits of the year (e.g., 98).
User	CN	Displays the user's full common name as it appears in NDS.
	FULL_NAME	Displays the user full name as it appears in the NDS and the bindery.
	LAST_NAME	Displays the user's last name as it appears in NDS or the user's full name as it appears in the bindery.
	LOGIN_CONTEXT	Displays the context where the user exists.
	REQUESTER_CONTEXT	Displays the context when login started.
	ALIAS_CONTEXT	Displays Y if the REQUESTER_CONTEXT is an alias.
	LOGIN_NAME	Displays the user's login name. It is truncated to only eight characters.
	USER_ID	Displays the user's hexadecimal ID number.
	MEMBER OF "group"	Displays the group object to which the user belongs.
	NOT MEMBER of "group"	Displays the group object to which the user does not belong.
	PASSWORD_EXPIRES	Displays the number of days before the password expires.
Workstation	MACHINE	Displays the type of computer the user has (e.g., IBM_PC or any other name specified in the NET.CFG file).
	S_MACHINE	Displays the type of computer the user has in short format.
	NETWARE_REQUESTER	Displays the version of requester for DOS or OS/2.
	OS	Displays the type of operating system used on the workstation (e.g., MSDOS, OS/2, etc.).
	OS_VERSION	Displays the operating system loaded on the workstation.
	STATION	Displays the workstation's connection number.
	P_STATION	Displays the workstation's 12-digit hexadecimal node number.
	SHELL_TYPE	Displays the version of the workstation's DOS shell for NetWare 2 and 3 users.
Miscellaneous	FILE_SERVER	Displays the name of the current file server.
	NETWORK_ADDRESS	Displays the 8-digit hexadecimal IPX external number for the cabling system.

ACCESS_SERVER	Displays "True" if the access server is functional; otherwise, it displays "False".
ERROR_LEVEL	Displays an error value ("value = 0" means no errors).
%n	Replaced by parameters the user enters after the login command, starting with %0.

Let us look at the following login script sample.

Script Commands	Descriptions
MAP F: =SYS: USERS\%LOGIN_NAME	Sets a network drive to the user's home directory.
MAP ROOT H: =SYS: USERS\%LLOGIN_NAME	Sets a pseudo root.
MAP G: =APPS: WP\DATA	Sets a network drive to the directory WP\DATA in the APPS volume.
MAP S1: =SYS: PUBLIC	Sets the first search drive to the PUBLIC directory.
MAP S2: =SYS: PUBLIC\%MACHINE\%OS\%OS_VERSION	Sets the second search drive to operating system directory in the PUBLIC directory.
COMSEC =S2: APPS: WP\WPDATA	WP\WPDATA is the directory location where the command processor COMMAND.COM will be reloaded if it was overwritten.
MAP DISPLAY OFF	Turns off echo of the map assignment.
LOGIN FS_2\GUEST /NS	Attaches to the server FS_2 and logs in as GUEST.
NO_DEFAULT	Does not execute the default login script.
DISPLAY F:\PUBLIC\SYSNEWS.TXT	Displays the content of the file SYSNEWS.TXT in the PUBLIC directory.
PAUSE	Waits for the user to press a key.
WRITE "GOOD %GREETING_TIME, %LOGIN_NAME"	Displays a greeting message using the user's login name.
WRITE "GOOD", greeting_time; ","; login_name	Same effect as above.
WRITE "%DAY_OF_WEEK, %MONTH_NAME, %DAY"	Displays today's date.
#COMMAND /C CLS	Executes the DOS command CLS to clear the screen.
IF "%HOUR24%MINUTE" . "0900" THEN BEGIN	Executes the WRITE statement "YOU ARE LATE !!!!" if the current system time is 0900.
WRITE "YOU ARE LATE !!!!"	
FIRE 5	Sounds phasors 5 times.

111

END
IF day_of_week = "FRIDAY" THEN BEGIN

Executes the WRITE statement "TODAY IS PAY DAY" if the current system date is FRIDAY.

WRITE "TODAY IS PAY DAY"
FIRE 3

Sounds phasors 3 times.

END
EXIT "NMENU CLASS.DAT"

Leaves the login script and executes the menu CLASS.DAT.

Now let us look at the steps it takes to create a login script in NWADMIN95:

Step 1: Double-click on the organization unit where the user is located.
Step 2: Double-click on the user.
Step 3: Click on the "Login Script" button on the right.
Step 4: Type the login script. See figure 4.1.
Step 5: Click on "OK".

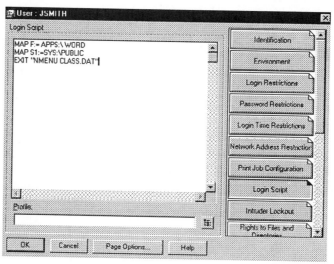

Figure 4.1 How to create a login script.

Let us say that you now want to copy JSMITH's login script into the user JDOE's login script. Here are the steps needed to do that:

Step 1: Double-click on the organization unit where the user JSMITH is located.
Step 2: Double-click on the user JSMITH.
Step 3: Click on the "Login Script" button on the right.
Step 4: Highlight JSMITH's login script by holding down and dragging the left mouse button to the end of the script.

Step 5: Press the keys <Shift> <Delete>.
Step 6: Press the keys <Shift> <Insert>.
Step 7: Click on "OK".
Step 8: Double-click on the organization unit where the user JDOE is located.
Step 9: Double-click on the user JDOE.
Step 10: Click on the "Login Script" button on the right.
Step 11: Press the keys <Shift> <Insert>.
Step 12: Click on "OK".

4.2 MENUS

Creating a menu allows you to automatically launch applications, perform special drive mappings, and utilize submenus. Menus can be user-specific or general to all the users. They are created in a effort to establish a turnkey system in which all users fit and to provide a user-friendly interface as they log in. Another important reason for using menus is to avoid forcing users to access the DOS prompt.

If you are using MS Windows, then you probably do not need to use a menu system, since MS Windows is a simple graphical interface. However, if you are not using MS Windows, then using a menu system is a great idea. Many people use menus to automate various tasks. In the process, complex scripts can launch commands simply by selecting a menu option. Novell has recognized the convenience of using menus and has licensed a menu system from Saber Software Corporation for its IntranetWare operating system. As with most things related to computing, planning is a critical phase in the development of your menus. Before you even start to write your menus, you should sit down with pad and pencil and draw out how you want the menus to look. Since IntranetWare menus can have several different layers of submenus, it is important to first visualize how the finished product will look. While you draw the first sketches of the menus, there are a few questions you should ask yourself:

- What do the users do at their desks? Knowing what the users are doing helps you understand what is required from a menu.

- What applications do the users use? Do not write menus that do not include all the different applications in use. Remember that the purpose of creating a menu is to make the user's life easier.

- Can you automate some of the redundant tasks? If there are tasks that users must do on a regular basis, see if you can automate these tasks as menu options. By automating these tasks, users will be able to perform their jobs more efficiently and minimize the chances of typos.

- How should the options be organized? Menus should be designed in a well-organized format. If users need in-depth training to figure out how you organized the menus, then your work has been wasted. Remember that the goal of using menus is to reduce the amount of work.

To customize your menu, you may include options, such as applications, network user utilities, e-mail, complex DOS commands, or access to other network directories. The menu is created using any standard ASCII text file that contains special commands. This text file can be created with the editor of your choice as long as the editor does not add any special formatting characters to the document. After the menu source file is written, it must be compiled using the MENUMAKE utility. There are some rules that need to be followed when writing a menu source file.

1) MENU commands are entered at the leftmost column.

2) Each MENU command must be followed by at least one ITEM command.

3) ITEM commands follow the MENU command and are indented one tab.

4) Each ITEM command must be followed by at least one executable (EXEC or LOAD) command.

5) Executable steps are any valid DOS or IntranetWare command line entries.

6) EXEC or LOAD commands should be indented two tabs from the left margin.

7) Remarks can be added to the menu as long as they are preceded by a semicolon (;).

8) The menu source file must have the extension .SRC.

9) The "%" sign should be used to identify a menu title.

10) The first menu must be defined fully before a submenu is defined.

11) Selections should consist of the choices that appear in the menu.

12) You should organize selections with your own numbering scheme or the letters A to Z. Otherwise, selections will be automatically alphabetized on the screen

13) Each menu must have at least one selection.

14) Submenus should be called through executable steps.

The IntranetWare menu system consists of four components. The first component is a main menu with a title and a list of options. The second is the set of control commands to be executed for each option. Third is the control commands used to prompt for input from the user. Finally, there is an optional submenu with titles, lists of options, and control commands. The basic format of a typical menu source file is as follows:

```
MENU menu_number, menu_name
    ITEM item_name, {option}
        Control Commands
    ITEM item_name, {option}
        Control Commands
```

There are two types of menu commands within a menu source file—organizational and control. Both types of menu commands must be entered in upper-case letters. Organizational commands establish the content and organization of the menu programs. Control commands give instructions to the menu program, NMENU.EXE, on how to process information and execute commands. The two organizational commands are MENU and ITEM. We will now explain these two commands.

In the above source file, the MENU command names and identifies the beginning of the menu or submenu. The menu_number is replaced with a number to identify the menu or submenu and the menu_name is replaced with a name to identify the name of the menu or submenu. Note that the numbers assigned to each menu have no bearing on the order in which they appear in the finished product. The ordering of menus and options depends on how the ITEM commands are included. But, for the purpose of organization, it is better if groups of menus and submenus are structured neatly. Therefore, you may want to number your menu commands in groups of five or ten. This makes life easier should you need to add new options down the road. Remember that you can have only 255 MENU commands in one menu file.

The ITEM command signifies the different options within each menu or submenu. You can have a maximum of 12 ITEM commands per MENU command, and each ITEM command must be indented one tab from the left margin. Item_name is replaced with the name or phrase you want to be used as the menu option up to a maximum of 40 characters in length. Option is a parameter used to change the way a command is displayed or executed. It must be enclosed with curly brackets {}. There are four option parameters used with ITEM commands as shown below:

Option	Example	Description
BATCH	ITEM WordPerfect {BATCH}	Added to the end of the ITEM line to tell NMENU to remove the menu system from memory temporarily when is executing a

		command. The BATCH option will save you 32KB of RAM, but slows down the reloading of the menus slightly. In addition, it will return the user to his/her prior directory automatically by running the CHDIR option.
CHDIR	ITEM LOTUS 123 {CHDIR}	Added at the end of the ITEM line to tell NMENU to return to the previous default directory after the processing is completed.
PAUSE	ITEM Directory Listing {PAUSE}	Added at the end of the ITEM line to stop the execution of a DOS command until a key is pressed. It will display the message "Press any key to continue".
SHOW	ITEM Copy a File {SHOW}	Added to the end of the ITEM line to have a command executed and displayed in the upper left corner of the screen.

You may add more than one option in the curly brackets. For example, you can execute the command ITEM Copy a File {SHOW PAUSE}. The menu program lists the item_names in the menu in the order shown in the source file. The menu program automatically assigns a letter to each item_name beginning with the letter A. To override the line assignments, you can insert your own using the carat "^" character. For example, if you want the letter W to stand for WordPerfect, you must enter the command ITEM ^W WordPerfect. When you precede the item_name with a "^", it must be a unique, not a duplicated item, and you must then use a carat "^" character throughout the item_names with the same menu or submenu.

The following are the six control commands that a source file can have. They all may be entered after an ITEM command.

- EXEC command—The EXEC command must be the last control command issued for any ITEM command. You can use the EXEC command to execute any .COM or .EXE program, an IntranetWare utility, or any of the following four commands:

Command	Example	Description
DOS	EXEC DOS	Allows the user to jump to a DOS shell from within the menu. If the user wants to return to the menu, he/she must type EXIT from the DOS prompt.
EXIT	EXEC EXIT	Exits the menu program completely and places the user at the DOS prompt.
LOGOUT	EXEC LOGOUT	Exits from the menu and logs the user out of the network, placing him/her at the DOS prompt.
CALL	EXEC CALL TEST.BAT	Calls a batch file from within a batch file

There is no limit to the number of EXEC commands that can follow an ITEM command. Remember that the ITEM command is followed by the command(s) you want to pass to DOS, up to maximum of 250 characters. Since DOS will not except commands of 250 characters on a single line, you can break up commands by using the plus "+" sign. As an example:

```
ITEM Capture to Print Q1
    EXEC CAPTURE +
    L=1 Q=PRINTQ1 TI=2
```

The above will execute the command CAPTURE to PRINTQ1, with a time-out value of 2. When entering the command you want to execute, specify the drive letter and directory where it can be found, if it is not in the path. NMENU does not recognize volume names. For example:

```
ITEM WordPerfect
    EXEC H:\APPS\WP
    EXEC WP.EXE
```

If you use the command EXEC LOGOUT in your menu file, selecting this option would produce the error "Batch File Missing" even though you would still be logged out. To get around this error, you could use the EXEC EXIT command with a batch file that contains the LOGOUT command. To do so, first create a batch file called FINISH.BAT in the LOGIN directory that contains the LOGOUT command. Then add the following test to your menu:

```
ITEM Logout from the server
    EXEC F:
    EXEC CD\LOGIN
    EXEC EXIT "FINISH.BAT"
```

Once you have added this test and you have recompiled the menu source file, users can select this option and log out of the server without getting an error message.

- LOAD file_name.dat—The LOAD file_name.dat command allows the user to create multiple menus in separate source files. You can use LOAD to start and run an outside menu that was compiled. NMENU will put the original menu on hold while executing the other menu.

- SHOW menu_number—The SHOW menu_number command will reference a submenu within the same menu script. You can create up to 255 submenus in a single source file. You must include the menu_number declared in the MENU command to execute that submenu.

- GETO instruction {prepend} length, prefill, Secure {append}—The GETO command prompts the user for additional information on an optional basis. The information is gathered and is added to the end of the following EXEC command.

- GETR instruction {prepend} length, prefill, Secure {append}—The GETR command prompts the user for additional information that is required. The program will not continue until the user enters a valid input. The user may press the <ESC> key to return to the main menu. The information is gathered and is added to the end of the following EXEC command.

- GETP instruction {prepend} length, prefill, Secure {append}—The GETP command prompts the user for additional information to be used later. After aa parameter is inputted, it is assigned to a variable (%0 to %9). These variables can then be called into the following EXEC command.

The GETO, GETR, and GETP instructions have the parameters "instruction {prepend} length, prefill, Secure {append}" following them. The user may use any of the three GETx commands to prompt for user input. They use the same options and execute in the same manner. The GETx commands will execute with the following user input:

- instruction—This is used to display text to the user.

- {prepend}—This is used to enter text before the user's text. Be careful with spacing. Any spaces between the curly brackets will be used.

- length—This is used to specify the number of characters the user can enter (up to 255).

- prefill—This is used to place a text in an entry window by default. You can call DOS environment variables as the default by enclosing them in percent signs "%", e.g., "%SERVERS%".

- append—This is used to enter text after the user's text. Again watch the spacing. Any spaces between the curly brackets will be used.

Here are some examples of how to use the GETx commands:

GETR Give me a name please: {} 80,%NAME%,{}
GETO Enter the print queue number: {PRINTQ_} 2, ,{}
GETP Enter the file name: {} 12,, {}

When using the GETx commands, you must observe the following five rules:

1) A GETx command is issued only between ITEM and EXEC commands.

2) A maximum of 100 GETx commands per ITEM command should be used.

3) Limit the length of each prompt to one line.

4) Only 10 prompts can be entered per dialog box.

5) You must include a carat "^" at the beginning of the prompt text if you want a prompt to appear in its own dialog box.

Remember that all of the GETx options will wait for the user to press the key <F10> to execute their input. The comman will normally use only the information you type in; if no information is entered, then the command will use prefill information. GETR will continue to wait for user input until typed information is entered. If you have upgraded from a previous version of NetWare, you may still be using the older menu system (MENU.EXE and MNU source menus). Instead of wasting time rewriting these scripts, you can convert them using the MENUCVT command. Once converted, they can be run in the same fashion as the newer menus. The syntax for the MENUCVT command is as follows:

MENUCVT oldfile_name.mnu newfile_name.src

After the newfile_name.src is created, you must use the MENUMAKE command to compile it. To create a new menu, you must follow the following three steps:

Step 1: Create a source menu using a text editor. Make sure to name it with the extension .SRC. Let us assume that you have created a source menu called TEST.SRC.

Step 2: Compile the source menu TEST.SRC using the command MENUMAKE TEST.SRC. If you used a different extension, you must specify the full file name. If there are no errors in your script, MENUMAKE will convert the script TEST.SRC and create a new file called TEST.DAT. If there are errors, MENUMAKE tells you in which line the errors occurred, so you can resolve them.

Step 3: Execute the compiled menu file TEST.DAT using the command NMENU TEST.DAT.

Let us see an example demonstrating the above three steps:

Step 1: Let us use the DOS editor to create the following menu source file called TEST.SRC.

Script command	Description
MENU 01, Administration Menu	Main menu called Administration Menu.
ITEM WordPerfect	Option item called WordPerfect.
EXEC CD\WP51	Changes to the directory WP51.
EXEC WP.EXE	Executes WP.EXE.
ITEM LOTUS 123	Option item called LOTUS 123.
EXEC CD\R123	Changes to the directory R123.
EXEC 123.EXE	Execute 123.EXE.
ITEM File Management	Option item called File management.
SHOW 15	Goes to and executes the submenu declared 15.
ITEM ^DDOS Prompt	Option item called DOS Prompt.
EXEC DOS	Exits to the DOS prompt temporarily
ITEM ^LLogout from the Server	Option item called Logout from the Server.
EXEC LOGOUT	Logs out from the network.
ITEM ^EExit from the Menu	Option item called Exit from the Menu.
EXEC EXIT	Exits to the DOS prompt permanently.
MENU 15, File Management	The submenu 15, called File Management.
ITEM Copy an entire directory {SHOW PAUSE}	Option item called Copy an entire directory.
GETP Enter the source: {} 80,,{}	Gets the source and assigns %1 to it.
GETP Enter the target:: {} 80,,{}	Gets the target and assigns %2 to it.
EXEC NCOPY %1 %2 /S	Copies the entire directory structure.
EXEC DIR %2 /W	Lists the target directory.
ITEM Directory Listing {SHOW CHDIR PAUSE}	Option item called Directory Listing.
GETO Enter name of directory: {} 80,,{}	Gets the directory name and assigns %1 to it.
EXEC NDIR	Lists the directory.

Step 2: After you have saved the TEST.SRC file, you must execute the command MENUMAKE TEST.SRC from the DOS prompt. If there are no errors, then a file called TEST.DAT is created.

Step 3: Execute the compiled menu file TEST.DAT using the command NMENU TEST.DAT. The menu will appear as shown in figure 4.2.

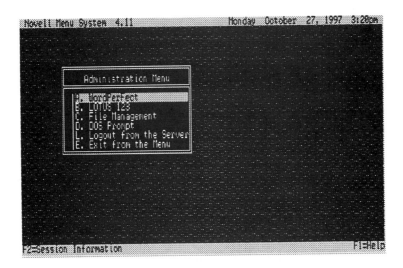

Figure 4.2 The output menu TEST.DAT.

To pick a choice on the menu, you can either press the letter that appears on the left side of the menu or use the arrow keys to move up or down. Once this is all done, you must then determine where you want the menu file to be stored. The menu file should be placed in one of the search drives where users have at least the [R] and [F] rights. It is normally placed in the directory PUBLIC for this purpose. Next, you must create a directory somewhere on the server that will be used for temporary files. NMENU creates temporary files whenever the users access the menu or shell to DOS. Since you usually have a search drive pointing to the PUBLIC directory, you can create the temporary directory called TEMP as a subdirectory of PUBLIC. You have to assign all users the rights [RWCEMF] in the temporary directory. Finally, there are two environment variable settings you should add to the system login script:

Command in Login Script	Description
SET S_FILE ="%STATION"	NMENU will use this variable for naming the temporary files.
SET S_FILEDIR = "Z:\PUBLIC\TEMP\"	This variable specifies where the temporary files should be stored. You should replace the directory name with the one you created. But you must ensure there is a back slash "\" at the end of the path.

If both of these SET parameters are not set, then the default directory for temporary files will be the directory from which the NMENU was executed, and the temporary filenames will be MENU$$.BAT, NMENU_O.BAT, and $$$.DAT. In order to implement NMENU properly, you must use the DOS SET parameters to set up the environment for NMENU, use the EXEC CALL command in the your menu file to call a batch file, and teach NMENU users how to exist the menu properly.

Otherwise, you may encounter problems, such as the old menu keeps coming up or you have trouble converting from the old menus. When NMENU is executed, it does the following:

- Creates a temporary xxxx.dat file if there is no xxxx.dat file.

- It uses the xxxx.dat file to refer to the menu filename file.

NMENU uses the menu filename file contained in the xxxx.dat file regardless of the menu filename specified on the command line. Hence, if the temporary files are not being deleted properly, the old menu keeps coming up. Here are some reasons that cause the temporary files not to be deleted properly.

1) The user reboots the workstation while still in the menu.

2) The user does not have rights to create and delete files in the temporary directory.

3) The user executes a batch file from the menu without using the EXEC CALL command.

4) The user exits the menu without using the EXEC EXIT command.

5) The user logs out of the menu without using the EXEC LOGOUT command.

Please notice that all EXEC commands are case sensitive and must be in upper case. NMENU may execute the commands EXEC exit and EXEC logout, but will not delete their temporary files. You could add a command to a container login script to ensure that everyone uses the new menus automatically by adding the command EXIT "NMENU menu_name.dat" to the end of the script. Again, you want to create menus with a turnkey environment to provide users, who do not use MS Windows, a quick and easy access to applications and network resources. The benefits of using IntranetWare menus are:

- The users' need to learn many commands is eliminated.

- The amount of information presented to a user at any one time is limited.

- Information is presented in multiple layers.

- The system supports the needs of many users at once.

Again, to create a turnkey environment, you must follow the following three steps:

1) Create a menu. You must create a menu using any text editor, compile it using the command MENUMAKE, test it using the command NMENU, and place it in a directory where all users can share it (preferably in the PUBLIC directory).

2) Modify the login script. You must create all the necessary search drives for the applications and menus. In addition, to make sure that all users have access to network printing, you should invoke the menu file in the login script using the EXIT command.

3) Assign security. Make sure that NMNEU.EXE is stored in the PUBLIC directory and that all users have the [R] and [F] rights to the PUBLIC directory. In addition, make sure that the users have the [R], [W], [C], [E], and [F] rights to their home directories.

4.3 OVERVIEW OF INTRANETWARE PRINTING

IntranetWare printing is a major service provided by the network. We can use the printing service on the network only if we have installed it after the installation of the file server. A user with a standalone PC can send a print job to his/her local printer directly from the local printer port as shown in figure 4.3.

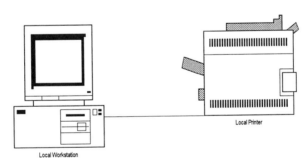

Local Printer

Local Workstation

Figure 4.3 A local workstation attached to a local printer.

When a user prints on the network, he or she sends a print job to a network printer or a print queue. The print job travels around the network in the following manner:

1) The print job travels to a print queue on the file server and is then prioritized.

2) The print queue stores the print job as a temporary file until the printer is ready.

3) The print server moves the job from the print queue and sends it to the printer that is ready for printing.

4) The print server then deletes the temporary print job file from the print queue. See figure 4.4.

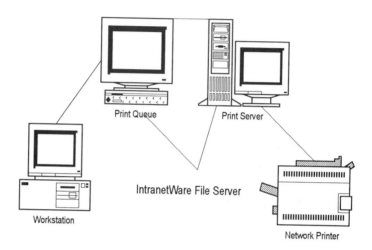

Figure 4.4 Understanding network printing.

IntranetWare printing consists of three components or three NDS objects. Each of the three components has a physical and a logical definition:

- Print queue—The print queue object stores information, such as the location of the physical print queue directory, verification of who can use and operate the print queue, and the status of the print queue. IntranetWare creates a print queue directory under the SYS: QUEUES directory on the file server automatically when a print queue object is created. The directory is identified by a unique hexadecimal identification number, and will have the extension .QDR. In addition, there are also two files created in the .QDR directory— the .SYS file to hold parameters of print jobs, and the .SRV file to hold print server information. When users send print jobs from their workstations, they send them to the print queue directory on the file server. The print queue stores the print jobs as temporary files until the printer servicing the queue is ready. Every print queue object must have a queue name to link the print queue to a printer, and a volume name to store the print queue directory.

- Printer—The printer object stores information, such as the printer name, the location of the printer, the printer specification for print configuration, and notification lists for printer problems. You can attach a printer to a print server, IntranetWare server, workstation, or directly to a network cable. Every printer must have the property printer name to link it to the print server. In addition, it must have a print queue name to link the printer to the print queue, the printer type (either serial or parallel), an LPT or COM port, and an interrupt for better performance (polled mode is set by default). Finally, it must have a location to auto-load for a printer that is attached to a print server. You will have to perform a manual load for a printer that is not attached to a print server.

- Print Server—The IntranetWare print server is a file server running PSERVER.NLM. PSERVER.NLM is located in the SYS: SYSTEM directory. When PSERVER.NLM (print server) is loaded, it loads the password needed to access the print server console menu, print server user and operator lists, and printers that the print server services to memory. You may service up to 255 printers using the IntranetWare print server. But, a maximum of five printers can be attached to a file server or a print server with the rest attached remotely to workstations or directly to network cables. The job of the print server is to monitor the print queue until it's ready for print servicing. Once ready, the print server takes the print job from the queue and sends it to the printer for printing. Every print server object must have the property print server name to link it to the print queue, and printers to add to the printer lists.

It is very important to plan carefully when creating and configuring printing objects. To begin with, you must collect all the critical properties about all the print objects. Second, you should create a print queue object, and pick a volume where the print queue or print queue directory will be created. Third, you must create a printer object. Make sure that you configure the printer object to match the physical device, and add the print queues to the Print Queues assigned list. Finally, you must create a print server object. Again, do not forget to add the printers to the Print List properties. In IntranetWare, you can use the NWADMIN and PCONSOLE utilities to manage all three NDS print objects: print queue objects, printer objects, and print server objects. Note that the NETADMIN utility cannot create or manage any of the network printing objects.

There are three basic configurations available for IntranetWare network printing:

1) PSERVER.NLM loaded on the print server with NPRINTER.NLM automatically.

2) NPRINTER.NLM loaded on the file server with an active print server running.

3) NPRINTER.EXE running on the client workstation side with an active print server running

Here are the four steps you need to set up a network printing service in IntranetWare:

1) Create and configure printing objects using the NWADMIN or PCONSOLE utilities. To do this, first, you must select a context in the directory tree by picking a container to store the printing objects. Then, you must create the print queue objects. Do not forget to assign a unique print queue name for each queue created. Also, specify the volume where the queue directory is to be stored, and assign users to the notification list. Figure 4.5 shows how to create a print queue object using NWADMIN.

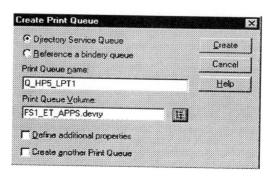

Figure 4.5 How to create a print queue object using NWADMIN.

Then, create the printer objects. Again, do not forget to assign a unique printer name for each printer created. If you are using NWADMIN, see figure 4.6.

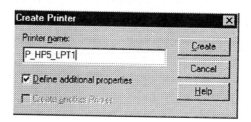

Figure 4.6 How to create a printer object using NWADMIN.

After pressing "Create", you must also specify all the parameters to match the physical printer, assign a print queue to the printer, and assign users to the notification list (optional) as seen in figure 4.7.

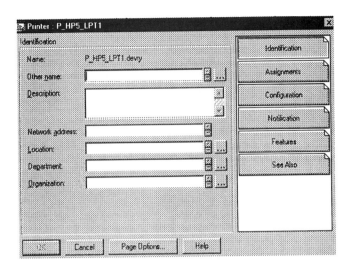

Figure 4.7 To set additional properties for the printer.

Finally, create a print server. When creating a print server, make sure that you assign a unique print server name for each print server created. If you are using NWADMIN, see figure 4.8.

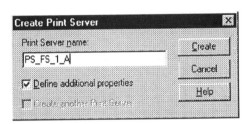

Figure 4.8 How to create a print server object using NWADMIN.

After pressing "Create", you must also assign a printer to service the print server, and assign the print server password, operators, and users. If you are using WADMIN, see figure 4.9.

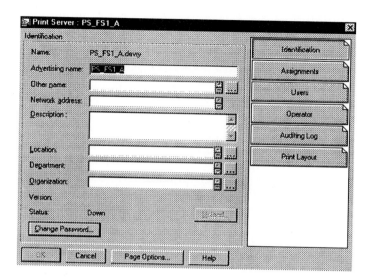

Figure 4.9 To set additional properties for the print server.

2) Activate the print server by loading PSERVER.NLM on the file server. Make sure to add PSERVER.NLM in AUTOEXEC.NCF to automate the print server loading process.

3) Set up and connect the printer on the network. You can connect printers to an IntranetWare file server. To do this, you must load NPRINTER.NLM to make the attached printers operate as remote network printers. Make sure to add the file NPRINTER.NLM in AUTOEXEC.NCF to automate the loading process. In addition, you can connect printers to workstations. To do this, you must first load the communication protocol NetWare DOS requester, and NPRINTER.EXE to make the attached printers operate as remote printers. Make sure to add the file NPRINTER.EXE in AUTOEXEC.BAT to automate the loading process.

4) Customize the print service environment. This step is performed only if needed. To customize the printing service, you must first define the print devices and printer forms using the NWADMIN or PRINTDEF utilities. Then, you must set up a print job configuration using the NWADMIN or PRINTCON utilities.

Now that you have learned how to set up a network printing services environment, it is time to learn the four steps it takes to activate it:

1) Physically attach the printer to a print server or some other IntranetWare server, a workstation, or a network cable.

2) Create an NDS printer object. If you attach the printer to a print server, then you must configure the NDS print object location property value as an auto load. On the other hand, if you attach the printer to another print server or DOS workstation, then you must configure the NDS print object location property value as a manual load. If you attach the printer to a network cable, then you must see the vendor manual for configuration instruction.

3) Activate the print server by loading PSERVER.NLM on the IntranetWare file server.

4) Activate the IntranetWare printers by loading NPRINTER.NLM. If a printer is attached to a file server and you want to make it a network remote printer, then activating PSERVER.NLM (with property value declared as auto load) will load NPRINTER.NLM to activate the attached printer. Otherwise, add the command NPRINTER.NLM in AUTOEXEC.NCF. If a printer is attached to a workstation, then you must add the file NPRINTER.EXE in AUTOEXEC.BAT to make the printer a remote network printer.

Remember, the IntranetWare print server is a file server running PSERVER.NLM. You must always load the print server on IntranetWare to activate the physical print server. You can make changes to the printing environment without downing the file server. However, you must down the print server and then load it again for the changes to take effect.

4.4 INTRANETWARE PRINTING UTILITIES

IntranetWare provides us with many printing utilities to manage printing services easily. These printing utilities include NWADMIN.EXE, PCONSOLE.EXE, PSERVER.NLM, NPRINTER.NLM, NPRINTER.EXE, PRINTDEF.EXE, PRINTCON.EXE, CAPTURE.EXE, NWUSER.EXE, NPRINT.EXE, NETUSER.EXE, and PSC.

- NWADMIN.EXE—You can use NWADMIN to perform the same tasks as in the PCONSOL, PRINTDEF, and PRINTCON utilities. You can use the "print layout" windows in NWADMIN to graphically display the logical layout between the print server, printers, and print queues. In addition, NWADMIN provides a status for each of the networking components. You can use NWADMIN to manage all the network print objects and their properties.

- PCONSOLE.EXE—You can use the PCONSOLE (Print CONSOLE) utility to manage and create NDS print objects. You can also use it to manage and issue commands to printers and print servers, as well as to manage and submit print jobs within the print queue. Finally, you can use PCONSOLE to manage and control access to the network printing services. In other words, PCONSOLE is the complete network printing management tool. Looking at figure 4.10, you'll notice that there is a choice that you can pick called "Quick Setup". You may want to use "Quick Setup" to create NDS print service objects or configure the basic components for the print objects.

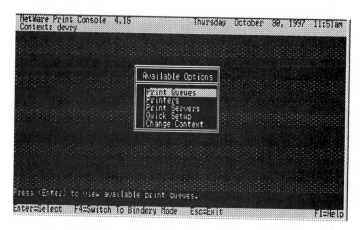

Figure 4.10 PCONSOLE menu.

If you pick the "Quick Setup" option, a new window will appear as shown in figure 4.11.

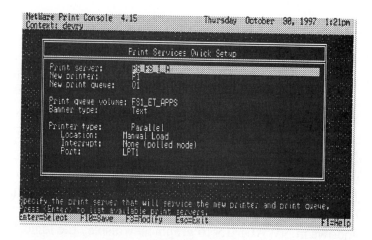

Figure 4.11 Choosing the option "Quick Setup" in PCONSOLE.

As shown above, the PCONSOLE option "Quick Setup" will automatically provide default names for each of the objects, add a print queue to the printer's list of print queues, add a printer to the print server's list of printers, and provide a default setting for the declared printer type.

- PSERVER.NLM—You load PSERVER.NLM on an IntranetWare file server to activate the print server. PSERVER.NLM provides network printing services. It is the utility that moves the print jobs from the queue to the network printer. Finally, it can manage printers and print servers.

- NPRINTER.NLM—When NPRINTER.NLM is activated on an IntranetWare printer, the printer attached to the IntranetWare file server will be activated and made into a network printer.

- NPRINTER.EXE—NPRINTER.EXE is an executable 8KB TSR (Terminate and Stay Resident) program that runs at a remote workstation where a printer is attached. The print server must be activated before you can activate NPRINTER.EXE.

- PRINTDEF.EXE—The PRINTDEF.EXE (Printer Definition) utility is used to create a database of print devices and printer forms for use in creating print job configurations. The utilities PRINTCON, CAPTURE, NPRINT, PCONSOLE, and NETUSER all use PRINTDEF to submit print jobs that need print job configurations, specific devices, modes, and printer forms. The database of PRINTDEF is called PRINTDEF.DAT. It is located in the directory SYS: PUBLIC. The database is an attribute of a container object in DS (Directory Service) mode. The print device definition files are files with the extension .PDF and are all saved under the directory SYS: PUBLIC. Figure 4.12 shows the PRINTDEF menu.

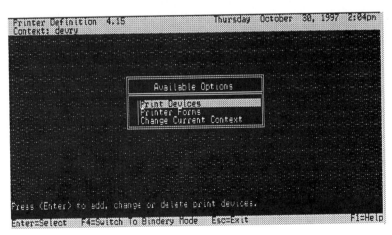

Figure 4.12 PRINTDEF menu.

The choice "Print Devices", which includes printers, plotters, and other print devices, allows you to import, export, edit, create, delete, or modify a printer name and definition on the current server. The choice "Printer Forms" allows you to create, delete, or modify form names and definitions on the current server. You can use six lines per inch for calculating the length of the paper, and ten characters per inch for calculating the width of the paper.

- PRINTCON.EXE—The PRINTCON.EXE (Print Jobs Configuration) utility is used to create print job configurations for simplifying the issuing of NPRINT and CAPTURE commands. The utilities PRINTCON, CAPTURE, NPRINT, PCONSOLE, and NETUSER all look for the print job configuration in the user object and its context, the container above the user. PRINTCON allows the user to create a custom print job configuration using the devices, forms, and modes defined in PRINTDEF. Most of the options in PRINTCON are used with the CAPTURE command. Figure 4.13 shows the PRINTCON menu.

Using the "Job" option in the CAPTURE utility to control how the job should be printed will result in replacing the complicated options used in the CAPTURE command. For example, suppose that you executed the command CAPTURE J=John. The job John must be created by choosing the option "Edit Print Job Configurations" from the PRINTCON menu. Complicated options are also eliminated in the NPRINT command when using print job configurations. PRINTCON will save each print job configuration as a database in bindery mode. The public database is saved in the PRINTJOB.DAT file in the SYS: \PUBLIC directory. The private database is saved in the PRINTJOB.DAT file in the user's mail identification directory. PRINTCON will also save print configurations as attributes of a container or user object in NDS mode. If you selected the option "Edit Print Job Configurations" from figure 4.13, and pressed the <Insert> key to create a new job called Joe, a window will come up as shown in figure 4.14.

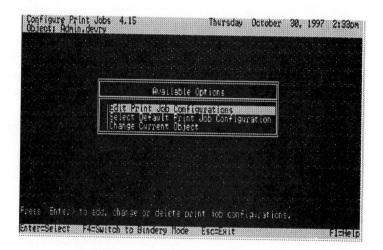

Figure 4.13 PRINTCON menu.

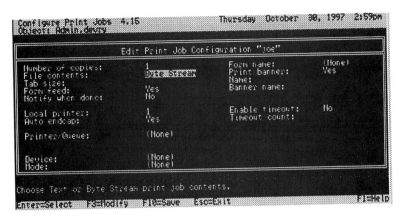

Figure 4.14 A print configuration file called "Joe".

Figure 4.14 shows the default values in "Joe's" print configuration file. The range and description of each option is as follows:

Option	Range	Description
Number of copies	1 to 65,000	
File contents	Text or Byte Stream	Text for converting tabs to spaces or Byte Stream.
Tab size	1 to 18	Used for "Text" file contents only.
Form feed	Yes or No	
Notify when done	Yes or No	
Form name		Declares the form for use.
Print banner	Yes or No	
Name		Declares a name up to 12 characters long.
Banner name		Declares a name up to 12 characters long.
Local printer	1 to 9	Uses LPT ports 1-9. It is used with the CAPTURE command.
Auto endcap	Yes or No	Used with the CAPTURE command.
Enable timeout	1 to 1,000 seconds	
Printer/Queue		Declares a printer queue to send job to.
Device		Declares a print device you want to use.
Mode		Declares a print mode you want to use.

- CAPTURE.EXE—The CAPTURE.EXE command line is used to set up print jobs redirection within IntranetWare DOS requester to allow network printing from within non-network-aware applications. In addition, the CAPTURE command is used to save data, such as screen captures, to a file or to print screens to a network printer. Instead of using the CAPTURE command with multiple variables on a regular basis, you can create print jobs with PRINTCON that group these commands into a single "job". Once created, you would only have to use the job parameter with CAPTURE. To use the CAPTURE command from the DOS prompt to redirect a print port to a print queue, you must use the following syntax:

CAPTURE [option(s)]

To use the CAPTURE command in a login script to redirect a print port to a print queue, you must use the following syntax:

#CAPTURE [option(s)]

Here is a list of options that can be used with the CAPTURE command:

Option	Abbreviated	Default	Example	Description
Auto endcap	A	Enabled	CAPTURE A	IntanetWare does not complete the print request until you exit from the application you are using. Useful for saving multiple screen dumps or files from the same application to the same network files. It will close the file, then print the data when you exit or enter an application. Auto endcap is the default setting for CAPTURE.
Banner	B=text	LST	CAPTURE B=CIS-238	Specifies up to 12

134

				characters to be printed on the lower half of the banner.
Copies	C=number	1	CAPTURE C=3	Specifies how many copies of each job that is sent. You can send a maximum of 65,000 copies.
Create	CR=text		CAPTURE CR=MI.TXT	Specifies the data to be sent to a file instead of a print queue.
Details	D		CAPTURE D	This lists the printing parameters of the job.
Endcapture	EC	1	CAPTURE /EC	Ends capture for the specified port.
EndcaptureALL	ECALL		CAPTURE /ECALL	Ends capture for all the LPT ports.
EndcaptureCancel	ECCA		CAPTURE /ECCA	Discards the capture data, then ends capture.
Form	F=number	0	CAPTURE F=10	Specifies a form created in the PRINTDEF utility. It is used to distinguish between different types or sizes of paper that should be loaded into the printer. You can

				specify either the form name or number with this option.
FormFeed	FF	Enabled	CAPTURE FF	Used to tell IntranetWare to issue a form feed command after the job is completed. This will cause a blank page to be issued after every print job.
Help	?		CAPTURE /?	This lists the available CAPTURE settings.
Hold	HOLD		CAPTURE HOLD	Sends a job to the queue without having it print.
Job=job_name	J=text		CAPTURE j=memo	Specifies a print job configuration created with PRINTCON that should be used. Print job configuration files contain the same type of information you should issue with the CAPTURE

Option	Abbreviated	Default	Example	Description
				command. Using the print job configuration file reduces the amount of work needed to issue a CAPTURE command, because you do not have to enter all the other variables at the command line.
Keep	K		CAPTURE K	Under normal situations, if the PC is disconnected from the network while sending a print job, such as during a power failure, IntranetWare discards the partial print job. Using the Keep option, you can instruct IntranetWare to print whatever it receives, even if it is a partial job. This option is

Local	L=#	1	CAPTURE L=3	mostly used when issuing a print request that could take a long time. Specifies which printer port you want to capture, such as LPT1=1, LPT2=2, LPT3=3. By capturing different ports, you can capture to multiple queues at the same time.
Name	NAME=text	Login_Name	CAPTURE NAM=JDOE	Specifies the name that should be printed in the upper half of the banner sheet, up to 12 characters.
NoAutoendcap	NA		CAPTURE NA	This tells IntranetWare not to send the print job to the queue when exiting or entering an application. It disables the Autoendcap and the Timeout options. The print job will not be closed until the workstation reboots, and it will be lost

				if CAPTURE did not include the K option. You must use the command CAPTURE /EC to close the file, then send the data to the printer.
NoBanner	NB		CAPTURE NB	Tells IntranetWare not to print a banner page before the print job.
NoFormFeed	NFF		CAPTURE NFF	Tells IntranetWare not to send a form feed after the print job.
NoNOTIfy	NNOTI	Enabled	CAPTURE NNOTI	Tells IntranetWare to send a message after the print job is completed. Use this option only when NOTI is enabled.
NoTabs	NT		CAPTURE NT	Tells IntranetWare not to replace the tab characters with spaces. Use this option if you are having problems printing graphics.
NOTIfy	NOTI	Disabled	CAPTURE NOTI	Tells

				IntranetWare to send a message after the print job is completed.
Printer	P=Printer_name		CAPTURE P=P1	Declares a printer for a print job.
Queue	Q=Queue_Name		CAPTURE Q=Q1	Declares a queue for a print job.
Server	S=Server_Name	Default Server	CAPTURE S=FS1	Declares a file server for a print job.
Show	SH		CAPTURE SH	Shows all the current CAPTURE settings.
Tabs	T=#	8	CAPTURE T=10	This tells IntranetWare the number of spaces you want CAPTURE to substitute for each tab. The range is from 1 to 18.
Timeout	TI=#	0	CAPTURE TI=30	This tells IntranetWare how many seconds to wait before closing the print request from the time the print request is actually made. Increase the number for this option if you are having problems

			with jobs not being sent in their entirety. The range is from 0 to 1,000.
Version	Ver	CAPTURE Ver	This displays the version information for this utility.

You may use the CAPTURE command to redirect print output to a network printer to print screen dumps, save data to a network file, or print files from a non-network-aware application. If there are no print job configurations defined, CAPTURE will follow the default values of the options. If there were no options specified in the CAPTURE command, then it will print the captured data based on the print job configuration declared in PRINTCON. You can use PRINTCON to define the print options as a print job configuration, then use the Job option to indicate which print job configuration to use. You must specify the file server name if the printer specified in the CAPTURE command is not the default printer. To make the CAPTURE command permanent, include it in the login script or a batch file. If the CAPTURE command is placed in a login script, then the pound "#" sign must precede it.

Remember that in IntranetWare CAPTURE does support printer names, but not printer numbers or print server names.

Another thing to remember: if you have not captured to a print queue and there are no printers attached to the workstation, the workstation may hang if the user attempts to print a screen. To alleviate this problem, add the command LOCAL PRINTERS=0 in the NET.CFG file.

Let us look at some examples of how to use the CAPTURE command:

Example	Description
CAPTURE Q=Q1 TI=10 NB	This captures the workstation to a print queue Q1 on the default server with a timeout of 10 seconds, and without a banner.
#CAPTURE L=LPT1 Q= .Q_TF.CLASS.TEST TI=30 NB NFF NOTI	Used in a login script. It captures the workstation to a port LPT1, a print queue

with the path
.Q_TF.CLASS.TEST
on the default server
with a timeout of 30
seconds, without a
banner, without a
form feed, and with a
notification message.

- NWUSER.EXE—The NWUSER.EXE (NetWare User Tools for Windows 3.1)
  utility is used to set up print job redirection within the NetWare DOS requester to
  allow network printing from within non-network-aware applications. Remember
  this: you cannot use NWUSER to redirect a print job to a file. You may use
  NWUSER to perform tasks, such as redirecting print jobs to a printer or a printer
  port, ending a print job redirection, configuring or setting print job redirection
  options, and making a permanent print job redirection. You must use Printers
  Dialog of the MS Windows Control Panel to select the corresponding parallel port
  and print driver for a Windows application. The print job redirection remains
  active even after we exit MS Windows 3.1 since all changes made with NWUSER
  and NETUSER utilities occur within the NetWare DOS requester. This software is
  installed as part of the IntranetWare DOS requester or Client 32 connectivity
  software. To start NWUSER, find the icon under the NetWare Tools Program
  Group, or launch File Manager and choose Disk/Network Connections.
  Remember, Windows 95 provides a native configuration screen for printer
  redirection by using the Printer Properties screen. To get there, just click on Start,
  Settings, and then Control Panel. Finally, click on printers and you'll get a list of
  available printers. Highlight your printer, click the right mouse button, and choose
  Properties.

- NPRINT.EXE—NPRINT.EXE is a command used when you want to print a DOS
  ASCII file or a file that has been properly formatted by an application for your
  printer to an IntranetWare print queue. The syntax for NPRINT is as follows:

  NPRINT path [option(s)]

  When using this syntax, replace "path" with the directory path of the file which
  you want to print, including the file name, and replace "option(s)" with one or
  more of the options shown below. If no options are present, NPRINT will use the
  default print configuration specified in PRINTCON.

Option	Abbreviated	Default	Example	Description
Banner	B=text	LST	NPRINT TEST.TXT Q=Q1 B=Immediately	Prints up to 12 characters on the lower half of the banner page.
Copies	C=number	1	NPRINT TEXT.TXT C=10 Q=Q1	Specifies how many copies of each job you want. A maximum of 65,000 copies.
Delete	DEL		NPRINT IBM.TXT DEL	Deletes the files you are printing as soon as the print job is sent to the queue.
Details	D		NPRINT IBM.TXT D	Lists all the printing parameters of the job.
Form	F= form or #	0	NPRINT IBM.TXT F=2	Specifies a specific form created in PRINTDEF. This way you can distinguish between different types or sizes of paper that should be loaded into the printer. You can specify either the form name or number.
FormFeed	FF	Enabled	NPRINT IBM.TXT FF	Feeds a blank page after a print job is done.

Help	?		NPRINT /?	This lists the available NPRINT settings
Hold	HOLD		NPRINT M.TXT HOLD	Sends a job to the queue without having it print.
Job	J = Job_config		NPRINT IBM.TXT J=ENG Q=Q1	Specifies a print job configuration file created in PRINTCON to be used.
Name	NAM=text	Login_Name	NPRINT M.TXT S=FS1 NAM=JDOE	Specifies the name that should be printed in the upper half of the banner sheet, up to 12 characters.
NoBanner	NB		NPRINT IBM.TXT NB	Tells IntranetWare not to print a banner page before the print job feed after the print job is complete.
NoFormFeed	NFF		NPRINT IBM.TXT NFF	Tells IntranetWare not to send a form.
NoNOTIfy	NNOTI	Enabled	NPRINT T.TXT NNOTI	Tells IntranetWare to send a message after the print job is completed. Use this option only

NoTabs	NT		NPRINT IBM.TXT NT	when NOTI is enabled. Tells IntranetWare not to replace the tab characters with spaces. Use this option if you are having problems printing graphics.
NOTIfy	NOTI	Disabled	NPRINT T.TXT NOTI	Tells IntranetWare to send a message after the print job is completed.
Printer	P= Printer_Name		NPRINT T.TXT P=P1	Declares a printer for a print job.
Queue	Q= Queue_Name		NPRINT T.TXT Q=Q1	Declares a queue for a print job.
Server	S= Server_Name	Default Server	NPRINT T.TXT S=FS1	Declares a file server for a print job.
Tabs	T=number	8	NPRINT T.TXT T=10	This tells IntranetWare the number of spaces you want CAPTURE to substitute for each tab. The range is from 1 to 18.
Version	Ver		NPRINT Ver	This displays the version information for this utility.

Remember that instead of using NPRINT command with multiple variables on a regular basis, you can create print jobs with PRINTCON that group these commands

145

into a single "job". Once these are created you only have to use the job option with NPRINT. In addition, you do not have to capture anything to run the NPRINT command, and you can print multiple files from the single command by separating each file name with a comma. Let us look at some examples of how to use the CAPTURE command:

Example	Description
NPRINT TEST.TXT Q=Q1 S=FS2 B=FAST	This prints the file TEST.TXT to a print queue Q1 on the file server FS2 with a banner called FAST.
NPRINT TEST1, TEST2 Q=Q1 C=3	This prints three copies of each of the files TEST1 and TEST2 to the print queue Q1 on the default file server.

- NETUSER.EXE—NETUSER (NetWare User for DOS) is a utility similar to the SEESION utility of NetWare3. You can use NETUSER to redirect a printer port to a network printer or a print queue. You can also use NETUSER to create, modify, or delete print jobs. The main menu of NETUSER is shown in figure 4.15.

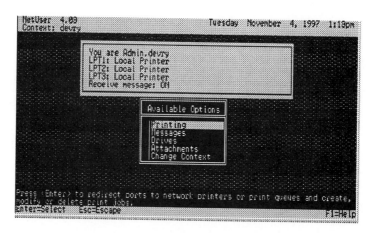

Figure 4.15 NETUSER main menu.

- PSC—PSC (Print Server Control) is a utility similar to PCONSOL. It performs tasks, such as checking the status of an attached printer, stopping the current print job, mounting forms, and making a remote printer private. To use PSC, you need the following information.

1) The print server name.

2) The name of the printer to manage.

3) The command desired (i.e. STATUS, DISMOUNT, and MOUNT).

4.5 MANAGING INTRANETWARE PRINTING

You may send print jobs from network-aware applications directly to network printers. Most DOS applications are not network aware. You can only print these DOS applications to a local device, such as LPT1, COM1, or a file on a disk. You can send a print job from a non-network-aware application to a network printer in two ways. First, you may redirect a print job sent to a local print port to a network printer or a print queue. Second, you can redirect the print file to a network printer or a print queue. You may configure the workstation so that print jobs sent to the local printer ports are redirected to a network printer or print queue by using the CAPTURE, NETUSER, or NWUSER utilities. These three utilities can redirect up to nine logical printer ports, namely LPT1 to LPT9, to network printers or print queues. You may also use the NPRINT and PCONSOLE utilities to redirect a print file to a network printer or a print queue. Remember that in PCONSOLE, you can use the "Print Queues" or "Print Jobs" options.

Here are the steps you should take to redirect a print job in DOS:

1) Log on to the network.

2) Redirect the printer ports before entering the application. You can do this using CAPTURE, NETUSER, or NWUSER to assign a parallel port name to a network printer or a print queue. The NetWare DOS requester will then store the printer ports redirection information temporarily. Hence, the printer ports redirection information is lost once you log out of the network. If you want to automate the printer ports redirection, use the CAPTURE command in the login script or a batch file.

3) Select a parallel port to print within the application.

4) Select a print driver within the application. The print driver within the application converts the print job into a printer language. Remember that the IntranetWare print utility can only redirect print jobs to network printers or print queue. Therefore, you must select a print driver within the application.

5) Print the print job to the printer port within the application. If you need to modify the print job redirection, then you must exit the application.

The steps it takes to redirect a print job in MS Windows 3.1 are as follows:

1) Activate NWUSER (NetWare User Tools for Windows).

2) Double-click on "Printer Connection" icon or press the keys <Alt> <P>.

3) Drag a queue from the Resource window to the printer port LPT1 for capturing.

4) Click on the "LPT Settings" box to modify the capture options.

5) Click on the "Permanent" box to make the capture permanent, then exit Windows.

The steps it takes to redirect a print file in DOS are as follows:

1) Select a print driver within the application.

2) Print the print job to a file on a disk within the application.

3) Log on to the network.

4) Send the print file to a network printer or a print queue. At the DOS prompt, you may use NPRINT or PCONSOLE to send the print file to a network printer or a print queue. The print file must be in a suitable format for the specific printer.

The steps it takes to redirect a print job or a print file in MS Windows 95 are as follows:

1) Click on "Start".
2) Choose "Settings".
3) Choose "Control Panel".
4) Choose "Printers".
5) Highlight your printer.
6) Click on the right mouse button.
7) Choose "Properties.

There are three different ways to customize a print job:

1) Use a print job configuration. The print job configuration determines how a job should be printed. It also simplifies the use of the commands CAPTURE and NPRINT using the "Job option". It is a named set of printing options. You can create a print job configuration at either the container or user object level. At the container object level, the print configuration will be available to all the users in that container. At the user object level, the print configuration will be available to

that specific user only. You may use the PRINTCON or NWADMIN utilities to create a print job configuration. Remember that you may declare a default print job configuration using PRINTCON. Hence, executing the CAPTURE command without any options will set up a printer redirection based completely on the default print job configuration.

2) Use a print device definition. Print device definitions are used to activate the printer function if the application does not have the correct driver. You can activate a print device definition with the PRINTCON utility. A print device definition is a set of printer control sequences used to change the print mode. All print device definitions are created at the container level. You may use the utilities PRINTDEF or NWADMIN to create a print device definition. You want to create a print device definition to produce a landscape printing, print condensed font, or reset the printer to the default configuration.

3) Use a printer form. A printer form is a print option that specifies the paper size. Printer forms are created at the container level. Again, you can use the PRINTDEF or NWADMIN utilities to create printer forms. Printer forms are activated with PRINTCON, CAPTURE, and NPRINT. You want to use printer forms to prevent print jobs from being printed on the wrong paper. A message will be sent to the operator if you specified a print form for a job. The operator then must confirm that the correct form is being used.

The three network printing management tasks are print queue management, printer management, and print server management.

- Print queue management—As an administrator, you must be able to control the print queue work flow by stopping jobs from entering and leaving the queue, or by stopping new print servers from adding jobs to the queue. In addition, you must be able to manage print jobs in the queue by viewing, adding, or deleting print jobs in a queue. You can modify print jobs in a queue by changing the print order of the print jobs, setting a job on hold for deferred printing, and viewing or modifying the print job attributes. Finally, an administrator must be able to control the access to the print queue by assigning a print queue user and operator. A print queue user has the ability to submit, delete, and manage his/her own jobs in the queue. A print queue operator has the ability to change the order of print jobs, edit another user's print jobs, delete print jobs, and change print queue flags.

- Printer management—As an administrator, you must be able to manage printer error messages by specifying who will receive printer error messages. In addition, you must be able to view and control printer status. IntranetWare allows you to view or control printer status from a server console or a DOS workstation. A printer's status can be active, not connected, or out of paper. For an active printer, an operator can change service mode, mount printer forms, pause, start, stop, and rewind the printer, mark the top of the form or force form feed, and abort a print job.

- Print server management—As an administrator, you must be able to view server status from a server console or a DOS workstation. The server status window displays data, such as print server type, version, and advertising name. It also displays the number of printers the server supports, and the current server status (running or down). In addition, an administrator must be able to bring down the print server. There are four ways to bring down a print server:

  1) Unload PSERVER, NLM at the IntranetWare server console.

  2) Unload the print server at the print server console.

  3) Down the print server with PCONSOLE.

  4) Down the print server with NWADMIN.

Finally, an administrator must have control of the access to the print server. You can do this by assigning users and operators on the print server. A print server user can only view the print server status. A print server operator can attach other IntranetWare servers to the print server or down the print server.

By default when you create a print server, you will automatically be added to the print server operator list, the print queue operator list, and the print queue user list. If you create a parent container, then you will automatically be added to the print queue user list, and the print server user list. If you create your own print job, you will automatically be added to the printer notification list. Below is a list of all the users and operators and what tasks they can perform:

- Supervisor to a container—A supervisor to a container will be able to create, delete, and manage printing objects. In addition, he/she can modify the print queue and the print server user and operator lists, modify print queue assignments, modify the printer notification list, and view or monitor the print server.

- Print server operator—A print server operator will be able to modify print queue assignments, modify the printer notification list, modify printer status, and down the print server.

- Print server user—A print server user will be able to view or monitor the print server, and receive printer error messages.

- Printer notification list user—A printer notification list user will be able to receive error messages only.

- Print queue operator—A print queue operator will be able to modify print queue operator flags, and manage others' print jobs in the print queue.

- Print queue user—A print queue user will be able to use, or send jobs to a print queue, and manage his/her own print jobs in the print queue.

Questions

1) What is the command that allows you to convert an earlier version of a NetWare menu to IntranetWare?
2) What is the command that allows you to compile an IntranetWare menu named TEST?
3) What is the command that allows you to run a compiled IntranetWare menu program?
4) Name the four components of an IntranetWare menu system.
5) What are the two command types that are contained in the menu script file?
6) What is the menu command that exits the menu program and displays the DOS prompt?
7) What is the menu command that exits the menu program temporarily and displays the DOS prompt?
8) Name the three IntranetWare menu commands that are associated with the EXEC control command.
9) What is the maximum number of GET commands per ITEM in an IntranetWare menu program?
10) In the GETx command "GETO Enter Name: {} 40, User Name, {}:", what name is used by the program if the user does not type anything in the dialog box?
11) What is the command that prompts the user for:

   a) required input in an IntranetWare menu program?
   b) input to be stored in a variable in the IntranetWare menu program?
   c) an optional user in an IntranetWare menu program?

12) How many IF statements can be nested while creating a login script?

13) What is the last step in IntranetWare menu creation?

14) What is the last step to ensure that all users can access the menu file?

15) To run a menu file, what rights to the user's current directory does the user need?

16) To run a menu file, what rights does a user need in the directory containing the compiled menu file?

17) The IntranetWare menu program automatically assigns a letter to each item in a menu; to assign a specific letter to an item, what character and the letter should you type in front of the option for the ITEM?

18) If you have IntranetWare menus in separate files, how can you load one menu from within another?

19) How many submenus can you create within a single menu script file?

20) What are the four types of login scripts used in IntranetWare?

21) In which two login scripts can the NO_DEFAULT command be placed to disable the default login script?

22) When is a default login script executed?

23) To execute an internal DOS command, such as DIR or CLS, from within a login script, what should precede the command?

24) What login script command sets the correct path for reloading the command.com file if it has been overwritten by an application?

25) What are the four options that alter the way the ITEM command is displayed or executed in an IntranetWare menu file?

26) What is the login script you should use to provide a general access to network resources?

27) What is the login script that may be used for a specific group's needs?

28) How many container scripts can you have per organization or organization unit container?

29) What are the three login restrictions set at container level?

30) When a login script is finished, the user's default drive will be the first available drive unless you specify a default drive with what command?

31) What are the four characters that denote a comment in a login script?

32) To remove printer codes and other garbage from the contents of a file displayed during execution of a login script, you can use what command?

33) What is the command used to display text enclosed in quotes on the screen during login script execution?

34) What are the four user account restrictions used by the network administrator to control the login process?

35) What does the CX login script command do?

36) What is the maximum number of search drives supported by IntranetWare?

37) What is the command used to map H: to the ENGIN directory on a volume VOL1?

38) If you have only three search drives mapped (e.g., X, Y, and Z), give three different commands that will create a search drive W: mapped to the WORD directory of the APPS directory on the volume APPLIC.

39) Name the three components that are necessary to allow access to network printing.
40) What three things do you need to know when setting up a network-printing environment?
41) Name the three major steps in setting up network print services.
42) Name five things you need to know about print servers.
43) What sends a print job from a queue to the printer?
44) What two things must be done to configure a print server?
45) In IntranetWare, a network printer can attach to what three devices?
46) In IntranetWare printing, how many printers can be attached to the print server?
47) If a workstation has two parallel ports, how many parallel port names can be assigned to network printers or print queues by the NetWare DOS requester?
48) The user object that creates a print server is automatically placed on which three printing lists?
49) What is the function of a print queue?
50) What is the information that is contained in the NDS print queue object?
51) Where are the IntranetWare print queues physically stored?
52) Are all users on the print queue user list print queue users?
53) How can you fix a high volume printing?
54) How can you fix a priority printing?
55) What are the two IntranetWare utilities that allow you to modify print object properties?
56) What is the option in PCONSOLE that allows you to create and add printer, queue, and print server objects and properties quickly?
57) What NLM can be used to enable an IntranetWare server to act as a print server?
58) What is the utility that can be used to connect users to a printer on a workstation?
59) Name the two steps you would perform at a workstation to configure a network printer?
60) In Intranetware printing, how do you set up a workstation printer as a network printer?
61) Name two things you need to know about NPRINTER.NLM?
62) What are the two conditions for PSERVER.NLM to automatically load NPRINTER.NLM?
63) Name two things you can do to send print jobs from non-network-aware applications to network printers.
64) Name three things you can use to set up print job redirection before opening an application.
65) What are the commands necessary to do the following:

a) View print port, or current network printer redirection status
b) Notify a user if the printer has a problem or if his/her job cannot be printed
c) Set up print job redirection based on a print job configuration named MIKE

    d) Redirect printing from LPT2 on your workstation to a network HP Laser Jet III printer named LPT1, print 3 copies of each print job with no banner page, and timeout in 30 seconds

    e) Send a print file to a network printer

    f) Print files from outside an application to a network printer?

66) What is a named set of printer control sequences used to change the printer mode, such as, bold, italic, print size, and font?

67) What is a named set of options that determine how a job is printed and simplify the use of CAPTURE and NPRINT?

68) What are the two utilities you can use to create print device definitions at the container level?

69) What is the utility that is used to specify font types, graphics, forms, and page orientation?

70) What can be used to fix a non-application-supported printing?

71) What are the two utilities that can be used to create print job configurations?

72) What is the IntranetWare utility used to preset options for the CAPTURE command?

5

NDS Security and Server Management

This chapter discusses how to manage and implement NDS security and resources. In addition, you will learn how to maintain and manage server security by using IntranetWare server utilities, executing console commands, and managing NLM utilities. Finally, this chapter will teach you how to protect data by learning server management on the IntranetWare network.

5.1 NDS SECURITY

NDS and file system securities are separate IntranetWare security systems. File system security controls access to the files on the IntranetWare server volumes, while NDS security manages who can access the objects and properties stored in the NDS directory, or NDS database. In addition, NDS security manages what objects or properties users can access, what kind of access users can have to those objects or properties, and how to view and modify the information stored in the NDS directory. The separation of file system and NDS securities allows us to have the option of assigning a "container" administrator. Hence, one network administrator can manage all the NDS object administration and file system administration, or have it divided among various network administrators. You may want to have one network administrator manage the network resources, or NDS objects, or have more than one container administrator manage containers and file systems.

NDS security differs from file system security in the following ways:

1) NDS security is based on two distinct sets of rights: object and property rights.

2) The lower levels of the directory tree can inherit NDS rights.

3) You can use IRF to block all the inherited rights, including the supervisory rights.

4) NDS rights do not flow from NDS into the file system except in one special instance.

Each NDS object has an object trustee property (sometimes referred to as ACL property). An object trustee is an object that is placed in the ACL property of another object. The ACL (Access Control List) property of the object records the trustees who can access or change information stored in the object properties, and who can manipulate the object. In order to access an NDS object or its property, a user must be made a trustee to the object and then be granted either object or property rights to the object. Object rights are the rights that control what a trustee can do with the object. Property rights are the rights that control access to the property values of an object.

NDS minimizes the individual rights assignments by using rights inheritance. NDS rights flow downward from a container to its contents. Only "Object" rights and "All Properties" rights can flow downward. Rights granted through the "Selected Properties" option cannot be inherited. In NDS, a user object is security equivalent to its parent containers. The effective rights of a user are the combination of rights received through the rights assignment minus any inherited rights blocked by the IRFs. Access to NDS objects is controlled by ten different NDS access rights. These rights are organized into two different functional groups:

1) Object rights—Object rights control what a trustee can do with any object. They control the object as a single piece in the NDS directory tree, and control the access to the object but not to the property values of the object. You must be a trustee of an object to be granted rights to the object. Following is a description of the five object rights and their functions:

   a) Browse—Grants the right to see an object in the directory tree.

   b) Create—Grants the rights to create a new object within the container. It is available on container objects only.

   c) Delete—Grants the right to delete an object from NDS.

   d) Rename—Grants the rights to change the name and the naming property of an object.

   e) Supervisor—Grants all the rights, or access privileges, to an object. Trustees with a supervisor object right have access or rights to "All Properties". Be aware that a supervisor object right can be blocked with IRF.

You can remember the object rights by remembering the word BCDRS. Object rights control the access to the object only. If you want to have control over the contents of the object, you will need to be granted property rights.

2) Property rights—Property rights control access to the information stored within an NDS object. In other words, they control access to the property values stored in the object. You have to be a trustee of an object to be granted rights to the

properties of the object. Following is a description of the five property rights and their functions:

a) Supervisor—Grants all the rights to object properties. The supervisor right can be blocked by an object's IRF.

b) Compare—Grants the right to compare any given value to the value within the property. With the compare right, an operation can return True or False, but it will not give the value of the property.

c) Read—Grants the right to read the values of the property.

d) Add Self—Grants the right to add or remove yourself as a value of a property. The add self right is meaningful only for properties that contain object names as values, such as group membership lists and mailing lists. This right is automatically granted with the write right.

e) Write—Grants the right to add, change, remove, or modify any values of the property.

You can remember the property rights by remembering the word SCRAW. You may assign property rights in one of two different ways:

1) All properties—Allows you to assign the rights you indicate to all properties of the object.

2) Selected properties—Allows you to assign rights independently to each property. The rights granted through the selected properties option override the rights granted through the all properties option for the selected property.

Here are the steps you need to do to assign object or property rights to a user using NWADMIN:

Step 1: Double-click on the container where the user resides.
Step 2: Right-click on the user name.
Step 3: Go down to the "Trustees of this object..." option.
Step 4: Highlight the user name.
Step 5: Assign the appropriate rights.

As you can see from figure 5.1, property rights can be granted in one of two ways—"All properties" and/or "Selected properties".

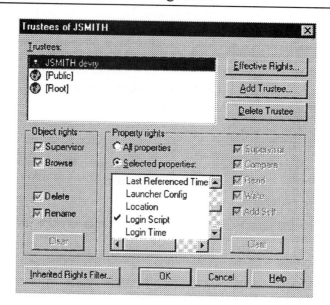

Figure 5.1 Assigning object and property rights in NWADMIN.

Let us now take a look at the default NDS security. This will help you determine if you need to assign additional object or property rights to a user. IntranetWare assigns default NDS rights during four major events:

- Initial NDS installation—When NDS is installed on the very first server on a network, two key objects are created—[Root] and Admin. [Root] represents the very top of the NDS tree, and Admin has supervisor control over the entire network. Incidentally, Admin is placed in the organization level of the first server's context. The following default rights are granted when NDS is first installed:

  1) Admin user object—Grants a supervisor [S] object rights to [Root]. This allows the first user object to administer the entire NDS tree.

  2) [Public] trustee—Grants the browse [B] object right to [Root]. This allows every object in the NDS tree to see every other object.

- New file server installation—When a new file server is installed in NDS, the following default NDS rights are granted to the creator of the server, server object, and [Public] trustee:

  1) Creator of the server object—The creator of the server object is the person who performed the server installation. This user is granted supervisor [S] object rights to the server. This allows the Admin or the container administrator to manage the server object.

2) Server object—The server is granted supervisor [S] object rights to itself. This allows the server to modify the parameters of its own object.

3) [Public] trustee—Grants the read [R] property right to a specific server property—the messaging server property. It allows any network client to identify the messaging server assigned to this server, or e-mail address.

- New user object creation—In general, when you create a new user object in NDS, certain rights are granted automatically:

   1) User object—Each user is granted three sets of property rights by default:

      a) Read [R] right to "All Properties" to allow the user to read the properties stored in the user object.
      b) Read and write [RW] rights to the login script and print configuration to allow the user to execute and change his or her login script and to create print jobs and send them to the printer.
      c) Browse [B] right to yourself. This right is not explicitly granted at user creation: it is inherited from the initial NDS installation.

   2) [Root] object—Grants the read [R] property right to the user "Network Address" and "Group Membership". This allows anyone in the tree to identify the user's network address, location, and any group the user belongs to.

   3) [Public] trustee—Grants the read [R] property right to the selected user property—default server. This allows anyone to determine the default server for this user.

- New container object creation—Any container you create will receive the default rights to itself. This allows all objects in the container to receive the rights they need to access their own family members.

Let us now look at the three steps needed to assign NDS security:

1) Assigning trustee rights—Remember, a trustee is any NDS object with rights to any other object. Trustees are tracked through the ACL (Access Control List) property. Every object has an ACL property, and the ACL lists the trustees of that object and the rights they have. IntranetWare supports a variety of trustees, including user, group, container, organizational role, and [public].

   If a trustee assignment or inheritance is not enough to do the job, then security equivalence may be the answer. Security equivalence simply states that one object is equivalent to another with respect to NDS rights. When you design the directory tree, you should consider using containers as natural groups to assign rights to the network resources. In NDS, a user object is a security equivalent to its parent container. A user object receives the rights granted to its parent container when the container is made a trustee of an object. In other words, making a container object a trustee of an object is the same as making all objects in the container trustees of the object. Remember, a user object is security equivalent to all parent containers in which the user object resides, up to and including the [Root]. IntranetWare provides us with four strategies for security equivalence:

a) Ancestral inheritance (AI)—This simply means that an object is security equivalent to its ancestor (parent container).

b) Organization role—This is designed for jobs that require multiple temporary users.

c) Groups—This is designed to allow us to distribute similar rights to unrelated users.

d) Directory map objects—This is designed to allow us to map directory paths to a centralized object instead of to a physical location.

2) Filtering IRF rights—You may block inherited rights using either one of the following two methods:

a) Make a new trustee assignment—Trustee assignments override inherited rights. A new trustee assignment of the same object at a lower level in the directory tree will change the rights of the object from that level down. Making a new trustee assignment is very useful for overriding property rights granted with the "All Properties" option.

b) Change the IRF—This overrides inherited rights for all objects in the tree. You may change the default IRF to block unwanted inheritance of either "Object" rights or "All Properties" rights in the directory tree. (Be careful: you can also block the supervisor [S] NDS right.)

3) Calculating effective rights—Remember that access to the NDS directory is controlled by object trustees, object rights, and property rights. A user must have appropriate NDS rights to do certain tasks, such as viewing other objects in the directory tree, using the login script stored in the user object, and obtaining other users' e-mail addresses to send messages. Usually users need only the default NDS rights; additional rights are given to administrators only.

The effective rights of a user are the combination of rights received through the following rights assignments minus any inherited rights blocked by IRFs:

a) Explicit trustee assignment to a user object.

b) Membership of a group object.

c) Occupant of an organizational role object.

d) Security equivalence to other user objects.

e) Trustee assignment to the parent container of the user object.

f) Rights granted to the [Public] trustee.

You may use the "Trustees of this…" option in NWADMIN to find a user's effective rights from the user object or from another object in the directory tree.

5.2 IMPLEMENTING NDS SECURITY

Usually, the default NDS rights provide users enough access to network resources. Again, users receive the browse [B] object right automatically through the [Public] trustee. The browse [B] object right allows users to see objects in the directory tree. With default NDS rights, users can see objects in the directory tree. NDS allows us to make additional rights assignments when the default NDS rights are not enough to carry out certain tasks. Most users need to create and delete objects, or modify property values. You should only grant additional rights to those who need to manage NDS objects frequently. You can use the following guidelines to assign additional NDS rights:

1) Start with the default NDS rights assignments. Usually, the default NDS rights provide users sufficient access to network resources.

2) Avoid using the "All Properties" option to assign property rights. To protect private data about a user and other NDS objects, you should use the "All Properties" option to assign property rights only when necessary. Always use the "Selected Properties" option to assign rights to the properties needed.

3) Avoid granting the write [W] property right to the ACL property of an object. Otherwise, you will be giving the trustee the ability to grant all rights, including the supervisor [R] right, to itself and any other objects. The ACL property of an object is the object trustees property of the object.

4) Avoid granting the supervisor [S] object right to a server object. Otherwise, you will be giving the trustee supervisor file system rights to all volumes linked to that server. It gives the trustee access to all files on all volumes linked to the server. Granting the write [W] property right to the ACL property of the server object also gives the trustee the supervisor [S] file system rights to all volumes linked to that server.

5) Avoid granting the supervisor [S] object right to any object. Otherwise, you will grant the supervisor [S] right to all properties. As a container administrator, you should consider granting all object rights except the supervisor [S] object right to an object first. Then, grant the specific properties with the "Selected Properties" option.

6) Be careful when filtering out supervisor [S] rights with an IRF. Usually the user object of the network administrator has the supervisor [S] rights of the network administrator from a branch of the NDS directory tree. The network administrator can no longer manage that particular branch of the directory tree if the network administrator deletes the user object of the container administrator later.

When a user object has common needs to the NDS or IntranetWare file system, you may add a user object to the member list of a group object or add or move user objects to the same container object. You may add users to following three different groups:

- Natural groups—Since a container acts like a natural group, the NDS rights and file system rights flow down to the user objects in the container. You may add or move user objects to the container to gain rights.

- Local groups—A local group is a group object used to grant members within a container additional NDS or file system rights.

- Global groups—A global group is a group object used to grant group members among different containers additional NDS or file system rights.

To be able to grant users in one context access resources in another context, you need to use one of the following three shortcuts in the network setup:

- Global group object—A global group object may contain members from multiple containers in the directory tree to regulate global access. You can use a global group object in any context to grant rights. The location of the global group object in the directory is not critical. However, the users in the member list, and where the global group object is granted rights are critical.

- Directory map object—This is a leaf object that represents another object in the directory tree. This object is used mostly with the login script MAP command to represent the locations for common applications. It allows you to map logical pointers to NDS objects instead of physical volume locations. In other words, it points to a file system directory on an IntranetWare volume. Hence, you may access the same file system resource regardless of where the actual location of the directory is. In addition, if you mapped a network drive pointer to a directory map object, then you do not need to update all the login scripts to reflect the location change of the directory, since you can have the directory map object point to the new directory location. Finally, you can use a directory map object to access a directory or an application under a directory from different containers when the directory can exist on only one volume. For example, if you create a directory map object pointing to a directory on a volume in another container in the current context, the user in the current context can then map a drive pointer to the directory using only the common name of the directory map object.

- Alias object—This is a leaf object that represents an object in a different location in the directory tree. By using alias objects, one object, such as an IntranetWare volume, can appear in several containers at one time, thus enabling users in each container to easily locate and use the original object. An alias object can point to the actual object in another container in the directory. This is helpful when you have a resource you need in multiple containers. For example, if you create an alias object pointing to a network printer in another container in the current context, the user in the current context can then redirect print jobs to the printer using only the common name of the alias object.

You as an administrator need to grant additional rights to users when the object or resource is in a container other than the user objects container. You must grant additional NDS rights to the following:

To enable the user to run a profile login script:

NDS resource	Rights required
Profile object	Read [R] property right to the login script property or read [R] property right to the "All Properties" option.
Profile object in same container	No additional rights are required, since the user already has the read [R] property right to any object in the container.
Profile object in different container	The user object must be added to the trustee list of the profile object. Hence, the browse [B] object right and create and read [CR] property rights will be granted by default.

To enable the user to map a drive pointer to the directory map object:

NDS resource	Rights required
Directory map object	Read [R] property right to the path or read [R] property right to the "All Properties" option.
Directory map object in the same container	No additional rights are required, since the user already has the read [R] property right to any object in the container.
Directory map object in different container	The user object must be added to the trustee list of the directory map object. Hence, the browse [B] object right and create and read [CR] property rights will be granted by default.

You as an administrator must have certain rights to grant a user access to an NDS resource. Below is a list of all the rights necessary to create and manage daily NDS resources:

NDS resource	Action needed	Rights required
Alias	Grant a user appropriate NDS rights to the alias object.	Authority to grant NDS rights to objects in other containers (i.e. write [W] right to the object's ACL property).
Application	Grant a user appropriate file system rights to the application referred to by the application object.	Supervisory [S] or access control [A] file system rights to the directory or file.
Application	Associate users with application objects	Write [W] property right to ACL property of the application user object.
Directory map	Grant a user the appropriate file system rights to the directory referred to by the directory map object.	Supervisory [S] or access control [A] file system rights to the directory or file.
Directory map	Grant users the read [R] property rights to the path property of the directory map object.	Write [W] property right to ACL property of the directory map object.
Group	Add users to the group membership list of the group object.	Write [W] property right to the ACL property of the group object.
Organization role	Add users to the occupant list of the organizational role object	Write [W] property right to the ACL property of the organizational role object.
Print queue	Add users to the print queue users list of the print queue object.	Must have a print queue operator status.
Printer	Add users to the print queue users list of the print queue object that services this printer.	Must have a print queue operator status.
Profile	Add a profile object to each user object's profile property or grant users the read [R] right to the	Write [W] property right to the ACL property of the profile object.

	login script property of the profile object.	
Volume /Directory	Grant users the appropriate file system rights to the directory or file.	Supervisory [S] or Access control [A] file system rights to the directory or file you want to target in the volume. Remember, no rights are needed for the SYS: PUBLIC directory since the read [R] and file scan [F] rights are granted by default.

There are some special circumstances that require a unique approach toward NDS security when dealing with traveling users. Before you grant any additional NDS and file system rights to traveling users, you must consider the following:

1) The number and types of traveling users.

2) What types of computer the traveling users use (i.e., laptop or desktop).

3) How to authenticate the user to NDS and NDS objects.

4) How to have the users access applications.

5) How to have the users access files stored in a directory.

6) How to have the users access files stored in different locations.

7) How to have the users access resources, such as e-mail and printers.

Here are three different types of travelling users you should consider when you want to grant additional NDS and file system rights:

- A user that spends equal time between two locations. If this user needs the same resources at both locations, you should do the following:

   a) Create a user object in each location.
   b) Grant each user the appropriate NDS and file system rights.
   c) Set up a profile object. Then grant each user the read [R] property right to the login script property.
   d) Set up a directory map object. Then grant each user the read [R] property right to the path directory.

- A user that travels to various locations regularly and needs similar resources in all locations, or a user that will be at one location temporarily. In these cases you should:

a) Create an alias object, or assign the user to a group object, or assign the user to an organizational role object.

b) Grant NDS and file system rights to the alias, or group, or organizational role object.

c) Set up a profile object. Then grant each user the read [R] property right to the login script property.

d) Set up a directory map object. Then grant each user the read [R] property right to the path directory.

Here are some guidelines you should follow when you are planning to set up resources in multiple containers:

1) Set up user accounts and login security. Each container should have its own User_Template and "Intruder Detection" option enabled. If users often log in from workstations with different default contexts, you should create alias objects to the user objects in the other contexts.

2) Plan the file system and its security carefully. Make sure to consider global objects such as group objects with global membership, [Root], [Public], when planning who should have rights. If you need to grant object rights to a volume in another context, make the object a trustee and grant the rights to the object. When mapping a network or a search drive, make sure to use the distinguished name of the volume object. In addition, make sure to create a directory map object in the current context if needed. Finally, make sure to create an alias object in the current context if needed.

3) Plan the network printing carefully. Make sure to have only one print server that manages printers and print queues in multiple contexts. You should grant more global access than local access. You may also add user, group, or container objects in the other contexts to the print queue user list to allow them to print. You can provide users in one context access to a printer in another context by using distinguished names or by creating an alias object to the printer in the context of the user.

4) Plan NDS and its security carefully. Stay with the default values if at all possible. You should give responsibilities by creating additional administrators. You can grant the supervisory [S] object right, or any other object right but the supervisory right to the newly created administrators.

One of the advantages of NDS is that it enables you to section off certain areas of the network administration tasks. In a distributed resource management environment, you may have multiple network administrators managing different branches of the NDS tree, or NDS containers. One network administrator may not have authority to manage objects in another container. You may not be able to create or edit objects in another container, grant user rights to the file system, or grant a user access to a network printer. If users need access to the resources in another container, you may have to request limited administrative rights to the resources or have another network administrator grant the users access to those resources. You should only grant NDS rights to allow an administrator to manage NDS objects and properties or to allow users to use certain network resources. NDS allows you to approach administration in one of two ways.

- Central administration—This means you have only one user (ADMIN) with supervisor [S] rights to the entire tree. This is the IntranetWare default. This is good for a company with a small directory tree or a company that wants to retain a central administrator. The ADMIN user is created during installation of the first server and initially has rights to manage NDS. ADMIN is granted the supervisor [S] object rights to the [Root] by default. Therefore, he/she will inherit rights to the rest of the tree unless an IRF is applied later. Some tasks that can be performed centrally are as follows:

  a) Naming the directory tree.
  b) Installing the first file server.
  c) Creating the top layers of the NDS tree.
  d) Managing NDS partitioning, time synchronization, and replication.
  e) Assigning container administrators.
  f) Issuing the initial auditor password.
  g) Upgrading server, clients, and applications.

- Distributed administration—This means that designated users are given enough NDS rights to manage distributed branches of the NDS tree. This special type of user is called a container administrator. You may grant any of the following NDS rights at container level to a container administrator to manage that branch of the directory tree.

  a) An explicit supervisor [S] object right to the [Root].
  b) [BCDR] object rights and [RW] property rights to the container.
  c) The [C] object right to the container.

Distributed administration generally allows you to respond to users' needs more quickly, especially in a large implementation. The following tasks can be performed by a container administrator:

  a) Creating users accounts and maintaining login scripts.
  b) Creating additional file servers.

c) Creating and configuring print services.
d) Backing up and restoring data.
e) Creating workgroup managers.
f) Assigning system trustees.
g) Upgrading servers, clients, and applications.
h) Monitoring server performance, errors, and disk space usage.

5.3 CONTAINER ADMINISTRATORS AND NETWORK AUDITING

You can assign container administrators to either a user object or an organizational role object. You may assign a container administrator to a user object if only one person is assigned to manage a container. To accomplish this, you need to make a user object the trustee of the container, then assign to it the supervisor [S], [BCDR], or [SBCDR] object rights. Finally, you must assign the needed rights to the file system to the user object. You may assign a container administrator to an organizational role if a group of user objects are assigned to manage a container. To accomplish this, you need to make an organizational role object as the trustee of the container, then assign to the object the supervisor [S], [BCDR], or [SBCDR] object rights. Assign the needed rights to the file system to the organizational role object. Finally, make the user objects occupants of the organization role object.

Specific issues must be considered while creating container administrators:

1) Grant all the container rights [SBCDR] to the user or organizational role object. With all the rights granted, the total administration of the container is still possible even if [S] is filtered out by an IRF.

2) Since the ADMIN object can be blocked using an IRF, you should consider making the ADMIN user object an occupant of the organizational role object. As an occupant of the organizational role object, the ADMIN object can still manage the container, even if IRF is used.

3) If a container administrator must manage the file system, make sure the administrator is a trustee of the server object. Also, grant the administrator the supervisor [S] right to the server object. If the container administrator does not need to manage the file system, make sure to remove the administrator from the trustee list of the server object. Then, edit the IRF of the server object to block the [S] right. Finally, grant the file system administrator the proper file system rights.

4) If you are using the organizational object role as a container administrator, you should always employ a user object as an explicit container administrator. This user object can prevent the administrative loss of the container in the event that the organizational role object is deleted.

If a container administrator is responsible for creating its own branch directory, you could grant the administrator the create [C] object right at the parent container of the tree. The supervisor [S] object right is always granted to the creator of the object by default.

Remember, the supervisor [S] right to the container flows downward to all objects in the container. The supervisor [S] right to the server object flows into its file system, or all volume objects attached to it. This is the only instance when NDS security affects file system security.

You might want to create a container administrator that is the only administrator who has the exclusive supervisor rights on a specific container. To do this, you must create an exclusive container administrator. You may have to filter out the rights inherited by the ADMIN user object to do this. The exclusive container administrator assignment may be useful in government organizations or a department of a company with highly sensitive information.

To create an exclusive container administrator, you need to follow the steps below:

1) Create a user object as a trustee of the container.

2) Grant all the container rights to the user object. You can grant [SBCDR] object rights and [SRCWA] property rights through the "All Properties" option.

3) Remember, with all the rights granted, the total administration of the container is still possible even if the supervisor [S] right is filtered out by IRF.

4) Modify the IRF to have only the browse [B] object right to allow other users see the tree. Also modify the IRF to have only read [R] property right.

5) Remove the ADMIN object from the trustee list of the container.

6) Make sure that the new container administrator has the supervisor [S] object right to itself.

7) Remove the ADMIN or other object from the trustee list of the new container administrator.

In addition to creating an exclusive container administrator, you may create other types of administrators, such as mailing list administrators, print queue operators, or print server operators.

- Mailing list administrator—You may add a user to the trustee list of each user object. The browse [B] object right and [CR] rights to all the properties will be granted by default. You may grant the user object the [RW] "Selected Properties" rights to the street, telephone, and other properties of each user object.

- Print queue operator—You must add the user or organization role object to the print queue operator property of the target print queue.

- Print server operator— You must add the user or organization role object to the print server operator property of the target print server.

IntranetWare auditing allows individuals, in addition to or other than the network administrators, to audit network transactions independently. A network transaction is any action that changes the NDS database or the content of a volume. To enable the IntranetWare auditing, you must do the following:

1) Create a user object for the auditor using NWADMIN.

2) Enable the network auditing for the auditor using AUDITCON.

3) Create a current password using AUDITCON.

4) Give the password to the auditor.

5) Disable the auditing on both containers and volumes after the auditing is completed using AUDITCON.

IntranetWare auditors may audit or track network events at a container or a volume level. On the other hand, auditors do not have the rights needed to open or modify network files other than the audit files. To audit at a container level, you must enable the auditing at a container level to monitor NDS events, such as user objects creation or login and logout activities of users. When you enable the auditing for an NDS container, you must enable the auditing for that specific container only and not enable any auditing for its subordinate containers.

To enable the auditing at a volume level, you must enable the auditing at a volume level to monitor the file system activities, such as the use of files, directories, queues, or servers. When you enable the auditing for a volume, you must enable the auditing for that specific volume only. For example, if you want to track the access use of Internet, you must use AUDITCON to enable audit at a container level for tracking the login and logout activities of users. Then, you must enable audit at a volume level for tracking the number of times a user opens a file.

During IntranetWare installation, AUDITCON is automatically installed in the SYS: \SYSTEM directory. IntranetWare auditors may use AUDITCON to audit the following three events:

1) Directory services events—If the auditing at a container level is enabled, then you may create, move, rename, or delete objects. You may also add or remove security equivalence of an object. Finally, you may track login and logout activities of users.

2) Server events—If the auditing at a volume level is enabled, then you may bring down the server, create or delete bindery objects, mount or dismount volumes, or modify security rights.

3) File or directory events—If the auditing at a volume level is enabled, then you may create, move, rename, modify, delete, or salvage directories or files. In addition, you may create, delete, or service print queues.

To enable AUDITCON, run the IntranetWare utility program AUDITCON.EXE from a workstation as shown in figure 5.2.

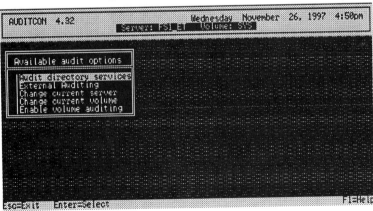

Figure 5.2 AUDITCON utility.

5.4 SERVER MANAGEMENT

IntranetWare is the main server software component that provides network services to clients. This software is modular, so it can be divided into two categories—the core operating system and the NetWare Loadable Modules (NLMs). The core operating system runs in the RAM of all IntranetWare servers. It provides basic network services to clients, such as the file system for shared file storage, IntranetWare directory services, security, authentication or packet signature, and routing. On the other hand, NLMs add functionality to the file system by loading or unloading the NLMs while the server is running. Some of the NLMs provided by IntranetWare are server LAN and disk drivers, network printing, storage management, server monitoring, remote server console, UPS monitoring, optional network management products, optional communication products, optional media management products, and optional data migration products.

The modular approach of IntranetWare provides the following three benefits:

a) You may reduce server workload or free up memory by removing inactive NLMs.
b) You may load and unload NLMs without bringing down the server.
c) Other vendors may supply NLMs, or add-on modules, for the IntranetWare operating system.

IntranetWare server management consists of three components:

- Console commands—This is part of the IntranetWare core operating system file (SERVER.EXE), used to keep the server running at peak performance. The following are four types of console commands:

Screen Display Commands:

Command	Description
BROADCAST or SEND	Used to send brief alert messages to all attached workstations. SEND is another related command used to send a brief message to a specific user. A BROADCAST message can be up to 40 characters long. A SEND message can be up to 55 characters long. The syntax is BROADCAST message or SEND message. The downside of BROADCAST and SEND is that they lock up the destination computer until <Ctrl> and <Enter> are pressed. To avoid having messages lock up machines, consider issuing SEND with the following parameters: /A=C—This parameter will only accept messages from the server console. /A=N—This parameter will accept no messages (be careful with this parameter). /A=P—This parameter will store the last message sent until polled to receive it. /P—This parameter will poll the server for the last stored message. /A=A—This parameter will accept all messages.
CLS	Clears the console screen.
EXIT	Returns to DOS partition after the server has been downed.
OFF	Clears the console screen.
PAUSE	Same as the DOS PAUSE command. This is used in .NFC files.
REM or ";"	Used for commenting a line. This is used in .NFC files.

Maintenance Commands:

Command	Description
CLEAR STATION	Abruptly clears the workstation's connection. It then closes all the files and server's internal tables for the workstation. This command is useful only if workstations have crashed or if users have turned off their machines without logging out. The syntax is CLEAR STATION n, where n is the connection number of the workstation.
DISABLE LOGIN	Prevents access to the server for troubleshooting or maintenance activities. It is useful when you are working on the NDS database, backing up files, loading software, or dismounting/ repairing volumes. Remember that this command does not affect users already logged in.
DISABLE TTS	Disables the Transaction Tracking System.
DISMOUNT	Makes a disk volume unavailable to the network users.
DSTRACE	Enables you to monitor NDS replica-related activities, including advertising, synchronization, and replica-to-replica communications.
DOWN	Completely shuts down file server activity and closes all open files in an orderly manner. Before DOWN shuts down the server, it clears all cache buffers and writes them to a disk, closes all open files, updates the appropriate directory and file allocation tables, dismounts all volumes, clears all connections, and closes the operating system.
ENABLE LOGIN	Enables the users to log on to the file server after it has been disabled.
ENABLE TTS	Enables the Transaction Tracking System.
MEMORY	Displays the amount of installed memory addressable by IntranetWare.
MEMORY MAP	Displays the amount of installed memory addressable by DOS and IntranetWare.
REMOVE DOS	Eliminates COMMAND.COM from the background server memory. This memory is returned to IntranetWare for file caching. When DOS is removed NLMs cannot be loaded from the DOS partition, and users cannot EXIT to the DOS partition; thus, the REMOVE DOS command can be used to increase server security.
RESET ROUTER	Resets the router table if it becomes corrupted.
RESTART SERVER	Reactivates the server after it has been downed. Consider the following parameters used with the RESTART SERVER command: -NS—Restarts the server without invoking the STARTUP.NCF file. -NA—Restarts the server without invoking the AUTOEXEC.BAT file.
TRACK OFF	Turns off the router-tracking screen.
TRACK ON	Activates the router information protocol (RIP) tracking screen. TRACK ON information is formatted according to whether the file server is receiving information or broadcasting information.
UNBIND	Disables the communication between the file server and workstation. It closes all the files and servers' internal tables for the workstation.
SECURE CONSOLE	Secures the file server from unauthorized system programs.
SET	Views the thirteen settable operating parameter categories.
SET parameter value	Configures the operating system parameter.
SET TIME	Declares the time and date kept by the file server
SET TIMEZONE	Declares the time zone kept by the file server.

Configuration Information Commands:

Command	Description
CONFIG	Displays hardware information for all internal communication components.
DISPLAY NETWORKS	Displays all networks and assigned network numbers recognized by the router.
DISPLAY SERVERS	Displays all servers recognized by the router.
LIST DEVICES	Displays all the physical devices on the system.
MODULES	Displays a list of currently loaded NLMs and some brief information about each, including the module short name, descriptive string for each module, and the version number if it's a disk driver, LAN driver, or management utility.
NAME	Displays the name of the server.
PROTOCOL	Displays a list of the protocols registered on the server.
SCAN FOR NEW DEVICES	Causes the operating system device drivers to look for new devices on the system.
SPEED	Displays the CPU running speed rating.
SPOOL	Redirects a printer number to a print queue.
TIME	Displays the current time and date of the file server.
UPS STATUS	Checks and displays the status of the UPS attached to the server.
UPS TIME	Displays the UPS discharge and recharge time in minutes.
VERSION	Displays the file server's version information.
VOLUMES	Displays the information of all the mounted volumes.

Installation Commands:

Command	Description
ADD NAME SPACE	Makes a volume available to store non-DOS files after loading the name space NLM.
BIND	Links the LAN driver to a communication protocol. Once the LAN driver is loaded, BIND must be issued to activate the LAN communications. The default IntranetWare communication protocol is IPX. The syntax is: BIND IPX to driver.
HELP	Views the available console commands.
HELP command	Views specific help about a command.
LOAD	Activates NLMs and attaches them to the core operating system.
MOUNT	Activates the internal IntranetWare volumes. You can mount all of the volumes on the server by executing the command MOUNT all.
REGISTER MEMORY	Makes the server recognize any installed memory above 16 MB.
SEARCH	Lists, adds, or deletes a search path for NLMs and .NCF files.
UNLOAD	Unloads NLMs to free up valuable server memory.

- NetWare Loadable Modules (NLMs)—NLMs are add-on modules to the IntranetWare operating system. As you know the core operating system provides only basic network services, such as NDS, file system, security, authentication, and routing. Without NLMs IntranetWare would be limited to communications and file storing. Here is a list of the additional services provided by IntranetWare NLMs:

a) Server customizing—SERVMAN.NLM.
b) Remote server console—REMOTE.NLM and RSPX/RS232.
c) Storage management services—SBACKUP.NLM and drivers.
d) Network printing—PSERVER.NLM
e) Server monitoring—MONITOR.NLM
f) Communications—NetWare connect (optional)
g) Messaging—Groupwise (optional)
h) Network management—Managewise (optional)

IntranetWare has four types of NLMs:

1) Disk drivers—These NLMs control the communications between IntranetWare and the internal shared disk. Disk drivers are the ones that activate the NetWare partition. They have the .DSK extension. Newer disk modules written to the Novell Peripheral Architecture standard come in pairs and have the extensions .CDM (Custom Device Module) and .HAM (Host Adapter Module).

2) LAN drivers—These NLMs control the communications between IntranetWare and the internal network interface cards (NICs).

3) Name space modules—These modules enable files using non-DOS naming conventions to be stored in the IntranetWare file system.

4) NLM utilities—These modules monitor and change the operating system configuration options. There are two types of NLM utilities—management and file server enhancement modules. You can always activate an NLM by loading it to the RAM and deactivate it by unloading it from the RAM. At the server console screen, you may view a loaded NLM screen by pressing the keys <Ctrl><Esc>, then selecting the desired screen from the menu displayed or by pressing the keys <Alt><Esc> to switch among the loaded NLM screens. Let us look at four types of NLMs, namely INSTALL.NLM, MONITOR.NLM, SERVMAN.NLM, and DSREPAIR.NLM.

a) INSTALL.NLM—You must load INSTALL.NLM to install, manage, troubleshoot, optimize, and maintain the IntranetWare server. If you type the command LOAD INSTALL.NLM at the server prompt, a screen containing 10 options will be launched as shown in figure 5.3.

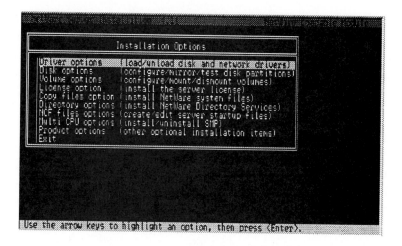

Figure 5.3 INSTALL.NLM.

You can perform some tasks after the IntranetWare installation using INSTALL.NLM. These tasks include: disk duplexing, adding drives and volumes, adding incremental server licenses, redefining the hot fix redirection area, editing server configuration files, and loading an upgrade IntranetWare license. In addition, you can install and configure additional products, including Web Server, NetWare/IP, additional languages, Macintosh connectivity, and UNIX support.

b) MONITOR.NLM—You want to load MONITOR.NLM to track resources that include file connections, memory, disk information, users, file lock activity, and processor usage. As seen from figure 5.4, MONITOR.NLM consists of two main menus—General Information and Available Options.

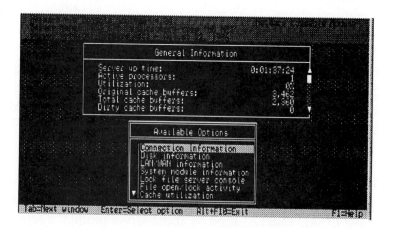

Figure 5.4 MONITOR.NLM.

Here are some of the General Information and Available Options statistics and descriptions:

<u>General Information:</u>

Statistic	Description
Utilization	This shows the CPU utilization. It is the amount of time the processor is busy.
Original cache buffers	Indicates the number of buffers (blocks) originally available for caching.
Total cache buffers	Indicates the number of buffers (blocks) available for file caching. You want this number to stay high, since file caching has a dramatic impact on server files. This number will decrease as NLMs and other resources are loaded.
Dirty cache buffers	Indicates the number of file buffers (blocks) in memory waiting to be written to a disk. If this number grows large, your server might crash and data might be corrupted.
Current service processes	Indicates the number of task handlers IntranetWare allocates to service incoming requests. The default maximum number of service processes is 50, with a possible range of 5 to 1000.

<u>Available Options:</u>

Statistic	Description
Connection information	This lists all the active connections and tracks their current activities. You can clear a user connection with this option.
Disk information	Lists all the available internal disks and available hot fix redirection area statistics. You can activate, deactivate, or modify internal disks with this option.
LAN/WAN information	Lists all LAN and WAN driver configurations and statistics, and workstation and network addressing statistics.
System module information	Lists all loaded modules by name, size, and version.
Lock file server module.	Enables you to protect the console by declaring a password.
File open/lock activity	Monitors file, lock activity, and status. In addition, it lists general information about mounted volumes and directory structures.
Cache utilization	Lists detailed caching statistics. This option enables you to assess the efficiency of the server memory.
Processor utilization	Lists a detailed histogram of all selected processes and their CPU usage.
Resource utilization	Shows the memory usage for the cache buffer pool, allocated memory, movable and non-movable memory pools, and code/data memory.
Memory utilization	Shows detailed memory statistics. This option enables you to activate garbage collection routines.

| Scheduling information | Shows and allows you to change the priority of a process by delaying CPU execution until a later time. |
| EXIT | Allows you to exit MONITOR.NLM. |

c) SERVMAN.NLM (SERver MANager)—You must load SERVMAN.NLM to provide you with a menu interface for SET parameters and to display valuable IntranetWare configurations. As seen from figure 5.5, SERVMAN.NLM consists of two main menus—General Information and Available Options.

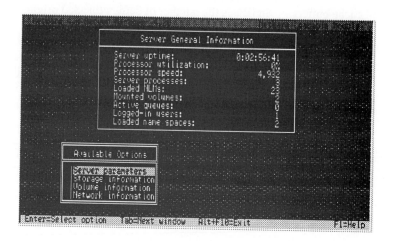

Figure 5.5 SERVMAN.NLM.

Here are some of the General Information and Available Options statistics and descriptions:

<u>Server General Information:</u>

Statistic	Description
Server uptime	This shows the length of time the server has been running since it was last loaded.
Processor utilization	Shows the percentage of time the server CPU is busy.
Processor speed	Shows the speed at which the processor is running based on the CPU clock, CPU type, and the number of memory wait states.
Server processes	Shows the number of task handlers currently available to handle incoming user requests.
Loaded NLMs	Shows the number of modules currently loaded on the server.
Mounted volumes	Shows the number of volumes currently active on the server.
Active queues	Shows the number of active print queues currently servicing user print jobs.
Logged-in users	Shows the number of users logged into the server.
Loaded name space	Shows the number of name spaces loaded on the server, including DOS.

Available Options:

Statistic	Description
Server parameters	This shows and allows you to configure most of the IntranetWare operating system parameters. These include the SET parameters which are automated by the AUTOEXEC.NCF and STARTUP.NCF files. Changes made in SERVMAN can optionally be reflected in the server configuration files.
Storage information	Shows adapter, device, and partition information. This is similar to INSTALL.NLM and MONITOR.NLM.
Volume information	Shows information about volumes mounted on the files server. This is similar to INSTALL.NLM.
Network information	Shows network information, such as the number of packets received and transmitted. This is similar to MONITOR.NLM.

d) DSREPAIR.NLM—You must load DSREPAIR.NLM to make repairs and adjustments to the NDS database and to solve inconsistencies with time and replica synchronization. Figure 5.6 shows the main menu of DSREPAIR.NLM and both synchronization options. Consider the following symptoms that indicate that the NDS is corrupted:

a) You cannot create, merge, or modify partitions.
b) You cannot create, delete, or modify objects even though you have sufficient rights.
c) Unknown objects appear in the tree that do not disappear after all servers are synchronized.

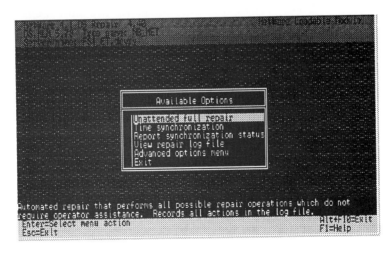

Figure 5.6 DSREPAIR.NLM.

- Remote server management—IntranetWare remote management capability allows network supervisors to manage all IntranetWare file servers on the internetwork from one workstation. Remote console makes a workstation acts as if it were a file server console, and then you may use console commands as you would at the file server. You have to load the appropriate remote management software on the servers. The remote console does not disable the console keyboard or bypass the MONITOR keyboard lock. Since remote console allows you to make a workstation act as a file server console, you may remove the keyboard and monitor from the server to provide greater file server security.

RCONSOLE transfers the screen and keyboard strokes data to and from a remote file server. Remote console supports concurrent connections to the server. This allows you to do remote troubleshooting and train other file server administrators and managers. RCONSOLE allows you to change screens and perform all tasks available at the file server console. In addition, you can scan directories and the DOS partition of the server, transfer files to the server, go to DOS to view a network directory, and copy an IntranetWare utility to the file system on the server. Remember this: RCONSOLE will not allow you to copy files from the server to floppy disks.

Users can access the server from a remote workstation only if they have the appropriate rights (i.e. read [R] and file scan [F] to the SYS: SYSTEM directory). In addition users must have a security password. There are two steps required to set up a remote console. First you must set up the file server for remote console. Then, you must execute the remote console software (RCONSOLE) at the workstation. You can establish a remote console connection in two ways:

1) Direct connection over the network cable system—To perform this connection, you must load REMOTE.NLM with a password onto the server. REMOTE.NLM is an NLM that manages the data exchange between the server and the remote workstation. Then, you must load the NLM RSPX onto the server to load the SPX drive for communication support and advertise that the server is available for remote access.

2) Asynchronous connection over a pair of modems—To perform this type of connection, you must first configure a modem attached to the remote workstation first. Then select a remote location to connect to. Finally, you can start to use the remote management console options. Once this is done, then you must load the following NLMs in the order shown below:
REMOTE.NLM—Manages the data exchange between the server and the remote workstation.
AIO.NLM—Invokes the communication port interface module.
AIOCOMX.NLM—Invokes the communication port drive.
RS232.NLM—Invokes the asynchronous communication driver to initiate the communication port of the file server and transfer the screen and keyboard stroke data to and from REMOTE.NLM.

You may automate the remote console setup procedures on the server by adding the appropriate command to the AUTOEXEC.NCF file on the file server. The entire set of remote console NLMs is located in the SYS: SYSTEM directory.

On the workstation end, you must copy the RCONSOLE.EXE to the local drive for asynchronous remote console. You may execute RCONSOLE at the DOS prompt of a workstation to turn the workstation into a virtual file server. You may use the following shortcut keystrokes while in RCONSOLE:

Keystroke	Function
<Alt> <F1>	Displays the RCONSOLE main menu.
<Alt> <F2>	Exits or clears the connection with the current server.
<Alt> <F3>	Scrolls forward through the active console screen.
<Alt> <F4>	Scrolls backward through the active console screen.
<Alt> <F5>	Displays the address of the workstation.
<Alt> <F7>	Sends if manual keystroke send is enables.
<Alt> <F8>	Enters a buffer command if On demand buffering is enabled.
<Esc>	Resumes the remote session with the server.

As a network administrator, you must be able to protect the server in one or all of the following ways:

1) Lock up the server in a safe room. This is the most secure way.

2) Lock the server console using the "Lock File Server Console" option in MONITOR.NLM. This way you can prevent unauthorized keyboard entries.

3) Use the SECURE CONSOLE command to remove COMMAND.COM from the server memory, prevent loading NLMs from any directory other than SYS: SYSTEM, prevent changing data and time, and prevent access to the DOS partition of the server.

4) Add a password to REMOTE.NLM to prevent unauthorized access to the server with RCONSOL. RCONSOLE will allow only the supervisor password or the password assigned when REMOTE.NLM is loaded.

5.5 STORAGE MANAGEMENT SERVICES

Storage Management Services (SMS) is a product provided by IntranetWare to allow you to back up and restore data. SMS consists of several related services that allow data to be stored and retrieved. The backup process involves an application on the server, which communicates with modules on a target device. The server application reads the target device data, then stores it on a storage media, such as an IntranetWare server, NDS, DOS workstation, OS/2 workstation, or Btrieve (SQL) database. Notice that backup cannot use a Macintosh or a UNIX workstation as a target device. There are three types of backup:

1) Full backup—This backs up all the data regardless of when it was backed up before. This type of backup will clear the Archive Bit or Modify Bit of the files. Although full backup takes the longest to perform, it is the fastest way to restore data, because it needs only the most recent backup tape.

2) Incremental backup—This backs up only data that is new or has been modified since the last backup. This type of backup will clear the Archive Bit or Modify Bit of the files. To use this type of backup, you should perform a weekly full backup followed by daily incremental backups. This type of backup takes the least time to perform, but it is the slowest to restore, because you must restore the last full backup and every incremental backup since then, in order.

3) Differential backup—This only backs up data that has been modified since the last full backup. This type of backup will not clear the Archive Bit or Modify Bit of the files. This way, the files that have been changed since the last full backup are copied each time. That is why full backup clears the Modify Bit. This type of backup provides a balance of efficiency and performance because it minimizes the number of restore sessions and copies only files that have been changed.

Remember these points when choosing a backup strategy. First, only a full backup can back up the NDS database. Second, you must never mix incremental and differential backups in your backup strategy. The best backup strategy is performing a full backup weekly and a differential backup every day. To be able to perform backup sessions, you need certain rights:

1) The read [R] and file scan [F] rights to the files on the IntranetWare file system..

2) The browse [B] object right and read [R] property rights to the IntranetWare NDS database.

3) The password on the workstation, if it is enabled.

4) The password to all the servers that act as hosts and targets.

IntranetWare implementation of SMS is the SBACKUP.NLM program. SBACKUP is an NLM that operates at the IntranetWare server and communicates directly with the host backup device. It is automatically installed on the file server during an installation or upgrade process. Following are four terms that you need to be familiar with when using SBACKUP:

1) Host—This is an IntranetWare file server running SBACKUP and having a backup device attached to it.

2) Target—This is any IntranetWare server, workstation, or NDS database that has the Target Service Agent (TSA) loaded.

3) Parent—This is a data set that may have subordinate data sets, such as directories, subdirectories, or a containers.

4) Child—This is a data set that has no subordinates, such as a file or a leaf object.

In addition to the preceding terms, you also need to be familiar with the modules that SBACKUP uses to carry out the backup and restore functions:

1) Device drivers—These control the mechanical operations of various storage devices and media, such as read, write, back, and stop. A backup utility uses SMSDI to communicate with device drivers.

2) SMSDI—This stands for SMS Device Interface. It is loaded on the host server to allow you to pass commands and information between the backup utility and storage devices.

3) SMDR—This stands for Storage Management Data Requester. It is loaded on the host server to allow you to pass commands and data among SBACKUP, TSAs, and SDI.

4) SBACKUP—This is the backup utility provided by IntranetWare. It is responsible for routing requests of data to the source and returning information to the SDI.

5) Server TSAs—This stands for Server Target Service Agents. These are modules used for specific operating system and data base types. Server TSAs are loaded on the target server to back up the server's file system. You must load the server TSAs on the host server if you want to back up the data on the host. Server TSAs use SMDR to communicate with backup software.

6) Database TSAs—These are loaded on a target server to back up a third-party database. You must load the database TSAs on the host if you want to back up the database on the host.

7) Workstation TSAs—These are loaded on a workstation to back up data on local drives.

8) Workstation manager—This where you receive the message "I am here" from workstations available to be backed up. The workstation manager keeps the names of the workstations available to be backed up in an internal list. Since SBACKUP displays this list, you may select a target for a backup or a restore procedure.

Since not all modules are used in all backup procedures, you should use only the ones needed for a specific backup task. Now it is time to learn some simple SBACKUP guidelines to ensure that backup and restore sessions are successful:

1) To load SBACKUP on the host server you need a minimum of 3 MB of additional RAM, 1 MB of disk space on the SYS volume for temporary files and log files, and backup devices attached to the host file server.

2) Limit the SBACKUP access to the ADMIN or supervisor equivalents only. Remember that all the SBACKUP utilities are stored in the directory SYS: \SYSTEM.

3) You may use SBACKUP to back up the file servers and workstations on the internetworks.

4) Use MONITOR to check for host memory.

5) Use MONITOR to check for the current loaded NLMs.

6) Know the session description and full path of the backup data.

7) Know the password of the user who has the rights needed to do backup.

8) Know the workstation password when backing up a DOS or OS/2 workstation.

9) SBCKUP will exit when a delayed backup is complete. This is a security risk. Therefore, to reduce the security risk, make sure you have enough space on the backup media to hold all the data for delayed backup, set append to "NO", and attend the backup session for inserting the next tape.

10) The SBACKUP interface can only support DOS file names and path conventions. Full name space is supported in backup and restore. You should use the DOS equivalent names when specifying names for non-DOS files. The backup log and error files will be displayed in both DOS equivalent name and name space.

11) The temporary files that are created by SBACKUP on the target server are located in the SYS :\SYSTEM\TSA$TMP.* directory. They are used to store data during

backup. Make sure to monitor the size of these files. They become large if files have extended attributes or are linked to UNIX files.

12) Never mount or dismount a volume or unload drivers during backup or restore sessions. This may corrupt data or ABEND (bring down) the host server.

To use SBACKUP, you must load the TSAs on the target devices, then load SBACKUP on the host server. The following is a list of TSAs that must be loaded on the target devices:

The Target Server to be Backed Up	TSA for Host	TSA for Target
NetWare 3.11 server		TSA311.NLM
NetWare 3.12 server		TSA312.NLM
NetWare 4.0 server		TSA400.NLM
NetWare 4.1 server		TSA410.NLM
NetWare 4.11 server		TSA411.NLM
NetWare 4.1 NDS		TSANDS.NLM
DOS workstation	TSADOS.NLM	TSASMS.COM
OS/2 workstation	TSAPROXY.NLM	TSAOS2.COM (icon)

Remember that when SBACKUP is loaded on the host it automatically loads the NLMs SMSDI, SMDR, STREAMS, TLI, SPXS, NWSNUT, and CLIB.

Below are the steps you need to follow to perform a backup using SBACKUP:

1) Load the backup device driver on the host server.

2) Load the appropriate TSAs on the target devices.

3) Load SBACKUP.NLM on the host server. See figure 5.7 for the SBACKUP main menu.

Figure 5.7 SBACKUP main menu.

4) Select a target to be backed up from the TSA list.

5) Select the backup device from the "Available Options" list.

6) Pick the "Log/Error File Administration" option to declare a directory where the session log and error files are to be stored.

7) Select "Backup".

8) Declare the type of backup you want (i.e. full, incremental, differential, or custom).

9) Use the "Custom: Only specified Data" option for backing up selected data on the volume.

10) Select "Start the Backup Now" or "Proceed with Backup". You may choose the "Start the Backup Later" option for scheduled backup.

11) When you are done, exit Backup.

12) Unload the NLMs in the opposite order they were loaded from the host server to free up memory. You may do this by:

   a) Unloading NLMs for the SBACKUP from the host server.
   b) Unloading TSAs from the host, if there is any.
   c) Unloading any drivers for your backup devices from the host.

13) Unload any TSAs from the target device to free up memory.

Below are the steps you need to follow to perform a restore using SBACKUP:

1) Load the backup device driver on the host server.

2) Load the appropriate TSA on all the target devices you wish to restore.

3) Load SBACKUP.NLM at the host server.

4) Pick the "Log/Error File Administration" option to declare a directory where the session log and error files are to be stored.

5) Select a target device to restore to.

6) Select "Restore".

7) Declare the type of restore you want.

8) Declare "Restore Options", then press the key <F10>.

9) Select "Yes" at the "Proceed with Restore?" prompt.

10) Once the restore is complete, press the <Enter> key to go back to the SBACKUP main menu.

11) Check the error log if needed.

12) Exit SBACKUP.

13) Unload the NLMs in the opposite order they were loaded from the host server to free up memory. You may do this by:

    d) Unloading NLMs for the SBACKUP from the host server.
    e) Unloading TSAs from the host, if there is any.
    f) Unloading any drivers for your backup devices from the host.

14) Unload any TSAs from the target device to free up memory.

SBACKUP always creates a backup log file for every backup session performed. This backup log file includes information, such as backup session data and time, backup session description, backup target name, media set identification information, and all the parent and children data sets backed up during the session.

SBACKUP also creates a backup and restore error file when a data set is initially backed up. The error file contains the same header information as shown in the backup log file. The error file also lists errors, such as the names of files that were not backed up. SBACKUP will append the errors that occurred during the restore session to the same file.

Session data is sent to the files on the host server each time a backup or a restore session is performed. Data is sent to the backup log file and error file during a backup session. Data is sent to the error file during a restore session. SBACKUP saves the session files in the default directory SYS: \SYSTEM\TSA\LOG. The backup session files contain data, which can help you to manage the network effectively, facilitate the restore process, and troubleshoot the backup session. You should always delete the session files that are no longer useful. The "Restore Without Session Files" option of SBACKUP allows you to restore backup sessions without the session files.

You can also use SBACKUP to back up and restore data on local disks of a DOS workstation. To do this, just follow the procedures below:

1) Load TSADOS.NLM on the host server.

2) Load TSASMS.COM at the target workstation.

3) Select the DOS TSA from the SBACKUP menu.

4) Run the DOS TSA at the workstation using the following command:

   TSASMS /SE=FS_1 /t /D=c /B=40 /options…

Questions

1) Name three things that pertain to security equivalence.
2) What is the minimum object right to rename an object?
3) What does Joe need in order to change some of Mike's object rights?
4) If you are assigned the write [W] right for the ACL property to the ADMIN user object, what functions can you do then?
5) Describe what auditing is.
6) Name three tasks an auditor does.
7) What three parameters in auditing configuration can be changed?
8) Name two ways to check the excess use of the Internet.
9) In what three ways does NDS security differ from file system security?
10) What is the process of verifying a user logging in to a network?
11) Describe what authentication is.
12) What right is required to change the IRF?
13) Give two methods to block the inheritance of rights in the NDS directory tree.
14) What default object right to [Root] is granted to ADMIN when NDS is installed?
15) What is the object that may be used to grant rights that are relevant to specific positions in your organization, such as managers or assistant administrators?
16) Name two good reasons for granting NDS rights.
17) Name three things that are true about right inheritance.
18) Name six things that are true about object supervisor right.
19) On what object can the [S] effective right flow into the file system?
20) Name three things about the property supervisor right.
21) What are the two NDS rights that are inherited?
22) What does ACL stand for?
23) Name three good guidelines to use in assigning NDS object and property rights.
24) Name the two options that you may use in assigning property rights.
25) What rights can be inherited through the selected properties option?

26) What is important to know about the write right to the ACL property of a server object?

27) What object right allows the object trustee to change an object property value?

28) It is a good idea to grant rights to what object, when multiple users within a container or across several containers need the same rights?

29) What two utilities allow the administrator to manipulate NDS objects?

30) Describe what console commands are.

31) What console commands do the following:

    a)   Displays the server name and LAN configuration?

    b)   Activates an NLM by placing it into server memory?

    c)   Deactivates an NLM by removing it from server memory?

32) What is the NLM that controls communications between the IntranetWare operating system and a hard disk?

33) Your workstation is connected directly to the network's backbone, and your server is locked in a closet on another floor of the building. What steps would you take to set up a remote console on your workstation?

34) Which two keys are used to switch between active NLM displays in RCONSOLE?

35) In what file can you add appropriate load commands so you can set your server to automatically load the NLMs required for remote console operation?

36) If SFT (System Fault Tolerance) is important when you are designing your network, what should you do?

37) Name the three best ways to protect the IntranetWare server.

38) Name two correct ways to back up the file system.

39) What is the correct way to restore the backup data after a full backup and several incremental backups?

40) What type of backup should you use if you do not want to clear the modify bit?

41) What is the reason that an error message shows up after loading SBACKUP.NLM, which indicated a problem at the backup target?

42) Where can you find the list of the names of files which were not backed up during the system backup?

6

NDS Design and Integrating Netware 3.1x

This chapter discusses how to design and manage NDS. In addition, you will learn how to partition and replicate NDS, synchronize time, and create a detailed design and troubleshooting scheme for NDS. You will learn the differences among the four types of replicas and the different types of time synchronization methods. Finally, you will learn how to use bindery services to integrate NetWare 3.1x with the IntranetWare 4.11 server.

6.1 DESIGNING NDS

For a small company, the default installation of IntranetWare provides enough features to administer NDS without any major design considerations. For a more complex installation, you can approach the design of NDS in two different phases:

- Structural design—The structural design approach focuses on the structure of the NDS tree and the process for implementing the directory structure. You can structure the directory tree by doing the following :

  1) Identify workgroups and workgroup needs. To accomplish this, you need to gather information about the organization charts, project team descriptions, and workflow analysis. Once the information been gathered, you may use NDS objects to organize the network resources. You may then plan or structure the directory tree based on the following criteria or considerations:

     a) The needs of workgroups and the management of the workgroups.

     b) The topology of the network.

     c) The information flow of the organization.

     d) The required access to network resources.

Identifying the workgroup needs is a crucial part in designing an effective directory tree. As you identify the work groups, you should consider how the users view themselves and the resources in their work environment and how the resources are accessed. An effective directory tree should uniquely identify all network resources as users see them and help users in completing their tasks. You can design the directory tree by grouping the organization as follows:

a) Administrative divisions—You may emphasize workgroups based on the management structure and design a directory tree that imitates the organization chart of a company, such as Accounting, Production, Sales, etc.

b) Workgroups across divisions—You may emphasize workgroups based on similarities in users' tasks and resources and design a directory tree that imitates the workgroups, such as Project1, Project2, Accounting, Sales, etc.

c) Geographical locations—You may emphasize workgroups based on their physical locations and design a directory tree that imitates the geography of a company, such as USA, Europe, Asia, etc.

d) Hybrid or mixed environment—You may emphasize the design of the directory tree based on a combination of the preceding three models.

2) Determine the topology of the network and organize objects in the directory tree. The NDS directory has no particular limits on the level it can handle. On the other hand, the length of the NDS path cannot be longer than 256 characters. You should always limit the directory tree to less than 8 levels, or layers to make management of NDS an easy task. As you determine the directory tree to structure, you should consider if you have WAN links as part of the network. If they do exist, then you should consider where are they located in the network. Finally, you should consider how the network resources are divided.

3) Specify naming conventions. You need to establish an NDS naming conventions standard, such as the conventions used in the directory tree and the conventions used in the property values with objects. Having consistent naming conventions provides you with a guideline for managing NDS objects, eliminates redundant planning for NDS objects, and helps users identify resources quickly.

4) Plan the implementation method. This all depends on the size and needs of the organization. You may select a directory tree implementation method once you have established the naming conventions and directory tree structure. The three implementation methods are as follows:

a) Departmental—Here you would create a small directory for a workgroup, if the coordination of planner, installer, and administrator is not practical or if the server cannot access the same directory over a WAN. You may use the departmental method to install multiple trees for small groups within a company without waiting for the organization networking goals to be established. If you do this, make sure that each tree has a unique name so that you can merge all the trees later.

b) Divisional—Here you would need to create a few large directory trees for many workgroups, but not for the entire company. Each directory tree must have a unique name so you can merge the entire directory tree easily later. You may create a directory tree in each location or region, for each division, or for a subsidiary.

c) Organizational—Here you would need a clear understanding of the organizational networking goals. Once you do, you would create a directory tree for the entire company. To accomplish this, you may use the top-down approach organizational method if all the servers are connected to each other via a LAN or a WAN, the network is small and simple, and a group administrator can manage the upgrade of IntranetWare.

- Detailed design—The detailed design focuses on how the directory is accessed by users, how the directory is stored on the server, and how the directory is coordinated to provide accurate data. You can perform a detailed design of the directory tree by using the following procedure:

1) Secure the NDS. You can secure the directory tree by picking a centralized or distributed administration approach, and organize and place workgroups in the directory tree by using containers or group objects. In addition, you can plan rights inheritance and security equivalence using containers or group objects, assign the server supervisor object right carefully, and provide access to network resources for traveling users.

2) Replicate the directory partitions. You can accomplish this by planning partition boundaries to prevent a single point failure, identifying the proper replica assignments, and balancing accessibility and fault tolerance versus

network traffic and performance. In addition, you can allow for WAN links and assign administrators for partitions and replicas.

3) Synchronize time. You can accomplish this by planning server time for the directory tree, synchronizing time source servers and time provider servers, reducing WAN traffic for synchronizing time, and planning a time synchronization strategy for directory merges.

If you plan to merge the entire tree later, you should give each directory tree a unique organization container name and add an extra organization unit to each directory tree. The extra organization unit allows you to move all the containers easily in the merged tree. To be able to merge a tree, you will need the following utilities:

1) SBACKUP—You want to back up the directory trees in case you encounter problems.

2) SET TIMESYNC—You need this command to establish time synchronization.

3) DSMERGE—You need this NLM to consolidate trees, check that the servers in the tree have the correct tree name, to check the time synchronization of the servers in the tree, to merge a tree into another, and to rename a tree.

4) NWADMIN—You need this utility to clean up the merged tree.

Before you consolidate the trees, make sure you have planned how to merge the trees, backed up the directory trees, synchronized the time, merged the trees, and cleaned up the merged tree. To plan how to merge the tree, you must consider which source tree should be consolidated into the target tree, and what the new tree should look like. The source tree should be the tree with fewer objects at the root. Both trees must use the same schema and use the same version of NDS. The schema is defined as object classes and rules of containment. Before synchronizing the time, make sure to perform the following tasks:

1) Pick source and target directory trees.

2) Create unique organization object names for the source tree.

3) Get the full name and password for the ADMIN object for both trees.

In order to merge both trees together, they need to agree on a correct time. Remember that NDS depends on time to make updates to the directory. You must make one of the target tree servers a single reference timeserver. You must change all the source tree servers to secondary timeservers and they must get their time from the single reference server. To establish time synchronization, issue the SET TIMESYNC command at every receiver or source tree server. Below is a list of the four SET TIMESYNC commands:

SET TIMESYNC Command	Description
SET TIMESYNC TIME SOURCE = time_source	time_source is the target tree server
SET TIMESYNC TYPE = SECONDARY	
SET TIMESYNC WRITE PARAMETERS = ON	Creates the TIMESYNC.CFG file with new parameters as type = SECONDARY, and time source = time_source.
SET TIMESYNC RESTART FLAG = ON	Makes the source server read the changes from the configuration file and make them immediately.

You can start merging the tree as soon as you receive the message "Time synchronization has been established". To merge the tree, you need to load DSMERGE.NLM from the source tree server. See figure 6.1 for the DSMERGE.NLM main menu. Make sure you do the following while merging the trees:

Figure 6.1 DSMERGE.NLM main menu.

1) Check the servers and time synchronization.

2) Track the merging progress of the trees. You may use the DSTRACE screen on the target server to monitor the merging process by entering the following command at the target server console:

SET DSTRACE = ON

This will display a message that the merge is complete once we exit DSMERGE.

3) Validate the merging by loading DSREPAIR.NLM and use the "Replica synchronization" option to check if there are any errors. See figure 6.2 for the DSREPAIR.NLM main menu.

Figure 6.2 DSREPAIR.NLM main menu.

4) Clean up the merged tree using NWADMIN. To accomplish this you may need to move containers with their objects, rename objects according to the naming conventions, copy existing container login scripts to the new containers if needed, and delete unneeded containers after their objects and information have been moved.

5) Modify the configuration files for login. NDS names and context will be changed as a result of the merge. You need to make some changes to the parameters on the server and client workstations as follows:

Location of file	File that needs to be changed	Command that needs to be changed
Workstation	NET.CFG	NAME CONTEXT = context
Workstation	NET.CFG	PREFERRED TREE tree_name
Server	AUTOEXEC.NCF	BINDERY CONTEXT = context

6.2 NDS PARTITIONS AND REPLICAS

The NDS directory has characteristics, such as it is a database that replaces the bindery and contains information on all objects in the directory tree. It also uses the directory for access control, uses the directory for authentication, which is a part of login security, and does not contain data on the file system except for the server and volume objects. A large directory may contain information on thousands of objects. You may divide (partition) the directory into multiple partitions to reduce network traffic and provide fault tolerance. You can only partition the directory along the boundaries of container objects. The partition is a part of the whole directory and it may contain one or more containers and their associated leaf objects. Make sure that you partition only containers that have no more than 5000 objects.

Here is a list of terms that are used throughout this chapter:

- Partition—This is a division of the directory along the boundary of a container object.

- Replica—This is a copy of all the information in a partition. It is an image or a snapshot of a partition. All of the replicas in the directory tree compose the directory.

- Root partition—This is the container in the partition which is closest to the [Root].

- Parent partition—This is a partition which is directly above the partition root of another container.

- Child partition—This is a partition which is subordinate to another partition in the directory tree.

Replicas are stored on any server on the network in the directory tree. You can store only one replica of a partition on one server. Remember that creating multiple partitions does not increase fault tolerance or improve performance by itself. Distributing the replicas on multiple servers does provide fault tolerance, because multiple replicas on various servers make NDS data always available. In addition, it reduces network traffic because you will be making NDS data accessible locally and enabling users to use the network services even if a server goes down.

There are four types of replicas:

- Master replica—A master replica is always created when you first define a
  partition. Each partition must have only one master replica. It can be used for login
  authentication, and any changes made to an object in the master replica will be
  propagated to all other replicas of that partition. You must be able to access the
  server that holds the master replica before you can split the partition or merge the
  partition with another.

- Read/write replica—You may have multiple read/write replicas for a partition.
  Read/write replicas may be used for login authentication. Any changes made to an
  object in the read/write replicas will be propagated to all other replicas of that
  partition. You cannot use read/write replicas to redefine the partition boundaries.

- Read-only replica—You may have multiple read-only replicas for a partition.
  Read-only replicas are used only for searching and viewing objects. You cannot
  modify objects on read-only replicas. They cannot be used for login authentication.
  They only receive and propagate changes made to the master of the read/write
  replicas.

- Subordinate replicas (Subordinate references)—Subordinate replicas are
  maintained by NDS automatically and can never be modified. NDS uses them to
  refer to other types of replicas and to facilitate tree connectivity. Subordinate
  replicas do not contain data about any object in a partition. They only point to
  another replica of a child partition. Subordinate replicas do not support login
  authentication or viewing or managing objects.

When the first IntranetWare server is created, the first partition is also created. In
addition the master replica of this partition is stored on the SYS volume of the same
server. If you installed another server in an existing tree, IntranetWare will expand the
partition to include the new server in the existing partition. It will not create any new
partitions. It will create and place a read/write replica on the second and third servers
in the partition. However, IntranetWare will not create or place any replicas on the
fourth or subsequent servers.

You can turn a read/write or read-only replica into a master replica if the server
that has the master replica goes down. The original master replica will become a
read/write once the server is back on line. NDS automatically places a subordinate
replica on a server if either the parent partition has a master, read/write, or read-only
replica on the server or the child partition does not have a master, read/write, or read-
only replica on the server. However, NDS will automatically delete any subordinate
replicas from the server if read/write or read-only replicas are added to the child
partition to the server.

When you merge trees together, servers in the source tree that contain the replica
of the [Root] partition receive a read/write replica of the new [Root] partition, and

receive subordinate replicas of the child partition to the [Root] partition. Servers in the target tree that contain a replica of the [Root] partition receive subordinate replicas of the top-level partitions of the source partition. When you upgrade a server from NetWare 3 to IntranetWare 4.11, the server receives a read/write replica of all partitions containing the bindery contexts of the server.

A replica ring is a ring that includes all the servers of the same partition. NDS periodically updates and synchronizes the replicas of a partition. Therefore, the more replicas you have in the ring, the longer it will take to synchronize them. Remember that it takes even longer to synchronize changes if you have servers in the replica ring separated by a relatively slow WAN link. Hence, the limiting factor in creating multiple replicas depends on how much synchronization cost the network can accommodate. This includes the amount of processing time required to synchronize and the amount of communication traffic required for synchronizing. Novell recommends that you only create between three to six replicas of each partition in one tree.

You should replicate partitions to create NDS fault tolerance and increase efficiency of users. You can manage partitions and replicas easily if you adhere to the following guidelines:

1) Create only three to six replicas for each partition to meet the needs of NDS fault tolerance. You may create additional replicas to make login and network resource access time faster for users.

2) Partition the directory along the boundaries of each workgroup and its associated resources. You should place replicas of each partition containing data used by a workgroup on servers that are physically close to that workgroup.

3) Make sure that each server contains a master or read/write replica that contains the bindery context if the bindery services are needed.

Make sure to replicate the [Root] partition properly. The [Root] is the most important partition of the directory tree. If the [Root] partition is lost, then the directory tree becomes inaccessible. The [Root] partition and high-level partitions often have multiple child partitions. When you place a replica of the [Root] partition on the server without placing the replicas of its child partitions, NDS creates subordinate replicas for all of its child partitions on the server. This may increase synchronization cost. Make sure not to replicate the [Root] or high-level partitions too many times.

Always consider subordinate replicas in the partition and replica design because any partition operation affects subordinate replicas as well as other types of replicas. For example, when you make a partition change, the directory will not be synchronized if you have subordinate replicas linked to other replicas across a WAN or if the other replicas are not available or the WAN link is down. To reduce the number of subordinate replicas, you must adhere to the following guidelines:

1) Create few partitions at the top levels of the tree. This will cause the NDS to create fewer subordinate replicas.

2) Avoid unneeded partitions. Workgroup boundaries should determine the number of partitions needed. You should always partition the tree according to how the network resources are used and where the network resources are located in the tree.

3) Avoid unneeded replicas of the [Root] partition or other parent partitions. Remember that when you place a replica of the [Root] partition on a server, NDS creates subordinate replicas for all of its child partitions on the server.

Moving a container object is considered a partition operation. You must make the container the root of a partition before you can move it. If you do not do this NDS will give you a warning message. After you move a container, the structure of the directory tree will change and the distinguished name for each object in the container will also change. Hence, to adapt to the directory changes after you have moved a container, each user in the container may log in to the network by using a new NDS distinguished name or using an NDS common name after you change the "NAME CONTEXT =" statement in the NET.CFG file. You may use the NDSMGR32.EXE utility (NDS Manager) to manage partitions and replicas. NDSMGR32.EXE is located in the directory PUBLIC\WIN95\NDSMGR32.EXE. Figure 6.3 shows the platform of NDSMGR32.

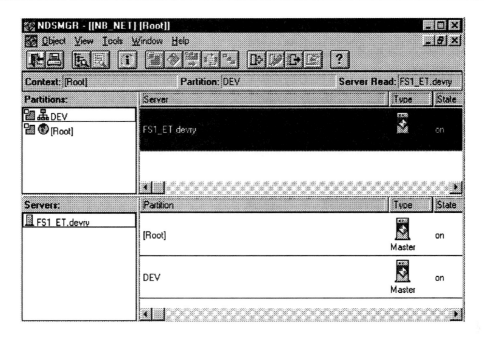

Figure 6.3 NDSMGR32.EXE.

You may use the following criteria to determine if you should partition the directory tree:

1) No new partitions are created automatically by default. Do not create any additional partitions if you have no WAN links, if 15 or fewer servers are holding replicas, or if you have 5,000 or fewer objects in a partition. The recommended maximum number of objects in a partition for IntranetWare is 5,000 objects

2) You should partition the directory by location to reduce WAN traffic. Hence, updates to the directory can occur on a local server since all objects in each partition are at a single location.

3) Split a partition to reduce the synchronization traffic if you have 15 or more servers holding replicas in the same partition.

4) Some servers will automatically receive numerous subordinate references if you have partitioned the directory by location. You may create a level of regional partitions above the physical locations to reduce the number of subordinate references.

6.3 TIME SYNCHRONIZATION

Time synchronization is performed to ensure that all servers in a directory report the same time. This is done to make sure that all time stamps among servers are accurate in the replica ring and to order the NDS events correctly. NDS events that rely on time stamps are file and directory operations, messaging applications, and any other NDS operation. A time stamp is a unique code that includes the time of the event and uses Universal Time Coordinated (UTC). UTC is a time system that adjusts time for the local time zone of the server and corrects the local time to get the equivalent of the Greenwich Mean Time (GMT). NDS uses time stamps to establish the order of events, record "real time" time values, and set expiration dates on events. NDS will always request a time stamp whenever events occur in the directory. A time stamp is always assigned to an NDS event so that the orders in which the directory replicas are updated or synchronized are correct. IntranetWare uses TIMESYNC.NLM, which is automatically loaded when the server boots up, to control time synchronization. TIMESYNC.NLM uses parameters that are stored in a file called TIMESYNC.CFG. You can edit TIMESYNC.CFG with any text editor, but remember that you have to reboot the server when you make changes to the file TIMESYNC.CFG file.

Every IntranetWare server is a timeserver of some kind. Timeservers are servers that provide a consistent source for the time stamps and ensure that each stamp is accurate. IntranetWare timeservers are divided into four different types:

- Single reference server—This is the default configuration for the first timeserver. It cannot coexist with any other reference or primary servers. It is mainly used for small networks without any WAN links. This timeserver determines the time for the entire network and is the only source of time on the network. It gets its time from a hardware clock or an external source and provides the time to secondary timeservers and workstations. You can have only one single reference server on the network. All other servers must be made secondary time servers.

- Reference servers—These are servers that vote with primary or other reference servers to decide what the common network time should be. You must have at least one primary server on the same network that the reference time server can contact for polling. A reference server provides a central point of time control for the entire network. It does not adjust its internal clock: it gets its time from a hardware clock or an external source and provides time to primary and secondary servers and to the workstations. Usually, only one reference timeserver is installed on a network. If you have more than one reference timeserver on a network, you must synchronize each reference server with an external time source.

- Primary servers—These are servers that vote with other primary or reference servers to decide what the common network time should be. You must have at least one additional primary or reference server on the same network that a primary timeserver can contact for polling. A primary timeserver synchronizes time with at least one other primary or reference server. It corrects 50% clock errors per polling interval and provides time to secondary timeservers and to the workstations.

- Secondary servers—This is the default configuration for the additional timeservers on a network. It does not participate in voting of correct network time. It gets time from a single reference, reference, or primary timeserver. It corrects 100% clock errors per polling interval and provides time to the workstations only.

If you have several servers on the network as primary or reference timeservers, you should make all other servers on the network secondary timeservers. To keep traffic to a minimum, you should connect secondary timeservers to primary or reference timeservers that are physically nearby. To optimize time synchronization, you should minimize the number of routers and slow LAN segments between time providers and secondary timeservers. There are two ways to keep timeservers synchronized:

1) Default configuration—When you install IntranetWare, the program will assume that only two types of timeservers are needed, single reference and secondary servers. This configuration is used primarily for small networks without any WAN links. The default method uses the Service Advertising Protocol (SAP) to advertise the time sources. Therefore, time providers know which server to arbitrate time with. In addition, secondary servers know where to get their time. If a single reference server goes down, you may use SERVMAN.NLM or the SET parameters to set up a secondary server as a new single reference server. The default configuration method is simple, efficient, and requires no redefinition of time synchronization when adding a new server. Below is a list of the advantages and disadvantages of using the default configuration method:

Advantages

a) It is easy to understand.

b) No planning is required.

c) There is no need to provide a configuration file for each file server.

d) Minimum errors, since the secondary server will talk only to the time provider.

Disadvantages

a) The single reference server must be contacted by every other server on the network.

b) One misconfigured server may disrupt the whole network.

c) Since the single reference server is the only time provider, it is a single point of failure.

2) Custom configuration—This type of configuration uses reference and primary servers as time providers to minimize the single point of failure. To customize time synchronization, you should decide on which servers will be time sources and which time provider individual servers will refer to, and you should give each server a configuration file using TIMESYNC.CFG. You may copy the same TIMSYNC.CFG file to several servers and change the contents of it including the authorized time sources and other parameters for the server. Custom configuration is usually used in large networks because it reduces network traffic, but it requires additional administration. Below is a list of the advantages and disadvantages of using the custom configuration method:

Advantages

a) It has complete control of the time synchronization hierarchy.

b) It optimizes the network traffic and distributes time sources in the network.

c) It provides alternate time sources to be used in case of network failure.

Disadvantages

a) It requires careful planning.

b) It requires updating the configuration files on several servers when adding new time sources.

You may reduce the administration of configured lists by using the command:

SET Directory Tree Mode = ON

This command allows timeservers throughout the tree to listen to a vote with time servers in the same directory tree. Another command to reduce the administration of configured lists is:

SET SAP mode = ON

This command allows timeservers to send and receive time broadcasts over SAP. To customize time synchronization, you need to adhere to the following guidelines to create a hierarchical structure based on the physical location of the servers:

1) Make sure to keep the number of time sources small to reduce network traffic. You should not have more than five references and primary servers on the network.

2) Make sure to distribute time sources to provide local access throughout the network. Other servers look for these regional time providers for their time. If the time sources are good timekeepers, you may increase the polling interval to an hour or more to reduce network traffic.

3) Make sure to have secondary servers synchronized to the closest time source. In each location, you should order the time source list as follows: the closest timeserver appears first, the lowest cost time providers appear next, and then the rest of the time providers.

You may want to create a time provider group at each location for a network that consists of a large number of servers at multiple locations. This will reduce time synchronization traffic across the WAN. Each time provider group should be composed of the following time server types:

1) There should be a reference server at each location using a dial-up time service, such as a radio clock. The reference server could then synchronize to a common clock without generating any synchronization traffic across the WAN.

2) You should have as few primary servers as you can manage at each location. Each primary server will use the local reference server as its time source.

3) All other servers at each location should be secondary servers. Each secondary server will have a list of the local primary servers as the time sources in its TIMESYNC.CFG file.

When you bring an IntranetWare 4.11 server online, the server sets its clock to the network time. A time provider will adjust to 100% when it comes on line with the network. You can minimize time synchronization problems by doing the following:

1) Before booting the server set DOS, or the hardware clock to the proper local time. Then execute SERVER.EXE.

2) During the server boot, check and make sure that the AUTOEXEC.NCF file has the correct time zone and daylight savings time information.

3) After the server boot, monitor the server console for a few minutes. Make sure that the time does not adjust by an hour or more. If it does, then down the server immediately, check the time, and check the time synchronization in the AUTOEXEC.NCF file. Never let the server run for more than 20 minutes with an excessively incorrect time. It may cause unpredictable problems with the network clock.

You may use the following procedures to change time synchronization parameters:

1) Load SERVMAN.NLM to change the TIMESYNC parameters. Remember that if you use this method, changes will be lost once the server is rebooted.

2) Issue the "SET TIMESYNC parameter" command at the file server console prompt. You may not include SET TIMESYNC commands in the STARTUP.NCF file. Again, if you use this method, changes will be lost once the server is rebooted.

3) Load and edit TIMESYNC.CFG from the SYS: \SYSTEM directory. TIMESYNC.CFG has all the time synchronization parameters. You may use any text editor to edit the TIMESYNC.CFG file. If you use this method, you have to reboot the server for the changes to take effect.

Below is a list of the SET TIMESYNC parameters with the default values shown:

Parameter	Description
Add Time Source	Adds a timeserver to the configuration list.
Configuration File = SYS: \SYSTEM\	Sets a path for different TIMESYNC.CFG files.
Configured Sources = Off	Does not use time sources in the configuration list.
Default Time Server Type = Secondary	Sets the default timeserver. This command can be set in STARTUP.NCF.
Directory Tree Mode = On	Synchronizes with servers in the same directory tree.
Hardware Clock = On	Used to have all servers in the same tree have the same setting. A single reference or reference timeserver reads the hardware clock at the beginning of each polling loop. A primary or secondary timeserver sets the hardware clock. Set it off if you are using an external time source.
Polling Count = 3	Sets how many times packets can exchange while polling. The range is from 1 to 1,000.

Polling Interval = 600 (seconds)	Used to have all servers in the same tree have the same value. The range is from 10 to 2,678,400 seconds (a maximum of 31 days).
Remove Time Source	Removes timeservers from the configuration list.
Reset = Off	Clears the configured list and resets values if Reset = On.
Reset Flag = Off	Reloads TIMESYNC.NLM after you have edited the TIMESYNC.CFG file without rebooting the server if Reset Flag = On. The flag automatically resets to off.
Service Advertising = On	Allows the time provider to use SAP. If it is set off, then the time provider will use a custom list of time sources.
Synchronization Radius = 2000	Used to set a margin of error for time synchronization. Some servers may not synchronize if Synchronization Radius is < 1000. The range is from 0 to 2,678,647 milliseconds.
Time Source	Displays or adds a timeserver to the configuration list.
Type = Secondary	Sets the timeserver type.
Write Parameters = Off	Changes the setting in TIMESYNC.CFG if Write Parameters = On.
Write Values	Modifies the TIMESYNC.CFG file. The range is between 1 to 3.

For a detailed directory tree design, you must consider certain issues, such as how NDS security affects the directory tree design and how to partition the directory. In addition, you should consider where to place the replicas, which timeserver types should be used for each server, and the possible conflict and network traffic needs for synchronizing time.

1) NDS directory security—First, you must decide on whether to use centralized or distributed administration. You can use the default ADMIN object for centralized administration, but you must set up container administrators with proper rights for distributed administration. Second, you must provide access to resources by placing groups in the directory. You can use containers for workgroups in a small company, and group objects for workgroups in a large company. Third, you must plan for the inheritance and security equivalence, since group and container design affects the directory tree design. You can use group membership, since groups supply rights to their members and are listed in the "Security Equal To List". You can also use parent containers (security equivalent is implied), since parent containers supply rights to their children containers and are not shown in the "Security Equal To List". Fourth, you must assign server object rights. Remember that rights to server objects will flow to the file system. Therefore, do not assign

the supervisor [S] right to the server object to any object. Finally, you must provide traveling users access.

2) Partitioning and replicating the directory tree—First, you must plan the partition boundaries by considering WAN topology and geographic locations, information flow, workgroup needs, required access to the directory information, and the number of objects in the containers in order to avoid single point failure and to reduce network traffic. Second, you must identify and assign the replicas properly. Remember that the default replicas help prevent a single point failure and that a master replica is placed on the first server in the partition by default. The read/write replicas are placed on the second and third servers in the partition by default. Make sure to place additional replicas for fault tolerance and accessibility. Third, you must balance access and System Fault Tolerance (SFT) versus performance by providing accessibility and fault tolerance, increasing network performance, and minimizing replica synchronization traffic. Fourth, make sure to allow for WAN links by minimizing replica synchronization traffic. You can make smaller partitions on a few servers to achieve this. Finally, assign partition and replica administrators to coordinate NDS changes to reduce network traffic.

3) Consider the possible conflict and network traffic needs for synchronizing time— First, you should plan timeserver types to provide a solid plan to all the network administrators. You can use the default timeservers for small workgroups and a custom timeserver configuration for a divisional or organizational directory tree. Second, coordinate time sources to coordinate the plan with other administrators. You can decide on what type of time provider groups you should have to maximize time synchronization, hence minimizing network traffic. Third, reduce WAN traffic: you should never let time providers communicate with secondary servers across WAN links in a large network. Finally, synchronize time for merging trees. To accomplish this, you must have the servers synchronized prior to the merger.

6.4 INTEGRATING NETWARE 3.1X

IntranetWare 4.11 bindery services make the IntranetWare server appear as a NetWare 3.1x server. Bindery clients and applications may then use limited NDS services. NetWare 2 and 3 have no NDS services. They use bindery as a flat database of objects. Since it is a flat database, the bindery objects do not relate to each other. NDS on the other hand is a hierarchical structure database where objects do relate to each other. Each bindery contains objects known to and associated with the NetWare 2 or 3 server, such as users, groups, print servers, and print queues. NetWare bindery does not contain IntranetWare NDS objects or provide NDS object properties. NetWare 2 and 3 bindery is server based. Hence, each NetWare 2 or 3 server must have its own bindery and network users must log in, or attach to each server separately.

IntranetWare bindery services associate NDS leaf objects within a server to create a flat structured bindery for that server on a container-by-container basis. All of the leaf objects in the bindery context are considered part of the bindery of that server. NDS objects or bindery clients, servers, or applications using bindery services may access all of the leaf objects within a bindery context. With bindery services, you may use applications written for NetWare 2 or 3, such as third-party print servers and backup applications in the IntranetWare network. These applications calls to the NetWare bindery to perform network functions. IntranetWare bindery services allow you to manage and use some, or limited NDS objects and properties as if they were part of a NetWare 3.1x bindery. Bindery services work by making NDS objects appear as if they were in a flat bindery. They work only on NDS objects that correspond to bindery objects. In order for NetWare 3.1x clients using old shell to log on to an IntranetWare server, you must place the corresponding user objects in a bindery context and use SYSCON to create the system and user login scripts for the users. Remember that when NetWare clients use the old NetWare shell, or NETx, to try to log on to an IntranetWare server which does not have a bindery context set, they will receive a "BINDERY LOCK" error message.

When you install an IntranetWare server in the directory tree, NDS creates a server object in a container object. It also sets the default bindery context at that container's object and activates the bindery services. The bindery context is a container object where you set the bindery services. All the leaf objects in the bindery contexts appear as a bindery to NetWare 2 and 3 clients. You must set the bindery context to the container objects where you have user objects that need resources through bindery services. Container, profile, and user login scripts are properties of the corresponding NDS objects. They are not available through bindery services. When you use bindery applications to create objects, all of the objects are placed in the bindery context. A server must have a master or read/write replica of all partitions that include the bindery contexts of the server.

You may set up to 16 bindery contexts for each IntranetWare 4.11 server. You can use the following SET command at the file server console to set the bindery context:

SET BINDERY CONTEXT = context_1; context_2 ...etc.

Make sure that there are no leading periods specified in "context". Use a semicolon ";"to separate each context. Another SET command you may want to use is:

SET BINDERY CONTEXT = ou=engin.o=acme;o=acme ...etc.

To set the contexts temporarily enter this command at the server console. To set it permanently, add the command in the AUTOEXEC.NCF file. You may also use SERVMAN.NLM at the server console to set the bindery context, make it effective immediately, and add the command to the AUTOEXEC.BAT file at the same time.

Bindery clients, servers, or applications can only view the objects with a bindery-compatible name. The name must be the common name of the objects among all the bindery contexts. Hence, you should name each object in the bindery context according to the bindery compatible naming rules. In addition, you must use a unique common name among all the possible 16 bindery containers. If there is a common name conflict among the bindery contexts, the first client will receive the service requested and any other objects with the same common name will be denied the services.

To synchronize binderies on NetWare 3.1x servers with the IntranetWare 4.11 server, you must use the NETSYNC program. You may use NETSYNC to synchronize up to 12 NetWare 3.1x servers with each NetWare 4.11 server. You may also load NETSYNC on all servers in the NETSYNC cluster. Once synchronized, you must manage all the objects in the NETSYNC cluster as NDS objects. You may use NETSYNC to copy NetWare 3.1x binderies into an IntranetWare NDS container. You must use NWADMIN or NETADMIN to manage all the users, groups, print services, and other bindery objects on the NetWare 3.1x servers in the NETSYNC cluster as part of the directory tree.

NETSYNC hardware requirements are an IntranetWare 4.11 server or up to 12 NetWare 3.1x servers. The software requirements are NETSYNC files or one unused licensed connection on the IntranetWare 4.11 host server. NETSYNC consists primarily of three NLMs:

1) NETSYNC4.NLM—This NLM must be loaded on the IntranetWare 4.11 host server first. IntranetWare uses NETSYNC4.NLM to control the NETSYNC cluster. You may also load NETSYNC4.NLM in the AUTOEXEC.NCF file. This NLM will use one licensed connection on the IntranetWare 4.11 host server. Each IntranetWare 4.11 host server can support up to 12 NetWare 3.1x servers.

2) NETSYNC3.NLM—This NLM may be loaded on each NetWare 3.1x server in the cluster only after NETSYNC4.NLM has been loaded on the IntranetWare 4.11 host server. You may also add NETSYNC3.NLM in the AUTOEXEC.NCF file. NETSYNC3.NLM uploads, or copies the NetWare 3.1x bindery information to the bindery context on the IntranetWare 4.11 host server initially. It will then keep a constant communication with its IntranetWare 4.11 host server and receive updates to its bindery.

3) REMAPID.NLM—NETSYNC3.NLM automatically loads REMAPID.NLM on each NetWare 3.1x server. REMAPID.NLM must remain loaded after you unload NETSYNC3.NLM because it is used to handle the password synchronization.

Remember that first you have to load NETSYNC (NETSYNC4.NLM) on the host server. Then you must load NETSYNC (NETSYNC3.NLM) on the NetWare 3.1x servers. If there is any print server defined in the NetWare 3.1x server, NETSYNC3.NLM will make the "Move a Print Server" option available. You may use the "Move a Print Server" option from NETSYNC3.NLM to either move a NetWare 3.1x print server to the IntranetWare 4.11 host server or merge the NetWare 3.1x print servers into IntranetWare 4.11 print servers. During the "Move a Print Server" operation, it creates an NDS printer object for each of the NetWare 3.1x printers. It will also create an NDS print queue object for each of the NetWare 3.1x print queue and create an NDS print server object if you have moved the NetWare 3.1x print server. After the "Move a Print Server" operation, the existing NetWare 3.1x print queues appear the same to the NetWare 3.1x users. The IntranetWare 4.11 print server now services the existing NetWare 3.1x queues. Finally IntranetWare 4.11 clients may print to the new NDS printer objects.

Below is a list of the times you should consider, or not consider using NETSYNC in a mixed NetWare 3.1x and IntranetWare 4.11 environment:

Consider using NETSYNC:

1) If you have NetWare Name Services (NNS) running and do not want to upgrade all servers in the NNS domain to IntranetWare 4.11 simultaneously.

2) If you plan not to upgrade to IntranetWare 4.11; that means you want to manage all the users, groups, and print servers on the NetWare 3.1x servers without upgrading to IntranetWare 4.11

3) If you want to centralize the network administration of a mixed network temporarily before full migration to IntranetWare 4.11.

Do not consider using NETSYNC:

1) If you plan to migrate all of the NetWare 3.1x servers to IntranetWare 4.11 shortly.

2) If you plan to separate administration and want to use NetWare 3.1x utilities, such as SYSCON, to manage all the NetWare 3.1x servers.

3) If you have no need to include NetWare 3.1x bindery objects in the IntranetWare 4.11 directory database.

4) If you have only IntranetWare 4.11 on the network.

To install NETSYNC on a mixed server's network, you need to adhere to the following steps:

1) Plan carefully. Resolve duplicate name conflicts between 3.1x and 4.11. Set bindery context at the 4.11 server console. The NetWare 3.1x bindery will copy to the first context in the list.

2) Install NETSYNC4.NLM on 4.11 on the host server.

3) Install NETSYNC3.NLM on the NetWare 3.1x server. REMAPID.NLM and NETSYNC3.NLM will be loaded from the AUTOEXEC.NCF file. You can move or merge print servers if required.

4) Check the NetWare 3.1x synchronization. Use NWADMIN to make sure that all NetWare 3.1x objects are added to the first bindery context. Also make sure that you can create a user object. You must use NWADMIN to create a server object for NetWare 3.1x and a volume object for each volume attached in the NetSync cluster. Finally check the login script and effective rights granted to all users.

Questions

1) Name three advantages to creating replicas.
2) What are the considerations if you down a server, which has the only replica of a partition?
3) Name four considerations for partitioning.
4) Give two statements that are true about default partitioning and replication.
5) Name four considerations for partitioning and replicating NDS.
6) What must you do first when you want to move a container?
7) Describe what a master replica is.
8) Describe what a read/write replica is.
9) Describe what a read-only replica is.
10) Describe what a subordinate replica is.
11) Give three ways to minimize the number of subordinate references on the network.
12) How many replicas of each partition in your directory tree does Novell recommend?

13) What are two tasks that must be performed when implementing changes to an NDS partition?

14) Describe what IntranetWare time servers are.

15) What is the time server type that can coexist with a single reference time server?

16) Give four advantages that the default method of time synchronization gives.

17) What is a time synchronization consideration when servers are linked across a WAN?

18) Which command causes an IntranetWare server to read changes from the commands in the TIMESYNC.CFG configuration file immediately?

19) When servers are installed into an existing directory tree, which servers receive a read/write replica of the partition?

20) What three things affect the amount of time required for a change to be replicated and synchronized throughout the "loosely consistent" NDS database?

21) Give three symptoms (problems) that may indicate that replicas are out of synchronization.

22) What two problems does the presence of unknown objects in the directory tree indicate?

23) Give three guidelines you should consider to avoid NDS database problems and inconsistencies.

24) Give four procedures that can be used to troubleshoot and repair NDS.

25) Give two procedures that can be performed to recover from a disaster when a server with a master replica is corrupted.

26) Give three steps you should take if a server containing the master replica for a partition goes down due to the failure of a hard drive containing the SYS: volume.

27) Server A has the master replica and server B has a read/write replica of the partition. The router linking the two servers has gone down. You will have someone to fix it this afternoon. What needs to be done?

28) A server that contains the only replica of a partition is going to go down for more than a week. What action should be taken?

29) If a server fails, what two actions must be taken?

30) To solve problems with your directory that cannot be repaired with DSREPAIR, what should you do as a last resort?

31) Why do you want to use bindery services to integrate a NetWare 3 client and an IntranetWare 4.11 server?

32) How does an IntranetWare 4.11 server SET bindery context for a NetWare 3 client?

33) What can be used to merge the printing service of NetWare 3.1x to that of 4.x servers?

34) Describe bindery services.

35) How many bindery contexts can be set for each IntranetWare server?

36) How does using a bindery-compatible naming convention help integrate NetWare 3 and IntranetWare?

37) What are the three NDS objects that can be seen and accessed by bindery users?
38) If bindery clients in two containers have the same common name and a server's bindery context is set to both containers, what happens if both users attempt to request bindery services?
39) How do you set bindery context in an IntranetWare network?
40) What are the primary software components of a NETSYNC cluster?
41) Name the four components that are needed to create a NETSYNC cluster.
42) How do you integrate 12 NetWare 3 servers into an IntranetWare network?
43) Give four statements that correctly describe the changes possible to the print services in a NETSYNC cluster.

7

Network Services and Optimizing the Network

This chapter discusses the functions of the MultiProtocol Router 3.1 (MPR), the concept of the NetWare Web Server, and how to enable internationalization. In addition, you will learn to how manage IntranetWare memory, and how to optimize the network and server.

7.1 INTRANET MANAGEMENT

An intranet is simply a Web server that is confined to a private internal network and publishes files to a private audience. The Internet publishes files to the world. IntanetWare has the following features for Intranet and Internet:

- IPX/IP Gateway—This enables administrators to allow IPX-based workstation to access TCP/IP-based resources, such as FTP and the World Wide Web (WWW), without having to install or configure TCP/IP on those workstations. It also allows administrators to implement access control by limiting users by TCP port number, IP address or target host, and the time of day. When the IPX/IP gateway is installed in the IntranetWare server, the server runs IPX to communicate with IPX workstations on the network, and runs TCP/IP so that it can communicate with the Internet. Using IPX/IP, you can run only IPX on the network workstations. Compared to IP, IPX is a lot simpler to manage. Finally, the IPX/IP gateway allows you to limit access to Internet services by the type of traffic (Web browser or FTP) and by remote host. You can configure the IPX gateway by choosing the "Protocols" option in the INETCFG.NLM utility (see figure 7.1).

- NetWare MPR (MultiProtocol Router 3.1)—This provides WAN connectivity, and routing of multiple protocols over leased lines, frame relay, or ISDN lines. This is what makes you able to connect to an Internet Service Provider (ISP). MPR includes a suite of software that provides internetworking between dissimilar types of systems, runs on standard PC-compatible hardware, and supports various transport protocols used in LANs. MPR provides three major services:

1) It connects dissimilar media, frame types, and transports at all levels in the ODI layers using the NetWare Link Services Protocol (NLSP).

2) It improves performance by off loading routing tasks from busy servers to dedicated machines.

3) It provides security by isolating traffic on LAN segments.

NetWare MPR 3.1 includes routing capabilities for several communications protocols including IntranetWare IPX/SPX (default), UNIX, TCP/IP, Macintosh AppleTalk, and NetWare Link Services Protocol (NLSP). It also allows you to connect network LANs over leased lines, frame relays, or ISDN. MPR is installed using INSTALL.NLM. Once installed it is managed and configured using INETCFG.NLM. You may load INTECFG.NLM from the server console to configure and manage MPR, or to set routing and bridging configuration on the server. INETCFG.NLM will build the correct LOAD and BIND commands in the AUTOEXEC.NCF file. You must reboot the server to activate the changes added to the AUTOEXEC.NCF file. When you load INETCFG.NLM for the first time, it performs the following initialization tasks:

1) It saves the AUTOEXEC.NCF file as AUTOEXEC.BAK in the directory SYS: \SYSTEM.

2) It creates a new AUTOEXEC.NCF file.

3) It imports the LOAD and BIND commands to the new AUTOEXEC.NCF file from the AUTOEXEC.BAK file.

4) It imports the LAN driver, protocol, and remote access commands to the new AUTOEXEC.NCF file from the AUTOEXEC.BAK file.

5) It inserts the following commands in the new AUTOEXEC.NCF file:

   a) LOAD CONLOG.NLM—This command enables the server to begin a log file of all messages that appear during the initialization. The console messages are stored in a console log file in the SYS:ETC directory.

   b) LOAD INITSYS.NCF—This command configures the server communications using the INET.CFG database. The network driver LOADs and BINDs are initiated using INITSYS.NCF. The actual LOAD and BIND commands are contained in the SYS:ETC\INITSYS.NCF file and the SYS:\INITSYS.CFG file.

c) UNLOAD CONLOG.NLM—This command stops the server from recording all console messages in the log file.

Figure 7.1 INETCFG main menu.

- FTP services for IntranetWare—This allows you to configure FTP access for your intranet network. With FTP services, users can use FTP to access and transfer files from the Intranet or Internet. If you wish, you can create your own anonymous FTP account for users to use.

- The NetWare Web Server—This is a Web server that allows you to publish HTML pages over the Internet and Intranet. It also has a Netscape browser that allows you to locate and read information from the Web. The NetWare Web Server 2.5 is a WWW server that comes with IntranetWare. A WWW server is a file server that serves or publishes files in HTML format. You can read the HTML files using applications called browsers. The difference between HTML files and text files is that HTML files do not contain any proprietary custom symbols or formatting characters. In addition, HTML files can include text or graphic links, which users can click on to move to another location in the same file or another file on any Web server in the world. A WWW Web server publishes files in HTML format, and communicates with browsers using HTTP (HyperText Transfer Protocol). HTTP runs over TCP/IP. To install the NetWare Web server, you need to configure your network to support TCP/IP and then run INSTALL.NLM to install the Web server product. Before installation, you must have the following hardware:

1) An IntranetWare server with a CD-ROM drive.

2) At least 2.5 MB of hard disk space, with additional disk space for new HTML files.

3) A workstation running Windows 3.x, Windows 95, or Windows NT. The workstation must be at least a 80386 machine with 4 MB of RAM, and 12.5 MB of hard disk space available for the Netscape Navigator browser (you can use a different browser if you prefer).

4) A Windows word processor with tools to create HTML files.

To install the Netscape Navigator browser on a Windows 3.1 workstation, execute the SETUP.EXE file, which is in the PRODUCTS\WEBSERV\BROWSER\N16E201 directory. To install the Netscape Navigator browser on a Windows 95 workstation, execute the SETUP.EXE file which is in the PRODUCTS\WEBSERV\BROWSER \N32E201 directory. To prepare the NetWare Web server installation, you must do the following:

1) Install the IntranetWare file server.

2) Establish IPX and TCP/IP communication between the two. You may do this by launching INTCFG.NLM to specify an IP address for the server and then bind it to the network board.

3) Launch PING.NLM to verify the TCP/IP communication with the workstation.

To install the NetWare Web server, you must do the following:

1) Load INSTALL .NLM.

2) Choose "Product Options".

3) Choose "Install NetWare Web Server".

4) Follow instructions until the NetWare Web server installation is completed.

Now you may press the keys <Alt> <Esc> at the server console to switch between the active services, such as the Novell HTTP server 2.5, which is the NetWare Web server NLM; the Novell Basic language interpreter, for dynamic Web page support; and the Novell Perl language interpreter, for dynamic Web page support. Now that you have created a Web site, you may launch your browser at a workstation, open a location from the file menu, and enter the Universal Resource Locator (URL), which is http://server_IP_Address. The default file INDEX.HTM is a file located in the directory SYS: \WEB\DOC that allows Web browsers to see when they access the site using the IP address. The Web server has three root directories.

1) SYS: root—This is the NetWare volume root directory.

2) SYS: \WEB server root—This directory contains all the configuration and control files associated with the Web site. Make sure that visitors to the site cannot access this directory.

3) Document root—This is a default path to all the files you want to publish. To protect the server configuration files, place this directory in a subdirectory of the server root directory or on a different volume.

After all this is done, you must configure name services on your Web server. If anybody wants to access your site, they must remember your IP address. To make this process easier, you can create a name service. A name service uses a table of IP addresses and names to establish names that can be used in place of the IP addresses. Each IP address can be associated with one or more names or aliases. There are two ways to create a name service on a network. The fastest way is to create a hosts file on your server. Or you can configure your server as a Domain Name Service (DNS) server or as a client of a DNS server. DNS is an Internet protocol that allows administrators to associate Internet addresses with names that people can remember. The hosts file approach provides name services only on your network and subnet, while DNS provides name service over an entire network or the Internet.

To create a table of IP addresses and host names, Create a file called HOSTS.TXT in the SYS: \ETC directory using a text editor. The file should look something like this:

#IP ADDRESS	ALIASES	COMMENTS
IP_Address	alias_1, alias_2	# the NetWare Web Server
IP_Address	alias_3	# ACME

Anything written after a "#" character will be ignored. To configure the NetWare Web server to use the name service of a DNS server, use a text editor to create a file named RESOLV.CFG in the SYS: \ETC directory. You must enter the following commands in this file:

Domain domain_name
Nameserver IP_Address

The domain_name is a variable used for the name of the domain in which the server is installed. The IP_Address is a variable used for the name of the IP address of the DNS server. It is time now to take a look at FTP services for IntranetWare.

Since IntranetWare extends the boundaries of your WAN, it needs to span the world. Hence, you are going to need to speak everyone's language.

Internationalization is a language support provided by IntranetWare. It can display text in non-English languages for utilities and system messages. In addition, it displays numbers, dates, times, and other parameters in alternative formats. It supports Asian languages, or double byte characters, and supports non-English filename characters and path names.

IntranetWare isolates all message strings from the source code. It places message strings in separate files called language modules. Message strings are text strings such as menu and error messages. It places all message strings in the source code with pointers to the location of the strings in the language modules. Language module file names are the names of programs with a .MSG extension. For example, SERVER.MSG is the language module for SERVER.EXE. Language modules for different languages all have the same name. Hence, you must keep language modules for different languages in different directories.

To set a different language for a server, you must down the server, copy the desired SERVER.MSG to the IntranetWare server boot directory, and reboot the server by executing SERVER.EXE. Changing the language of the server will change the language for the NLMs loaded later. The language designator determines the languages for the NLMs. The language designator directs the NLM loader to the NLS subdirectory for the language module. You may use the command LANGUAGE language_ designator to change the language. Here is a list of the language designators that IntranetWare supports:

Language Designator	Language
0	Canadian French
1	Chinese (Simplified)
2	Danish
3	Dutch
4	English
5	Finnish
6	French (France)
7	German
8	Italian
9	Japanese
10	Korean
11	Norwegian
12	Portuguese (Brazil)
13	Russian
14	Spanish (Latin America)
15	Swedish
16	Chinese (Traditional)
17	Polish
18	Portuguese (Portugal)
19	Spanish (Spain)
20	Hungarian
21	Czechoslovakian

The NLM message search hierarchy is based on the fact that every server has a default language for loading NLM messages and help files. This default language is based on the language designator. The NLM search hierarchy uses the language designator in connection with the directory structure SYS, SYSTEM, NLS, then language designator. IntranetWare uses this directory structure to load various languages on a server. The INSTALL.NLM automatically copies language modules to the proper NLS subdirectories each time a new international version is installed.

International server keyboard types are activated using KEYB.NLM. For example, you would type the following at the server console to define a French keyboard:

LOAD KEYB France

Here is a list of the IntranetWare international keyboard types:

Belgium	Norway
Brazil	Portugal
Canadian French	Russia
Denmark	Spain
France	Sweden
Germany	Swiss French
Italy	Swiss German
Japan	United Kingdom
Latin America	United States
Netherlands	US International

Note that the keyboard types are dependent on the code page set by DOS. Code pages are available to IntranetWare only if you have the correct UniCode files that match your code page number and country code. Most keyboard types work with the default code page.

The IntranetWare locale formats are in C:\NWSERVER\LCONFIG.SYS. Locale formats for international languages determine how time, dates, and numbers are formatted. IntranetWare packages each international version with its own LCONFIG.SYS file. You may use the following SET parameter at the workstation to set the language support for the client:

SET NWLANGUAGE = language

"language" can be replaced with English, Deutsch, Espanol, Francais, Italiano, and Portuguese. NWLANGUAGE is a DOS environment variable that tells the client to look for a specific message file for the utilities. You must set this language support to access online support within utilities. DynaText also uses the NWLANGUAGE variable to access the proper online manuals. The default English message files are used if no message files exist. You may include this language support command in the AUTOEXEC.BAT file.

7.2 MESSAGE HANDLING SERVICES

Message Handling Services (MHS) is an "engine" that provides messaging capabilities. MHS includes the capacity for storing, accessing, and delivering text, graphic, video, and audio data. MHS is slightly different from file services. MHS deals with communication and interaction between computer users. It also deals with transporting data from point to point and notifies the user of awaiting messages. For a simple local delivery, MHS has the following three components:

- Messaging server—This is an IntranetWare implementation of the MHS "engine". It accepts data from a variety of e-mail or messaging applications. The messaging server delivers messages to local user mailboxes and routes messages to other messaging engines for eventual delivery. The users may then use their own messaging applications to retrieve messages from their mailboxes.

- User mailboxes—This is the physical location on the messaging server where messages are delivered. You may use any e-mail and messaging application to send MHS messages to any NDS objects that can be assigned a mailbox.

- Messaging applications—IntranetWare includes two messaging applications: FirstMail for DOS and FirstMail for Windows. FirstMail is an NDS-aware e-mail application from Novell. MAIL.EXE is the DOS version of the FirstMail program and WMAIL.EXE is the Windows version of the FirstMail program. FirstMail is automatically installed in the SYS: PUBLIC directory of the messaging server during the MHS services installation. You can use any message-enabled application to exchange e-mail, share calendars, schedule facilities, and carry out other tasks.

In order to install MHS services for IntranetWare, you must identify the hardware and software requirements for MHS installation and install MHS services during or after initial IntranetWare installation. The software for MHS services is provided on the IntranetWare CD-ROM disk. MHS services for IntranetWare has no limits on mailboxes, but the license limits the number of concurrent users of MHS services. Before installation, the host IntranetWare server on which you are installing MHS services must have the following hardware requirements:

1) A minimum of 500 KB of additional free RAM.

2) 2.5 MB of free disk space for program storage.

3) Additional free disk space for user mailboxes.

After installation, the host IntranetWare server must meet the following hardware requirements. These depend on how many users and how many messages are exchanged daily:

Category	File server if less than 10 users and having 100 messages daily
CPU	A minimum of 80386, and above
Memory	A minimum of 12 MB
Additional hard disk space	A minimum of 65 MB
CD-ROM for installation	Yes

Category	File server if more than 10 users and having 100 messages daily
CPU	A minimum of 80386
Memory	A minimum of 16 MB
Additional hard disk space	A minimum of 65 MB and a minimum of 5 MB per mailbox
CD-ROM for installation	Yes

MHS for IntranetWare 4.11 provides a store-and-forward messaging engine. You may start messaging services as soon as MHS is installed. You do not need to configure FirstMail since it is an NDS-aware application. In Windows, you may use "File" then "New" program item option to create a FirstMail icon for WMAIL.EXE. If you are using a mail-enabled application that is not NDS-aware, you must register the application with MHS for IntranetWare 4.11 and add the application name to each user's list of applications.

IntranetWare provides the following four NDS objects especially for use with MHS services:

- Messaging routing group—This is a collection of interconnected messaging servers. IntranetWare creates a default messaging routing group during the first MHS installation. By default, it adds the subsequently installed MHS messaging engines to this group. You may want multiple MHS engines to route messages to each other using messaging routing groups by assigning all the desired messaging servers to the messaging routing servers list, or to use the messaging server by assigning the same messaging object to the messaging server.

- Messaging server—This identifies the host IntranetWare server and the location of the MHS directory structure (SYS: MHS). All the users mailboxes are located in SYS: MHS. It also enables the messaging services. It is created during MHS installation and does not require any configuration.

- Distribution list—This forwards messages to numerous user mailboxes. Only one copy of the message is delivered to the distribution list mailbox. The message is then replicated for every mailbox in the distribution list. Since multiple messages are routed with only one packet, network traffic is reduced. You may create a distribution list object to simplify the addressing of messages. You can use a distribution list to address mail to multiple mailboxes. Members of a distribution list object do not share login scripts or trustee assignments. A distribution list object may contain, or nest, other distribution list objects. You must associate a distribution list with a mailbox location or a messaging server object. You may use group objects to address mail to multiple user mailboxes, but remember that the member list of a group can not contain other groups.

- External entity—This represents a non-native NDS object. It is a placeholder that allows you to send messages to users who would otherwise not be listed in NDS. External entity objects are mostly imported into NDS for use with gateway software. Hence, objects are not created during MHS services installation.

Installing MHS during initial intranetWare installation is very similar to adding MHS after the initial IntranetWare installation. You must use the "Customized Installation" option to install IntranetWare 4.1.z and use "Product Options" to install MHS. Below are several examples on how to install and manage MHS services:

Example 1: How to install MHS after the Initial installation of IntranetWare.

Step 1: Load INSTALL.NLM.
Step 2: Choose "Product Options".
Step 3: Choose "Choose an item or product listed above".
Step 4: Choose "Install NetWare MHS".
Step 5: Specify the path to the MHS software.
Step 6: Enter the distinguished name for the postmaster general in the name field of the "Postmaster General Authentication" window. Usually, the ADMIN user object is the postmaster general.
Step 7: Enter the password for the Postmaster General in the "Postmaster General Authentication" window.
Step 8: Press the <Enter> key to continue.
Step 9: Choose the volume on which to install the MHS database.
Step 10:Add the statement "LOAD MHS" in the AUTOEXEC.NCF file.
Step 11:Exist the INSTALL.NLM menu.

Example 2: How to create a distribution list in NWADMIN.

Step 1: Invoke NWADMIN.

Step 2: Click on the "Object" menu.

Step 3: Click on "Create".

Step 3: Pick the "Distribution List" object.

Step 4: Click on the "OK" button.

Step 5: Enter a unique name in the Distribution List Name.

Step 6: Pick the "Browse" button to the right of the Mailbox Location field.

Step 7: Choose the desired Messaging Server object.

Step 8: Click on the "OK" button.

Step 9: Pick the "Define Additional Properties" option.

Step 10: Click on the "Create" button.

Step 11: Choose the "Members" property page button.

Step 12: Choose the "Add" button.

Step 13: Pick the desired objects from the objects list box.

Step 14: Click on the "OK" button.

Step 15: Click on the "OK" button to complete the settings.

Example 3: Since you can assign mailboxes to user, group, organization role, and organizational unit objects, show how to assign a mailbox through the users property of messaging server.

Step 1: Invoke NWADMIN.

Step 2: Pick the messaging server icon.

Step 3: Choose the "Users" property page button from the right.

Step 4: Click on the "Add" button.

Step 5: Pick the desired object from the objects list box.

Step 6: Click on the "OK" button.

Step 7: Click on the "OK" button to complete the assignment.

Example 4: Show how to assign mailboxes through the mailbox property page of an object.

Step 1: Invoke NWADMIN.

Step 2: Choose the desired user, group, organizational role, or organizational unit object.

Step 3: Pick the "Mailbox" property page from the rights.

Step 4: Click on the "Browse" icon to the right of the Mailbox Location field.

Step 5: Pick on the messaging server object from the object list box.

Step 6: Click on the "OK" button.

Step 7: Click on the "OK" button to complete the assignment.

Example 5: Since MHS automatically installs FirstMail in the SYS: \PUBLIC directory and the default path to the mailbox user is SYS: \MHS\MAIL\USERS\user_name

\DOCUMENT.DOC, MHS links the mailbox location through NDS to the corresponding messaging server object. Show how to use FirstMail to read or send an e-mail.

Step 1: Launch FirstMail in Windows by double-clicking on the FirstMail icon.
Step 2: Read a message as follows:

a) Click on the "Read New Mail" icon from the button panel.
b) Double-click on the desired message to read.

Step 3: Save the message as follows:

a) Highlight the message.
b) Click on the "Move" icon from the New Mail folder.
c) Double-click on the Mail folder and the message will be saved there.

Step 4: Send a message to a user object as follows:

a) Choose "File" from the menu bar.
b) Pick "New Message" from the option list.
c) Type the user object name in the "To" field.
d) Type a title for the message in the "Subj" field.
e) Type and complete the message in the message box.
f) Click on the "Send" icon, which is located to the left of the message box.

Step 5: Send one message to a distribution list object as follows:

a) Click on the "Send Mail" icon from the button panel.
b) Type the distribution list object name in the "To" field.
c) Type a title for the message in the "Subj" field.
d) Type and complete the message in the message box.
e) Click on the "Send" icon, which is located to the left of the message box.

Step 6: Exit FirstMail and Windows.

Example 1 showed how to install MHS services after the initial installation of IntranetWare. During the MHS installation, several events take place:

1) The default message routing group object is created. "MHS_ROUTING_GROUP" is assigned as the default object name and the ADMIN object is assigned as the default owner of the message routing group.

2) The default messaging server is then created.

3) A Postmaster General is assigned for the messaging server, as well as the default mailbox location for ADMIN to the messaging server and the default mailbox identification. If you delete the ADMIN user object later, you must reassign the owner of the message routing group and the postmaster for the messaging server. Failure to do so will cause extensive troubleshooting problems.

4) The property value is assigned to the object property. For the default messaging routing group object, the Admin object is assigned as the Postmaster general and the default messaging server to the messaging server's property. For the default messaging server object, the Admin object is assigned as the Postmaster General, the local IntranetWare server to the IntranetWare servers property, and the default messaging routing group to the messaging routing groups property. For the local IntranetWare server object, the default-messaging server is assigned the messaging server property.

5) Finally, both FirstMail for DOS and FirstMail for Windows are installed.

7.3 OPTIMIZING THE SERVER MEMORY AND DISK SPACE

In IntranetWare, memory management tasks are handled automatically. You may fine-tune an IntranetWare system using MONITOR.NLM, SERVMAN.NLM, or SET commands. IntranetWare assigns physically noncontiguous pages of memory in a logically contiguous range. It uses paging to allocate all memory resources in the system. A page is a 4-KB block of RAM supported in 386 systems and up. This results in efficient memory utilization.

Memory allocation reserves a specific RAM location for processes, instructions, and data. In the IntranetWare memory architecture, the network operating system gives each process its own allocation pool. IntranetWare maps the process allocation pools to the global pool of memory pages. Each process requests memory from its own allocation pool. Each process returns memory to the same allocation pool. The IntranetWare memory allocation scheme and memory protection features minimize memory fragmentation and maximize memory efficiency. They also allow the expedient development and optimization of third-party applications or NLMs. IntranetWare optimizes the combined function calls, or APIs, in the memory management scheme for NLMs. This is because NLMs tend to make a set number of allocations and use the same pool of memory over and over during the life of the process.

IntranetWare has only one memory pool, the cache buffers. Cache buffers consist of 4-KB memory blocks, or pages. IntranetWare gives each loaded NLM its own memory pool. Each NLM memory pool consists of three allocation lists:

1) An array of 64 linked lists in 16-byte increments for blocks up to 1 KB.

2) An array of 21 linked lists in 256-KB increments for blocks up to 4 KB.

3) A single linked list for blocks 4 KB and larger.

An NLM uses its memory-linked lists to manage its memory until the NLM is unloaded. It will borrow memory from the cache buffers in 4-KB pages if more memory is needed, or if memory fragmentation occurs in the NLM's memory pool.

Reclaiming unused memory addresses is important to maintain performance. IntranetWare uses memory deallocation garbage collection to collect unused segments of memory and return segments of memory to a common memory pool. The API named Free must deallocate memory. The API name Free simply labels the memory as deallocated. Then the deallocated memory must be recovered. Garbage collection reclaims the deallocated and available system memory. Hence, the system memory does not become depleted over time. Garbage collection should run frequently. In fact, it runs in the background and its process is interruptible.

IntranetWare uses garbage collection to defragment the memory in the NLM's memory pool. When IntranetWare invokes garbage collection for an NLM, the following events happen:

1) It examines the blocks on the NLM's allocation lists.

2) It combines the blocks on a linked list into a larger block if possible.

3) It places the larger block on the linked list corresponding to the new block's size.

4) It returns blocks with 4-KB or larger size to the cache buffers.

Hence, garbage collection returns all memory blocks on the third allocation list to the cache buffers. IntranetWare uses three counters within each NLM to track the statistics since the last time garbage collection has been carried out for the NLM. IntranetWare compares the NLM's three counters with the corresponding system SET parameters. IntranetWare starts garbage collection for an NLM when certain criteria are met. You may use the following three SET commands to set the three counters at the console to optimize garbage collection:

SET parameter	Default	Range	Description
Garbage Collection Interval	15	1 to 60 minutes	Sets the maximum time interval between collections.
Number of Frees for Garbage Collection	5000	100 to 100,000	Sets the number of NLM calls for triggering collection.
Minimum Frees Memory for Garbage Collection	8000	1,000 to 1,000,000	Sets the minimum number of bytes in the allocated memory pool needed for triggering collection.

You may issue the above three SET commands at the server console, in the AUTOEXEC.NCF file, or in the STARTUP.NCF file. The NLM loading and unloading process provides the flexibility needed for high performance. Many NLMs rely on prerequisite NLMs. The NLMs can be loaded in available memory space. They return memory right away once they are unloaded. Before unloading an NLM, make sure that it is not a prerequisite for other NLMs. You may use MONITOR's "Resource Utilization" option to check the memory requirement for an NLM before unloading it. While loading an NLM, the memory needed is the sum of:

1) Memory needed for the NLM, which is about the same size as its file size.

2) Memory needed for all of the prerequisite NLMs.

3) Any additional memory that may be needed for some of the NLMs as they are running.

When name support is added to the volume, it creates another entry in the Directory Entry Table (DET) for the directory and file naming conventions of that file system. Hence, IntranetWare requires a minimum of 10 MB of free disk space to add name space to a volume. Macintosh files consist of two parts or forks. One is the data fork, which is similar to DOS file data. It holds application-specific information and file data. Second is the resource fork. It stores icon information, drivers, and fonts specific to the MAC operating system. Since the DET also holds the native file name and other information, volumes with name space support need more memory to cache the directory tables.

IntranetWare structures the memory resources in such a way that processes are kept from corrupting each other's memory space and the memory space of the network operating system. IntranetWare allows you to establish a safe area, sometimes referred to as the OSP domain. The OSP (Operating System Protected) domain runs untested third-party NLMs until you are sure of their integrity. (Domain is a legal addressing memory space for a process.) Application or NLM developers can test

NLMs in the OSP domain before running them in an unprotected production environment. NLMs loaded into the OSP domain cannot corrupt the NetWare operating system.

To create the OSP and enable memory protection, you must include the command LOAD DOMAIN in the STARTUP.NCF file before other modules are loaded. It may not be possible to unload the domain if an NLM fails. When you execute the command LOAD DOMAIN, it creates OS and OS_PROTECTED domains. It also automatically loads NWTIL.NLM and NWTILR.NLM. These two NLMs may be unloaded once all modules are loaded. IntranetWare copies the DOMAIN files DOMAIN.NLM, DOMAIN.MSG, NWTIL.NLM, and NWTILR.NLM to the server boot directory. You may use the following commands with DOMAIN:

Command	Description
DOMAIN	Views available domains and modules in the domains.
DOMAIN HELP	Views the online help for DOMAIN.
DOMAIN = OS	Changes the current domain to OS.
DOMAIN = OS_PROTECTED	Changes the current domain to OS_PROTECTED.

IntranetWare memory protection uses the ring protection model. The ring protection model is a logical model of concentric circles. Each ring has a different privilege level. You may run programs at different privilege levels, or rings, and the programs will remain isolated from one another while they are running. The isolation prevents the processes from accessing NLMs in the OS domain. The OS domain runs in ring 0, where it has the highest privilege. Ring 0 does not have segment limits and read/write restrictions. Code and data are not protected in ring 0. The OSP domain runs in ring 3. A process cannot gain access to memory at a greater level unless explicitly allowed. You may move a tested NLM from the OSP domain, or ring 0, to gain performance. At ring 0, processes are trusted and are not slowed down by validation processes.

IntranetWare protects processes from each other within a ring through memory segmentation. Memory segmentation limits the memory a process can address. It implements the limits as a set of bits in the code and data segment. The size limits create a fence around the domain of the system. Segmentation prohibits the processor from executing instructions or accessing data above a certain memory location for each process. The IntranetWare memory protection scheme provides the following benefits:

1) It secures services and operating system environments.

2) It protects against any loss of data due to ill-behaved NLMs.

3) It allows graceful termination for services that fail.

4) It allows services in ring 0 to keep running during failure of NLMs in the OSP domain.

5) It allows testing of new services.

The disk system is a typical bottleneck in the server. The disk drivers and controllers used in the server affect the server performance. A disk driver is the interface, or software program that controls the hardware. A controller is the hardware that regulates disk drives. You may improve the file read and write times by using high-end driver/controller configurations. High-end servers using SCSI boards will use an intelligent device driver. Some advanced disk controllers use bus mastering and 32-bit technologies to optimize the transfer of data to and from disk. To balance the number of disk read or write requests and to improve the overall performance of the server, you should consider using multiple HBAs and drives or balancing the number of disk requests across multiple drive channels. In addition, you may place heavily used drives on a separate disk channel, or place a slow drive, such as a CD-ROM, on a separate disk channel.

IntranetWare manages its memory based on three memory components:

- Tables—Tables contain the address information that tells the operating system where the data can be read from or written to on a volume. Each IntranetWare volume contains two copies of two tables:

  a) File Allocation Table (FAT)—The entries in the FAT correspond to the blocks for the volume. The first entry corresponds to the first block on the volume. The second entry corresponds to the second block, and so forth. FAT keeps an index or a list of the blocks used to store files and directories. When retrieving a file, IntranetWare searches through the FAT entries until it finds all the FAT entries and corresponding blocks for the requested file.

  b) Directory Entry Table (DET)—This is a table that contains all the directories, subdirectories, and files which are located on each volume. During server startup, the DET for each volume is loaded into the server memory. IntranetWare volumes are always cached, meaning the DET is always placed in memory. IntranetWare accesses the FAT from the DET.

- Disk blocks—IntranetWare organizes or divides each disk volume into disk allocation blocks. IntranetWare stores files on disk volumes using disk allocation blocks. If a file is stored in more than one block, the blocks used need not be adjacent. The FAT links the file together. You may use INSTALL.NLM to set block sizes to 4, 8, 16, 32, or 64 KB. Block size may vary from volume to volume. However, all the blocks on any given volume must be the same size. The larger the block size, the fewer the FAT entries.

- Cache buffers—Cache buffers are segments of server RAM allocated to store the most frequently used files or modified files until they can be written back to the disk volume. You must set file cache buffer size equal to or smaller than the smallest disk allocation block size, or volume block size, among all volumes. IntranetWare will not mount any volume if its disk allocation block size is smaller than the cache buffer size.

To optimize indexing and accessing very large files, IntranetWare builds Turbo FAT for files that exceed 64 FAT entries. It will not build Turbo FAT for files that are accessed sequentially. Turbo FAT is an index of blocks and redirection, which pertain to the file only. Turbo FAT makes access to the file faster since it does not have to scan through the entire FAT and it can index the table without any scanning. When a file is closed, IntranetWare uses an aging process to flush the Turbo FAT from the memory. You may change the SET Turbo FAT Re-Use Wait Time parameters if large files will be reused quickly or you want to ensure that the Turbo FAT will remain in the memory. The default Turbo FAT Re-Use Wait Time is 5 minutes and 29.6 seconds. You may increase wait time if the files will be reused very quickly or decrease the wait time if the memory will be needed to index the next file.

IntranetWare optimizes permanent memory storage, or disk space using block suballocation or file compression. You may maximize disk saving if you select file compression enabled and block disk suballocation enabled, and set the disk allocation block size to 16 KB or larger.

- File compression—You may enable or disable this scheme at volume creation time using INSTALL.NLM. It is a background process that has minimum impact on server performance. It optimizes disk space by compressing files. IntranetWare manages file compression internally by first reading and analyzing the file, then building a temporary file used to describe the original file. Then, it decides if any disk sectors can be saved (there must be at least 2% savings before a file is compressed). Then, it starts the creation of the compressed file. Finally, it swaps the original file with the compressed one. It replaces the original file with the compressed file after the error-free compressed files are built. The original file is retained in case an error occurs or a power failure occurs during compression.

The average file compression ratio is 63% in a volume. The compression ratio is the difference in file size before and after compression. IntranetWare file compression ratio has priority over compression speed volume because compression usually runs during off hours on files that have not been accessed for some time. Decompression has no noticeable effect on system performance. You may load INSTALL.NLM to enable or disable file compression. The default is that file compression is enabled at volume creation. You may enable the file compression on an existing volume later, but you cannot disable the file compression once you have enabled it on the volume.

However, you can disable file compression at the directory and file level for an entire server by using the command SET ENABLE FILE COMPRESSION = Off. Immediate compress requests will be queued until compression is enabled. You may use SERVMAN.NLM or SET commands to control file compression. In addition, you may save the SET parameters settings in the AUTOEXEC.NCF file. Below is a list of the SET parameters you can use to control file compression.

SET Parameter	Description
Compression daily check starting hour	Specifies when to search for unopened files. It specifies the hours in military time. The default is 0.
Compression daily check stop hour	Specifies when not to search for unopened files. It specifies the hours in military time. The default is 0.
Convert compression to uncompressed option = 1	Specifies how to store a compressed file after the server compresses a file. The range is from 0 to 2. The default is 0. 0 means to always leave the file compressed. 1 means to leave the file compressed, if it has been read only once. 2 means to always leave the file uncompressed.
Days untouched before compression	Specifies when an unmodified file should be compressed. The range is between 0 to 100,000 days. The default is 7 days.
Decompress free space warning interval	Specifies an interval between displaying warning alerts when a volume has sufficient space for uncompressed files. The range is between 0 to 30 days. The default is 30 minutes and 18 seconds.
Decompress percent disk space free to allow commit	Specifies the percentage of free space needed on a volume before an uncompressed file can be committed to a disk. This prevents newly uncompressed files from filling up the disk.
Deleted file compression option	Specifies how to compress unpurged deleted files. The range is between 0 to 2. The default is 1. 0 means to not compress. 1 means to compress the next day. 2 means to compress immediately.
Enable file compression	Enables or disables file compression on an entire server. The default is ON.

Maximum concurrent compressions	Specifies the number of volumes that can be compressed concurrently. The range is between 1 to 8. The default is 2. Novell recommends using the default value. Increasing this number will slow down the compression.
Minimum compression percentage gain	Specifies the minimum percentage gain for a file to get compressed. The range is between 0 to 50%. The default is 2%.

In addition to the SET commands, you may use NWADMIN and the NDIR command to view compression statistics. In NWADMIN, you may pick the volume object. Then you can pick the object's details and click on the "Statistics" page button. Using the NDIR command, you may use NDIR SYS: /VOL to list statistics for the entire volume or use NDIR SYS: APPS COMP to list statistics for a directory.

You may use NWADMIN and the FLAG command to control attributes for file compression. Using the command FLAG SYS:APPS\DATA IC will compress files in the directory SYS:APPS\DATA immediately after they are closed. The immediate compression starts the file compression immediately regardless of the time set for daily compression or how the ENABLE FILE COMPRESSION parameter is set. You may notice a high CPU utilization when compression occurs. Using the command FLAG SYS:APPS\ DC /S will not compress files in the directory SYS:APPS. The DC attribute is used to prevent the compression of files.

- Block suballocation—You may enable or disable this scheme at volume creation time using INSTALL.NLM. In the IntranetWare block suballocation scheme, in addition to allocated block size, IntranetWare further divides the disk blocks into smaller segments, or suballocations. The default suballocation block size is 512 bytes. IntranetWare uses this block suballocation scheme to increase IntranetWare server speed and to ensure more efficient memory usage, or disk space usage. If suballocation is enabled, when a file is smaller than the allocated size, the beginning of the file is stored at the beginning of an allocated block, and the remainder of that block is used for suballocation. If suballocation is enabled, when a file is larger than the allocated block size, the beginning of the file is stored at the beginning of an allocated block, and the remainder of the file is placed in suballocation blocks.

  Without block suballocation, a full block is required to store a file even if the file is much smaller than the block size. In any case, IntranetWare stores the beginning of every file at the beginning of an allocation block. Since thousands of files may be saved on a large IntranetWare server, block suballocation can save a large amount of disk space. You may load INSTALL.NLM to enable or disable block suballocation. The default is that block suballocation is enabled at volume creation. You may enable block suballocation on an existing volume later, but you cannot disable the file compression once you have enabled it on the volume.

7.4 EVALUATING SERVER STATISTICS USING MONITOR.NLM

As shown in figure 7.2, MONITOR.NLM allows you to obtain detailed information about available options. The available options are as follows:

1) Connection information—This option allows you to list or delete connections on the server.

2) Disk information—This option allows you to list statistics about mounted volumes.

3) LAN/WAN information—This option allows you to list statistics about a LAN or a WAN.

4) Lock file server console—This option allows you to lock the server option.

5) File open/lock activity—This option allows you to list the lock information about a file.

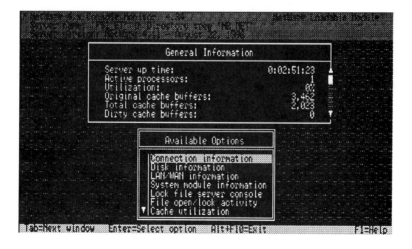

Figure 7.2 MONITOR.NLM.

6) Cache utilization—This option allows you to list disk cache utilization statistics as shown in figure 7.3. You may use "Cache utilization" option to display the percentage of cache hits. IntranetWare uses caching to speed up reads and writes on the server hard disk. A cache is a temporary space in RAM that holds blocks of

disk space. IntranetWare can access data in a cache much faster than in the hard drive. A cache hit means that the server or Intranetware has found data in RAM. This represents a large performance increase.

Having sufficient RAM to cache disk data results in a higher percentage of cache hits. The more NLMs are loaded, the less RAM is available for cache disk blocks. This will lower your cache hits and slow network performance. Be careful: if "Long term cache hits" falls below 90%, you should unload unneeded NLMs or use the command REMOVE DOS to free memory as a short-term solution. For a long-term solution add more RAM. In order to optimize the server read and write performance, you should set the cache buffer size equal to the disk allocation block size.

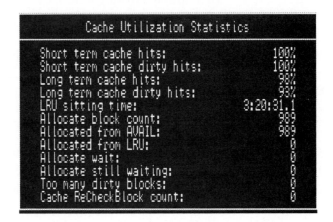

Figure 7.3 Cache utilization option.

7) Processor utilization—This option allows you to list the CPU utilization statistics for processes and interrupts. A heavy loaded CPU can drastically impact network performance. You may choose the "Processor utilization" option to view a utilization histogram. Processor utilization lists the CPU usage and identifies excessive use by specific processes. It also displays one-second snapshots of the selected processes. You may press the key <F3> to view all the available processes and interrupts. The "Count" column shows the number of times a process ran during the time sample. The "Load" column shows the percentage of the CPU used per second. The "Idle Loop" process shows processor utilization percentage. Idle loop percentage is inversely related to the CPU utilization. Therefore, when the CPU utilization is high, idle loop percentage is low. When the CPU utilization is low, idle loop will be over 90%.

8) Resource utilization—This option allows you to list memory and server resource utilization. You may choose "Resource utilization" to display "Track Resources", "Resource Tags", and "Memory Statistics" as shown in figure 7.4.

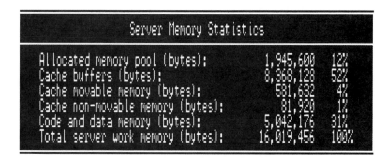

```
              Server Memory Statistics

Allocated memory pool (bytes):        1,945,600   12%
Cache buffers (bytes):                8,368,128   52%
Cache movable memory (bytes):           581,632    4%
Cache non-movable memory (bytes):        81,920    1%
Code and data memory (bytes):         5,042,176   31%
Total server work memory (bytes):    16,019,456  100%
```

Figure 7.4 Server Memory Statistics.

As shown in the figure above, IntranetWare tracks the following resource types:

a) Allocated memory pool—This is RAM used by NLMs for short-term memory requests, such as drive mappings, service requests, open and locked files, service advertising, user connection information, messages waiting to be broadcast, loadable module tables and queues manager tables, and previous menu information for loaded NLMs.

b) Cache buffers—This is RAM used for file caching, such as loading applications, accessing data files, and printing documents. Add more RAM immediately if this percentage number goes below 40%.

c) Cache movable memory – This is RAM used by FAT, DET, and other system tables.

d) Cache non-movable memory—This is RAM used for loading NLMs and allocating large memory buffers.

e) Code and data memory—This is RAM used for the IntranetWare operating system and loaded NLMs.

f) Total server work memory—This is the installed RAM minus DOS, ROM BIOS, and the operating system.

9) Memory utilization—This option allows you to list memory statistics for all loaded NLMs. MONITOR.NLM displays the following "Allocated Memory For All Modules" window on the console once you pick the "Memory utilization" option from the "Available Options" menu. This window is shown in figure 7.5. Available memory affects performance since it affects the number of cache buffers. The NLM loading and unloading process provides flexibility in managing memory to

ensure high performance since NLMs immediately return memory when they are unloaded. The "Percent free" option in figure 7.5 should not be low. If it is, then check the NLMs, add more RAM, or unload NLMs.

10) Scheduling information—This option allows you to measure the total CPU utilization.

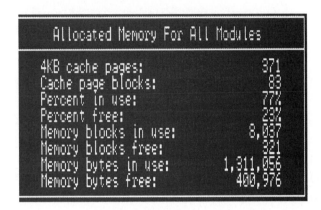

Figure 7.5 Allocated Memory For All Modules.

Once MONITOR.NLM is loaded, the main "General Information" screen, as shown in figure 7.6, displays the following server performance components to help you to effectively manage the server.

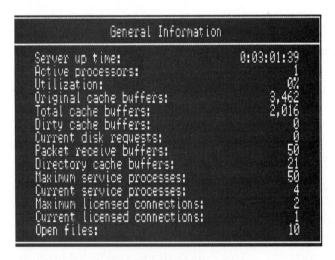

Figure 7.6 General Information screen.

General Information Options	Description
Server up time	Indicates the server running time since it was last booted.
Active processors	Indicates how many processors are active.

Utilization	Indicates the CPU utilization. It is the amount of time the processor is busy. It indicates the percentage of time the CPU is being used. A high CPU usage percentage, 60% or higher, may indicate heavy usage of the file system by a lot of users and/or heavy usage by too many services or NLMs. These excess services could be print servers, database servers, or communications services such as routers or gateways. You may correct the high usage, 60% or higher, by checking if an underperforming NIC or ill behaved NLM exists. In addition, you can upgrade the server to a faster computer and/or move some of the services to another servers.
Original cache buffers	Indicates the number of buffers (blocks) originally available for caching. This is the total installed server RAM minus the DOS and IntranetWare operating system kernel.
Total cache buffers	Indicates the number of buffers (blocks) available for file caching. You want this number to stay high, since file caching has a dramatic impact on server files. This number will decrease as NLMs and other resources are loaded. Server performance suffers if the percentage of memory available for cache buffers gets too low. Rebooting the server will increase this value. The ideal level is between 40% to 60% of the total server work memory. If the total cache buffers fall below 40% of the "Original cache buffers", then you should consider adding more RAM and/or unload unnecessary NLMs. You may temporarily increase the number of cache buffers by unloading NLMs that are not currently needed, rebooting the server to recover unused RAM from the memory pools and or/ using REMOVE DOS to free the memory used by DOS. You must add more RAM immediately if this value goes below 20%.
Dirty cache buffers	Indicates the number of file buffers (blocks) in memory waiting to be written to a disk. If this number grows large, your server might crash and data might be corrupted. A dirty cache buffer will be written to disk before a regular cache buffer. If the number of "Dirty cache buffers" is consistently at over 70% of the number of "Total cache buffers", you should evaluate the disk system. You may use the SET command to increase the "Maximum Concurrent Disk Cache Writes" value and/or increase the "File Services Processes value. In addition, you may want to consider upgrading to a faster disk system.
Current disk requests	Indicates the disk read or write requests that have not been completed. The current disk requests will increase as we increase the "Maximum Concurrent Disk Cache Writes" value. If this value is consistently high, you should evaluate the disk system.

Packet receive buffers	Indicates the number of buffers available to serve the client stations. You must reboot the server to decrease this value. If you need more "Packet Receive Buffers", then use the SET command in AUTOEXEC.NCF to set the "Maximum Packet Receive Buffers". In addition, you can use the SET command in STARTUP.NCF to increase "Minimum Packet Receive Buffers".
Directory cache buffers	Indicates the number of buffers allocated to cache directory table. If this value is over 100, you should use the command "SET Minimum Directory Cache Buffers" to increase the value.
Maximum services processes	Indicates the number of task handlers allocated to service client requests.
Current service processes	Indicates the number of task handlers IntranetWare allocates to service incoming requests. The default maximum number of service is 50, with a possible range of 5 to 1000. When service processes reaches the maximum services allowed, you may reboot the server to decrease this value, increase the "Maximum Received Buffers" to 500, or/and increase the "Maximum Services Processes Allowed". When "Current service processes" reaches the maximum value, "Dirty cache buffers", "Current disk requests", and "Packet receive buffers" will also increase. If this value approaches 40 and the server has enough RAM, you may use the command SET "Maximum Services Processes" to increase the value by 5. This will decrease file cache buffers. The only way to remove this memory allocation is to reboot the server.
Maximum licensed connections	Indicates the maximum number of client connections that can be attached to the server.
Current licensed connections	Indicates the number of client connections that are currently attached to the server. This value affects other parameters such as "Utilization", "Dirty cache buffers", "Current disk requests", and "Packet receive buffers".
Open files	Indicates the number of files currently opened on the server.

You should always use base lining to spot potential problems on the system before they cause a crisis. Base lining means documenting the typical usage (usually at 10:30 AM or 2:30 PM) for the file server by using the statistics of MONITOR.NLM on a weekly basis.

7.5 INTRANETWARE PERFORMANCE COMPONENTS

Server packet and buffer parameters are critical factors for improving server performance. You may need to modify the server packets and buffers to increase server performance. IntranetWare displays the SET console screen if you issue SET commands without a parameter. The SET console screen consists of 13 categories of server configuration parameters.

SET Parameter	Default	Range	Description
Maximum Physical Receive Packet Size	4,202	618 to 24,682	Must be set in STARTUP.NCF.
Maximum Packet Receive Buffers	100	50 to 4,000	Use 300 to 500 for a busy server. Must be set in AUTOEXEC.NCF.
Minimum Packet Receive Buffers	50	10 to 2,000	Increase this value if the server is slow to respond soon after it has been booted. Must be set in STARTUP.NCF.
Maximum Concurrent Disk Cache Writes	50	10 to 4,000	Increase this value for write-intensive applications.
Maximum Directory Cache Buffers	500	20 to 4,000	Increase this value if the directory searches become sluggish.
Minimum Directory Cache Buffers	20	10 to 2,000	This should be high enough so that directory searches can be done quickly. As directory cache buffers increase, file cache buffers decrease.
Immediate Purge of Deleted Files	Off	On or Off	Set this "On" for write-intensive applications.
Maximum Services Process	40	5 to 100	Increase this number to support many users and if the server experiences heavy usage daily. Must be set in AUTOEXEC.NCF.

You may use SERVMAN.NLM or the SET commands to set the "Maximum Physical Receive Packet Size" value to the largest client packet size available on the network. This parameter must be set in STARTUP.NCF file and should also specify the maximum packet size for the NIC card. The server uses the value of "maximum Physical Receive Packet Size" to set the packet receive buffers and negotiate the packet size with the clients. You may always use the SET command or SERVMAN.NLM to view or change the server configuration parameters.

Packet receive buffers are server memory set aside to hold data packets. The default maximum packet sizes for some network protocols are different:

Network protocol	Default maximum packet size (Bytes)
ARCnet	4,202
Ethernet	1,514
Token ring (4 Mbps)	4,202

Token ring (16 Mbps)   4,202

If the number of the allocated service processes is approaching the maximum service process number, you should increase the value of maximum service process. This will decrease the need for more packet receive buffers. You may increase the cache utilization and server read and write performance by setting the cache buffer size equal to the disk allocation block size. Using SET commands or SERVMAN, you may set the following parameters at the console to increase the server performance by increasing the speed of reads and writes:

SET Parameter	Default	Set to if write intensive	Set to if read intensive
Dirty disk cache delay time	3.3	7	
Dirty directory cache delay time	0.5	2	
Maximum concurrent disk cache writes	50	50	10
Maximum concurrent directory cache writes	10	25	5
Directory cache buffer non-referenced delay	5.5		60

By analyzing the path of a client's request to the server, you can better understand the role of service processes, packet cache receive buffers, file cache buffers, and No ECB available count. The basic path for a read request from a client to the server is as follows:

1) The client requests to open an existing data file.

2) The DOS requester encapsulates the request into an NCP request.

3) IntranetWare checks to see if there is an ECB (Event Control Block) available. Remember that ECB is also a term for packet receive buffer.

4) If there is an ECB, then IntranetWare drops the request packet, and it increases the number of "No ECB available count".

5) The request is placed in an ECB.

6) The ECB is given to the appropriate protocol stack.

7) IntranetWare checks to see if the request is for the server. If it is not, then the request is routed to the specified server or router.

8) IntranetWare checks to see if the server process is available. If the server process is available, then it holds the request in the packet receive buffer until a server process is available.

9) IntranetWare looks in the FAT table for the block's location on the hard disk.

10) IntranetWare checks to see if the block is in the cache. If it is not, it reads the block from the disk into the cache.

11) The server sends a reply to the client.

12) It checks to see if the client has more read requests.

The basic path for a write request from a client to the server is as follows:

1) The client requests to open an existing data file.

2) The DOS requester encapsulates the request into an NCP request.

3) IntranetWare checks to see if there is an ECB (Event Control Block) available. Remember that ECB is also a term for packet receive buffer.

4) If there is an ECB, then IntranetWare drops the request packet, and it increases the number of "No ECB available count".

5) The request is placed in an ECB.

6) The ECB is given to the appropriate protocol stack.

7) IntranetWare checks to see if the request is for the server. If it is not, then it is routed to the specified server or router.

8) IntranetWare checks to see if the server process is available. If the server process is not available, then it holds the request in the packet receive buffer until a server process is available.

9) IntranetWare looks in the FAT table for a block location on the hard disk.

10) IntranetWare checks to see if the block has been allocated. If it is not it then allocates hard drive space and cache space.

11) IntranetWare checks to see if the block is in the cache. If it is not it then gets the block from the hard drive.

12) IntranetWare writes the request to the cache.

13) The server sends a reply to the client.

14) It checks to see if data has been in the cache for more than 3.3 seconds. If data has been in cache for more than 3.3 seconds, that cache buffer is flagged as dirty and write this cache buffer to the disk as soon as possible.

15) It writes the cache block to the hard drive.

16) It checks to see if the client has more write requests.

The network board handles traffic between the server and the workstation. You may pick "LAN/WAN Information" from MONITOR.NLM to list the LAN/WAN statistics such as, total packets sent and total packets received. The statistics indicate trends in communication or problem areas that need to be addressed. You must review network board statistics to monitor the network performance. Rebooting the server will decrease all LAN statistics. The "No ECB available count" indicates the number of packets that are being dropped. ECB is another term for "Packet Receive Buffers". You must reboot the server to decrease the "No ECB available count".

Most network board drivers can provide 15 different statistics, including general error entries, total packets sent and received, and total packets dropped due to no available communication buffers. Some NICs may even provide additional custom statistics. You must upgrade the NIC if the parameters show a value of 100. The "Enqueued Sends Count" is a custom statistic for the Ethernet NE2000 NIC. The "Enqueued Sends Count" indicates the number of packets that the NIC had to buffer because the driver was too busy to send a packet the processor had prepared. If "Enqueued Sends Count" increases regularly, it indicates that the NE2000 NIC is having trouble keeping up with the server, and/or the NE2000 NIC is reaching its limits. To fix this problem, you should replace the NE2000 with a 32-bit NIC.

LIP (Large Internet Packet) should always be used with PBP (Packet Burst protocol). When both are used together, data transmission on the network will increase and the number of packets exchanged will be reduced.

- LIP (Large Internet Packet)—NetWare 3.11 sets the packet size to 576 bytes if it identifies a router between itself and the client. 512 bytes are allocated for the data portion; 64 bytes are allocated for the header information. By default, IntranetWare enables LIP at both the server and the client. It is included in SERVER.EXE and the client connection software. It works to increase the speed of data transmission over a router. You may enable LIP to enhance the throughput on FDDI, token ring, or Ethernet networks only.

LIP allows clients and servers to negotiate packet size when a client attaches to a server. The negotiated packet size will depend on the "Maximum Physical Packet Size" of the server. The maximum packet size is 4,202 bytes. Enabling LIP causes the server to ignore the router check during packet size negotiation. Setting the routers to handle larger packet sizes allows servers and workstations to negotiate the largest packet sizes possible. Hence, in order to support LIP on FDDI, token ring, or Ethernet networks, you must enable LIP on all the servers, workstations, and routers on the network. You may set the "Maximum Physical Receive Packet Size " in all routers on FDDI, token ring, and Ethernet networks as shown below:

SET maximum physical receive packet size = value

The above command must be placed in STARTUP.NCF. You may enable or disable LIP at the server console or in the STARTUP.NCF file using the following commands:

SET ALLOW LIP =ON
or
SET ALLOW LIP = Off

- PBP (Packet Burst Protocol)—The NetWare 3.11 server uses the "stop and wait" flow control technique. The server communicates with the client in the "one request/one response" mode. The IntranetWare server uses PBP as the default protocol. PBP uses sliding "window flow" control techniques to reduce network traffic. It allows server and client to send multiple packets before it requires a reply. It monitors communication and retransmits only the dropped packets. Any given request must have a maximum of 64 KB. PBP determines how much data is exchanged per burst transaction by using:

  a) Burst grasp time—This is a time delay requested by clients before packets are placed back to back on the media. It prevents fast servers from overrunning the client's buffers.

  b) Burst window size—This is the number of packets contained in a burst. PBP can have up to 128 packets. Each packet is 512 bytes.

  The server and client negotiate to see if each device can support PBP and the maximum burst size allowed at connection time. Hence, it is possible to use PBP with one client but not with another. Therefore, PBP removes the need to sequence and acknowledge each packet, but it will default to normal NCP mode if

PBP is not enabled. By default, IntranetWare enables PBP both at the workstation and at the server. You can not disable PBP at the server, but you can disable PBP at the workstation on a client-by-client basis. You may include one of the following commands in the NetWare DOS requester's section of the NET.CFG file on the DOS workstation to enable or disable the PBP.

PB BUFFERS = 0
or
PB BUFFERS = n

The value 0 means to disable the packet burst. The value n is a variable that ranges from 0 to 10. The default is 2. A higher number does not always result in better performance. It may even degrade performance if the hardware can not handle the additional memory requirement.

Packet burst protocol is particularly useful in areas within a network where high bandwidth exists on the media, wide area lines are used, and packets are distributed on the network; these include fast links (T-1), multiple routes (X.25), and multiple hops over routers and /or bridges. Packet burst may increase performance in these areas from 10 to 300 percent. It may also increase the performance on local FDDI, token ring, or Ethernet networks because multiple packets are transmitted as a unit. However, packet burst may decrease the performance on networks that are heavily loaded and/or have no extra bandwidth available on the media.

Questions

1) What must you do if you want Russian as the server language?
2) What are the two utilities that may be used to install, configure, and manage MPR?
3) Give three features of MPR.
4) How does MPR enhance network security?
5) What type of data may be delivered by NHS services?
6) What should you use to begin the MHS installation process on an existing IntranetWare server?
7) What happens when you install the first MHS service on an IntranetWare network?
8) What is the name of the object that can be used to address mail to multiple mailboxes?
9) What is associated with the distributed list object?
10) You are managing the IntranetWare directory tree of an international corporation. What step would you take to better server the needs of multicultural users in your department?

11) What is the name of the NLM that initializes a modem in a file server?

12) List the proper steps that allow you to down a server and have it reboot immediately.

13) How do you increase IntranetWare read/write performance?

14) How do you fix a server that is slow to respond after you have just booted it up?

15) What must you do to increase the maximum service processes if the server is busy?

16) What is the name of the NLM that must be loaded to have the operating system run in the protected ring for beta type NLM?

17) What must you do if the server containing the master replica fails?

18) You have a tree with 2 organizational units (OU=ENGIN, O=ACME and OU=SALES, O=ACME). You want to merge them so that your organizational name is .ENGIN.SALES.ACME. What is the procedure you must follow?

19) How do you enable the Large Internet Packet on the server?

20) What happens to loading NLMs when you use Secure Console?

21) A server has several volumes and their disk block sizes are 4 KB, 8 KB, 16 KB and 32 KB. What is the maximum size of cache buffers you can specify?

22) You have just created an object user called Mike. What rights does Mike have?

23) You want to create an administrator to a container and you want the administrator to be able to create new user objects anywhere under his/her container. Give two steps you should perform to ensure that the administrator has rights to create new user objects with the existing IRFs.

24) Describe what OSP is.

25) You can fine-tune server memory management with what three IntranetWare utilities?

26) Describe IntranetWare memory management.

27) What two things are used to collect unused memory and return it to the memory pool?

28) What are the three SET command parameters that are used to optimize Garbage Collection?

29) How do you ensure that an IntranetWare server/router will route maximum packet sizes?

30) What is the name of the file that you may include with the SET Maximum Physical Receive Packet Size command?

31) What are the ideal settings for server where their default maximum packet receive buffers settings is too low for busy server?

32) Where is the minimum packet receive buffer parameter set?

33) What enables a server to quickly locate files that require more than 64 FAT table entries?

34) Using TRACK ON, what does the entry BADBAE12 1/2 indicate?

35) How do you determine if SAP filtering is enabled on a server?

36) What do the following statistics show:

    a) Utilization
    b) Original cache buffers
    c) Total cache buffers
    d) Dirty cache buffers
    e) Packet receive buffers
    f) Maximum services processes

37) How do you decrease the system's need for more packet receive buffers?

38) Name three settings you can change to improve read/write performance on a server that supports many small read/write operations?

39) What can optimize IntranetWare system performance (increase read/write activities)?

40) If the network experiences slow response time and the Long Term Cache Hit is 75%, what are two actions that will improve response time?

41) What should you do if the Enqueued Sends Count on your server's network interface card is steadily rising?

42) Give four strategies you could use to avoid the problems caused by running out of space on the SYS: volume.

43) What are the three protocols that support LIP?

44) What three devices may be used to enable LIP?

45) What must you do to enable LIP on a workstation?

46) What is the new IntranetWare core protocol technology that expedites large file read/writes?

47) Packet burst protocol enables IntranetWare to support data based on what?

48) What three devices may be used to enable Packet Burst?

49) What enables Packet Burst on a DOS Requester client that accesses an IntranetWare server?

50) What are the two features that help optimize disk storage?

51) How do you increase disk storage efficiency when a server holds primarily 1 KB files?

52) What is the default size of a suballocation block?

53) What happens when a large file is stored on the disk if block suballocation is enabled?

54) When do you enable file compression?

55) How do you ensure that all of the files and subdirectories in the SYS: APPS directory remain uncompressed on a volume that supports compression?

56) What is the name of the utility that enables and disables data migration?

57) Give ways you can use to edit server configuration.

8

IntranetWare Installation and Configuration

This chapter discusses IntranetWare hardware and software components and requirements, server installation, configuration, and upgrade. You will have an overview of IntranetWare architecture and technical specification. In addition, you will learn IntranetWare server installation options and their usage. Finally, you will learn IntranetWare upgrade methods and their usage, and have an overview of migration.

8.1 AN OVERVIEW OF AN INTRANETWARE NETWORK

All IntranetWare networks are a combination of several hardware and software components. Novell IntranetWare networks are dedicated file server networks. The hardware components of an IntranetWare network consist of a workstation computer, file server computer, network interface card, and cabling.

- Workstation computer—This is a computer where the user's applications run in the workstation microprocessor and memory. The workstation might be an IBM or a compatible PC, IBM PS/2 or compatible, Apple Macintosh, or a UNIX-based computer.

- File server computer—This computer stores all the network's shared files. The operating system runs in the server memory. The file server might be a 386 machine or better with a large hard disk and memory capacity.

- Network interface card—Every computer in the network must have a network interface card (NIC) installed. An NIC allows the servers and workstations to communicate with each other. Some computers, such as a Macintosh, have built-in NICs.

- Cabling—Cables are types of transmission media that connect the NICs of all the computers in a network. These provide the communication link for the computers in the network. The choice of network board determines the type of cable used.

The available types of cables include Unshielded Twisted Pair (UTP), Shielded Twisted Pair (STP), COmmon AXis (COAX), and Fiber Optic.

IntranetWare software components include the NetWare Operating System (NOS), hardware drivers, and workstation files.

- NetWare Operating System—NOS runs on the file server and maintains the network file storage. SERVER.EXE is a NetWare 3.x and above executable file used to launch the operating system. It is based on a 386 machine.

- Hardware drivers—Hardware drivers provide an interface between the operating system and hardware devices. Hardware drivers include disk drivers and LAN drivers. Disk drivers allow the operating system to communicate with disk drives. LAN drivers allow the operating system to communicate with NICs.

- Workstation files—The workstation files provide interfaces between local applications and the NetWare operating system. For DOS workstations, you have the DOS requester or the NetWare shell. For OS/2 workstations, you have the OS/2 requester. For Macintosh or UNIX workstations, you have a protocol converter at the file server level. There is no need to communicate with the file server.

IntranetWare servers, network boards, and communication protocols must have unique network addresses to identify themselves. A network address is a unique eight-digit hexadecimal number. The server is assigned the IPX internal network address, which must be unique to the server. It is used to identify the core services of the server to the network. You must declare the IPX internal network address number as SERVER.EXE loads. The network board is assigned a node address, which must be unique to the NIC. It is used to identify the board to the host or other network devices. This address may be hard coded into the board, set with dip switches, or provided by software.

The communication protocol is assigned the IPX external network address (number), which is used to identify the communication protocol used to transport packets. A packet is a unit of data that contains addressing information. The external network address must be the same for all the servers on the same network. You must declare the external network address as you bind the protocol to the LAN driver. The IPX external network address is an eight-digit hexadecimal number. The addresses 00000000 and FFFFFFFF are illegal.

Each NIC must be attached to a network cabling system. Each network cabling system must have a unique network address. When you configure a NIC, you must declare the network address of the cabling system. Hence all the NICs must assign to the same network address if they are on different cabling systems. You must declare the network address when you generate the operating system software for NetWare 2.x, or bind the protocol to the LAN driver NLM for IntranetWare/NetWare 4.11 and NetWare 3.1x, or generate the router software for external routers.

A group of network hosts (nodes) may communicate with another group of nodes that does not use the same physical cabling system or the same topologies. A multiple-server network is a network that has more than one file server, and all the servers are on the same physical cabling system. Hence, on a multiple-server IntranetWare/NetWare network, each server must have a unique server name, a unique serial number for the operating system, a unique IPX internal number, and the same IPX external network (address) number.

An internetwork is a network that has at least one router. A router is a node with two or more network interface cards (NICs). Each of the NICs connects to a separate cabling system. Router software routes network communications from one board to the others. The router translates the packets into each board's physical "language". An IntranetWare router may be internal or external. An internal router is a router that has its software running on the file server. An external router, on the other hand, has its software located on a different computer other than the file server. Therefore, an InternetWare internetwork must have a unique server name, a unique serial number for the operating system, a unique IPX internal number, and the same IPX external network (address) number.

8.2 TECHNICAL SPECIFICATIONS OF AN INTRANETWARE NETWORK

NetWare 4.x and 3.1x are based on the 80386 microprocessor. IntranetWare (NetWare 4.11) is an open server platform. It can use protocols other than the traditional Novell IPX/SPX protocol. The IntranetWare operating system is not linked to any specific LAN or disk drivers. IntranetWare server applications, as well as LAN drivers, disk drivers, and server utilities, come in the form of NetWare Loadable Modules (NLMs). These NLMs are configured when loaded. This modular structure of IntranetWare provides flexibility to the NetWare 3.x environment. It allows you to load and unload NLMs while the file server is running.

An IntranetWare file server is a server running the NetWare 4.11 operating system (SERVER.EXE). It is used for managing the file system and network security, and it provides communication services for clients and other devices. Following are the hardware requirements for an IntranetWare/NetWare 4.11 file server and workstation installation and operation:

Category	File server	Workstation
CPU	80386 or above	8086 or above
RAM	8 MB (operating system only)	640 KB
Hard drive	115 MB	Not required

- DOS partition   15 MB   N/A
- NetWare partition   100 MB   N/A
- DynaText viewer   60 MB   N/A
  and NetWare 4.11
  documentation

Network Interface Card	Yes	Yes
Cables and connectors	Topology dependent	Topology dependent
CD-ROM	Yes (if installing from a CD-ROM)	Yes (if installing from a CD-ROM)

The hardware requirements listed above are minimums only. Realistically, you'll want a faster processor, more RAM, and a larger hard drive. The amount of RAM needed in addition to the required 8 MB of RAM is determined as follows:

1) Since the NetWare operating system itself uses 7 MB of RAM, 8 MB is the minimum requirement. Therefore, a server running with 8 MB of RAM cannot do any actual work.

2) The RAM required for disk caching is approximately 1 to 4 MB. The more RAM available for disk caching, the better the performance.

3) You can calculate the additional RAM (RAM above the minimum required 8 MB) using the hard drive size. The total hard disk size in megabytes should be multiplied by 0.008. For example, the recommended memory if you have a 1-Gig hard drive is calculated as follows:

   A 1-Gig hard drive = 1000 MB hard drive
   $1000 \times 0.008 = 8$ MB of additional RAM
   Therefore, the recommended memory is 8 MB (for the operating system only) + 8 MB (for a 1-Gig hard drive) = 16 MB.

The following are the technical specifications for an IntranetWare/NetWare 4.11 server:

Feature	Maximum	Minimum
Logical connections supported per server	1,000	N/A
Concurrent open files per server	100,000	N/A
Concurrent TTS transactions	10,000	N/A
Directory entries per volume	$2^{21} = 2,097,152$	N/A
Volume per server	$2^6 = 64$	N/A
Volume segments per hard disk	8	N/A
Hard disk per volume	$2^5 = 32$	N/A
Hard disk per server	$2^{11} = 2,048$	N/A
Volume size	$2^{45} = 32$ TB	N/A
Addressable disk storage	$2^{45} = 32$ TB	N/A
File size	$2^{32} = 4$ GB	N/A

Addressable RAM memory	$2^{32} = 4$ GB	N/A
CPU	N/A	80386
RAM memory	N/A	8 MB
Disk storage	N/A	115 MB
DOS partition	N/A	15 MB
NetWare partition	N/A	100 MB
DynaText documentation per language	N/A	60 MB
Number of network boards	16	N/A

The IntranetWare file server is a server running the IntranetWare operating system (SERVER.EXE), and it is used for managing the file system and network security and for providing communication services for clients and other devices. Before the installation of an IntranetWare/NetWare 4.11 file server, you must have the following information:

a) Server name
b) IPX internal network number
c) Disk driver type, such as ISADISK, IDE, DCB, PS2MFM, PS2SCSI, PS2ESDI
d) I/O port address and interrupt setting of hard disk controller
e) LAN driver type, such as NE2000.LAN and 3C5X9.LAN
f) I/O port address and interrupt setting of the network interface card
g) IPX external network number

During the installation, you must execute the following files in the order shown:

- INSTALL.BAT—This is a front end to INSTALL.NLM. INSTALL.BAT automates many of the steps that were carried out manually in the NetWare 3.11 installation. It performs tasks, such as copying the server boot files to the C:\NWSERVER directory on the DOS partition, and it assigns locale information and file format. In addition, it assigns the server name and IPX internal network number, and invokes SERVER.EXE.

- SERVER.EXE—This is the primary NetWare operating system. It is a DOS-based program. It takes over computer operation from DOS and identifies the server as a NetWare 4.11 server. It does not require the services of DOS. You may remove DOS from RAM to save memory. SERVER.EXE also acts as a software bus to which you may attach other services by loading additional NLMs. Once SERVER.EXE is running, you must load the NLM for NetWare disk drivers, and load the NLM for the LAN driver. Once the NetWare operating system (SERVER.EXE) is executed, it will call the STARTUP.NCF file to load the disk drivers first. It mounts the SYS: volume next, then turns control over to the AUTOEXEC.NCF file. If neither of the .NCF files exists, SERVER.EXE will prompt you for a unique file server name between 2 to 47 characters long and a unique IPX internal network number.

253

- Disk driver (*.DSK)—The disk driver is an NLM with a .DSK extension. The disk driver works with the disk controller to provide the interface between the NetWare operating system and the hard drive system. To allow the server to communicate with the installed hard disks, you must store the disk driver in the server boot directory on the DOS partition, and load it after SERVER.EXE is executed. You may then mount all NetWare volumes on the NetWare partition only. Common disk driver types include ISADISK, IDE, DCB, PS2MFM, PS2SCSI, and PS2ESDI.

- INSTALL.NLM—This module sets up the file server including disk partitions and startup files. A disk partition is a logical unit of the hard drive. A server's internal hard disk can have both DOS and NetWare partitions. You may create network volumes after the disk driver is loaded.

- LAN driver (*.LAN)—This is an NLM with a .LAN extension. The LAN driver provides the control interface to the NIC. To allow the server to communicate with the installed NICs, you must load the LAN driver after SERVER.EXE is executed and bind the communication protocol to the LAN driver after it is loaded.

- STARTUP.NCF—This file is generated by INSTALL.NLM during server installation. It normally loads the disk driver and mounts the SYS: volume.

- AUTOEXEC.NCF—This file is generated by INSTALL.NLM during server installation. It runs after STARTUP.NCF and completes the boot process.

8.3 SERVER INSTALLATION

Before we discuss server installation, it is important to understand volume parameters. You may optimize permanent memory storage, or disk space, by using file compression, block suballocation, and data migration. The default settings for volume parameters during server installation are that file compression is enabled, block suballocation is enabled, and data migration is disabled.

- File compression—You may enable or disable file compression during volume creation using INSTALL.NLM. File compression optimizes disk space by compressing files. It is a background process that has minimum impact on server performance. IntranetWare file compression ratio has priority over compression speed because compression usually runs during off hours and it only compresses files that have not been accessed for some time. Decompression has no noticeable effect on system performance. The default volume block sizes are as follows:

Volume Size	Default Block Size
0 to 31 MB	4 KB or 8 KB
32 to 149 MB	16 KB
150 to 499 MB	32 KB
500 MB and up	64 KB

- Block suballocation—You may enable or disable block suballocation during volume creation using INSTALL.NLM. In addition to the allocated block size, IntranetWare further divides the disk blocks into smaller segments, or suballocation blocks. The default suballocation block size is 512 bytes. IntranetWare uses block suballocation to increase IntranetWare server speed and to ensure more efficient memory usage and disk space usage.

  If a file is smaller than the allocated block size while suballocation is enabled, IntranetWare stores it at the beginning of an allocated block and uses the remainder of that block for suballocation. If a file is larger than the allocated block size while suballocation is enabled, IntranetWare stores the beginning of the file at the beginning of an allocated block, and then stores the remainder of the file in suballocation blocks. Without block suballocation, IntranetWare allocates a full block to store a file even if the file size is much smaller than the block size. In any case, IntranetWare stores the beginning of every file at the beginning of an allocation block.

- Data migration—Enabling data migration allows you to move less frequently used data to an external storage device, such as a hard disk, tape, or an optical disk. The IntranetWare operating system still perceives the data as residing on the volume. IntranetWare data migration allows you to free up disk space for frequently used files and still have access to less frequently used files. If you decide to use Novell's HCSS (High Capacity Storage System), you must turn file compression to "Off", turn block suballocation to "Off", and turn data migration to "On".

You may also optimize permanent memory storage or disk space by always reserving volume SYS: for the NetWare system files only. Create additional volumes for applications and data. If fault tolerance is more important than performance, you may create one volume per disk. If performance is more important than fault tolerance, you may span one NetWare volume over many hard disks with one segment of the volume on each hard disk.

If both performance and fault tolerance are important, you should span one NetWare volume over many hard disks and duplex every hard disk partition of the spanned volume. This way you can isolate network problems more easily. If you want to add name space for MAC or OS/2 workstations, you should create a separate volume for each name space support since long file names take up more disk space. If you plan to use the IntranetWare auditing feature and to have two or more auditors do the work, you should create a separate volume for each auditor.

In addition, you may maximize disk space by turning file compression to "On" to enable file compression, turn block suballocation to "On" to enable block suballocation, and set the disk allocation blocks to 16 KB or larger. Remember that you may only enable file compression or block suballocation of an existing volume by using the "Volume" option of the INSTALL.NLM program. The only way to disable file compression or block suballocation of an existing volume is by backing up the data on the volume, deleting the volume, and creating the volume again using INSTALL.NLM.

Now let us look at the step-by-step procedure to install a server. There are two server installation options with NetWare 4.11:

- Simple installation—Simple server installation is used only when the following criteria are met:

  a) The server must boot from the DOS partition.
  b) You must have a minimum of 15 MB of active DOS partition on the server.
  c) You must have a minimum of 100 MB of free disk space for NetWare partition.
  d) Each hard disk must contain only one NetWare volume.
  e) No disk duplexing or disk mirroring is allowed.
  f) You must use the default IPX network number without change during the installation.
  g) You must use IPX protocol only.
  h) You must use the default NDS directory with a single container.
  i) You must use STARTUP.NCF and AUTOEXEC.NCF without change during the installation.

The following are the steps required to install a simple NetWare 4.11 server:

1) Configure and install the file server hardware.

   a) Physically install the hard drives.
   b) Configure and install all the NICs (Network Interface Cards).
   c) Install the network cable, connectors, and terminators.
   d) Perform the computer setup utility to declare or configure the hardware.

2) Boot DOS, then prepare the file server hard disk.

   a) Insert a DOS boot disk into the floppy drive and boot the server.

b) Use the DOS command FDISK to create an "Active" primary DOS partition.

c) Use the DOS command FORMAT to format the "Active" DOS partition as a bootable DOS partition.

d) Install DOS and CR-ROM drivers if required.

e) Edit the CONFIG.SYS and AUTOEXEC.BAT files, if required.

f) From the CD-ROM drive, enter the command INSTALL (INSTALL.BAT) to run the file server installation program.

g) Select the option "NetWare Server Installation" to install a NetWare server.

h) Select the option "NetWare 4.11" to install a single system running NetWare 4.11.

i) Select the option "Simple installation of NetWare 4.11" to install NetWare 4.11 with default settings.

3) Copy the necessary NetWare system (server boot) files to the DOS partition.

a) Declare a unique server name.

b) Copy the server boot files to the directory C:\NWSERVER on the DOS partition.

c) SERVER.EXE will automatically run to start the server.

4) Configure and set up the NetWare server.

a) Pick the disk driver. Pick IDE.DSK as a disk driver for an installed IDE drive. Otherwise, pick Novell's ISADISK driver. The program copies the disk driver selected to the server boot directory.

b) Declare the disk driver parameters. The program will prompt you with the current disk driver settings, then prompts you for an option. You may select the option "Save parameters and continue" to continue the installation. It will then prompt you for additional disk drivers. You may pick "No" to continue the installation.

c) Declare the LAN driver. The program will scan the system and prompt for a LAN driver next. You may pick NE2000.LAN for a NE2000 network interface card.

d) Declare LAN driver parameters. It will display the current LAN driver settings and prompt for an option. You may select "Select/Modify driver parameters" then change the "Interrupt number" to 2. You may then pick the "Save parameters and continue" option to continue the installation. The program will prompt you for additional parameters. You may pick "No" to continue installation.

e) Continue installation. The program will then display the summary of current selections for the server drivers. It then prompts you for an option. You may pick the "Continue Installation" option to continue the installation.

f) The drivers are loaded.

g) Pick "Continue Accessing the CD-ROM via DOS" to continue installation.

h) Reconnect server to server if installing NetWare 4.11 across the network. The installation program will prompt you for the user password to log in to the source server again.

i) Install NDS. IntranetWare starts to scan the network for a directory tree.

j) Declare a server location in the NDS tree. If the installation program detects multiple NDS trees on the network, it will prompt you for an option to choose one of the existing trees. If it detects a single NDS tree on the network, it will prompt you for one of two options. You may pick "Install into tree_name" to continue installation.

k) If you chose the "Select another tree" option, you may press <Insert> and <Enter> at the confirmation. Pick "Yes" to create a new tree. Enter the new name.

l) Declare and save time zone information.

m) Specify the organization object.

n) License the operating system. The installation program then prompts you for the license for the NetWare 4.11 server. Insert the "Server Connection License" diskette into the "A" drive, then press <Enter>. The license file on the diskette is called SERVER.MLS.

o) Specify the login name and password of the NDS administrator.

p) Copy the NetWare system and public files to the SYS: volume.

q) Pick "Continue Installation" to end the installation.

r) Down and reboot the server. You must type "DOWN" to bring the server down. Type "EXIT" to exit to the DOS prompt. Cold boot the server. Type "CD NWSERVER". Type "SERVER" to start up the server.

5) Configure and set up the workstation. See chapter 2.

6) Test the network.

- Custom installation—Custom server installation should be used only after performing the following steps:

a) Boot the server from boot disks.

b) Assign a specific or registered IPX internal network number.

c) Use TCP/IP or AppleTalk protocol.

d) Partition the hard disks.

e) Perform disk duplexing or disk mirroring.
f) Assign specific volume names.
g) Span volumes across multiple drives.
h) Disable the disk partition.
i) Disable the block suballocation.
j) Enable the data migration.
k) Modify the time zone parameters in NDS.
l) Edit the AUTOEXEC.NCF and STARTUP.NCF files.

The following are the steps required to install a custom NetWare 4.11 server:

1) Configure and install the file server hardware.

   a) Physically install the hard drives.
   b) Configure and install all the NICs (Network Interface Cards).
   c) Install the network cable, connectors, and terminators.
   d) Perform the computer setup utility to declare or configure the hardware.

2) Boot DOS, then prepare the file server hard disks.

   a) Insert a DOS boot disk into the floppy drive and boot the server.
   b) Use the DOS command FDISK to create an "Active" primary DOS partition.
   c) Use the DOS command FORMAT to format the "Active" DOS partition as a bootable DOS partition.
   d) Install DOS and CR-ROM drivers if required.
   e) Edit the CONFIG.SYS and AUTOEXEC.BAT files, if required.
   f) From the CD-ROM drive, enter the command INSTALL (INSTALL.BAT) to run the file server installation program.
   g) Select the option "NetWare Server Installation" to install a NetWare server.
   h) Select the option "NetWare 4.11" to install a single system running NetWare 4.11.
   i) Select the option "Custom installation of NetWare 4.11" to install NetWare 4.11.
   j) Declare two parameters before you copy the boot files to the DOS partition. You must declare the server name and IPX internal network number before INSTALL.BAT copies the NetWare 4.11 server boot files to the DOS partition.

3) Copy the necessary NetWare system (server boot) files to the DOS partition.

    a) Copy the server boot files to the C:\NWSERVER directory on the DOS partition.

    b) Declare the following four parameters after you have copied the boot files to the DOS partition:

        1) Locale settings—You may press the key <Enter> to accept the locale settings for the country code, code page, and keyboard mapping.

        2) File name format—You may pick "DOS Filename Format" as recommended at filename format prompt.

        3) Start up commands— Enter the start up commands in the STARTUP.NCF file, if needed.

        4) SERVER.EXE command— Enter the SERVER.EXE command in the AUTOEXEC.BAT file. Enter the startup commands in the AUTOEXEC.NCF file, if needed.

    c) SERVER.EXE will automatically run to start the server.

4) Configure and set up the NetWare server.

    a) Pick the disk driver. Pick IDE.DSK as a disk driver for an installed IDE drive. Otherwise, pick Novell's ISADISK driver. It copies the selected disk driver to the server boot directory.

    b) Declare the disk driver parameters. The program will prompt you with the current disk driver settings, then prompt you for an option. You may select the option "Save parameters and continue" to continue the installation. It will then prompt you for additional disk drivers. You may pick "No" to continue the installation.

    c) Declare the LAN driver. The program will scan the system and prompt for a LAN driver next. You may pick NE2000.LAN for a NE2000 network interface card.

    d) Declare LAN driver parameters. The program will display the current LAN driver settings and prompt for an option. You may select "Select/Modify driver parameters" then change the "Interrupt number" to 2. You may then pick the "Save parameters and continue" option to continue the installation. It will prompt you for additional parameters. You may pick "No" to continue installation.

    e) Continue installation. The program will then display the summary of current selections for the server drivers. It then prompts you for an option. You may pick the "Continue Installation" option to continue the installation.

    f) The drivers are loaded.

    g) Pick "Continue Accessing the CD-ROM via DOS" to continue installation.

h) Create NetWare Disk partitions. Pick "Manually" from the "Create NetWare Disk Partitions" prompt to specify the NetWare partition size.

i) Pick "Create, Delete, and modify disk partition" from the disk partition and mirroring option menu. Specify or change the NetWare partition size if necessary.

j) Press the <F10> key to save the changes made to the partition size. Pick "Yes" at the "Create NetWare Partition" prompt. Pick "Continue with Installation" from the disk partition option menu.

k) Manage NetWare volumes. The program will then display the screen "Manage NetWare Volumes". For servers with one hard disk, the installation utility assigns all disk space to the SYS: volume. For servers that use more than one hard disk, the installation utility creates one volume per hard disk. You may delete one or more of the volumes and reallocate the resulting space.

l) Set the file compression, block suballocation, and data migration. You may highlight the SYS: volume or any volume and press <Enter> to make the changes.

m) Press the <F10> key to save the changes made to the volume. Pick "Yes" to save the volume information. The installation utility will then mount all volumes.

n) Reconnect server to server if installing NetWare 4.11 across the network. The program will prompt you for the user password to log in to the source server again.

o) Press the <F10> key to accept the marked groups and continue. Wait while the preliminary files are copied to the SYS: volume. NetWare copies only the SYSTEM and LOGIN files needed to continue the installation.

p) Install NDS. IntranetWare starts to scan the network for a directory tree.

q) Declare a server location in the NDS tree. If it detects multiple NDS trees on the network, the program will prompt you for an option to choose one of the existing trees. If it detects a single NDS tree on the network, it will prompt you for one of two options. You may pick "Install into tree_name" to continue installation.

r) If you choose the "Select another tree" option, you may press <Insert> and <Enter> at the confirmation. Pick "Yes" to create a new tree. Enter the new name.

s) Declare and save time zone information.

t) Specify a context for this server and its objects.

u) Specify the organization object and organization unit objects.

v) License the operating system. It then prompts you for the license for the NetWare 4.11 server. Insert the "Server Connection License" diskette into the floppy drive, then press <Enter>. The license file on the diskette is called SERVER.MLS.

w) Specify the login name and password of the NDS administrator.

x) Edit the server boot files. You may modify and save the STARTUP.NCF and AUTOEXEC.NCF files before you copy the NetWare System and Public files.

y) Copy the NetWare SYSTEM and PUBLIC files to the SYS: volume. Pick "Continue Installation" to end the installation.

z) Down and reboot the server. You must type "DOWN" to bring the server down. Type "EXIT" to exit to the DOS prompt. Cold boot the server. Type "CD NWSERVER". Type "SERVER" to start up the server.

5) Configure and set up the workstation. See chapter 2.

6) Test the network.

You may also use the RCONSOLE (Remote Console) utility to install NetWare 4.11. In this case you will need two systems for installation or upgrade. One system must meet the NetWare 4.11 hardware component requirements, but does not need to have a CD-ROM. The other system, which is a workstation, must have a CD-ROM installed to run RCONSOLE. All you have to do is to follow the steps listed below to use RCONSOLE to install a NetWare 4.11 server:

At the workstation:

1) Install the DOS client software on the workstation from the CD-ROM.

2) Copy the following boot files from the CD-ROM to a floppy diskette:

a) SERVER.EXE
b) .DSK and .LAN drivers
c) REMOTE.NLM and RSPX.NLM
d) INSTALL.NLM and any other support NLMs

At the file server:

1) Copy and set up the server hardware. At this point, you may want to set up the DOS time using the CMOS setup routine.

2) You must partition the hard drive. In addition, you must format and activate the DOS bootable partition.

3) Copy all the server boot files from the floppy diskette to the server boot directory.

4) Boot the server by executing SERVER.EXE.

5) Declare the server name and IPX internal network number.

6) Load the disk driver to activate the hard drive.

7) Declare the disk driver parameters.

8) Load the LAN driver to activate the network interface card.

9) Declare the LAN driver parameters.

10) Bind the protocol to the LAN driver and declare the network number.

11) Load REMOTE.NLM, RSPX.NLM, and/or RS232.NLM.

At the workstation:

1) Run the DOS client software.

2) Log in to the server.

3) Run RCONSOLE.

4) Load INSTALL.NLM.

5) Pick "Server Options".

6) Pick and install a new NetWare 4.11 server.

8.4 SERVER UPGRADE

There are four methods you may use to upgrade or migrate an existing server to a NetWare 4.11 server:

- INSTALL.NLM—You may use INSTALL.NLM to upgrade a NetWare 3.1x, NetWare 4.0x, or NetWare 4.1 server to a NetWare 4.11 server. The existing server hardware must meet NetWare 4.11 requirements. You must perform the upgrade at a NetWare 3.1x, 4.0x, or 4.1 server console. You may use INSTALL.NLM to:

a) Copy the NetWare 4.11 boot files to the C:\NWSERVER directory on the DOS partition.
b) Install NDS and upgrade the 3.1x bindery to a NetWare 4.11 NDS database.
c) Copy the NetWare 4.11 SYSTEM and PUBLIC files to the SYS: volume.

Using INSTALL.NLM to upgrade a NetWare 3.1x, 4.0x, or 4.1 server has the advantage of being the most convenient way to upgrade an existing NetWare 3.1x, 4.0x, or 4.1 server. In addition, using INSTALL.NLM has the advantage of not requiring any additional hardware if the existing hardware meets NetWare 4.11 requirements. The disadvantage of using INSTALL.NLM to upgrade a NetWare 3.1x, 4.0x, or 4.1 server is that it cannot upgrade a NetWare 2.x server or a non-NetWare server. INSTALL.NLM also has the disadvantage of risking data loss if no good backup is available and the server crashes.

- In-Place Upgrade—You may use In-Place Upgrade to upgrade an existing NetWare 2.x server to a NetWare 4.11 server. The existing NetWare 2.x server must meet the NetWare 4.11 hardware requirement. You cannot use the In-Place Upgrade method to upgrade a NetWare 2.x server with an IDE disk drive without a DOS partition to NetWare 4.11. This is because the NetWare 2.x IDE disk driver does not meet the DOS IDE disk driver specification.

  You must use 2XUPGRDE.NLM from NetWare 3.1x to upgrade the NetWare 2.x file system to a NetWare 3.1x file system first. You may use the upgrade option of the NetWare 4.11 installation program, INSTALL.NLM, to upgrade the server from 3.1x to NetWare 4.11. You may use the In-Place Upgrade method to upgrade, or convert, an existing NetWare 2.x server to a NetWare 4.11 server by following the steps listed below:

  a) Back up the complete NetWare 2.x server (both network security and file system information).
  b) Reboot the NetWare 2.x server as a DOS device.
  c) Run the NetWare 3.1x operating system file, SERVER.EXE, then load the disk driver.
  d) Load 2XUPGRDE.NLM to upgrade the NetWare 2.x file system to the NetWare 3.1x file system.
  e) Reboot the new NetWare 3.1x server as a DOS device.
  f) Use FDISK to create an active DOS partition on the server.
  g) Use FORMAT to format the partition to a DOS bootable partition.
  h) Load NetWare 4.11 INSTALL.NLM on the server then pick the upgrade option.
  i) Copy the NetWare 4.11 boot files to the C:\NWSERVER directory on the DOS partition.

j) Install NDS and upgrade the NetWare 3.1x database to a NetWare 4.11 NDS database.

k) Copy the NetWare 4.11 SYSTEM and PUBLIC files to the SYS: volume.

Using In-Place Upgrade to upgrade a NetWare 2.x server has the advantage of being able to migrate NetWare 2.x to NetWare 4.11. In addition, In-Place Upgrade has the advantage of not requiring any additional hardware if the existing hardware meets NetWare 4.11 requirements. A disadvantage of using In-Place Upgrade to upgrade a NetWare 2.x server is that it cannot upgrade a NetWare 2.x server using an IDE disk drive with no DOS partition. In-Place Upgrade also has the disadvantage of risking data loss if no good backup is available and the server crashes.

- Across-the-Wire Migration—You may the Across-the-Wire Migration method to upgrade NetWare 2.x and NetWare 3.1x bindery and data files to IntranetWare (NetWare 4.11) by running MIGRATE.EXE on the DOS client. It can also be used to upgrade non-NetWare servers, such as LAN manager, LAN server, VINES, or Windows NT to IntranetWare (NetWare 4.11). This method is considered a migration rather than an upgrade because information is copied across the network during the process. Using the Across-the-Wire Migration method to upgrade an existing server requires the following three computers:

a) An existing source server.

b) A NetWare 4.11 destination server.

c) A workstation running Client 32 for Windows or a DOS Client workstation with a local hard drive running MIGRATE.EXE.

The migration utility MIGRATE.EXE can be found in the MIGRATE directory on the CD-ROM, under the MIGRATE directory on the SYS: volume, or on the migration diskettes. The migration diskettes can be created using the NetWare 4.11 installation utility. The MIGRATE.EXE utility will perform the following four tasks:

a) Discover the bindery information from the source server. It will display in a directory tree.

b) Copy and translate the bindery files from the source server to the DOS client workstation.

c) Copy the translated bindery from the DOS client to the NetWare 4.11 server using bindery services.

d) Copy the data files from the source server to the NetWare 4.11 server.

You may format the source server disks and use them for other purposes once it has been verified that the NetWare 4.11 server contains all the bindery information and data files. Formatting will destroy the bindery information and data on the source server disks. Some of the advantages of the Across-the-Wire Migration method are as follows:

a) It is the safest upgrade method because the source server remains intact.
b) It can migrate NetWare 2.x data on an 80286 machine to a NetWare 4.11 server.
c) It can migrate multiple servers to a single NetWare 4.11 server.
d) It can migrate all or only selected information.
e) It can migrate data on a non-NetWare network operating system to a NetWare 4.11 server.

The disadvantages of using the Across-the-Wire Migration method are that you will need additional hardware to install a new NetWare 4.11 server and a large hard disk on the workstation side to hold bindery data temporarily.

Here are the steps to prepare the three machines needed for Across-the-Wire Migration:

NetWare 4.11 server:

a) Create volumes for the migrated data.
b) Make sure that you have enough disk space and memory.
c) Log out all the users.

Source server:

a) Log out all the users.
b) Verify that all files are closed.
c) Delete all unneeded files.
d) Rename the DOS directories and files that have long names. Move the directories that are deeper than 25 levels to lower levels.
e) Clean up the bindery using BINDFIX.
f) Back up the data.

Workstation:

a) Make sure that you have at least 480 KB of free RAM and 5 MB of free disk space.
b) Make sure to include the statement FILES=20 in the CONFIG.SYS file.

c) Make sure that you have the statement IPX RETRY COUNT=60 in the NET.CFG file.

d) Run workstation files.

e) Log in to a NetWare 4.11 server using the command LOGIN FS1_SERVER_NAME/SUPERVISOR/B or MIGRATE.EXE.

f) Run MIGRATE.EXE.

- Same-Server Migration—You may use the Same-Server Migration method to upgrade NetWare 2.x and NetWare 3.1x bindery and data files to IntranetWare (NetWare 4.11) by running MIGRATE.EXE and INSTALL.NLM. It can also be used to upgrade non-NetWare servers, such as LAN manager, LAN server, VINES, or Windows NT to IntranetWare (NetWare 4.11). The method is considered a migration rather than an upgrade because information is copied across the network during the process. Using the Same-Server Migration method to upgrade an existing server requires the following two computers:

a) An existing server that meets NetWare 4.11 hardware requirements.

b) A DOS/Windows 3.1 or Client 32 for Windows 95 workstation with a local hard drive running MIGRATE.EXE.

You may use the Same-Server Migration method to upgrade, or convert, an existing server to a NetWare 4.11 server by following the steps listed below:

a) Back up all the data files on the existing server using a backup device.

b) Use MIGRATE.EXE to copy the bindery from the existing server to the client workstation, which is running DOS/Windows 3.1 or Client 32 for Windows 95.

c) Translate the bindery into the IntranetWare format (NDS).

d) Use INSTALL.NLM to install NetWare 4.11 on the existing server.

e) Restore the data files from the backup media to the new NetWare 4.11 server.

f) Use MIGRATE.EXE to move the translated bindery information from the client workstation to the new NetWare 4.11 server.

Here are some of the advantages of the Same-Server Migration method:

a) It can migrate NetWare 2.x data on an 80386 machine to a NetWare 4.11 server.

b) No additional hardware is required if the existing server meets the NetWare 4.11 server hardware requirements.

c) It can migrate data on a non-NetWare network operating system to a NetWare 4.11 server.

Some of the disadvantages of using the Same-Server Migration method are listed below:

a) Possible risk of bindery data loss during the conversion process if you have no good backup available and the server is destroyed.
b) Possible risk of file attributes loss since data files are backed up and restored rather than migrated.
c) The DOS workstation requires a large hard disk to hold bindery data temporarily.
d) Possible risk of backup tape device failure.

You must perform the following tasks to confirm the NetWare 4.11 upgrade:

a) Check the login to the NetWare 4.11 server.
b) Check the drive mapping assignments.
c) Validate the sample user account and its restrictions. You should create a sample user account prior to server migration for the purpose of validating the success of the migration.
d) Examine the trustee rights, IRF, and attributes on directories and files. You may check the security setup of the sample user account.
e) Test and run all applications.
f) Check and test printing through all the print queues.

After confirmation of the NetWare 4.11 upgrade, you must complete the following tasks to allow the users to log in:

a) Change the user password.
b) Upgrade the workstation files, such as the CONFIG.SYS, AUTOEXEC.BAT, and NET.CFG files.
c) Assign new NDS rights.
d) Update the container, profile, and user login scripts.
e) Copy the NetWare 4.11 LOGIN.EXE to both the PUBLIC and LOGIN directories of the NetWare 2.x and 3.x servers on the same network.
f) Back up the server.
g) Enable login.

The migrating utility will migrate the following NetWare 3.1x objects to a NetWare 4.11 server:

File System:

a) Directories and files—Any DOS, MAC, or OS/2 directories and files with their corresponding naming conventions will be migrated.
b) Attribute of data files—Both DOS and NetWare attributes will be migrated.
c) Trustee rights—User and group trustee rights for directories and files will be migrated.

User Information:

a) User login name—The user login name is merged with the same login name.
b) User login script—The user login script is merged and becomes a user object property.
c) User print job configuration—The user print job configuration is merged and becomes a user object property.
d) User account restrictions—The user account restrictions, such as login time and station restrictions, are merged and become a user object property.

The migrating utility will not migrate the following NetWare 3.1x objects to a NetWare 4.11:

a) Printing environment—Print servers, printers, and print queues will not be migrated using MIGRATE.EXE. You may use MIGPRINT.EXE to migrate the printing environment.
b) User passwords—User passwords will not be migrated using MIGRATE.EXE. MIGRATE.EXE provides you with two options. You may assign no password to users, or you may assign randomly generated passwords to users. MIGRATE.EXE will save the randomly generated passwords in a file named NEW.PWD in the directory SYS: \ SYSTEM.
c) System login script—The system login script will not be migrated using MIGRATE.EXE because NetWare 4.11 does not have a system login script.
d) Directories over 25 levels deep—Any directory and files that are deeper than 25 levels will not be migrated.

8.5 NDS TROUBLESHOOTING

NDS provides tools and strategies for troubleshooting areas, such as NDS database inconsistencies, unsynchronized replicas, and server downtime. To prevent inconsistencies in the database, one needs to understand how the NDS works.

• The NDS database is a hidden file which is stored on the SYS volume. Even the NDIR command cannot find the NDS database file. It is protected by the TTS

(Transactional Tracking System). Every server must have TTS running if it contains active replicas. If the SYS: volume becomes full, TTS shuts down and the directory closes its files to any changes. If TTS shuts down, unpredictable results and possible damage to the replicas on the server may occur. To manage the NDS database and SYS: volume, you must perform the following steps:

a) Include the statement SET AUTO TTS BACKOUT FLAG=ON in the STARTUP.NCF file to back out any incomplete transactions and to prevent inconsistencies in the NDS database.

b) Set a minimum space requirement on the SYS: volume so that you will receive a warning if the SYS: volume is out of space.

c) Place print queues and user files on volumes other than SYS: to save space.

d) Do not replicate the server if the SYS: volume is small.

e) Do not attach a CD-ROM to a server that has a small SYS: volume. A CD-ROM often creates a large index file on the SYS: volume. Limit the auditing file size to save space for NDS data space.

- The time NDS needs to replicate and synchronize the servers depends on the types of changes, the size of the partition, and the number of servers that hold the replica. Simple changes, such as modifying a user object or creating a partition, need little time to replicate and synchronize since all the data needed are already replicated. Complex changes on the other hand take time to synchronize the changes among the replicas. For example, when two partitions are joined on two sets of servers, NDS will do the following:

a) Determine where all the replicas of each partition exist.

b) Replicate the data of both partitions to the server.

c) Complete the joining of both partitions.

- To ensure partition fault tolerance, make sure that you have three replicas of every partition in the directory tree to provide the best backup of the directory tree. In addition, you can place replicas and store backups on- and off-site.

- Back up the directory tree on a regular basis. If you have any NDS database inconsistencies later, you may recover the database by making a read/write replica into a master replica from an off-site server or use the backups of the directory.

- Remember that a partition locks during a merge, split, move, or join operation. Since two simultaneous NDS operations cannot be performed at the same time, you should perform the partition management tasks or NDS operations from only one workstation at a time.

The NDS database is only loosely consistent. Complex NDS changes may temporarily cause NDS inconsistencies. These happen because it takes time to synchronize the complex changes among replicas. You may find persistent problems, which might indicate that the replicas are out of synchronization. Here are some symptoms that indicate replicas are out of synchronization:

Client Symptoms:

a) Prompts for a user password when the user object does not require one.
b) Changes made to the directory seem to have disappeared.
c) NDS rights assigned to the object seem to have disappeared.
d) Performance is inconsistent and errors cannot always be duplicated.
e) Unknown objects may indicate a problem with NDS synchronization. However, unknown objects do not always indicate a problem. Objects sometimes become unknown when a partition root is changing during the merging or creation of partitions. The objects will return to normal when the operation is completed.

Server Symptoms:

a) To track replica synchronization from the server console, you must execute the SET command   SET DSTRACE = ON. If the message "SYNC: END sync of partition <name>. All processed = NO" is displayed and persists for more than 20 minutes, you must take action immediately.
b) You should let the server run for a few hours, it may correct itself.
c) If it fails to correct itself, then load DSREPAIR.NLM on the server to fix the problem.

The directory database is designed to withstand periods during which servers that store replicas are unavailable, or are down. All servers have a back-off algorithm that tells them not to send changes to an unavailable server, or a down server. In addition, all servers have an algorithm that requests changes periodically if no changes have been received for a set of period of time. The down server relies on this algorithm to synchronize its database once it comes back online. When an unavailable server becomes available again, the directory on the unavailable server automatically synchronizes itself.

If a downed server contains the master replica of a partition, you may not perform any partition operation on that partition until that server comes back online. If a downed server contains the master replica and the only replica of a partition, the services and user accounts on that partition are not available until the server is back online. You must use the NDS partition manager to move the master replica to another server.

The following are two instances of how you can maintain database integrity and recover from disaster when server downtime affects replicas:

Downtime due to maintenance:

a) Remove NDS—You may back up NDS, then use INSTALL.NLM to remove NDS from the server if you have to down the server or WAN link temporarily or replace the hard drive that contains the SYS: volume.

b) Remove replicas—You may remove replicas from the server if you have to down the server or WAN link temporarily to relocate a server to another site, perform a partition operation, or add, delete, or modify replicas.

Downtime due to failure:

a) Use other servers—A server can cause directory loss if that server contains replicas of the directory database or if it fails due to hard drive loss or some other problem. Usually, users still be able to access network resources if you have other replicas of the partitions on the other servers.

b) Remove server—Since the other servers in the same replica ring will continue to try to contact the failed server, in a busy network, you should remove the server using NDS partition manager and use DSREPAIR to remove the server from the replica ring.

You may use the following procedure to troubleshoot NDS:

1) Determine the synchronization state of a partition. Since NDS is global, you should use DSREPAIR.NLM to check the synchronization state of a partition before performing certain NDS operations. To do this, the user must have the [S] right to the [Root] of the tree.

2) Remove the server from the directory tree. Since IntranetWare/NetWare 4.11 servers may contain replicas and other essential references to the directory, if you delete a server, these references must be deleted too. You cannot use the normal interfaces of the NETADMIN or NWADMIN utilities to delete a server. You may use the NDS partition manager to delete a server (Windows version) or use PARTMGR at the NetWare prompt. Once the server is deleted, the server is removed from all replica rings immediately, and the volumes on the server are represented with an unknown object icon. You must use either NWADMIN or NETADMIN to remove the volume objects from the tree.

3) Send an update to synchronize corrupted replicas. Sending updates is a nondestructive way to force all replicas to update to the master replica of a

partition, regardless of time stamp; but it may cause excessive network traffic since it sends the entire replica that is affected. Hence, you should only use "Sending Updates" to all replicas as the last option to synchronize replicas if you have a problem with a directory and you cannot solve the problem using DSREPAIR. You may use the NDS partition manager to send updates.

4) Remove system software and NDS after a SYS: volume failure. Remember that the SYS: volume contains the NetWare operating system and utility files. It also contains the hidden file for NDS database partitions and replica information. If the server hard drive that contains the SYS: volume crashed, you have to reinstall the NetWare 4.11 and NDS first. Then restore the application and data files next. If the server hard drive that contains a master replica has crashed, you have to find another replica from the same replica ring. Upgrade the master replica ring using the NDS partition manager or DSREPAIR.NLM. After the server has crashed, you may install IntranetWare/NetWare 4.11 and NDS following the steps below:

a) Record the replicas and decide on the master replica status. You may do this by finding the replicas located on the server by using PARTMGR (Partition Manager) or the NDS partition manager. Then, if any of the list replicas is a master replica, change the replica to a master replica by loading DSREPAIR.NLM on a server with a replica in the same replica ring.

b) Delete the server and its volume objects. You may use the NDS partition manager to do this.

c) Fix any NDS errors and remove the replica pointers. You may load DSREPAIR.NLM on a server with a replica on the same replica ring. Do not forget that the user of DSREPAIR must have the [S] rights to the [Root] of the tree. You may use DSREPAIR.NLM to remove the deleted server from the replica pointer list on the master replica if a 625 error occurs while NDS is trying to connect to the server and the error remains for a while.

d) Reinstall the IntranetWare/NetWare 4.11 operating system and NDS on the new hard drive.

e) Place the replicas back on the server.

f) Restore the applications and data from backup.

g) Set the bindery context if needed.

Now we will discuss troubleshooting NDS rights. The most common problems related to NDS rights are as follows:

1) Unauthorized access to resources—The best method to find out why a user has access rights to resources is to check the effective rights of the user. You may have to walk up and down the tree to do this. You may also need to check trustees in the NDS objects, inherited rights from the NDS objects, and trustees on file

system directories. Finally you may need to check security equivalence. The user will get rights to a container or directory if the user has security equal to a container or a group, or the container or group has rights to the container.

2) Inability to access resources—The best method to find out why a user cannot access a resource is to check the effective rights of the user. You may have to walk up and down the tree to do this. You may also need to check the trustee assignment on the resource, such as, user, parent container, group, organizational role, and security equivalence rights. Finally, you have to check IRF on the resource.

You may use the NWADMIN or NETADMIN utility to check explicit trustee assignments, inherited rights, and effective rights on objects, such as, user, group (if the user object is a member), and organizational role (If the user object is an occupant). In addition, you may check explicit trustee assignments, inherited rights, and effective rights on an object, such as security equivalence (if it is on the "Security Equal To" property page of the user), parent containers, [Public] trustee, and [Root].

8.6 SERVER PERFORMANCE TROUBLESHOOTING

IntranetWare provides a SET console screen that consists of 13 categories for server configuration. The following are several server configuration parameters that you can use the SET command or SERVMAN.NLM to view or change:

Parameter	Default	Range	Description
Maximum Packet Receive Buffers	100	50 to 4,000	Uses 300 to 500 for busy server. Must be placed in AUTOEXEC.NCF.
Minimum Packet Receive Buffers	50	10 to 2,000	Increase this value if the server is slow to respond soon after it has been booted. It must be placed in STARTUP.NCF.
Maximum Directory Cache Buffers	500	20 to 4,000	This value is the maximum number of cache buffers the server has allocated for the directory tree. Increase this value if you notice that the directory searches is sluggish.
Minimum Directory Cache Buffers	20	10 to 2,000	This value is the minimum number of cache buffers the server automatically allocates for DET/FAT searches at

			startup. This number should be high enough so that the directory searches are performed quickly. As directory cache searches increase, file cache buffers decrease.
Maximum Physical Receive Packet Size	4,202	618 to 24,682	The server uses this to set the packet receive buffers and negotiate the packet size with the client. It must be placed in STARTUP.NCF.
Maximum Concurrent Disk Cache Writes	50	10 to 4,000	Increase this value for write-intensive applications.
Maximum Service Process	40	5 to 100	This is the maximum number of task handlers for station requests. Increase this value for server support with many users and/or if the server experiences heavy usage regularly.
Immediate Purge of Deleted Files	Off	On or Off	This will automatically purge files once they are deleted. This parameter prevents you from salvaging any files. Set this to "On" for write-intensive applications.
Fast Volume Mounts	On	On or Off	Set this to "On " to increase the speed of volume mounts by only checking the most important volume fields. Turn it "Off" if the volume dismounts abnormally.
Auto restart ABEND	Off	On or Off	When "On", this automatically restarts the server after it ABENDs (ABnormal END).

By analyzing the path of a client's request to the server, you can better understand the role of service processes, packet cache receive buffers, file cache buffers, and No ECB available count. The basic path for a read request from a client to the server is as follows:

1) The client requests to open an existing data file.

2) The DOS requester encapsulates the request into an NCP request.

3) IntranetWare checks to see if there is an ECB (Event Control Block) available. Remember that ECB is also a term for packet receive buffer.

4) If there is an ECB, then IntranetWare drops the request packet, and it increases the number of "No ECB available count".

5) The request is placed in an ECB.

6) The ECB is given to the appropriate protocol stack.

7) IntranetWare checks to see if the request is for the server. If it is not, then it is routed to the specified server or router.

8) IntranetWare checks to see if the server process is available. If the server process is available, then it holds the request in the packet receive buffer until a server process is available.

9) IntranetWare looks in the FAT table for the block location on the hard disk.

10) IntranetWare checks to see if the block is in the cache. If it is not then, it reads the block from the disk into the cache.

11) The server sends a reply to the client.

12) It checks to see if the client has more read requests.

The basic path for a write request from a client to the server is as follows:

1) The client requests to open an existing data file.

2) The DOS requester encapsulates the request into NCP request.

3) IntranetWare checks to see if there is an ECB (Event Control Block) available. Remember that ECB is also a term for packet receive buffer.

4) If there is an ECB, then IntranetWare drops the request packet, and it increases the number of "No ECB available count".

5) The request is placed in an ECB.

6) The ECB is given to the appropriate protocol stack.

7) IntranetWare checks to see if the request is for the server. If it is not, then it is routed to the specified server or router.

8) IntranetWare checks to see if the server process is available. If the server process is available, then it holds the request in the packet receive buffer until a server process is available.

9) IntranetWare looks in the FAT table for the block location on the hard disk.

10) IntranetWare checks to see if the block has been allocated. If it is not it then allocates hard drive space and cache space.

11) IntranetWare checks to see if the block is in the cache. If it is not it then gets the block from the hard drive.

12) It writes the request to the cache.

13) The server sends a reply to the client.

14) It checks to see if data has been in the cache for more than 3.3 seconds. If data has been in the cache for more than 3.3 seconds, that cache buffer is flagged as dirty and it must be written to the disk as soon as possible.

15) It writes the cache block to the hard drive.

16) It checks to see if the client has more write requests.

Here are some server performance troubleshooting techniques you might use to fix and optimize your server:

Slow server response to user requests:

Probable Cause 1: High LAN traffic

Solution:

Use a protocol analyzer to check for faulty LAN components, such as, a chattering LAN board, bad concentrator, or faulty cabling. Make sure that the topology is able to handle the traffic. You may have to split the cable system with an additional NIC in the server or replace the topology with a high-performance topology. Server configuration parameters that indicate trouble are as follows:

Probable Cause 2: "Utilization" constantly high

Solution:

If this value is constantly high, you should move excess users to other server, move excess services to other server, replace the CPU and/or redesign the disk system, or remove misbehaving NLMs.

Probable Cause 3: "Dirty cache buffers" constantly high

Solution:

If this value is constantly high, consider dirty cache writes over dirty cache reads. Retrieve unused but allocated RAM by unloading unused NLMs. Make sure that you configure and register the memory properly. Make sure that all RAM is good and with the same speed. Add additional RAM if needed.

Probable Cause 4: "Packet receive buffers" reaching maximum

Solution:

If this value is reaching its maximum, check to see if there is any bottleneck between the server NIC and the processor. Consider increasing the "Maximum Packet Receive Buffers" parameter if it reaches a maximum over a period of days or months. You may also reboot the server and watch the packet receive buffers. Replace any LAN driver or NIC if it constantly reaches the maximum in a matter of minutes or hours.

Probable Cause 5: "Current disk request" slow

Solution:

This may indicate that you may have a slow disk system. In that case, make sure that you use the current version of the disk driver. Install faster drives. Install multiple disk channels. Move a slow drive, such as a CD-ROM, to another disk channel.

Probable Cause 6: "Service process" reaching maximum

Solution:
If this value is reaching its maximum, you can adjust it using SERVMAN or the SET command as long as there is enough RAM left over for file caching. If not, consider adding more memory. You can also move excess users to other server, move excess services to other server, replace the CPU and/or redesign the disk system, or remove misbehaving NLMs.

Probable Cause 7: "No ECB Available Count" constantly increasing

Solution:

If this value increases constantly and the packet receive buffers do not reach the maximum, you should have short bursts of high LAN traffic. To fix this problem, increase the minimum and maximum packet receive buffers.

Probable Cause 8: Directory tables are not all cached

Solution:

If this happens then increase the directory cache buffers.

Server crashes:

If the error is an error specific to an NLM, then

Probable Cause 1: Misbehaving NLMs

Solution:

Make sure that the system runs properly by rebooting the server without loading the suspect NLM. Contact the NLM vendor for a remedy, if needed.

Probable Cause 2: Negative Interaction between NLMs

Solution:

Recopy the NLMs from the original disk to check for possible file corruption, then load the NLMs. Contact the NLM vendor for remedy, if needed.

If the error is a GPPE (technical name) error, then

Probable Cause 1: NLM version is too old

Solution:

Make sure that the support NLMs are the correct versions required for the other NLMs that are loaded. Contact the NLM vendor for remedy if needed.

Probable Cause 2: Corrupted NLM

Solution:

Recopy the NLM, then reload it.

Probable Cause 3: Corrupted SERVER.EXE

Solution:

Recopy the server, then reboot it.

Server crashes with an ABEND (ABnormal END):

If the error is an NMI parity error generated by the I/O, then

Probable Cause 1: Bad memory on the interface board

Solution:

Troubleshoot and replace the network board, video boards, HBAs, and any other board that uses memory.

Probable Cause 2: Bad power source

Solution:

Add a UPS (Uninterrupted Power Supply) to prevent spikes, surges, brownouts, etc.

Probable Cause 3: Bad power supply

Solution:

Replace the power supply.

If the error is an NMI parity error generated by the system board, then

Probable Cause 1: Bad memory on the system board

Solution:

Troubleshoot and replace the system memory.

Probable Cause 2: Bad system board

Solution:

Troubleshoot and replace the system board.

Probable Cause 3: Bad power source

Solution:

Add a UPS (Uninterrupted Power Supply) to prevent spikes, surges, brownouts, etc.

Probable Cause 4: Bad power supply

Solution:

Replace the power supply.

Users lose connection to server or drive deactivation:

Probable Cause 1: Hardware problems in the disk channel

Solution:

Check the error log and make sure that the hardware is set up properly.

Probable Cause 2: Driver problems in the disk channel

Solution:

Make sure that you use the current version of the disk driver. Contact the vendor for remedy if needed.

NLM not loading:

Probable Cause 1: Supporting NLMs were not loaded
Solution:

Recopy and reload the supporting NLMs.

Probable Cause 2: Not enough RAM

Solution:

Add additional RAM if needed.

Probable Cause 3: Memory is not registered properly

Solution:

Make sure that you have configured and registered the memory properly.

NetWare 3.11 NLM not loading properly:

Probable Cause: ALLOC memory usage reached maximum

Solution:

Increase the ALLOC memory in 1-MB increments.

Servers are lost in NetWare 3.11 RCONSOLE:

Probable Cause: NetWare 3.11 RCONSOLE does not support NetWare 4.11 packet signature feature

Solution:

Copy the NetWare 4.11 RCONSOLE.EXE onto the 3.11 server. NetWare 4.1 RCONSOLE.EXE is backward compatible. If security is not an issue, disable the packet signature on the NetWare 4.11 server by using the command LOAD RSPX SIGNATURE OFF.

Cache memory allocator is out of available memory:

Probable Cause 1: Board cannot address buffers above 16 MB

Solution:

Configure and register the memory properly.

Probable Cause 2: Available buffers below 16 MB are in use

Solution:

Reserve the buffers below 16 MB.

Server does not recognize all the RAM installed:

Probable Cause 1: Memory is not registered properly

Solution:

Configure and register the memory properly.

Probable Cause 2: SIMM chips are not seated properly

Solution:

Reseat the SIMM chips properly.

Probable Cause 3: SIMM chips with different speed

Solution:

Replace them with SIMM chips of the same speed.

Probable Cause 4: Bad memory on the system board

Solution:

Troubleshoot and replace the faulty memory.

Probable Cause 4: Bad system board

Solution:

Troubleshoot and replace the system board.

8.7 DESIGNING, INSTALLING, AND MAINTAINING AN INTRANETWARE SERVER

Before we end this chapter, you should have some ideas on strategies for designing, installing, and maintaining an IntranetWare/NetWare 4.11 network. You must consider the following strategies for designing a NetWare 4.11 network:

- Design rules of thumb—You should follow the following rules of thumb to design your network:

a) Keep the network design simple. Make sure to keep the resources close by reducing the distance to all servers by creating a backbone for the servers. In addition, minimize the number of hops from users to the server. Keep commonly used servers no more than two hops away. Standardize network hardware and software setup on clients. You can do this by using similar workstations, NICs, and routers for hardware and similar software drivers, operating systems, and applications for software. Dedicate network segments for high-usage network users, such as CAD systems, imaging systems, multimedia system, and others. Distribute users to balance LAN segments.

b) Protect the network. Decide on the degree of protection or fault tolerance needed. You may use the following to prepare for disaster recovery:

   1) Use UPSs (Uninterruptible Power Supplies) for alternative power supplies.
   2) Provide redundant paths to ensure lines of communications.
   3) Keep spare systems or spare parts on the network.
   4) Use disk mirroring.
   5) Check for viruses in new applications.
   6) Test and verify the backup system for the server.
   7) Replicate and back up the NDS database.

c) Increase the network performance. Do not use production and application servers for routing. Determine a baseline performance for the network. Design the network for performance and growth needs. Create SAP filters across slow links to remove traffic from local servers, local routers, and other local resources on the main network.

d) Pick routable transport protocols. Select routable transport protocols if possible. IPX and IP are routable protocols. NetBIOS and LAT are not routable.

e) Use standard base technology. Implement standard base technology, such as 10BaseT and SNMP. Avoid proprietary technology that can limit your interoperability.

f) Test new technology before use. Research and test new technology before integrating it.

- Keep Detailed Records—You should keep a log book of what exists on the network, such as:

a) Physical map of the network. Keep a floor plan to show where the equipment is.

b) Logical map of the network. Use management tools to get information and keep design simple.

c) Installation information. Record critical parameters for installation procedures.

d) Backups of NDS and data files. You may use SMS (Storage Management System) to back up the NDS database.

e) Configuration parameters. You should keep printouts of the following:

1) Network configuration—Network numbers, NIC settings, and others.
2) Workstation configuration files—AUTOEXEC.BAT, CONFIG.SYS, and NET.CFG files.
3) File server configuration files—AUTOEXEC.NCF and STARTUP.NCF files.
4) Login scripts—container, profile, and any other standard user login script.

• Ensure Server Security—You may perform the following tasks to protect the server:

a) Lock the server keyboard. To prevent access to the server keyboard, you may lock the console keyboard with password protection using MONITOR.NLM.

b) Load REMOTE with a password. This will prevent unauthorized use of RCONSOLE utilities.

c) Secure the ADMIN password. This will prevent serious security breaches.

d) Keep a backup administrator. Keep a backup network administrator and seal the password.

e) Run SECURE CONSOLE. You may run the console command SECURE CONSOLE to do the following:

1) Remove DOS from the server memory.
2) Prevent unauthorized loading of NLMs.
3) Prohibit changing of system date and time.
4) Block access to the DOS partition of the server.

Remember that the best way to secure the server is to lock the server in a room away from the users. You must consider the following strategies for installing a NetWare 4.11 network (refer to sections 8.2 and 8.3 for more details):

- Simple installation—Simple server installation is used only when the following criteria are met:

  a) The server must boot from the DOS partition.
  b) You must have a minimum of 15 MB of active DOS partition on the server.
  c) You must have a minimum of 100 MB of free disk space for the NetWare partition.
  d) Each hard disk must contain only one NetWare volume.
  e) No disk duplexing or disk mirroring is allowed.
  f) You must use the default IPX network number without change during the installation.
  g) You must use IPX protocol only.
  h) You must use the default NDS directory with a single container.
  i) You must use STARTUP.NCF and AUTOEXEC.NCF without change during the installation

- Custom installation—Custom server installation is used only when the following criteria are met:

  a) The server must boot from boot disks.
  b) You must assign a specific or registered IPX internal network number.
  c) You must use TCP/IP or AppleTalk protocol.
  d) The hard disks must be partitioned.
  e) You should perform disk duplexing or disk mirroring.
  f) Specific volume names must be assigned.
  g) Volumes should be spanned across multiple drives.
  h) The disk partition must be disabled.
  i) Block suballocation must be disabled.
  j) Data migration should be enabled.
  k) You should modify the time zone parameters in NDS.
  l) You must edit the AUTOEXEC.NCF and STARTUP.NCF files.

- INSTALL.NLM—You may use INSTALL.NLM to upgrade a NetWare 3.1x, NetWare 4.0x, or NetWare 4.1 server to a NetWare 4.11 server. The existing server hardware must meet NetWare 4.11 requirements. You must perform the upgrade at the NetWare 3.1x, 4.0x, or 4.1 server console.

- In-Place Upgrade—You may use In-Place Upgrade to upgrade an existing NetWare 2.x server to a NetWare 4.11 server. The existing NetWare 2.x server must meet the NetWare 4.11 hardware requirement. You cannot use the In-Place Upgrade method to upgrade a NetWare 2.x server with an IDE disk drive without a DOS partition to NetWare 4.11. This is because the NetWare 2.x IDE disk driver does not meet the DOS IDE disk driver specification.

    You must use 2XUPGRDE.NLM from NetWare 3.1x to upgrade the NetWare 2.x file system to a NetWare 3.1x file system first. You may use the upgrade option of NetWare 4.11 installation program, INSTALL.NLM, to upgrade the server from 3.1x to NetWare 4.11. You may use the In-Place Upgrade method to upgrade, or convert, an existing NetWare 2.x server to a NetWare 4.11 server.

- Across-the-Wire Migration—You may use the Across-the-Wire Migration method to upgrade NetWare 2.x and NetWare 3.1x bindery and data files to IntranetWare (NetWare 4.11) by running MIGRATE.EXE on the DOS client. It can also be used to upgrade non-NetWare servers, such as LAN manager, LAN server, VINES, or Windows NT to IntranetWare (NetWare 4.11). This method is considered a migration rather than an upgrade because information is copied across the network during the process. Using the Across-the-Wire Migration method to upgrade an existing server requires the following three computers:

    a) An existing source server.
    b) A NetWare 4.11 destination server.
    c) A workstation running Client 32 for Windows or a DOS Client workstation with local hard drive running MIGRATE.EXE.

- Same-Server Migration—You may use the Same-Server Migration method to upgrade NetWare 2.x and NetWare 3.1x bindery and data files to IntranetWare (NetWare 4.11) by running MIGRATE.EXE and INSTALL.NLM. This method can also be used to upgrade non-NetWare servers, such as LAN manager, LAN server, VINES, or Windows NT to IntranetWare (NetWare 4.11). This method is considered a migration rather than an upgrade because information is copied across the network during the process. Using the Same-Server Migration method to upgrade an existing server requires the following two computers:

    a) An existing server that meets NetWare 4.11 hardware requirements.
    b) A DOS/Windows 3.1 or Client 32 for Windows 95 workstation with a local hard drive running MIGRATE.EXE.

You must consider the following issues for maintaining a NetWare 4.11 network:

- Server interdependence—You should make sure that replicas are removed from the server if a server must be downed for an extended period of time or if you want to split or join partitions while a server is down.

- Server synchronization—You should check the following if NDS cannot synchronize with a server:

  a) Is the server running NDS software, or DS.NLM?
  b) Are the hardware, routers, and bridges functioning?
  c) Does a downed server contain a master replica?

- Changing the server name, IPX address, or server context—Before changing the server name, IPX number, or server context, you should make sure that the server has a replica of the partition in which it is contained and that the replicas on the server are synchronized.

- Ensure the DOS clock accuracy—You should check the DOS clock in the CMOS.

- NDS database and SYS: volume—The NDS database is a hidden file, which is stored on the SYS: volume.Even the NDIR command cannot find the NDS database file. It is protected by the TTS (Transactional Tracking System). Every server must have TTS running if it contains active replicas. If the SYS: volume becomes full, TTS shuts down and the directory closes its files to any changes. If TTS shuts down, unpredictable results and possible damage to the replicas on the server may occur. To manage the NDS database and SYS: volume, you must perform the following steps:

  a) Include the statement SET AUTO TTS BACKOUT FLAG=ON in the STARTUP.NCF file to back out of any incomplete transactions and to prevent inconsistencies in the NDS database.
  b) Set a minimum space requirement on the SYS: volume so that you will receive a warning if the SYS: volume is out of space.
  c) Place print queues and user files on volumes other than SYS: to save space.
  d) Do not replicate the server if the SYS: volume is small.
  e) Do not attach a CD-ROM to a server that has a small SYS: volume. A CD-ROM often creates a large index file on the SYS: volume. Limit the auditing file size to save space for the NDS database.

Questions

1) Give three good network design goals.
2) Give three good planning strategies for IntranetWare.
3) Name four things you must keep as part of a detailed documentation.
4) Name the four major steps in configuring a network.
5) What is the minimum RAM required for an IntranetWare server?
6) What happens if you install the same license on more than one server?
7) What are the network protocols that are always loaded during an IntranetWare installation?
8) What must you know about the IPX internal network number?
9) What is the name of the configuration boot file that contains commands to load the disk driver and mounts the SYS: volume?
10) Give some reasons why you would select the NetWare 4.11 custom installation option.
11) If you create a 400-MB IntranetWare volume using the defaults during a custom NetWare 4.11 installation, what are the settings for file compression and block suballocation?
12) A NetWare 4.11 server consists of two volumes: a SYS: volume and a DATA volume. The DATA volume has its block suballocation turned off. What can be used to enable the block suballocation?
13) A NetWare 4.11 server consists of two volumes: a SYS: volume and a DATA volume. Both volumes have their block suballocation turned on. What can be used to disable the block suballocation on the DATA volume?
14) What do you need to know about volume block size?
15) What is the IntranetWare default block size for a 750-MB volume?
16) What is the size of an IntranetWare suballocation block?
17) If an IntranetWare volume is created with the file compression enabled, how can you change the compression status?
18) Describe data migration.
19) What are the three computers that allow you to perform an Across-the-Wire upgrade?
20) Give two advantages and disadvantages of upgrading an existing server to IntranetWare using the upgrade option in the IntranetWare installation program INSTALL.NLM.
21) Give three places where you might find the migration utility files.
22) What is the safest upgrade method?

23) Give three advantages and disadvantages of using the Across-the-Wire Migration method.

24) What are the three requirements for an IntranetWare server using Across-the-Wire migration?

25) What are the four requirements for an IntranetWare workstation using Across-the-Wire migration?

26) What are the three steps you should do before upgrading from NetWare 3.1x to IntranetWare?

27) What are the four steps you should do on the source server when upgrading from NetWare 3.1x to IntranetWare using Across-the-Wire Migration?

28) During an Across-the-Wire Migration from NetWare 3.1x to IntranetWare, what are the three tasks that are performed?

29) What are the things that migrate from NetWare 3.1x to IntranetWare?

30) What are the two advantages of the Same-Server Migration method?

31) What are the four things that allow you to verify that an IntranetWare upgrade has been successful?

32) Suppose that you are upgrading from a 3.12 server into a 4.11 server, and 14 users have the same names on both servers. What will happen to the server accounts after the upgrade?

33) What is the command(s) that allows you to do each of the following:

    a) Determine what your current context is.
    b) Use the [Root] as your point of reference.
    c) Change your context from OU=SW to [Root]
    d) Make [Root] your current context and view all of the containers in [Root] if your current context is OU=SW.
    e) View all objects below the OU=SW context.
    f) Change your context from OU=SW to OU=NW.
    g) Change your context from OU=SW to O=ENGIN.
    h) Change your current context from OU=SW to C=US.
    i) Verify which bindery contexts are actively being used.
    j) Check your effective rights for the current directory.

34) What three things should you do if NDS cannot synchronize with a specific server?

35) If a server containing a master replica goes down, what two things should you do?

36) Describe NetWare Directory partitioning.

37) What are the three allocation lists used by NLMs to manage unused memory blocks?

38) You are viewing the MONITOR General Information screen of your IntranetWare server and notice that the "Maximum Services Processes:" equals 40, but the "Current Service Processes:" is only 3. What should you do?

39) The number of current licensed connections shown in MONITOR should be taken into account when evaluating what parameters?

40) What MONITOR server memory statistic shows how much memory is being allocated for the short-term needs of server-based applications or NLMs?

41) What MONITOR server memory statistic represents the amount of memory available to users for file-caching purposes?

42) What is the MONITOR server memory statistic that shows how much memory NLMs are using?

43) What MONITOR server memory statistic shows how much memory is being used for the NetWare operating system and loaded NLMs?

44) What is the MONITOR server memory statistic that indicates how many NetWare memory managers it has to network resources, such as volume tables?

45) What is the memory that is set aside to temporarily hold data packets from a workstation?

46) What does the "Redirection Blocks" statistic show?

47) To improve the response to DOS requests in NetWare, you should _____ the minimum packet receive buffers and set the maximum packet receive buffers value to _____.

48) The number of directory cache buffers can be increased to speed up directory searches, but this increase may do more harm than good. Why?

49) What may be used to disable SALVAGE?

50) Your server crashes with an ABEND, and an NMI parity error generated by I/O is indicated. What three things could be the problem?

51) Your server crashes with an ABEND, and an NMI parity error generated by the system board is indicated. What four things could be the problem?

52) What are the three things that can cause your server to crash with a GPPE error?

53) If the packet receive buffers value consistently rises to the maximum over a period of a few minutes or hours, what two things are most likely to be the cause?

54) If the number of cache buffers falls below _____ percent of total cache buffers, you may need to add server memory or unload unnecessary NLMs.

55) You investigate slow response to user requests on your network and find that service processes are at maximum. What could be causing the problem? (If your network response is slow and utilization is consistently too high, what four things may be causing this problem?)

56) Describe dirty cache buffers.

57) What two actions can you take to avoid a disk system "bottleneck" in your IntranetWare server?

58) What are the four steps you should take to make sure that the SYS: volume does not run out of space?

59) What happens to a read request in an IntranetWare server if a server process is not available?

60) When a client sends a file read request to an IntranetWare server, what happens if NO ECB is available?

61) In almost all cases, reaching the maximum services processes indicates what?

62) If an NLM needs more memory than currently exists in the memory pool, what will happen?

63) A remote office has a 256-KB, or slow, leased link to the main office. In order to obtain better performance across the link, what should you do?

64) What is the best way to protect a file server?

65) What three things might cause the packet receive buffer to reach its maximum value?

66) Describe garbage collection?

67) What is the disadvantage of using custom installation to install TCP/IP?

68) Give two things that can optimize network performance.

9

Troubleshooting an IntranetWare Network

In this chapter, you will learn how to integrate IntranetWare administration, installation, and configuration, and basic troubleshooting skills. Novell defines service and support as configuring, installing, and troubleshooting hardware and software for NetWare 3.12 and NetWare 4.11 networks.
In this chapter, we will learn the basic meaning of service and support as it pertains to NetWare 3.12 and NetWare 4.11 networks

9.1 INTRODUCTION TO NOVELL SERVICE AND SUPPORT

To be able to perform service and support on a Novell 3.12 or a NetWare 4.11 network, you must be able to configure hardware such as network boards, hard disks, disk controllers, and to configure server and other network software, as taught in other courses. You must also be able to install various network hardware components and be able to troubleshoot or investigate whether a problem is related to software or hardware, diagnose the problem, fix the problem, and document the problem. Finally you must be able to upgrade hardware and software as a means of supporting the network. Here are some of the subjects on which you should be informed:

Subject	Description
Introduction to service and support	Using a troubleshooting model. Avoiding problems with electrostatic discharge Documenting and recording network problems Using diagnostic and system information software
Install and troubleshoot cabling and NICs	How to eliminate the common problems that occur with various network topologies and identify issues and specifications of the FDDI standard. How to select, configure, and install network boards.
Install and troubleshoot network storage devices	How to configure, install, and troubleshoot various network storage devices, including hard disks and CD-ROM drives. Using partitions and

	volumes for NetWare file storage. Using spanning and mirroring hard disks in NetWare.
Troubleshooting the DOS workstation	Reviews three NetWare clients. How to use TRACK ON to troubleshoot the login process. How to find and fix workstation resource conflicts.
Troubleshooting the server & the network	How to diagnose and troubleshoot common NetWare server and network problems. How to create a disaster recovery plan and employ the utilities used for disaster recovery.
Troubleshooting network printing	How to prevent, diagnose, and resolve common network printing problems.
Introduction to network management	Explains the role and importance of network management and how to develop a network management strategy. Introduces Managewise, a network management tool.

Troubleshooting is part art and part science. Many attempts have been made to reduce troubleshooting to a set of procedures or flowcharts. However, no one can create a procedure or flowchart to deal with every possible problem. The key to troubleshooting is to develop the ability to break down a problem into its parts and see the interrelationships between those parts. It is a combination of knowledge and experience that will help us develop an efficient on-the-spot strategy to tackle each unique problem. Before you start, you should look for the common causes of problems before you do anything else. Depending on the type of problem you are facing, you should try the following steps first:

Step	Description/Usage
Eliminate user error	There are three possibilities when someone tells us that a network problem exists because somebody tried to use a procedure and got a result different from what he or she expected, or got no result at all: the user did not do the procedure correctly; or the procedure is working fine, but the user does not realize it; or a problem actually exists. The way to determine which of these applies is to do the procedure once more, carefully thinking through each step. If the result is the same, we should ask ourselves the question, "How do I know this is not working correctly?"
Check the inventory	You should ask the following questions: Are all the parts, such as cables, present? Are they the right parts? Are they connected properly to each other?
Back up the disks	If disks are involved, we should back up the data before proceeding.
Cold boot the system	Turn the power off and turn it back on again.
Remove elements	Simplify the system by removing unneeded elements. For

	example, remove TSR programs that are running in the background; remove the AUTOEXEC.BAT and CONFIG.SYS files to free memory; or remove expansion slot boards one at a time to expose conflicts.
Check the application	Suspect a rights problem if you can run one application successfully, but have trouble running another application.
Check software version	Make sure that the most current version of the software is being used.

You may use the following four steps for systematic network troubleshooting:

- Gather basic information— Determine what the symptoms are and who on the network is being affected by the problem. Determine usage at the time when the problem occurs. Is the network broken or just saturated with activity? Protocol analyzers, such as LANalyzer for Windows, may be useful in verifying usage. Check network logbooks and record-keeping devices to determine what the normal or baseline performance is for the network. The activity and configuration information records may help us answer the critical question, "What has changed since the last time it worked?"

- Develop a plan to isolate the problem— Come up with two or three hypotheses using the basic information you have gathered and the background knowledge you have about the LAN to decide whether the problem came from a user error, application software, or equipment. You should prioritize your hypotheses to decide which one to work on first based on the likelihood that a given solution is the right one and the cost of trying the solution. Suppose, for example, that we have three hypotheses about a problem. Based on our experience, we guess that hypothesis A has a 50% chance of being the problem, hypothesis B a 30% chance, and hypotheses C a 20 % chance. You would probably want to try them out in the order of A, B, then C. Now imagine the preceding scenario with one additional factor: assume that hypotheses A and C will be time-consuming to test, but hypothesis B is a one-minute quick fix. Now it makes sense to try them out in the order of B, A, C.

- Execute the plan—You should break down each hypothesis into the smallest reasonable, testable concepts. For example, if you have identified your problem as an interruption of network traffic between node X and node Y, you might want to consider the following possibilities:

  a) Node X is having trouble transmitting the signal.
  b) The cable segment to the backbone is having trouble carrying the signal.
  c) The router going to the backbone is having trouble carrying the signal.
  d) The backbone is faulty.

e) The router going to Y's cable segment is having trouble routing the signal.
f) Node Y's cable segment is having trouble carrying the signal.
g) Node Y is having trouble receiving the signal.

Test out your hypothesis by changing only one thing at a time Otherwise, you will never know which change was the solution. After making one change, test the system to find out if the problem has been affected. When dealing with network communication problems, you should start working at the source device and check the testable concepts by moving toward the destination device. Working from the source device toward the destination is called forward chaining. Working from the destination device towards the source is called backward chaining.

You should use only reliable test equipment, software, and procedures. If you test a system with faulty equipment or utility disks, you will be more confused about what is actually wrong. The NSEPro is valuable in working through a troubleshooting plan. User groups can also be very helpful when you do not know what to do next.

- Document the solution—You should document the solution and take steps to avoid or prepare for recurrence. You should record the nature of the problem and its solution in the network logbook. This record will provide a quick fix if a similar problem occurs in the future. The best predictor of future performance in a computer is its past performance. You should do what can be done to prevent or prepare for a recurrence of the problem. If a certain component burns out regularly, we may want to try installing a cooling fan. If prevention is impossible, we should replace the unit, or have a lot of spare parts handy.

Static charges are generated whenever two objects are joined together and then separated. Upon separation, the atoms of one object will take electrons and become negatively charged, while the atoms of the other objects will give up electrons and become positively charged. Normal movements such as lifting a foot or moving a chair will generate charges in the range of 1,000 volts, which we do not notice. To be felt, the charge of an electrostatic discharge or ESD must be about 3,000 volts.

As electronic components such as microchips have become smaller and denser, they have become susceptible to damage from ESD events of very small voltages. Computer components may be degraded or destroyed by discharge as low as 20 to 30 volts. ESD may cause failures in computer equipment during all stages of production, handling, shipping, and field maintenance. Direct physical contact is not required for static charges to build.

About 90% of the time, ESD events cause the component to degrade but not fail testing procedures, resulting in failure at a later date. Since components do not fail immediately, technicians often underestimate the cost of not using ESD prevention measures.

You should practice ESD prevention and encourage your customers and suppliers to do so. There are many benefits of a good ESD control program as shown below:

a) Less need for spare hardware inventory
b) Less downtime
c) Fewer difficult-to-trace intermittent problems
d) Fewer unnecessary service visits
e) Fewer disgruntled customers

You should follow the static prevention rules listed below to protect your equipment from ESDs:

Rule	Description/Usage
Use a wrist strap and mat	Use proper wrist strap and mat to ground yourself and your equipment before working on any device containing a printed circuit. But you should never use a wrist strap when working with monitors. They may carry a large voltage that can reach us through the strap. Test daily to make sure that the grounds have not become loose or intermittent.
Do not touch leads of ICs	Never touch component or integrated chips by their electrical leads.
Use no conductive surfaces	Never place components on any conductive surface.
Keep nonconductors away	Keep nonconductors, such as plastic, styrofoam, synthetic clothing, and polyester ties, away from open computers and components. Nonconductors are a source of static charges.
Keep people away	Do not let anyone touch you while you are working on boards that contain ICs. They may cause static charge.
Keep humidity at 70-90%	Keep the humidity of any area with open computers at 70 to 90 percent. Static problems are much more likely to occur in low humidity.
Use static shielding bags	Always transport and store boards and ICs in static shielding bags. No pin holes are allowed in the bags since it will defeat the purpose. Static shielding bags and anti-static bags are not the same. Proper static shielding bags often have a gray-silver color. Anti-static bags, usually colored pink or blue, do not shield their contents from external static fields and should not be used.

Keeping necessary system documentation may save you many hours in troubleshooting problems. You may divide the system documentation into three categories:

a) The LAN system.
b) The history of the LAN.
c) Resources used with the LAN.

You may document the following to help you solve physical network problems:

Documentation type	Description/usage
The LAN map	A detailed graphic record of the LAN that identifies the location of all users, user groups, servers, printers, repeaters, bridges, gateways, and wiring centers.
The LAN inventory	A record of the hardware, software, and peripherals used in the LAN. You can purchase software that maintains records of the hardware, software, and peripherals on the system.
Cabling documentation	A record of the actual cabling, or of which wire goes where, in the LAN. Accurate documentation is critical in solving cable problems
Workstation documentation	A record of each workstation configuration and its role in the network. The configurations and roles of individual workstations can be critical to a network's health and should be documented.
Chronological change log	A record of changes in the LAN configuration, including software upgrades and hardware that has been added or removed.

You should document the history of the LAN as shown below to help you solve a problem that may occur more than once.

Documentation Type	Description/Usage
The business environment	Many network administrators concentrate too much on the technology and forget that the real system is the whole business environment.This document should answer questions such as the following: How is this LAN being used? What is the relationship between the LAN and the company? These are important things to know in dealing with the human aspects of troubleshooting.
User information	This document lists user's names and the following information: Where the users are located. What the users typically do on the system. What training the users received.
Baseline information and user patterns	This document indicates how the network functions under normal circumstances, and it includes statistics on network traffic, CPU usage, bandwidth utilization, and errors and other information.
Log of past problems and trouble reports	This document should include details about what has happened over the past two years, including: Problem descriptions and resolutions Downtime incurred Performance analysis of devices such as printers and routers

You should document the resources used with the LAN to help you track down resources or people who might know the answer to your problem:

Documentation Type	Description/usage
Technology documentation	This document includes the protocols, routing, LAN architecture, and other technical materials specific to your network.
Technical support	This document should include key contacts in the vendor's service departments and current technical bulletin board numbers.

The purpose of diagnostic software is to quickly provide information about your system that can assist you in isolating and solving problems. When acquiring a diagnostic utility, you should look for a package that:

a) works with many aspects of your system
b) is known to work with your hardware
c) has a good user interface
d) meets your reporting requirements
e) has adequate and timely support available

You may use CheckIt PRO and WINCheckIt (the Windows 3.1 version), system information tools for PCs, to accomplish the following tasks:

Task	Description/Usage
Get system information	Gets information on system hardware and operating system. The report becomes part of the LAN network's record-keeping system.
Take system inventory	Takes inventory of the internal components of computer, such as the date of BIOS, type of CPU, and the amount of RAM.
Edit and view CMOS	This allows you to protect your CMOS against battery loss and to restore CMOS to other machines with the same configuration. This can be useful in a large networked organization where many nodes may have identical configurations.
Check IRQ, I/O, & ROM	Provides information on IRQs, I/O addresses, and memory addresses. This helps us avoid incompatibilities when we add a network board or other peripheral device to our system.
Test hardware components	This allows you to test and diagnose the following components: system board, hard disk, floppy disk drive, serial port, parallel port, and memory.
Check drivers and TSR	Collects system information, including information on device drivers and TSRs. This helps you to determine conflicts between software components.
Benchmark system	Takes benchmark readings on system performance. This allows you to compare our system to it or to other systems. Preventive maintenance could include generating performance data at regular intervals and comparing it to earlier data.

In addition, WINCheckIt has the following features:

Feature	Description/usage
Enhanced performance	It provides many system utilities to enhance workstation performance.
A clean-up utility	This removes unneeded files.
An uninstall utility	This identifies and deletes files for any Windows 3.1 program.
A memory tune-up utility	This consolidates Windows 3.1 memory fragments and increases the largest memory block available.
A setup advisor (Hardware compatibility)	You may use the setup advisor to report on compatibility between existing hardware and items from a list of over 200 expansion boards and peripherals we may want to install in the system.
A software shopper (Software compatibility)	You may use the software shopper to report on the compatibility between approximately 1,500 software files.

9.2 TROUBLESHOOTING AN ETHERNET AND A TOKEN RING NETWORK

Each network topology and access protocol has its own special characteristics. And so selecting and configuring NICs is also critical while setting up a network environment. You will now learn the skills required to install network boards such as:

a) Identifying the appropriate board type
b) Setting the IRQs, memory addresses, and port addresses
c) Setting jumpers and DIO switches
d) Ensuring network board and slot compatibility

You will also examine the issues and specifications of the FDII and ATM standards. FDII will play a growing role in the LANs and WANs of the future.

Ethernet has the following advantages:

a) It is an inexpensive way to get high-speed transmission.
b) It is a proven technology that supports various cabling configurations.
c) It works well with a large number of LAN and microcomputer to mainframe applications.
d) It is easy to install.

Ethernet has the following disadvantages:

a) It suffers performance degradation under high loads or high network traffic.
b) Its common cabling system can sometimes make it difficult to isolate problems.

Ethernet moves messages around the network in datagrams. A datagram is a self-contained packet of information that includes the source address, the destination address, the type of data that must be moved, and the data itself. Because packet size is limited, multiple packets are needed to move messages. To send a datagram, a network node must first listen to see if any other node is using the cable. When the cable appears to be clear, the node can send its datagram. The packets may collide with each other if two stations are transmitting at the same time. The result can be damaged and unreliable packets, which leads to wasted bandwidth.

When a collision occurs, a signal is broadcasted around the network. The nodes which have been competing for the cable's bandwidth will retransmit. Each node will delay its retransmission by a random amount of time to assure that eventually collisions will be avoided. When the nodes receive a packet, they will check to make sure the packet is not a fragment due to a collision. They will then check its address to see if it is a whole packet. The station will process the packet for use if the address matches its own address.

Ethernet uses transceivers to convert signals on the wire to a form that the workstation may use. Transceiver is an acronym for transmitter and receiver. Transceivers can be external devices or they can be built into the NIC.

The IEEE802.3 specification provides seven standards for Ethernet as shown below:

Standard	Description
10BASE2	10BASE2 uses a 50-ohm thin coaxial cable. The RG-58A/U cable is not a true 10 BASE2 cable since it has only a single shield. But the RG-58A/U cable is widely used anyway. Do not use RG-58A/U cable since it does not meet IEEE specifications. You must connect a 10BASE2 node to the bus with T connectors. You must turn off the Signal Quality Error test, SQE or heartbeat, on the NIC, if there is one, when repeaters are used. You must use repeaters when mixing 10BASE2 or 10BASE5 with fiber-optic cable.
10BASE5	10BASE5 uses 50-ohm RG-11 thick coaxial cable. You must use a drop cable, a 4 pair AUI cable, to connect nodes to the network cable. You may use a clamp, a "vampire tap", to connect drop cable to the bus. This vampire tap can penetrate the insulation of the cable without cutting it.
10BASE-T	This uses category 3 or better data grade phone cabling and a centralized wiring hub. The standard wiring involves 2 to 6 twisted pairs with a solid copper core. The wire should be AWG #22, #24, or #26, with 85 to 100 ohms at 10 MHz. You must connect all the 10BASE-T nodes to the wiring hubs or concentrators. The hub may have intelligence to route traffic around a defective cable segment. This star topology eliminates the single point of failure found on bus topologies. The concentrators or hubs may also have management firmware in ROM. By tapping the management information provided by the hub through a workstation or management node, you may locate and repair the defective cable much easier. 10BASE-T cable is particularly susceptible to EMI from fluorescent light ballast.
10BASE-F	This is the new standard for using fiber-optic cable and network boards with Ethernet. The use of fiber-optic cable for Ethernet is growing rapidly

	because it can greatly increase the distance and bandwidth of an Ethernet network.
10BASE-FOIRL	Fiber-optic inter-repeater link for using fiber-optic cable with the AUI.
AUI	Specification for the Attachment Unit Interface, also known as a DIX connector. AUI is the connector to Ethernet cable when using external transceivers.
Concentrators and Repeaters	Specifications for concentrators and repeaters.

Following are some of the rules used in the Ethernet cabling schemes:

Item	10BASE2	10BASE5	10BASE-T
Cable	RG-58A/U or RG-58C/U	0.4" dia RG-8 or RG-11	Level 3 and up: 100 ohm
Impedance	50-ohm thin coaxial	50-ohm thin coaxial	Unshielded twisted-pair
Physical topology	Linear bus	Linear bus	Star
Logical topology			Logical bus
Connector	BNC; T-connector	15-pin DIX	RJ45
Transceiver setting	Internal; on NIC	External	N/A
Max. number of trunk segments	5 segments: 3 for network nodes 2 for distance	5 segments: 3 for network nodes 2 for distance	5 segments: 3 link or tap hubs 2 link nodes to hubs
Max. number of repeaters	4 repeaters used to link segments	4 repeaters used to link segments	4 concentrators maximum between any 2 PCs
Max. length of a trunk segment	185 meters 607 feet	500 meters 1,640 feet	100 meters (unshielded)
Max. length of entire network trunk	925 meters 3,035 feet	2,500 meters 8,200 feet	N/A
Max. length from node to transceiver	N/A (on board transceiver)	50 meters 164 feet	N/A
Min. cable length between transceivers	N/A (on board transceivers)	2.5 meters 8 feet	0.6 meter, or 2 feet between hubs
Min. cable length between stations	0.5 meter 1.5 feet	N/A	0.6 meter, or 2 feet, between node and hub
Max number of nodes per trunk segment	30 nodes including repeaters	100 nodes including repeaters	512 nodes per segment 1,024 nodes per network
Terminating both ends of the trunk segment	yes	yes	N/A
Grounding one end of the trunk segment	yes	yes	N/A

You may troubleshoot an Ethernet network, or any other network, in two ways. You may use a sophisticated protocol analyzer, such as LANalyzer for Windows, to take measurements and draw inferences. You may also use simpler tools and your knowledge about a particular type of network and what is most likely to go wrong with it to guide you to appropriate solutions. In addition, you may use these two troubleshooting approaches together. Following are some of the troubleshooting tips for Ethernet hardware:

a) Make sure that the frame type used in the workstations and servers is matched. A mismatch of frame type will give the error message "FILE SERVER NOT FOUND".

b) Make sure that the network components are physically connected.

c) Make sure that Ethernet and manufacturer's specifications have been met. Make sure that cables and devices do not exceed the length and spacing limitations.

d) Isolate and divide the network to find a faulty NIC or transceiver. Faulty hardware, such as a bad NIC or transceiver, may cause gibberish to appear on the network. This is called "jabbering".

e) Check the connecting devices and terminators. Connecting devices and terminators are more likely than the Ethernet cable to go bad. Check for improperly removed T-connectors.

f) Use a VOM to check terminators for the proper resistance (VOM is an acronym for Volt-Ohm-Meter). Make sure that the T-connectors and terminators are good on a 10BASE2 network. Do not use ARCnet cables and terminators for Ethernet cables and terminators. You may check for proper termination by measuring the resistance at a connection point. It should read about 25 ohms. If it does not, we may have a faulty or missing terminator.

g) Use COMCHECK or other testing devices to check the continuity of the cables.

h) Use TDR to check cables for crimps, shorts, or breaks. TDR is an acronym Time Domain Reflectometer.

i) Swap out the NIC or transceiver if only that workstation can not connect to server.

j) Use the diagnostic diskette from the vendor to test the board. Use the diagnostic diskette that came with the board, if available, to check a problem board without removing it from the computer.

k) Make sure that the settings on the multi-port NIC are set to the port used. You may use on-board jumpers that need to be set for the computer.

l) Make sure there is good contact between the NIC and expansion slot. You may clean the NIC's connector fingers, then reset the NIC in the PC. Do not use a pencil eraser to clean the connector fingers.

m) Make sure there are no conflicts among NIC's, or add-in cards. You may remove all add in cards, then add one board back at a time. Watch for common interrupt conflicts. For example, interrupts 3 and 4 can be used for both Ethernet boards and COM ports. Stay away from IRQ 3, IRQ4, and IRQ 7 at all times.

Most token networks use a star-wired ring configuration. The token ring is built using wiring concentrators called MSAUs or CAUs. It uses patch cables to wire MSAUs to form a ring and uses adapter cables to attach stations to the MSAUs. MSAU is an acronym for Multi-Station Access Unit. CAU is an acronym for Controlled Access Unit. MSAUs are passive concentrators that have no power plug or internal intelligence. CAUs are powered concentrators that can play a role in physical network management. Token ring has the following advantages:

a) It offers excellent throughput under high-load conditions.
b) It facilitates the LAN to IBM mainframe connections.
c) It has built-in beaconing and autoreconfiguration troubleshooting mechanisms.
d) It is now available with unshielded twisted-pair cable.
e) It offers fault tolerance through automatic ring reconfiguration, or ring-wrap.

Token ring has the following disadvantages:

a) It is relatively expensive.
b) A token ring system administrator must have considerable management expertise.

Token ring uses the token passing method to move data from active station to active station. Each active station functions as a repeater. Each active station receives a series of bits from the preceding station, reads them, and then retransmits each bit to the next station on the ring. The passing of a free token controls media access. A token, a 3-byte MAC frame, provides an active station with permission to transmit. In a 4Mbps token ring, only one token is allowed to be on the ring at a time. In a 16Mbps token ring, a new free token can be released after the transmitting station has finished sending the last bit of a frame. This is called token release. When a station wants to transmit on the ring, it waits for a free token to pass by. This source station takes the free token and makes it busy by adding data to the frame. It then sends the token out on the ring.

As the busy token is passed to each active station around the ring, each station checks the token's destination address. If a station is not the intended recipient of the token, it sends the token out on the ring. If a station is the intended recipient, it will copy the data from the frame. The intended recipient will reverse two bits of the frame, to indicate that it has recognized the address and copied the data, before sending the altered frame back out to the ring. The frame continues around the ring until it reaches the source station. The source station releases a new free token when it sees that the frame it originally generated has been received and copied by its intended recipient.

IEEE 802.5 and IBM token ring are the two most popular token ring networks. IEEE 802.5 and IBM token ring specify token ring passing as their media access method. IEEE 802.5 is compatible with IBM's token-ring network since IEEE developed its 802.5 standard based on the IBM token ring. The specifications for IEEE 802.5 and IBM token ring are not identical, as can be seen below:

Parameters	IBM token ring	IEEE 802.5
Logical topology	Ring	Not specified
Media	Twisted pair	Not specified
Stations	260 (shielded T.P.) 72 (unshielded T.P.)	250
Data rate in Mbps	4, 16	1, 4
Access method	Token passing	Token passing
Signaling	Baseband	Baseband
Encoding	Differential Manchester	Differential Manchester

The IBM token ring network uses a star-wiring configuration. At the wiring centers are MSAUs (multi-station access units). It uses patch cables to wire the MSAUs to form a ring and uses adapter cables to attach stations to the MSAUs.

- MSAU—The IBM 8228 MSAU is a passive element in the main ring path. A MSAU comes with 10 ports to support 8 stations: 1 port labeled RI, or ring in; 1 port labeled RO, or ring out; and 8 ports labeled 1 to 8 for node attachment.

    The 8228 MSAU provides both a primary path and a backup path for the ring. The backup path is activated when a MSAU is used and the RI/RO ports are empty. You may use patch cable to connect the RI port on one MSAU to the RO port on another MSAU to form a physical ring. The MSAUs include bypass relays for removing stations from the ring when a workstation has failed or a port is not in use. Empty positions are automatically bypassed. Positions with cables installed will be bypassed until the board becomes active. Ring diagnostics are run between the device and the 8228.

    If the diagnostics yield no problems, a 5-volt signal called the phantom signal is used to open the relay for the node to become part of the ring. An audible click can be heard as the station is inserted into the ring. You may also use a special tool called a set-up aid or initialization aid to reset the relays.

    When a station is removed from the ring, the 5-volt signal ceases. This causes the MSAU to drop the relay from the ring. The MSAU bypasses the port so the ring can still function without interruption. By maintaining the continuity of the ring, the bypass relays of the MSAUs increase the ring's reliability and make it easier to maintain.

- Patch cables—These are normally IBM type 6 cable, but other types can be used. Patch cables are used to connect MSAUs to each other and have IBM cable system connectors on both sides.

- Adapter cables—These are normally IBM type 6 cable, but other types can now be used. Adapter cables are used to attach stations to the MSAU directly or via wall jack. An IBM cable system connector is at one end and a NIC connector is on the other end. The maximum distance between an MSAU and a station is 100 meters or 328 feet.

Token ring uses several types of cable as shown below:

Cable type	Description
Type 1 cable	Made of braided cables shielded around two twisted pairs of # 22 AWG copper. Type 1 cable may be used for interconnection.
Type 2 cable	Same as type 1 with additional four twisted pairs of telephone conductors. Type 2 cable may be used for the interconnection of terminal devices located in work areas and distribution panels located in wiring closets.
Type 3 cable	Made of braided cables shielded around two twisted pairs of #22 AWG copper.Made of solid unshielded twisted pair, or UTP, of #22 or #24 AWG copper with at least two twists per twelve inches. Type 3 cable is a less expensive, but more limited alternative. It is susceptible to noise and crosstalk and is subject to greater distance restrictions also.
Type 5 cable	Made of fiber-optic cable. Type 5 cable is used only on the main ring path.
Type 6 cable	Type 6 is also shielded twisted pair. But type 6 cable has a higher loss per unit of length than type 1 or 2. Type 6 cable is typically used for patch cables and extension cables that are used in work areas and wiring closets.
Type 8 cable	Type 8 cable is used for data communications under carpeted floor.
Type 9 cable	Type 9 is a plenum version of type 6 used for fire retardant.

Using token ring over UTP is becoming increasingly popular. MSAUs are now available that will accept both type 1 and type 3 cabling. A new IEEE specification for UTP/TR at 16 Mbps is replacing the 4 Mbps specification. The new specification includes the use of Level 5 UTP wire and has the advantage of less attenuation at 16 Mbps (limiting crosstalk) and distances comparable to type 1. Type 1 cable is still the media of choice in extremely noisy industrial environments where shielded wire is required. Type 1 cable is also very common in large installations.

Troubleshooting a ring is somewhat different than troubleshooting linear Ethernet. When a problem is detected on a token ring, all stations including the active monitor and standby monitor stations will attempt to deal with problems in the background. Normally, the first station turned on is the active monitor. All other stations are standby monitors. Every seven seconds, the active monitor sends out a frame to the next active device in the ring. The frame tells this device which station is the active monitor and requests that the device introduce itself to the next active device on the ring. The process lets each active device that has contacted it. This information is essential in identifying the fault domain. The fault domain is the portion of the ring where a problem may be occurring.

- Beaconing—Token ring allows some automatic error recovery as, for example, when a fault occurs in the cabling of the ring between two stations. Whenever a station does not receive a message from its nearest active upstream neighbor, or NAUN, the station sends out a beacon frame. The beacon frame identifies the approximate area of failure. It also initiates a process called autoreconfiguration. The beacon frame defines a failure domain, which includes the station reporting the failure, the nearest active upstream neighbor (NAUN), and anything in between the station and the NAUN. Nodes within the failure domain will attempt to reconfigure the network.

- Autoreconfiguration— Although we must often examine the addresses and diagnose a beaconing problem, the network board may attempt to fix the problem by itself without our intervention. This process is called autoreconfiguration. The board will disconnect itself from the ring, perform internal diagnostics, and put itself back on the ring if it can safely do so. You must manually reconfigure the token ring board if automatic reconfiguration fails to remove the error from the ring.

    Following are some troubleshooting tips for a token ring network:

a) Reset ports on MSAUs. A useful solution for small non-bridged, non-routed token ring networks is to remove all drop cable connectors, reset all the ports with the initialization or setup tool, and reconnect the drop cables to the MSAU.
b) Make sure the board speed is set correctly. Compare the network speed, either 4 or 16 Mbps, to the token ring board speed. If the board speed is different, all network traffic will stop as a beacon is sent.
    The board speed is displayed on your workstation when you load the token ring driver. The IBM PS/2 Reference Diskette "Autoconfigure" routine may set your board to 4 MBPS. You must override this manually if you want 16 Mbps.
c) Check internal errors in custom statistics for the malfunctioning board.
d) Isolate and divide the network to find faulty NIC or MSAUs. You may adjust the cabling to bypass a single unit failure. You may use special cable testers to work with token ring.
e) Make sure there is no conflict among NICs, or add-in cards. You may remove all add-in cards, then add one board back at a time. Three parameters can be configured with the token ring device drivers: board addresses, shared RAM locations, and early token release. If you have multiple NICs, you must set each board individually.
f) Make sure that the token ring address is set correctly. Token ring addresses are burned into ROM on the network board. If you have to overwrite the address of a token ring board, the new address should be unique on the network and fall into the legal range specified.

g) Mixing MSAUs from different vendors can cause problems. Differences in electrical characteristics, such as impedance, can cause errors.

9.3 TROUBLESHOOTING AN ARCNET AND AN FDDI NETWORK

ARCnet is the oldest of the LAN options. ARCnet is an acronym for Attached Resource Computer network. ARCnet is an ANSI standard 878.1. The core concept of ARCnet is to combine the token passing element of token ring with the star and bus topologies. ARCnet is known for being slow but reliable. That is changing with the newer and faster implementations of ARCnet. ARCnet has the following advantages:

a) It inexpensive.
b) It is extremely reliable.
c) It is easy to install and troubleshoot.
d) ARCnet supports a variety of cables, including fiber-optic and UTP.
e) ARCnet has good interoperability using ARCnet components from various manufacturers.

ARCnet has the following disadvantages:

a) The standard ARCnet speed, 2.5 Mbps, is slow.
b) ARCnet was not designed with interconnectivity in mind.

ARCnet is normally distributed in a cluster of hubs on one or more buses. The hubs may be active or passive. Every workstation in a network must be connected to a hub. Active hubs are powered and normally have eight ports.Each active hub regenerates the signal before distributing it. Passive hubs are not powered and simply distribute the signal to their four ports. Like token ring, ARCnet eliminates contention for the cable by circulating a token. ARCnet is sometimes called the token-bus network. TCNS is a derivative of standard ARCnet that can be used to achieve higher speeds. TCNS is an acronym for Thomas-Conrad Network System. TCNS can achieve 100 Mbps. Because it is built on the simplicity of ARCnet, TCNS is currently the least expensive of the high-speed solutions. TCNS concentrators cost much less than their FDDI equivalents.

ARCnet is a token-passing star bus network using RG-62A/U 93-ohm coaxial cable. From the file server, the cable attaches to either a passive or an active hub. These hubs act as signal splitters. For an active hub, it acts as a signal also. From a hub, the cable connects to another hub or network node (PC). Unused nodes on an active hub should be terminated, although this is not required. Unused nodes on a passive hub must be terminated using a 93-ohm terminator. A passive hub cannot connect to another passive hub. A passive hub cannot connect to two or more active hubs.

Although active hubs are self-terminating, this termination can fail. When it does, the failure may be difficult to detect. Hence, terminating of unused active hub ports is a wise and inexpensive investment. The ARCnet RG-62A/U 93-ohm coaxial cable length limitations are as follows: 100 feet is the maximum at either side of the passive hub; 2,000 feet is the maximum at either side of the active hub; and 20,000 feet is the maximum between any two nodes in the network

From	To	Maximum Length
Network node	Network node	20,000 feet
Network node	Active hub	2,000 feet
Network node	Passive hub	100 feet
Active hub	Passive hub	100 feet
Active hub	Active hub	2,000 feet
Passive hub	Passive hub	Does not work

An ARCnet node address may be from 1 to 225 and must be unique in a network. The Network Time-out setting, a unique setting to ARCnet, is the time a board will listen before it assumes the next node is no longer there. Its default setting is 31 microseconds. A longer time will allow a longer distance network. A longer time will slow the network communications. When stations enter or leave the network, or when certain faults occur, ARCnet networks perform autoreconfiguration, or recon. ARCnet supports a variety of cables, including fiber-optic and UTP:

Cable Type	Description
Twisted pair	You must use special boards and hubs with twisted-pair ARCnet cable. Cable lengths can be up to 400 feet, or 120 meters. Allow a maximum of 32 stations on a cable. TCNS equipment permits 800 feet, or 240 meters. The standard cable specification calls for #22-24 AWG made of solid copper. Two twisted pairs are in a shielded cable with a solid copper core. A minimum of two twists per foot is required. The impedance is 105 ohms +/– 20 percent running at 5 MHz.
Linear bus	Linear bus ARCnet cable requires special boards that permit multiple nodes, up to a maximum of eight boards on a bus, to share the same cable. It uses BNC T-connectors for attachment. It requires termination. The trunk cable can be up to 1,000 feet, or 302 meters long. Some of the newer boards have built-in termination which can be activated by a jumper when the boards are used for nodes at the end of the chain.
Fiber-optic	This greatly increases the distance and bandwidth of an ARCnet network.

The star topology of ARCnet lends itself to speedy problem isolation because we can easily disconnect most parts of the network. Following are some of the troubleshooting tips for an ARCnet network:

a) Some ARCnet hardware from certain vendors does not work with passive hubs.
b) Do not connect two hubs into a ring.
c) Make sure that the ARCnet board IRQ, DMA, and base I/O address settings are correct.
d) Be careful not to duplicate addresses on ARCnet boards.
e) Replace or check terminators using a VOM. Failure to terminate unused ports on a passive hub will cause signal reflections.
f) Check the hubs. LEDs are often used on active hubs to monitor their status. Because active hubs are powered, the problem may be as simple as a blown fuse or an incorrect voltage setting for a local power source.
g) Check for autoreconfigurations. Whenever a node is activated on an ARCnet segment, a system reconfiguration occurs. Some ARCnet drivers, such as the ARCnet ODI drivers from SMC (PC500 and PS110), have custom statistics regarding these autoreconfigurations. These statistics indicate how many times the network has had to reconfigure. They may indicate a cable disconnect in the case of constant reconfiguration.
h) ARCnet is not compatible with SFT III.

FDDI (Fiber Distributed Data Interface) is a LAN standard using fiber-optic cables. The standards are under the guidance of ANSI Committee X3T9.5. The fiber-optic cable carries a light source, which is generated by a laser or an LED. FDDI uses a timed token rotation, rather than multiple tokens, to achieve high data rates. An FDDI ring never has more than one token at a time. All stations negotiate for level of service, or how soon they need to have possession of the token. FDDI bypasses low-priority stations to speed up high-priority work.

FDDI has the following advantages:

a) It is designed to run at 100 Mbps.
b) It supports long cable distances.
c) Network management has been built into the FDDI specification.
d) Its standard ensures fair access to the medium, unless the operator intervenes.
e) Fiber-optic cable increases reliability by eliminating cable breaks and EMI.
f) Fiber-optic cable is difficult to wire tap.
g) Fiber-optic cable can maintain ground isolation, since it does not conduct electricity.
h) The cable cost is comparable to that of a UTP.

The disadvantages of an FDDI are as follows:

a) Its concentrators can cost over $1,000 per port.
b) Its network boards are also relatively expensive.
c) Substantial expertise is needed to install and maintain an FDDI network.

TP-PMD (Twisted Pair-Physical Medium Dependent), a short-distance form of FDDI using copper cables, is also available. TP-PMD exists under an informal standard in the marketplace. It is a proposed ANSI standard, X39T.5/93-TP-PMD/312 Rev2.1. TP-PMD is much less expensive than FDDI. It does not provide the same security advantage or resistance as FDDI.

FDDI networks consist of dual counter-rotating rings. The primary ring moves data in one direction, while a backup ring performs backups and other services in the opposite direction. You may attach workstations and other devices, such as bridges and routers, to one or both rings through the concentrators. Class A stations are stations connected to both rings. Class B stations are stations connected in only one direction. Class A stations have to be very stable because failure could mean a break in both rings.

FDDI supports up to 1,000 connections with a maximum fiber-optic path length of 200 km. It uses frames of up to 9,000 symbols. A symbol is 4 bits. Therefore, it takes two symbols to make a byte. An FDDI frame can be 4,000 bytes. Its frame is smaller than the maximum available for 16 Mbps token ring. FDDI handles network access in the same way the token ring standard does. A station must capture the token before it can transmit frames. Like IEEE 802.5, FDDI uses beaconing to isolate serious failures, such as breaks in the ring. Each station monitors the ring for problems that might require ring initialization.

Under normal conditions, traffic flows only in the primary ring. The secondary ring stays idle. When a fault occurs, FDDI can automatically reconfigure, or wrap the network so that the operation is still possible in the event of a failure of the primary ring. The stations immediately before and after the problem reroute the data they receive onto the other ring, sending it in the opposite direction and, thereby, reconstructing the broken ring. For example, a ring of 500 Class A stations and having a total circumference of 100 km becomes a ring of 1000 stations and 200 km of cable upon failure of a segment. Therefore, 500 stations and 100 km of cable are cited as the limits for an FDDI ring.

Here are some troubleshooting tips for an FDDI network:

a) Match the fiber-optic cable type with the intended distance between nodes. Multimode fiber is acceptable for distances up to 2 km.
b) Use an OTDR (Optical Time Domain Reflectometer) to test breaks on a fiber-optic cable. You may also use an optical power meter and a known source of light energy. You may use a light source as simple as a flashlight.
c) Look for bad connectors, bad connections, or an open condition on the cable. A loss of optical power greater than 11 decibels is serious.

d) Clean the connectors with a lint-free cloth dipped in alcohol. Since data is carried by light in FDDI, dirty connectors can cause problems.
e) Use glass fiber-optic cable instead of plastic optic cable. Plastic fiber-optic cables are available, but are much less robust than glass cables.
f) FDDI has an unavoidable delay factor of much as 4 milliseconds.
g) Use a source routing bridge when using FDDI with NetWare.

9.4 TROUBLESHOOTING THE WORKSTATION

After completing this section, you should be able to do the following:

- Troubleshoot IPX-based and ODI-based DOS workstations.
- Install and troubleshoot a remote boot workstation.
- Use TRACK ON to troubleshoot workstation connection and login problems.
- Diagnose and fix workstation conflicts based on resources such as IRQ, memory, and DMA.

There are three common types of NetWare clients: IPX/NETX, IPX/ODI, and NetWare DOS requester. In a client/server interaction, a client requests services from a server. For example, a DOS-based application residing on the client workstation can request file services, such as writing to and reading from files, from the NetWare file server. In order to do this, the workstation must have the following two programs running:

Program	Description/Usage
IPX.COM	IPX, or internetwork packet exchange, is a Novell proprietary communication protocol. NetWare lets us use IPX to manage the connections between network devices, such as workstations, file servers, routers, etc.
	IPX uses a LAN driver, software, to control the network board for data delivery. IPX.COM assigns source and destination addresses to a data packet ,and it addresses and routes outgoing data packets across the network. IPX also directs the returning data by reading the data addresses assigned and assures correct delivery by using the SPX protocol to monitor the transmissions. You must use WSGEN.EXE to create a custom IPX.COM for each network board. Because the driver cannot be separated from the protocol stack, the use is limited to one protocol stack per network board.
NETX.EXE	NETX.EXE, or NetWare Shell, establishes, maintains, and terminates the connection between the applications on the workstation and the server.

If a workstation cannot establish a connection to the file server, perform the following procedure:

a) Make sure to match the IPX/NETX Workstations. You may check your IPX configuration with IPX –i.
b) Check for IRQ, DMA, and memory conflicts.
c) Check for frame type conflicts on Ethernet topologies.
d) Make sure IPX is properly bound to the LAN driver at the file server.
e) Load each LAN driver individually, rather than with a batch file. This will permit you to see the result of each step.
f) Run the diagnostic utilities to verify the NIC setting. A very common error is to use UTP cable when the board is set for coaxial.
g) Determine whether a good physical connection exists. Run the COMCHECK diagnostic program to circumvent NETX.
h) Make sure the network board is properly seated.
i) Make sure the cables are properly connected.

You may attach to a file server other than the currently attached server as follows:

Option	Description/Usage
Login command	Includes the new preferred server name in your LOGIN command.
NET.CFG file	Designates the new preferred server in the NET.CFG file.

With the right parameters set, the shell polls up to five servers, searching for an available connection. This designates the server that we want to attach first. This helps assure our connection to the network. If the specified server has a connection available, the shell attaches to that server.

The ODI specification is designed to simplify support for multiple protocols on a single network. You may use ODI to consolidate the support for multiple protocols that have less than one driver installed. Any LAN driver communicates with any ODI protocol stack, such as IOX or TCP/IP. With ODI, one network board in the server can support various clients on the network.

The NetWare 3.12 and NetWare 4 operating systems are shipped with only ODI drivers. An ODI driver has several advantages over IPX.COM. It simultaneously supports multiple protocols and frame types, simplifies support of multiple protocols on a single network, and facilitates the integration of new protocols as they emerge. It allows software drivers to be upgraded without regenerating the shells. It provides improved memory management due to modularity and can be unloaded in reverse order for troubleshooting. It allows up to four active network boards in the client station and supports LANalyzer for Windows. DOS ODI clients require the following software to establish a connection with the network:

Layer	Description/Usage
NIC and MLID layer	MLIDs are LAN drivers that support the ODI specification.
NE2000.COM	MLID is an acronym for Multiple Link Interface Drivers

	NetWare 3.1x requires MLID. A LAN driver connects the software and the physical network components. It is the software that activates and controls the NIC and provides communication between the LSL and the NIC. MLIDs accept packets in any communication protocol, such as IPX packets from IPX workstations, AppleTalk packets from Macintosh workstations, and TCP/IP packets from any workstation.
Link support layer (LSL)	The LSL acts as a switchboard to route network packets from different protocol between the LAN drive and the communication protocol by identifying the type of packet received and passing the packets to the right protocol in the protocol stack layer. When network information arrives at a workstation, LSL enables the workstation to communicate over several protocols by routing IPX packets to IPXODI or by routing UNIX data to software support TCP/IP protocol.
Protocol stack layer IPXODI.COM	This layer manages communication among network stations. It includes protocol stacks such as IPX, AppleTalk, and TCP/IP. IPXODI delivers packets. Once a packet arrives, it will either be passed to the DOS requester or it will be sent back down to another network. IPXODI can deliver the packets only on a best effort basis. Delivery is guaranteed only when using the SPX protocol.
NetWare shell NETX	NETX intercepts requests for DOS services at the workstation. NETX provides services for files and printing.

Following are the basic steps for installing a DOS ODI workstation:

Layer	Description/Usage
Check workstation	Verify that the workstation is functional.
Get ODI LAN driver	Make sure that a DOS ODI LAN driver for the NIC is available.
Configure and install NIC	Make sure that the NIC is appropriate for your cabling topology.
Copy ODI files to disk	Copy ODI files to either a FD or hard disk. These include: LSL.COM The LAN driver IPXODI.COM NETX
Create the CONFIG.SYS file	This file specifies devices and device drivers in DOS.
Create AUTOEXEC.BAT	This autoloads NetWare files each time the workstation is booted.
Create the NET.CFG file	This sets parameters for DOS ODI files.

You may use the following commands in the Link Driver section of the Net.CFG file:

Link Driver Option	Description/usage
INT [#1	#2] interrupt_#	Configures the NIC's interrupts.
PORT[#1|#2] hex_start_address[hex_#_length]	Declares the starting port and number of ports of the NIC.

DMA [#1|#2]channel_#	Configures the NIC's DMA channels.
MEM[#1|#2]hex_starting_address_[hex_length]	Declares memory range for NIC use.
PROTOCOL name hex_protocol_ID frame_type	Lets the existing LAN driver handle the protocol.
FRAME frame_type	Declares the frame type used by the NIC.
NODE ADDRESS hex_address	Overrides the hard-coded NIC address.
SLOT number	Disables the fault scan.
SAPS number	Sets number of service access points for the LANSUP driver.
LINK STATIONS number	Sets number of link stations needed for the LANSUP driver.
ALTERNATE	Makes LANSUP, token ,or PCN2 use another NIC.
MAX FRAME SIZE number	Maximum number of bytes put out by token ring adapter.

The following is a sample NET.CFG file using ODI drivers with the NE2000 board.

Sample Command	Description/Usage
LINK DRIVER NE2000	Declares ODI driver for NE2000 NIC.
INT 2	Declares interrupt at 2.
PORT 300	Declares port address at 300 hex.
FRAME Ethernet_802.3	Declares frame type.
FRAME Ethernet_802.2	Declares frame type.
DMA 3	Declares the DMA channel as 3.
MEM D000	Declares memory address.
LINK SUPPORT	
BUFFERS 8	Sets the # of LSL receive buffers. NetWare TCP/IP requires 2 minimum.
MEMPOOL 4096	Sets the size of the memory pool buffers (IPXODI protocol does not use this.) NetWare TCP/IP needs 2048 bytes minimum
NetWare DOS requester	
FIRST NETWORK DRIVE = F	Declares F as the first network drive.
PREFERRED SERVER =FS_EET	Sets FS_EET as the default server.
CONNECTIONS = 50	Sets maximum connections at 50.
SHOW DOTS = ON	

The NetWare DOS requester replaces the previous NetWare shell and all its variants. It is shipped with all versions of NetWare from 3.12 on up. The NetWare DOS requester has several new features:

Feature	Description/Usage
Modularity	Enables adopting third party and future functionality.
Memory swapping	Enables efficient memory usage.

DOS redirection	Eliminates the duplication of effort between the shell & DOS.
System optimization	Includes packet burst and large internet packet support.
Compatibility	NETX.VLM provides backward compatibility with previous versions of NetWare. NDS.VLM provides compatibility with NetWare 4.

There are three ways for applications and users to make calls to the DOS requester:

a) Call the DOS requester before calling DOS.
b) Call the DOS requester through DOS using the INT 2FH redirector.
c) Call the DOS requester without going through DOS.

The NetWare DOS requester is composed of two main components:

Component	Description/usage
VLM.EXE	VLM.EXE is the VLM manager that loads and manages the VLMs. It handles DOS redirection differently then NETX.EXE: VLM.EXE works with DOS to handle file and print requests, but NETX.EXE handles file and print requests without involving DOS. For existing applications that require specific APIs used in NETX.EXE we should use NETX.VLM the with the DOS requester to provide the shell functionality of NETX.EXE.
VLMs	VLM is an acronym for Virtual Loadable Module. A VLM is a TSR program that performs related functions.

VLM.EXE, the VLM manager, is responsible for handling requests from applications and routing them to the proper VLM. It is also responsible for managing communications between modules, including multiplexor and child modules. Finally, it is responsible for controlling memory services, allocation, and management. You must run VLM.EXE to enable the DOS requester. The VLM manager will load a default sequenced series of VLM files. VLM.EXE supports DOS.3.1 and above. VLM.EXE works with XMS 2.0, EMS, and conventional memory, but by default it selects XMS first. VLM.EXE selects EMS if XMS is not available, and selects conventional memory if both XMS and EMS are not available.

You may use VLM.EXE to load VLMs in three ways:

a) Load VLMs found in the current directory if "VLM" is used.
b) Load VLMs as specified in the NET.CFG if the "USE DEFAULT = OFF" setting is used.
c) Load VLMs listed in the directory, or file_spec, if the "VLEM/C=file_spec" setting is used.

There are two categories of VLMs:

316

VLM category	Description/usage
Parent VLMs	Also called multiplexors; these route requests to the applicable children VLMs.
Children VLMs	These handle particular implementations of logical grouping functions.

There are several types of VLMs available:

VLM type	Description/usage
DOS redirection VLMs	The DOS requester makes a NetWare server look like a DOS drive to the user by having REDIR.VLM provide the redirector level of client services.
REDIR.VLM	REDIR.VLM is responsible for DOS redirection services.
Service protocol VLMs	Handles requests for specific services such as broadcast messages, file reads and writes, and print redirection.
NWP.VLM	This is the NetWare Protocol Multiplexor that establishes and maintains connections, logins, and logouts. It handles broadcasts. NWP.VLM also handles the particular network server implementation by coordinating services with its children VLMs: NDS.VLM for NetWare 4.0 NDS, BIND.VLM for bindery services, and LITE.VLM for NetWare Lite Services.
FIO.VLM	The file input/output module implements the basic file transfer protocol. FIO.VLM handles cached, non-cached, or burst mode reads and writes.
PRINT.VLM	The printer redirection module provides printing services using the FIO.VLM for file write.
Transport protocol VLMs	These provide packet transmission and other transport-related services. FIO.VLM is responsible for maintaining server connections.
TRAN.VLM	The transport protocol multiplexor supports transport modules. TRAN.VLM is responsible for routing transport protocols to its child VLMs: IPXNCP.VLM for IPX services, and TCPNCP.VLM for TCP/IP services.

VLMs are load-order dependent:

a) You must load children VLMs before parent VLMs.
b) You must load the preferred NetWare protocol first.
c) You must load BIND.VLM before NDS.VLM if you use the bindery instead of using NDS.
d) You must then load the multiplexor, NWP.VLM.

Keep the following in mind when working with the NetWare DOS requester:

a) VLMs will load from the current directory unless you specify another directory in the configuration file.
b) You must load the children VLMs before the parent VLMs.
c) You can not load a VLM with a file extension other than ".VLM". To avoid loading an unwanted VLM, rename it with a different extension or do not include it in the NET.CFG file.
d) NETX.COM or NETX.EXE causes conflict with the DOS requester. You should use NETX.VLM to provide the shell function of NETX.EXE.
e) IPXODI.COM must be loaded before loading the IPXNCP.VLM. The IPXNCP.VLM is the transport protocol implementation using IPX.

9.5 DISKLESS WORKSTATIONS, VIRUS PROTECTION, AND TRACK ON

Computer viruses spread by changing files based on potential rights of the user. Blocking access points to the network can prevent viruses. Major access points are floppy disk drives and modem connections. Hence, personal diskettes and downloaded software should be restricted and screened. You may protect client workstations by setting up diskless workstations or remote booting of workstations.

You must follow the following virus prevention guidelines to protect your server and workstations:

a) Limit supervisor account usage. Limit workstations where supervisors can log in. Use the supervisor account only when needed. Assign workgroup or user account managers rather than supervisor equivalent.
b) Do not grant supervisory or access control rights in personal directories.
c) Flag executable files to the Read Only (RO) attribute.
d) Use diskless workstations with remote booting capacity. Do not install floppy drives on client stations.
e) Control modem use on the network.
f) Use virus-scanning software.
g) Screen or restrict personal diskettes and downloaded software.
h) Scan software before installing it on the network.
i) Use write-protected working copies of original software diskettes.
j) Back up the system after scanning for viruses.

The advantages of using diskless or remote boot workstations are:

Advantage	Description/file
Greater security	Since workstations do not have floppy drives, the use of unauthorized programs is prevented as well as the introduction of computer viruses.

Speedy boot	Some Ethernet remote boot chips are faster than hard disks.
Less expense	Diskless workstations are less expensive than workstations with large disk drives.
More convenience	No need to handle floppy disks or hard disks.

You may use the following steps to set up a file server for diskless workstation login:

a) Load RPL.NLM on the file server.
b) Bind RPL.NLM to the NIC.
c) Make sure the SYS:LOGIN directory contains the bootstrap program files.
d) Run DOSGEN.EXE to create the remote boot disk boot image files in SYS:LOGIN.

You must install and enable a remote boot PROM on the NIC in the diskless workstation. Sometimes, it may be necessary to install diskless or remote boot workstations. You must install and enable a remote boot PROM on the NIC in the diskless workstations. A boot PROM is a read-only memory chip that resides on the NIC. The boot PROM allows the workstation to remote boot from a remote boot disk image file stored on the NetWare server's hard disk. The code in the boot PROM is executed during the boot sequence on the workstation. The boot PROM establishes communication with the server and returns the appropriate boot information to the workstation.

When a diskless workstation is started, it requires information, including system sectors, File Allocation Tables (FATs), and directory tables. The requested information is accessed from a remote boot disk image file on the server. The boot disk image file contains the information that would normally be found on the workstation's hard disk or boot diskette. Whenever the workstation makes a read request, the boot PROM intercepts the request and converts it into a network read request. You must create a workstation boot diskette for each diskless workstation.

The workstation boot diskette must contain the following files:

Category	Description/Usage
DOS boot files	IBMBIO.SYS, IMBDOS.SYS, COMMAND.COM, CONFIG.SYS, AUTOEXEC.BAT.
Workstation files	Files such as LSL, NE2000, IPXODI, and NETX.EXE.
Optional files	Files such as a mouse driver, Mouse.COM.

You may use the DOSGEN utility to create the diskless workstation remote boot files by compiling all the files saved on the floppy diskette. DOSGEN.EXE is stored under the SYS: SYSTEM directory. These remote boot files must be placed on the file server and run from the file server. Following are the diskless workstation remote boot files:

Category	Description/File
NET$DOS.SYS	File for single remote boot workstation.
BOOTCONF.SYS and .SYS files	Remote boot image files for multiple workstations.

The RPL.NLM, or Remote Program Load NLM, acts as a protocol stack and responds to the IBM Remote Program Load frames as defined in the IBM Remote Program Load User's Guide. RPL is used in networks that have diskless workstations using the RPL BIOS module. RPL is supported on IBM Token Ring boards, IBM PC network boards (older IBM systems), some IBM Ethernet network boards, and Novell or OEM network boards that have the Remote Boot PROM installed.

RPL has five bootstrap programs, each of which is used with a specific type of network board. Following are the basic steps for installing RPL.NLM on a NetWare server:

a) Install RPL in the SYS:\SYSTEM directory.
b) Type LOAD RPL at the console prompt.
c) Make sure that the proper .RPL files are in the SYS:\LOGIN directory. The .RPL files are the bootstrap program files.
d) Bind RPL to a board. Since RPL.NLM is a protocol stack, we must bind it to all network boards that have RPL clients attached to them.

Sample Command

Bind RPL TO board_name[ACK],[FRAME=ff],[GNS],[NODEFAULT], [PTOTECT],[PS=server],[TRO],[WAIT TIME=sss]

e) Install the RPL PROM on the network board if it did not come pre-installed. You may need to set up a DIP switch or jumper block.

Following are the basic steps for setting up a remote boot workstation:
a) Set up remote boot PROM on NICs. For token ring networks, we must load RPL.NLM at the file server before booting the workstation.
b) Load TOKENRPL.NLM.
c) Log in as SUPERVISOR from another workstation with floppy drive.
d) Create, then insert the workstation boot disk into drive A.
e) Copy the AUTOEXEC.BAT file to both SYS: LOGIN and the user's default directions. You must copy the AUTOEXEC.BAT file from the boot disk in drive A to both the SYS: LOGIN directory and the default directory declared in the user's login directory. Be careful: the user may get a "batch file missing" error at login if the AUTOEXEC.BAT file is missing from either SYS: LOGIN or the user's default directory.

f) Run DOSGEN from the SYS: LOGIN directory. It creates, then saves a boot image file, NET$DOS.SYS, in the SYS: LOGIN directory.

Following are sample commands to run on the DOSGEN utility after logged in:

Sample command	Example/description
MAP F:=SYS:SYSTEM	Maps drive F: to SYS:SYSTEM.
Map G:= SYS.LOGIN	Maps drive G: to SYS:LOGIN.
G:	Changes the directory to SYS: LOGIN.
F: DOSGEN.EXE	Runs DOSGEN.EXE from the SYS:LOGIN directory.
Copy A:\AUTOEXEC.BAT	Copies AUTOEXEC.BAT to the SYS: LOGIN directory.
Copy A:\AUTOEXEC.BAT user_dir	Copies AUTOEXEC.BAT to the user's default directory.
Flag NET$DOS.SYS S	Flags the NET$DOS.SYS FILE as Shareable.
Grant M to user_name	Grants the modify right to a remote boot user in SYS:LOGIN.

g) Flag the NET$DOS.SYS file in SYS:LOGIN directory as a Shareable file:

Flag NET$DOS.SYS S

h) Grant the modify right to the remote boot user in SYS:LOGIN:

Grant M to user_name

Following are the basic steps for setting up multiple remote boot workstations:

a) Set up the remote boot PROM on NICs.
b) Log in as SUPERVISER from a workstation with a floppy drive.
c) Create, then insert the workstation boot disk into drive A. You must create a workstation boot diskette for each diskless workstation. You must rename the AUTOEXEC.BAT file on each diskette to a unique name with the .BAT file extension:

Rename AUTOEXEC.BAT new_name.BAT

You must record the network address and node address for the corresponding workstation that will use the batch file on the workstation configuration sheet. You have to declare this information when we create the BOOTCONF.SYS file. You must create a new AUTOEXEC.BAT file on each diskette with only one command to execute the renamed batch file.

d) Copy each batch file to both the SYS: LOGIN and user's default directories. You must copy each of the renamed batch files from the boot disk in drive A to both the SYS: LOGIN directory and the default directory declared in the user's login directory. Be careful: the user may get a "batch file missing" error login if the renamed batch file is missing from either the SYS: LOGIN or the user's default directory.

e) Run DOSGEN from the SYS: LOGIN directory. It creates, then saves a boot image file, new_name.SYS, in the SYS:LOGIN directory. You must record the network address and node address for the corresponding workstation that will use this file on the workstation configuration sheet. You have to declare this information when you create the BOOTCONF.SYS file. Repeat this and previous steps for each remote boot workstation.

f) Create or modify the BOOTCONFIG.SYS file. The BOOTCONFIG.SYS file must contain an entry for each customized boot file image. You can not create a multiple remote boot image file, BOOTCONFIG.SYS, if one already exists in the SYS: LOGIN directory. But you can use any text editor to modify this file. Use the text editor to add an entry for each remote boot image file:
0x[network address],[node or station address]=[boot image file name]

g) Flag the .SYS files and .BAT files as shareable. You must flag the .SYS files and .BAT files in SYS:LOGIN directory as shareable files as follows:

Flag *.SYS S
Flag *.BAT S

h) Grant the Modify right to the remote boot user in SYS: LOGIN. Change the directory to SYS:LOGIN directory, then enter:

Grant M to user_name

In order to let some of the remote boot workstations attach to another file server on the same network, you must do one of the following:

1) Create remote boot .SYS and .BAT files on the target server.
2) Copy remote boot .SYS and .BAT files from the default server to the target server.

RPLFIX allows workstations to load remotely with DOS 5.x and above. You need to run RPLFIX after you create the boot disk image file.

RPLFIX[f:]<boot image file name>

The remote workstation may hang during the reset process if we are resetting using DOS 5.x or above and the boot image file has not been loaded. The combination of DOS 5.0, ODI drives, and remote boot can cause problems with some revisions of remote boot PROMs. Be sure to check with the boot PROM vendor. Because RPLFIX modifies the boot disk image, we only have to run it once. Also, if you are using ODI drivers with this boot PROM, you need to load RPLODI.COM after LSL.COM and before the network board driver.

Keep the following tips in mind when the remote boot workstation can not boot:

a) If you get the "error opening boot disk image file" message, you may attach to another file server that does not contain the remote boot image files. You may solve this problem by copying the remote boot image files from the default file server to the other file servers on the network.

b) If you get the "batch file missing" message, make sure that the AUTOEXEC.BAT file is in one of the following directories:

SYS: LOGIN	For every file server we could possibly attach to.
Default/first mapped	For every file server we normally log in to.

c) If only one workstation can remote boot at a time, make sure that the .SYS files are flagged as shareable and that users are assigned the modify right to the SYS: SYSTEM directory.

d) If you can not remote boot a token ring workstation, make sure that TOKENRPL.NLM is loaded on the NetWare server.

e) Use track on to check if the boot prom is sending packets.

f) Use the track on console command at the NetWare server console and watch for "get nearest server" requests from the remote boot workstation.

g) Load the monitor at the server to see which remote boot file the workstation opens.

h) Verify the files on boot diskettes.

If a workstation can not remote boot and you have another workstation with an identical configuration and a floppy disk drive, you may try with the boot diskette created for the first workstation on the second workstation. NetWare servers and routers track routing information through RIP and advertised service information through SAP. Each server and router records the RIP and SAP information to identify:

a) the final destinations of packets

b) the fastest route to a device

c) the locations of network services

You may use the following commands at any server or router to list RIP and SAP information:

Command	Description
Display networks	Lists all networks and assigns network numbers (internal and cabling system); lists the number of hops and ticks needed for a packet to reach the network.
Display servers	Lists all servers and services advertised with SAP and the number of hops needed to reach each server. It will not list a server if its SYS: volume is not mounted.
Reset router	When file servers or routers on the network go down, and packets sent to or through their routers are lost due to inaccuracy of the router tables, you may use reset router to reset the router tables. This command resets the router in each file server on the network and the router will send a request to other servers for known networks; it then builds a new accurate router table.
TRACK ON	You may use TRACK ON on at a file server or a router console to display the continuous flow of incoming and outgoing RIP and SAP information for investigation of problems with workstations trying to connect to a server and for diagnosing problems with routers and servers on the internetwork. Track on creates a router tracking screen and displays information on the Server Network layout (route). A connection request is broadcast on the network. On the router tracking screen, track on shows "in" for a NetWare server receiving information and "out" for a NetWare server that is sending or broadcasting information. FFFFFFFFFF indicates that a message is for all nodes on the network. "Get nearest server" is for receiving a connection request from a client. "Give nearest server" is for responding to a connection request from a client. It also lists the number of hops (number of routers crossed) and the estimated time in ticks (number of 1/18 of a second) required for a packet to reach its destination.
TRACK OFF	Disables TRACK ON; turns off the tracking function.

IPX routers use RIP (Router Information Protocols) to exchange route information. IPX clients use RIP to find the fastest route to destination networks.

Servers, print servers, gateways, and other services use SAP (Service Advertising Protocols) to advertise their services, names, and addresses around the network. IPX packets can be addressed to a server that has been advertised because its routing information has been placed on the servers that received the SAP.

A file server must be broadcasting SAPs to be seen by or to respond to a workstation. Routers use SAPs to exchange server information. Workstations use SAPs to locate servers. You may use TRACK ON to verify that SAPs are being broadcast. If TRACK ON displays an outbound line with a file server's name in it, the file server is successfully broadcasting SAPs. A file server may not be sending SAPs if IPX is not bound to the board in the server or if the server's volumes are not mounted. You may decode a router-tracking screen using the information shown below:

Category / code	Example / description / usage
Sample incoming SAP	In [00200090:00102315378d] 11 :42am FS_ET 3 Fs12_25b 3 fs4_100b 3 caddsco2 2
In	Indicates an incoming message.
00200090	The network number of an external router sending the packet.
001023515378d	The network node of the server sending the packet.
FS_ET	The server name known by the sending router.
3	The number of hops from the sending router to this file server.
Sample incoming RIP	In 00000099:004509515346c 11:43am 0000002 2/3 00000003 3.4 00000099 5/6 0951127b 2/3
In	Indicates an incoming message.
2	The number of hops from the sending router to this network.
/3	The number of ticks from the sending server to this network.
Category / code	Example / description / usage
Outgoing RIP sample	Out [0950121b:FFFFFFFFFFFF 11:43:04am 0000002 2/3 000000003 ¾ 0000009 5/6 0875226c 3/2
Out	Indicates an outgoing message.
0875226c	The network number of the device sending the packet.
FFFFFFFFFFFF	Indicates a broadcast message.
00000002	The network number of a network known

	by the sending server.
3/	The number of hops from the sending server to this network.
/2	The number of ticks from the sending server to this network.

Keep the following in mind when diagnosing workstation problems:

a) When the workstation loads the client software and hangs, or displays the "A file server could not be found" message, you may have a communication problem on the LAN. You may complete the following tasks to diagnose this problem:

1) Make sure that IPX is properly bound to the LAN driver on the server.

2) Run TRACK ON on the file servers and routers involved.

3) Run workstation files as the DOS requester or NetWare shell is running on the workstation. The router tracking screen should display the messages "Get nearest server", "Give nearest server server_name", and "Route Request". If these messages appear, you have established communication.

4) Look for messages from the router tracking screen:

   a) There may be a physical problem if messages do not appear on the router tracking screen. In this case, suspect a problem such as a bad cable, hub, or connection.
   b) The server has a problem if only the statement "Get nearest server" appears repeatedly. The workstation has successfully requested the connection. The server received the request, but could not respond. You might have a network transmission problem in the file server, such as a faulty or improperly configured network board or driver.
   c) The client has a problem if the "Get nearest server" and "Give nearest server" messages appear repeatedly before a "File server not found" message. The workstation might have a physical or configuration problem. The server NIC or its driver might also be causing the problem.

B) If you get the "Unknown file server" error message while a file server is running, and the file server is not listed in the list of the servers when a user initiates the SLIST or NLIST command from a NetWare workstation, an incorrectly configured network number on a server or router may be causing the problem. You may complete the following tasks to diagnose this problem:

1) Run TRACK ON on the file servers and routers involved.

2) Look for messages from the router-tracking screen.

   a) If more than one server have the same internal network number, the screen displays "Warning!!! Multiple router with same Internet address".
   b) If a server has the wrong external network number, the screen displays "Router configuration error!!! Router XXX claims LAN a is YYY".

9.6 TROUBLESHOOTING THE SERVER

When you experience server problems, you should always make sure that you have the latest server software loaded. This software includes the operating system, device drivers, and NLMs.

Novell provides patches for known SERVER.EXE problems. On NETWIRE in the NOVLIB and Novell files or the NOVFILES areas on the NSEPro CD-ROM, Novell provides the following naming conventions for the patch files:

Convention	Description
Sample file names	311ptd.exe
First 3 digits	First 3 digits of the operating system version.
Pt	For passed test.
It	For in test.
D	Revision number of letter.

Novell uses 5 types of patches:

Patch Type	Description
Static patch	A DOS-executable patch that modifies the SERVER.EXE file. You must back up the original SERVER.EXE before using it.
Dynamic	Can be loaded and unloaded while the server is running since dynamic patches are implemented as NLM files. These do not modify the operating system and must be loaded every time the operating system is brought up.
Patch Manager	The NLM which tracks and manages all official patches for NetWare. Patch Manager is available in the same files as the

	patches.
Auto load patches	You should include the loaded patch_name in the server boot file. Some patches should be loaded by the STARTUP.NCF file, while others can be loaded by the AUTOEXEC.NCF file.
List loaded patches	Enter patches at the NetWare server console to list the loaded patches.

You should always load all patches in a kit. The following are basic steps to apply a static patch:

Step	Description
Back up SERVER.EXE	Copy SERVER.EXE to SERVER.OLD.
Copy new patches	Copy static patches to the same server boot directory as SERVER.EXE.
Run new patches	Apply the static patches by typing the following command at the console: Patch_name SERVER.EXE.

Following are basic steps to ensure that a dynamic patch is autoloaded:

Step	Description
Copy new patches	Copy the patch manager and new patches into a directory on the server dos partition which contains the server boot directory.
Edit server boot file	Include the load patch name commands in a server boot file. Some commands are loaded in the STARTUP.NCF file, others in the AUTOEXEC.NCF file.

Device drivers are NLMs that form the communications interface between the NetWare operating system and peripheral devices such as hard disks or network boards. There are two types of device drivers that are supported by a NetWare server:

Type	Description
Disk drivers (*.DSK)	Disk drivers allow hard drive controllers to communicate with hard disks (loaded on system startup).
NPA drivers .HAM .CDM	NPA drivers help the NetWare media manager keep track of and communicate with a variety of storage devices and media.

	NPA is an acronym for NetWare peripheral architecture. HAM is an acronym for host adapter modules. CDM is an acronym for custom device module. You should contact third-party vendors to obtain the newest device drivers.

You may locate the latest versions of NLMs on NetWire in the Novell library NOVLIB area. You may then download them to your hard disk. These files are self-extracting archives: when you type the name of the file, the NLM is automatically extracted. You may then copy the extracted NLM to the SYS: SYSTEM directory on your server.

The following presents recommended guidelines and procedures and a few advance precautions, we will be better prepared to handle server ABENDs and lockups. The primary reason for ABENDs in NetWare is to ensure the stability and integrity of the internal operating system in the event of an abnormal end of a program. The NetWare 3 and NetWare 4 operating systems continually monitor the status of various server activities to ensure proper operation. If NetWare detects a condition that threatens the integrity of its internal data, it abruptly halts the active process and displays an abend message on the screen.

There are two types of errors that may cause ABEND in NetWare:

Error type	Description
CPU-detected error	The CPU can interrupt program execution by issuing an interrupt or an exception when the server's CPU detects an error. An interrupt is generated by an external device that needs attention. An exception is caused by the CPU responding to a condition it detected while executing an instruction. Exceptions are classified as faults, traps, or aborts, based on how they are reported and whether the failed instruction can be restarted. The types of exceptions that are related to abends are the non-maskable interrupt, or NMI, and processor-detected exceptions. NMIs are hardware-specific errors and not related to NetWare.
Consistency check error	Consistency checks are internal tests in the NetWare OS code used to ensure the stability and integrity of internal operating system data. Numerous consistency checks

	are interlaced throughout NetWare to validate critical disk, memory, and communications processes. A failed consistency check is always a serious error because it indicates some degree of memory corruption. A corrupted operating system file, or corrupted or outdated drivers and NLMs might cause consistency check errors, as well as bad packets formed at the client, or hardware failures. Consistency check errors might also be caused by defective memory chips, static electricity discharges, faulty power supplies, or fluctuations in commercial power.

Before NetWare displays an ABEND message on the file server screen, several actions occur. The actions vary, depending on whether the error was CPU detected or code detected. However, the type of information provided on the screen is identical in both cases:

Item	Description
ABEND message string	The text of the ABEND message may help us determine whether it is a CPU-detected ABEND or a core-detected error. The ABEND page fault processor exception (error code 000000000) message is provided to the operating system by the CPU. We may use the error code to learn additional information about the exception.
OS version	Shows the version of the NetWare operating system running on the server.
Running process	Indicates which process was running at the time of the ABEND. A process is a thread or path of execution that runs in the OS. It can be an internal OS process or an NLM process, but the running process may not be the cause of the ABEND.
Stack	The 30 hexadecimal bytes represent part of the CPU's stack for the current running process at the time of the ABEND. All three lines of the stack dump may be useful to technical support people in diagnosing

	the cause of the ABEND.

The same problems that cause server ABENDs may also cause server lockup. There are two types of server lockups that may take place:

Type	Description
Full server lockup	You may receive no response at all from the server console or other NLM screens. Nothing can be done at the server console or other NLM screens. No processes are allowed to run. Connections that are currently logged in or attached are dropped. No one can log in to do work on the server.
Partial server lockup	After partial lockup, you might still be able to log in to the server and do work. In addition, you might be able to toggle to different servers or NLM screens and do
	work. A partial lockup might eventually clear itself up, or it might lead to a full system lockup.

Software or hardware problems may also cause server lockup. One possible cause of server lockup is a server or NLM instruction that becomes caught in a tight loop and does not relinquish control of the CPU.

A process may also lock up resources by blocking access to these resources. Sometimes, you might want to generate a memory image file, or core dump, that lists the entire contents of the server's RAM to diagnose the cause of a server lockup. You may use the following six basic steps to troubleshoot server ABENDs or lockups:

Step	Description
Gather information	You must gather information about the problem.
Identify probable causes	Understand the problem and identify probable causes.
Test possible solutions	You may use several methods or techniques to test your hypotheses.
Use debugging tools	You may use some debugging tools to get additional information.
Solve the problem	You may solve the problem with patches, drivers, and workarounds. Also, you may replace any hardware that is causing the problem.

Document the problem	This will reduce the time needed to solve the same problem if it occurs again.

You should gather the following information for troubleshooting server ABENDs or lockups:

Fact	Description
Error messages	You may get error information from several sources including the ABEND information screen and the server console screen. Two others are the system error log and the volume error log after the server is brought back up.
Changes made recently	Check the server log to view the most recent changes made to the system. The server log should record both hardware and software changes. These records can help us determine if the system has a history of stable operation, and whether this problem has been seen before on this system.
Events before crash	Documents the activities that occurred prior to the server ABEND or lockup. These activities might include events, such as system backups, database rebuilds, and other maintenance; installation or changes in software of hardware; system failures, errors, and warnings; high system workload caused by month end closing, and others.
Hardware configuration	Get a complete list of hardware configuration of the server. Find certification and testing information on these components.
NLMs and NCF files	Get a complete list of NLMs running on the server. Include date and version information for each NLM. Also obtain a list of the STARTUP.NCF and AUTOEXEC.NCF files.

Novell support provides CONFIG.NLM to help us gather this information. You may download CONFIG.NLM from the NSD area of the NetWire. The self-extracting file is named CONFIG.EXE. To run this module, you must have the latest CLIB.NLM loaded on the server. Updates to CLIB can be found on NetWire in LIBx.EXE. You may load CONFIG.NLM to create a text file called CONFIG.TXT in SYS: SYSTEM. A CONFIG.TXT file contains a list of all modules loaded on the server at the time CONFIG.NLM runs. The contents of the CONFIG.SYS and AUTOEXEC.BAT files for the server are a directory listing of SYS: SYSTEM and the local drive.

Once you understand the problem, you may try to identify some possible causes by drawing conclusions from the information gathered and forming one or more hypotheses. You may better understand the problem by asking the following questions:

a) When did the ABEND problem start? Did it coincide with the installation time or with changes made to the hardware or software, etc?

b) Is the server partially or totally locked up?

c) How often does the ABEND occur?

d) Is the ABEND message always showing the same ABEND type or running process?

e) Does it always happen at a certain time of day or during a certain activity? What events occur prior to the ABEND or lockup? Are there any noticeable changes in monitor statistics?

f) What other symptoms or error messages occur prior to the ABEND?

g) Can the problem be duplicated at will, or is it intermittent?

h) Have the latest patches for the NetWare OS been applied?

i) Are all the NLMs and drivers up to date? Are they all certified?

j) What are the details of the server hardware and configuration? These include the type of machine, RAM, controllers, network boards, .NCF files, types of clients, and so on. You may load CONFIG.NLM to find this information.

k) Has the hardware configuration been certified and tested?

l) How are the drivers and NLMs loaded for this hardware configuration?

m) Are any printers, such as a HP jet direct, connected directly to the network? Have you modified this configuration recently?

n) What other information could relate to the ABEND message or lockup? You should check the server error log file, the volume error log file, and other audit type files.

Option	Description
Apply current patches	Over half of the server ABENDs and lockups reported to Novell technical support are resolved by patches and fixes that have already been written. You should always apply known patches, drivers, NLMs, and fixes first. Doing so may save many hours of unnecessary troubleshooting.
Replace components	When we are familiar with the expected

	behavior of each component and already have a good idea of what could be causing the problem, swapping the suspected faulty component is most effective
	It is vital that we swap out only one component at a
	time. This technique is effective for both hardware and software problems.
Simplify configuration	To isolate a problem, remove components from the system one at a time. This technique is effective for both hardware and software problems.
Discuss with peer	We may gain valuable feedback about a problem by discussing possible solutions with other CNEs and Novell support engineers.

If you do not have enough information to make conclusions about an ABEND or lockup, you may use the following debugging tools to help you resolve it:

1) MONITOR.NLM. You may check the LAN statistics in this NLM for high-utilization memory issues and resource conflicts.

2) Network analyzers. You may use a network analyzer to gather troubleshooting information such as LANAnalyzer for Windows from Novell. In many cases knowing about the behavior of protocols and packets on the network can help speed up the resolution of a problem.

3) Memory image file. You may create a memory image or core dump file of the server and send it to Novell technical support for analysis if the problem still exists. You should always apply all the tested and approved NetWare patches to the server before creating and sending in a memory image file. A memory image file is a snapshot of the server at the time of the abend. It shows what was occurring at the time of the abend. It does not provide much of a history. However the memory image often provides enough information for Novell engineers to correctly diagnose the problem.

Since the primary function of a file server is to move data from disk storage to attached users, we need to resolve any performance bottlenecks as quickly as possible. Server performance bottlenecks can be grouped into four basic categories.

1) Disk I/O problems. Disk speed, the number of hard disks, and the intelligence and speed of disk array controllers all play an important role in the efficiency of the disk subsystem. You may load MONITOR at the system console and check the number of dirty cache buffers and the number of current disk requests the system is processing. You may have a disk I/O problem if these numbers are continually growing. In addition you may check the disk light. You may also check to see if the disk light is constantly flashing. This could be an indication of an overloaded hard disk.

2) Network I/O problems. These usually occur in applications, such as file and print services, video servers, and imaging systems, that have a high network utilization rate. To check these problems, you may load MONITOR through the LAN/WAN information screen. In MONITOR we may check:

   a) Send packet to big count
   b) Receive packet overflow count
   c) Receive packet too big count
   d) Send packet miscellaneous errors
   e) No ECB available
   f) Packet receive buffers
   g) Receive packet miscellaneous errors

   You may have a network I/O problem if these numbers are high or growing.

3) CPU problems. Most 486 and above CPUs can handle most of the network requests for CPU-intensive applications. Check with the software vendor for the proper configuration to minimize as many CPU performance problems as possible.
4) Bus I/O problems. Distinguishing between bus I/O and CPU problems is difficult since these components work so closely with each other.

You may solve server performance bottlenecks as follows:

1) Disk I/O problems. Upgrade to fast SCSI II or fast wide SCSI II for disk drive subsystems. Fast SCSI II controllers transfer data at 10 MB/second. Fast/Wide SCSI controllers transfer data at 20 MB/second. You may also use other faster controllers. Other types of controllers have on-board processors to allow CPU-to-memory and disk-to-memory transactions to happen simultaneously. You may use faster disks or replace one large disk with many smaller disks. Multiple small disks are faster because more than one set of read/write heads can be active at one time. The heads do not need to reposition themselves as often.

2) Network I/O problems. Upgrade to a faster NIC that has one channel per bus interface. However, installing additional NICs in the server may result in diminishing returns due to the increased load of servicing the boards. You may also divide overloaded network segments with a bridge or router.

3) CPU problems. Bus master LAN and disk controller boards are capable of doing unassisted data transfers, thus freeing the CPU to perform other tasks. Bus master boards can reduce CPU utilization by a factor of 6 to 1.

4) Bus I/O problems. You may use a bus master. Bus mastering I/O devices contend with cache systems for access to main memory, but run much slower than the CPU. You can also upgrade the server. Most high-performance servers are manufactured to allow I/O devices and the CPU memory to run simultaneously.

Hardware failures can occur due to power fluctuations, viruses, or misuse. When faced with data loss, we generally have a few options:

- Use VREPAIR to repair a damaged volume. You may load VREPAIR.NLM to repair a volume or remove the name space entries from a volume:

  load [path] VREPAIR   load will search SYS:SYSTEM for VREPAIR

  You must use the correct version of VREPAIR to repair a dismounted bad volume while other NetWare server volumes are functioning. After you have finished running VREPAIR, you may mount the required volume. If the damaged volume contains additional name space, you must load the matching NLMs, such as V_MAC.NLM, V_OS.NLM, etc., after loading VREPAIR. NetWare 4.11 attempts to autoload these NLMs. In NetWare 3.12, you must manually load these NLMs. You may use VREPAIR to fix disk problems due to:

Option	Description
Hardware failure	A hardware failure either prevented a volume from mounting or caused a disk read error.
Power failure	A power failure corrupted a volume.
Disk has bad blocks	The volume has bad blocks.
Add name space	The server is displaying memory errors and cannot mount a volume after a name space is added to the volume. If this occurs, we must either add more memory to the server or use VREPAIR to remove the newly added name space.

You may need to run VREPAIR several times to repair heavily damaged volumes. VREPAIR should be run repeatedly until no errors are reported. Following are basic steps to run VREPAIR to repair the SYS: volume:

a) Make sure that VREPAIR.NLM is copied to the DOS partition.
b) Run SERVER.EXE.
c) Make sure that the SYS: volume is dismounted.
d) Load VREPAIR.NLM.
e) Select "repair a volume" from the Options menu.
f) Select the SYS: volume to repair from the list.
g) Change the Current Error Settings, if necessary.
h) Choose the option to continue with the repair.
i) A screen appears listing total errors and current error settings. You may press <F1> anytime to change the settings for not pausing on errors.
j) Press any key to return to the Options menu.
k) Choose the appropriate option to exit.

- Use DSREPAIR to repair damage to NDS in NetWare 4. You may load DSREPAIR.NLM to repair problems in the NDS database.

Load [path] DSREPAIR [-u]

The –u parameter instructs DSREPAIR to run, exit, and then unload from memory without further user assistance. DSREPAIR.NLM can repair records, schema, bindery objects, and external reference.

- Use backups. The most important element of a successful disaster recovery plan is a good backup of NDS and critical data. You should back up your system as often as you can afford to lose the data. Many people have backed up their data faithfully, only to discover later that their backup procedures or media were seriously flawed. You should always test backups in the backup process. Invalid backup files are of no use when you experience a data loss on a volume.
  You may then remedy the disk drive failure with the reliable backup. Before attempting a full restoration from backups, try to recover a volume using VREPAIR or a third-party tool such as ON TRACK Data Recovery for NetWare. If these utilities are unsuccessful, you may have to reformat your hard disk, re-install the operating system, and recover data from your backups. If the data on the server is valuable and the backups are not reliable, you should have experienced data recovery professionals handle the data recovery.

- Use third-party software to recover data. ODR for NetWare is an example of third-party data recovery and protection utilities. ODR is an acronym for ONTRACK Data Recovery and protection utilities. We may use data recovery and protection utilities to do the following:

Option	Description
Recover files	Recovers files without the backup from any volume with errors. Recovers files to another active server through a workstation connection, to a DOS partition, or to a floppy disk.
Rebuild the file system	Rebuilds the file structure within a server volume.
Modify disk sector	Examines, modifies, and saves any sector of a server device.
Check disk media	Does nondestructive disc media analysis to redirect defective sectors to NetWare hot fix areas.

ODR for NetWare is made up of three utilities:

Utility	Description
NetFile 4	NetFile 4 is a file recovery tool and file editor. You may use NetFile 4 to access files in a corrupted NetWare volume or you may use NetFile 4 to save a file to another NetWare server.
NetScan 4	NetScan 4 is designed to examine and nondestructively repair NetWare structural errors that can occur in a NetWare volume. It will examine a NetWare volume for defective sectors and will redirect data in defective blocks to NetWare hot fix areas.
NetDisk 4	NetDisk 4 is a sector editor. NetDisk 4 examines and modifies the data in any sector of a device, hard disk or optical disk. NetDisk 4 can access data from a file server, even if DOS and NetWare can no longer recognize partitions. NetDisk 4 can save track 0, the master boot record to a DOS partition, and later restore it if it becomes corrupted.

You may use ODR for NetWare to create a set of emergency diskettes that can be used to boot the server in the case of a serious SYS: volume or DOS partition corruption. These two diskettes contain SERVER.EXE, STARTUP.NCF (stored as STARTUP.OFF), CLIB.NLM, STREAMS.NLM, and any applicable device drivers.

- Use professional data recovery services. If the data is irreplaceable and valid backups are unavailable, you should not attempt repairs on what has now become the only available copy of your critical data. You should send the damaged disk to the professional data recovery company. Some companies offer onsite service at an additional charge. Professional data recovery services are generally able to recover any data that is still physically recorded on the disk. In the event of a head crash, data may be recoverable from the data areas not directly affected by the crash. If you use utilities that write to the disk or recreate a volume, you will eliminate the option of professional data recovery: you should use utilities only to read or copy data from damaged disks.

9.7 TROUBLESHOOTING THE NETWORK PRINTING

You may find network printing problems in various places, such as a workstation, a print queue, a printing server, a remote printer workstation, or a printer itself. You need to know the following in order to troubleshoot NetWare printing problems:

1) NetWare printing concepts. You must understand the network printing process and components required.

2) NetWare printing setup. You should know the steps to set up NetWare for network printing.

    a) NetWare 3.12 printing. The following are the basic steps for the NetWare 3.12 network printing setup:

        Step 1: Create print queues.
        Step 2: Create a print server.
        Step 3: Configure printers and protocols.
        Step 4: Assign print queues to the printer.
        Step 5: Assign a print server to service multiple file servers, if needed.
        Step 6: Spool printer number to print queue for compatibility, if needed.
        Step 7: Activate the print server by running PSERVER and NPRINTER.

    b) NetWare 4 printing utilities. The following are the basic steps for theNetWare 4.1 network printing setup:

        Step 1: Create print queue objects and specify the volumes for queues.
        Step 2: Create printer objects.
        Step 3: Configure printers and ports.
        Step 4: Assign print queues to the printer.
        Step 5: Create a print server object.
        Step 6: Assign printers to the printer list of the print server.
        Step 7: Activate the print server by running PSERVER and NPRINTER.

3) NetWare printing utilities. You must know how the print utilities function in NetWare 3 and NetWare 4 NWADMIN for NetWare 4.11 only, such as PCONSOLE, PRINTCON, PRINTDEF, NetWare User Tools (NetWare user tools for Windows), CAPTURE, ENDCAP (For NetWare 3 only), and NPRINT.

The following are some tips and techniques for troubleshooting network printing problems:

a) Install the latest software. You may find the most recent printing software in NOVLIB on NetWire.
b) Make sure that he print queue is assigned to the printer.
c) Make sure the printer is assigned to the print server.
d) Check the server's disk space. The NetWare column with the print queue directory must have enough disk space for holding all the possible print jobs.
e) Name the print queue. Use short print queue names.
f) Check the redirected port. Make sure that CAPTURE, NPRINT, or some other application is sending the print job output to the desired redirected LPT port.

Typically, when we begin troubleshooting a network printing problem, we should gather information about the problem first and then try some quick fixes. The following are some quick fix techniques for troubleshooting a network printing problem:

a) Check for any change. Ask "What changed?"
b) Check the cabling.
c) Power the printer off and on.
d) Check the printer cover and paper feed.
e) Check the workstation printer port redirection.
f) Check printing forms.
g) Check the error message. Look for console messages and tools for printer error conditions and printing error messages such as beeps or LCS panel lights.

The following are basic steps we may use to identify if the printing problem occurs before the print job reaches the print queue or after the print job leaves the print queue:

a) Stop print jobs from leaving the print queue. Set the "Allow services by current Print Servers" option to "No".
b) Send a print job to the print queue.
c) Check the print status to see if the print job is in the print queue job list. Redirect the print job to another print queue or printer to see if the print job is corrupted.
d) Identify the problem area. The network printing problem is probably at the workstation if the print job never arrives at the print queue or the print job status indicates adding or hold and never moves to ready. Otherwise, the printing problem probably occurs in the queue after the print job has left the queue.

The following symptoms indicate that the network printing problem may be occuring at the workstation:

a) The printing problem is specific to one workstation only.
b) The print job does not arrive at the print queue or arrives corrupted.
c) The job status never changes. The print job status remains in the adding or hold mode.
d) Jobs are merged together. The print job arrives at the printer, but merges with another print job.

The following are some basic steps for troubleshooting network printing problems:

a) Network-aware applications. Make sure that the correct print queue or printer is selected and also make sure we have the most current printer driver installed. Using an incorrect or out-of-date driver is a common mistake. Verify that the application can print to other network printers.
b) Non-network-aware applications. Make sure that the printer setup is not conflicting with TSRs, NICs, and others. Check printing setup, such as the LPT port and printer driver, inside the application. Try to print to the printer attached directly to the workstation. Verify the print job redirection parameters outside the application.

The following are advanced troubleshooting techniques we may use to solve printing problems at the workstation:

a) Move print queues to a different volume if the volume containing the queue does not have enough disk space.
b) Increase the disk space available on the volume to a user if the user does not have enough allocated disk space.
c) Assign a queue to the printer. Make sure the users know which queue goes with each printer.
d) Create a custom menu. Provide a menu-driven configuration file to allow users to change printers.
e) Use the /keep switch with the CAPTURE command for overnight print jobs if a backup system clears all connections at a set hour.
f) Turn off the TAB. Use the /NT switch with the CAPTURE command to turn off the tabs if TAB parameters cause undesirable laser printing results.
g) Manage the printers or jobs. You may use PRINTDEF and PRINTCON to manage advanced printers and create the needed printer and job definitions.
h) Increase the print buffer size. To accommodate the change made by PRINTDEF and PRINTCON, we may increase the buffer size up to a combined maximum of

255 bytes using the PRINT HEADER and PRINT TAIL commands in the NET.CFG file.

i) Increase the timeout count. If large graphics files are being printed partially or with premature page breaks, increase or disable the timeout count in the job definition.

j) Limit users to 37 job configurations. Each user ID may have up to 37 print job configurations.

k) Share job configurations. You may let users share PRINTCON job configurations by placing the supervisor's PRINTCON.DAT file in SYS: PUBLIC. Use NB to avoid printing the supervisor's banner page. You must delete the PRINTCON.DAT file from each user's mail directory or it will preempt the supervisor's PRINTCON.DAT file. Then change the search mode to 5 for CAPTURE, NPRINT, and PCONSOLE. Use the SMODE command in NetWare3.12, or FLAG in NetWare 4.

l) Check the plotting program. When some applications plot, they expect direct interaction with the plotter. This is a problem when an application's output goes to a queue file on disk rather than to the plotter itself.

    a) Plotting from AutoCAD. For example, when you are plotting from AutoCAD directly to a COM port, AutoCAD will wait for a replay from that port to continue the plot. Since NetWare only redirects printing to LPT ports, AutoCAD ends up waiting for COM port activity when there will not be any.

    b) Saving the plot to a file. You may handle this problem by saving a print job to a file and then using NPRINT OR PCONSOLE to print the job.

    c) Saving the plot to LPT1. You may also save the plot to a file named LPT1 after capturing the LPT device with the CAPTURE command.

Print jobs are saved in the print queue until they are ready to be serviced by a print server. The following symptoms indicate that a network printing problem may be occurring at a print queue:

a) The print job was sent uncorrupted but is corrupted at the print queue.
b) The print server ABENDs when accessing the print queue.
c) Printing orrurs sporadically

We may fix the printing problems at a print queue as follows:

1) Install the latest software. Use the latest versions of workstation files, printer drivers, and utilities. Out-of-date versions of IPX can cause queue errors when using NPRINT.

2) Move the print queues to another volume if the volume containing the queue does not have enough disk space.

3) Check the print port. CAPTURE, NPRINT, or other applications should print to the same LPT port.

4) Shorten the queue name.

5) Rename the print queue. Non-alphanumeric characters in the queue name may cause problems. Try renaming any queues that use non-alphanumeric characters.

6) Fix the corrupted queue. If print jobs that have been captured to a particular queue are not showing up in the queue, the queue may have become corrupted. Use CAPTURE with the show switch to verify where jobs are going. Delete the corrupted queue, then recreate the print queue. All print jobs in the corrupted print queue will be lost.

The following symptoms indicate that a network printing problem may be occurring at the print server:

a) The print job status is active, but the print job is never printed.
b) The print job leaves the print queue, but it is never printed.

The following are basic steps for troubleshooting a printing problem at the print server:

1) Check the queue status to make sure the print server is attached to the print queue.

2) Check the server status. Make sure the print server is running.

3) Restart the print server. Bring down the print server and reinitialize it.

4) Call the vendor for third-party server support.

5) If the problem persists, contact Novell technical support.

You may fix the printing problems at a print server as follows:

Print Servers:

1) Install the latest version. Installing the latest PSERVER can solve a lot of printing problems. You may download the new PSERVER.NLM from the NOVLIB on NetWire.

2) Check spelling. A misspelled print server name or a print server configuration error may cause the system to prompt for a password when loading a print server.

3) Add more RAM. Lack of RAM in the server may cause graphics to slow down the server. Adding more RAM can increase the number of cache buffers.

4) Plot to a file. When some applications plot, they expect direct interaction with the plotter. This is a problem when an application's output goes to a queue file on disk rather than to the plotter itself. You should plot to a file or LPT1.

5) Raise the IPX retry count. When you have PCONSOLE or PSERVER running across a router, an SPX connection may have trouble crossing routers. Asynchronous routers do not support SPX.

6) Recreate the print server. A corrupted print server definition can cause slow or erratic printing.

7) Reboot the print server to make the necessary changes take effect.

PSERVER.NLM:

1) Install the latest version of PSERVER.NLM. This can solve a lot of printing problems.

2) Down the server in an orderly manner. You may hang the print server if you interrupt an active print job.

PSERVER.EXE:

1) Install the latest version. NIC conflicts or older versions of IPX or the NetWare shell may cause PSERVER.EXE to hang the workstation.

2) You should have 52 KB RAM minimum. PSERVER.EXE with DOS and the NetWare shell may cause the PSERVER.EXE to hang.

3) Set IPX connections to at least 60 when working with PSERVER.EXE.

4) Reboot the print server. When PSERVER.EXE hangs we might notice that one printer is having problems while the other printers are still functioning properly.

5) Autoreboot to have the print server automatically reboot after an interruption. Use the utilities NETERR.ZIP file from NOVLIB on NetWire.

The following symptoms indicate that the printing problem may be occurring at a remote printer workstation:

a) The print job arrives corrupted at a remote printer.
b) The print job contains dropped characters or random errors.
c) The print job status goes to active or leaves the print queue, but is never printed.

You may perform the following tasks to determine if a network printing job is leaving the print queue. Attach a good printer to the same port of the workstation and try printing to this printer. The following are some troubleshooting techniques that we may use to solve the printer initialization:

1) Install the latest software. Use the latest RPRINTER.EXE, NPRINTER.EXE, and NPRINTER.NLM. These files can be found on NetWire in compressed format. Novell uses the following naming conventions for these files: PU for Print Utilities, PS for Print Server, OS for Operating System version and revision number.

2) Copy the remote printer files to the local drive or LOGIN directory. This will eliminate the security risk and user error problems that can occur by leaving a workstation logged in and unsupervised.

3) Activate a remote printer. You may run RPRINTER.EXE or NPRINTER.EXE only if PSERVER is running. We may create a workstation batch file using an if statement to check if PSERVER is running. If it is running, then load the remote printer software.

4) The following may cause RPRINTER to fail. Lack of memory, incompatible clone, or obsolete software such as RPRINTER, NPRINTER, or NetWare client.

5) Change the NIC settings. Sometimes RPRINTER or NPRINTER conflicts with the network board settings and hangs the remote printer workstation. You may change the network board settings to avoid this conflict.

6) Check the configuration. If a remote serial printer completes a self-test but is not working as a network device, the problem may lie in the printer hardware and software configurations.

7) Use polled mode. If you are working with Windows 3.1 or are experiencing persistent port conflicts, using RPRINTER and NPRINTER in polled mode may solve this problem.

8) Set to a local printer. Use the PSC private command from the DOS prompt to do this. PSC private is reversed with PSC shared.

9) Look for an inactive remote printer. The message "Not connected" indicates that running RPRINTER or NPRINTER on a workstation has not activated the remote printer.

10) Reboot the workstation. When you reboot the workstation to re-establish the lost connection, you might get a message that the remote printer is still in use. This is because the previous SPX connection has not timed out and torn down the session information, which usually takes at least 30 seconds. The time-out-before-tear-down sequence might be longer, up to five minute, if you have increased the SPX abort and IPX retry counts.

The following are some troubleshooting techniques we may use to solve printing process problems at a remote printer workstation:

1) If printing through the remote network printer is slower than printing to the same printer locally from DOS, you might try the following solutions:

   a) Try a new cable. Some printers require nonstandard parallel cables to work effectively.
   b) Change IRQ. An IRQ conflict might exist in the workstation.
   c) Change to poll mode. The workstation may not support hardware interrupts. You may configure printer to polling mode. You may add I/O boards for interrupt support also.

2) RPRINTER and NPRINTER may potentially conflict with other TSRs and compete for resources. Some programs also may overwrite RPRINTER or NPRINTER stored in RAM. Stacker is one of these utilities. Check TSR conflict. You may unload one TSR at a time to check if there is a problem. Run NPRINTER or RPRINTER only after running the competing programs.

3) If remote printers across router print periodically and at random, try increasing the following two parameters in the NET.CFG file: the IPX retry counts, when you have NPRINTER or RPRINTER running; and the SPX count across routers, since SPX connections may have trouble crossing routers.

4) Non-certified hardware or older drivers can cause RPRINTER and NPRINTER to behave erratically. Faulty hardware, such as cable, concentrators, terminators and NICs, can impede the SPX connection made by RPRINTER or NPRINTER.

Network printing problems occurring at the printer are characterized by the following symptoms:

a) The print job never prints or is corrupted when it prints.
b) The print job prints properly when a different printer is attached to the same printer port.

You may use the following troubleshooting techniques and tips to solve printing problems at the network printer:

1) If the print jobs arrive at the print queue but do not get printed, look for simple physical problems at the printer, including the following:

    a) The printer is not turned on.
    b) The printer is not online.
    c) A cable is loose.
    d) The paper is jammed.
    e) The toner cartridge is empty.

    You may use the self-test function of the printer to verify that the printer is operational. Sometimes the "Out of paper message" appears, even when plenty of paper is available. This may indicate a physical problem with the printer.

2) Static may be causing the problem. If a network printer sometimes goes offline for no apparent reason, but works fine when it is reinitialized, we might have a static problem. Some types of paper, such as carbonless forms, can generate large amounts of static. Try attaching a ground to a metal part of the printer.

3) Use parallel printing for time-critical output. Parallel printing is faster than serial printing. The difference between the two is substantially greater on 386 computers and above.

4) Use the latest printer driver from the application to speed up the printing. Some word processor drivers, such as those associated with WordPerfect 5.1 and above, are substantially faster than earlier versions.

5) Verify the pinouts on a suspect print cable. A network printer cable contains several wires, each of which is connected to a particular pin on the cable connector at the computer side and printer side. Each type of printer may require a printer cable with different pinouts. For example, the IBM 3816 page printer requires a printer cable with pinouts 2, 3, 4, 5, 6, and 7 at the computer side and with pinouts

3, 2 5, 20, 4, and 7 at the printer side. If the cable pinouts are not matched, print jobs will have errors or will not be printed.

6) Increase printing throughput. You may do the following to increase the printing throughput:

    a) Use high-speed printers.
    b) Add multiple printers to a queue.
    c) Add more queues.
    d) Change the physical design of the printing workgroups.

7) Change the print server's internal buffer for the printer. You should use the printer configuration option in PCONSOLE to increase the print server's internal buffer size for the printer in small increments until the problem goes away. This may help if the printer often stops and starts during the job or the print jobs are missing characters or words.

Novell recommends using parallel printers instead of serial printers whenever possible. Parallel printers offer speed and trouble-free installation. Serial printers offer greater cabling distances, but these distances are usually not needed because network printers can attach to any DOS or OS/2 workstation or NetWare server. The following table presents the basic differences between parallel and serial printers:

Item	Parallel printers	Serial printers
Speed	4 to 6 times faster than serial	Slower than parallel
Cable length	10 feet maximum standard distance; some cables are guaranteed for 150 feet	50 feet standard maximum distance; some cables are guaranteed for 500 feet
Error checking	Limited but relatively error free	Uses parity, can reduce speed by 10%
Parameters	IRQ	IRQ, XON/XOFF, Parity, Baud rate, Data Bits, and stop bits
Compatibil-ity	Universally compatible	Compatibility can be a problem

PostScript is a page description language that interfaces with high-quality printers. PostScript is especially useful when documents require sharp graphics and many printing fonts. Postscript is interpreted by built-in hardware, an add-on cartridge, or a system board chip. Installed on the printer, PostScript printers may have a problem dealing with information sent to them that is not in the expected format. Some solutions to PostScript problems are as follows:

a) Update the PostScript drivers.

b) Make sure that the PostScript cartridge is installed properly. You should hear a click when it snaps into place on a HP LaserJet or similar. If the cartridge is not properly installed, the PostScript code coming from the application will be unintelligible and the print job will not print correctly.

c) Make sure that the SYS switch is ON. Some printers, such as the HP IIISi models, require a switch to be set to enable PostScript.

d) Use the /NB and /NT parameters for all PostScript print jobs or Byte Stream Mode. Sending a NetWare banner page can cause the PostScript printer to see the print job as a non-PostScript file. The printer will delete the job before it discards the files sent to it that contain initial data that is not in PostScript.

e) Use the No Form feed (/NFF) parameter in NPRINT and CAPTURE commands.

f) Limit the shell header buffer size to 64 bytes. A problem may occur if PRINTDEF is used to create PostScript definition files or PDFs that include modes larger than the default shell header buffer of 64 bytes. This also applies to CAPTURE, but not to NPRINT.

Questions

1) You are installing a network in a rural area, and the system goes down intermittently. What two things could be the problem?

2) You are setting a network in a very dry power plant. What are four static precautions should you take?

3) What are the four steps of systematic network troubleshooting?

4) When looking for a diagnostic utility, what are three important things to consider?

5) You have been called in because of your troubleshooting ability. What is the first thing you should do before troubleshooting?

6) What are four things that should be avoided to prevent damage to your computers?

7) What are the four sources of problems for computers in an electrical environment?

8) You are called to a site that is having problems. They relate to you that the problems all started after the power went off and came back on. At that point, you suspect a transient. What is the characteristic of a transient?

9) To minimize the effect of transients in an electrical environment, what three steps should you consider when installing a network?

10) What are eight of the procedures that you should follow to prevent ESD damage?

11) To actually feel an ESD event, the charge must be equal to approximately how many volts?

12) You are consulting for a power generating company and they want you to set up a network. What topology do you recommend?

13) A firm is heavily into graphical applications and wants to expand into another building four miles away in the near future. What technology should you recommend to this company?

14) A credit union needs to install a highly fault-tolerant and very high-traffic LAN. You recommend a token ring LAN. What are five valid reasons for your recommendation?

15) What are the two file attributes that should be flagged for .EXE and .COM files for virus protection?

16) What is the last step in troubleshooting?

17) What are five good reasons to recommend an ARCnet network?

18) Name three tools you may bring with you to troubleshoot a 10Base2 network.

19) You have the message "TOKEN-DOS-201: DIR.OPEN.ADAPTER error code = 07. Try again" on the screen when you attempt to load your workstation boot files. What is the possible cause for this error message?

20) How often does an "ACTIVE MONITOR" send out a frame to the next active device?

21) When designing a bridged LAN, what should be the ratio of local traffic to crossover traffic?

22) What are the four steps you should consider to protect your workstation from viruses?

23) Your network is currently unreliable. All the stations are equipped with ARCnet cards. Stations D and E have both ARCnet and Ethernet cards. How would you attempt a "quick fix"?

24) What are the important points to remember when running a 10Base2 Ethernet?

25) What are the important points to remember when running a 10Base5 Ethernet?

26) What are the important points to remember when running a 10BaseT Ethernet?

27) Up to how many nodes may populate a segment using 10BaseT guidelines?

28) In 10BaseT, the distance between a hub and a workstation must be a minimum of _____ meters, and a maximum of _____ meters.

29) Name four Ethernet troubleshooting tips.

30) What are the four Token Ring functions or processes that are used to maintain and monitor the ring?

31) What is the maximum length of a patch cable connecting all MSAUs in a token ring network?

32) What are eight token ring troubleshooting tips?

33) What is the maximum number of stations on an IBM token ring network using shielded twisted pair cable?

34) What is the maximum number of stations on an IEEE 802.5 Token Ring network using shielded twisted pair?

35) What is the maximum allowable distance between an MSAU and a workstation?

36) What are the two built-in troubleshooting mechanisms in token ring networks?

37) You have a Novell 3.12 LAN installed that spans three buildings in a very light-intensive environment. What is the best way to maintain ground isolation between the server?

38) What are five FDDI troubleshooting tips?

39) What are eight ARCnet troubleshooting tips?

40) What are the three tools you should bring with you to troubleshoot a printer?

41) Your customer complains that his workstation is running NetWare 3.11 print server and it is not printing. What should you bring with you to troubleshoot this type of problem?

42) What is the last step in troubleshooting a printer?

43) PSERVER.EXE is being used to support multiple printers attached to workstations. One printer is having a problem, while the others are not. What is a quick fix for this problem?

44) How do you fix a white streak on a Laser Jet printout?

45) How do you fix a repetitive pattern smudge on a Laser Jet printout?

46) What three ways can you fix a fuzzy Laser Jet printout?

47) What three things should you look for if a dot matrix printer does not print, but it self-tests OK?

48) How can you fix a dot matrix printer if the last part of the multiform is scribbled?

49) How can you fix a dot matrix printer if it shuts down and recovers frequently?

50) Give three fixes for the error message "File Server Not Found"?

51) Data redundancy is reliable and very critical to a bank. The administrator wants to mirror all the volumes. What should be considered in the network design?

52) A server, which contains very critical data, has crashed. You are not sure about the integrity of the existing backup. What should you do to recover from the damage?

53) A non-Novell-aware print job is sent to print. It does not print when a CAPTURE /SH command is used. What would you do to solve this problem?

54) You suspect a cable problem when moving a printer to another department. What tools should you bring with you?

55) What are the four questions you should ask about a security program you are trying to purchase?

56) You are the system administrator for a NetWare 3.12 network. Users are complaining that their print jobs sometimes get damaged. You determine that this is because the station to which the printer is physically attached does not always have CAPTURE invoked. Which utility could you use to prevent this problem?

57) You have a network job that arrives at the print queue but does not get printed. What four items are a possible cause of this problem?

58) Mike brings you a piece of paper output from his printer. There is a "smudge" repeated over and over every two inches down the length of the paper. What action should you take?

10

TCP/IP

This chapter discusses the TCP/IP protocols supported on the IntranetWare server. You will learn the four layers of the TCP/IP protocol suite (DoD model), the major TCP/IP protocols and their applications. In addition, this chapter discusses how to assign and maintain IP addresses for hosts on the internetwork. Finally, you will learn how to configure TCP/IP on an IntranetWare server, and how to connect, manage, and troubleshoot IP intertnetworks.

10.1 INTRODUCTION TO TCP/IP AND THE INTERNET

TCP/IP (Transmission Control Protocol/Internet Protocol) was introduced by an experiment conducted by the DoD (Department of Defense) and several universities in the mid 1970's. DoD was looking for a way to connect all of their computer systems using existing resources. To have an internetwork of the many devices currently in place, the individual networks needed to be connected. The devices that connected these individual networks were called gateways, and a packet-switched network was the specific implementation that was chosen to exchange data.

TCP/IP is a set of common networking protocols used by computers for exchanging data. DoD defines TCP/IP as a four-layer networking model. Each layer of the TCP/IP model consists of a number of protocols. These protocols are collectively referred to as the TCP/IP protocol suite. TCP/IP was developed to interconnect computers and networks with widely different operating systems throughout the world on the Internet. It offers users immediate access to a complete spectrum of services and information. It has evolved into today's Internet connecting thousands of computers and networks throughout the world.

TCP/IP is the standard networking protocol for UNIX systems. It comes as a built-in part of many versions of UNIX. It is a standard part of 4.2 and 4.3 BSD UNIX. It has been added to many AT&T UNIX System V implementations as well, and it has become synonymous with UNIX networking. Specifications have been written for a complete set of TCP/IP applications for file sharing, terminal emulation, file transfer, printing, messaging, and network management. The specifications are freely available to any developer wanting to write an application. Today you can find commercial, shareware, and public domain versions of TCP/IP for all types of computers including PCs, SUNs, VAXs, Macintoshes, minicomputers, and mainframes. More than 100 vendors offer products supporting TCP/IP and related protocols.

In summary, the combination of TCP/IP networks together with an open-door policy allowed commercial research networks and academic facilities to connect to the DoD generated "information super highway" called the Internet. A set of protocols was needed for convenient and reliable communications. Out of this need came the TCP/IP protocol suite.

When you connect to the Internet, you can access thousands of computers throughout the world. Below are the most popular services available on the Internet:

- WWW (World-Wide-Web)—WWW is a tool for easily traveling (surfing) across the Internet. It is a type of data service running on many computers on the Internet. It uses a hypertext to associate text with URLs (Uniform Resource Locators) that can point anywhere on the Internet. Using browser programs, such as Netscape or MS Explorer, you may access WWW servers to obtain the latest information. From Novell's anonymous FTP server at FTP.NOVELL.COM, you may find a freeware version of the Mosaic browser. The /PUB/WWW directory contains versions of Mosaic compiled for use with Unixware, LAN WorkPlace for DOS, and Macintosh systems. The source code is also available for other platforms. You may access Novell's online services at HTTP://WWW.NOVELL.COM to obtain the latest information about IntranetWare.

- Gopher—Gopher is another tool on the Internet. It was created at the University of Minnesota, where the school mascot is the gopher. It organizes topics into a menu system and allows you to access the information on each topic listed. The menu system includes many levels of submenus, allowing you to burrow down to the exact type of information you are looking for. Gopher actually uses the Telnet protocol to log the user in to other systems. Gopher servers act as master directories of the Internet. Those directories can provide the specific location of a file or topic. Novell maintains a gopher server at GOPHER.NOVELL.COM.

- Telnet—Telnet is a protocol that you may use to log on to any host attached to the Internet by providing an account name and password for the host. You may access NetWire from the Internet by creating a Telnet connection to the COMPUSERVE.COM host.

- FTP (File Transfer Protocol)—FTP is a protocol that allows you to transfer files between any two computers that are using FTP. Hundreds of public domain, freeware, and shareware programs are available on anonymous FTP servers located throughout the Internet. These FTP servers are called anonymous because anyone can log on to the server using an "anonymous" account name and e-mail address as the password. Novell maintains anonymous FTP servers at

<u>FTP.NOVELL.COM</u> or <u>FTP.NOVELL.DE</u>. These servers contain files, patches, and documents for all Novell products. These file and patches are also available from NetWire.

- USEnet—USEnet is a very large bulletin board system made up of thousands of different conferences. It currently offers over 8,000 bulletin boards and forums. Forum members may exchange data on any topic. Novell users can receive technical support by posting messages to the forums COMP.SYS.NOVELL, COMP.UNIX.UNIXWARE, and BIT.LIDYDRTB.NOVELL.

- E-mail—E-mail is when a user sends an electronic mail to any user connected to the Internet. Messages may contain text, graphics, voice messages, or application databases.

As you can see from above, Internet users may access Novell resources from USEnet, FTP servers, Gopher servers, and WWW. Now let's answer the question "How are computers able to talk to each other despite their distance and diversity?" The answer is a common set of protocols, which enables all TCP/IP hosts to talk to each other. These protocols have specific formats and conventions that all TCP/IP hosts follow. There are four layers of protocols that make up the TCP/IP or the DoD model. Each layer is responsible for performing specific networking functions. Each layer may include several protocols. To understand TCP/IP, it is important to examine the function of each layer and identify the individual protocols that collectively make up TCP/IP. The four layers of the DoD model are as follows:

Layer 4: Process/Application
Layer 3: Host-to-Host
Layer 2: Internet
Layer 1: Network Access

Here is the best way to remember the order of the layers:

<u>Statement</u>	<u>DoD layers</u>
Put All	Process/Application
Hardware	Host-to-Host
Into	Internet
Networking	Network Access

The DoD model compares favorably with the OSI model in many aspects, with some exceptions. Below is a chart to remember the OSI model layers and their primary functions:

Layer Number	Layer Name	Layer Function
7	Application	User interface. Command interfaces with network.
6	Presentation	Data translation. Data is converted to and from computer code.
5	Session	Dialogue Management. Sender and receiver connections are set up.
4	Transport	Reliability. Quality and reliability of data transmission is managed.
3	Network	Routing. Data is routed through the network.
2	Data-Link	Packaging. Data is packaged for transmission.
1	Physical	Real connection. Bits and bytes are transferred from the sender to the receiver.

The chart below shows how the OSI model and the DoD model compare:

DoD Model	OSI Model
Process/Application	Application
	Presentation
	Session
Host-to-host	Transport
Internet	Network
Network access	Data-link
	Physical

The specifications for each protocol within the TCP/IP suite are defined within one or more RFCs (Request For Comments). Various users on the Internet submit these RFCs for proposing new protocols, suggesting improvements of existing protocols, and/or offering comments on the state of the network. You may obtain electronic copies of all RFCs from the anonymous FTP server at DS.INTERNET.NET or other servers throughout the Internet. Here is a list of the most commonly used protocols and the layers at which they function.

Layer 4: Process/Application Protocols:

This layer is responsible for the user's interface with the network. TCP/IP applications usually include a client and a server program. A user can execute the client program when access to the server is desired. The server program is often referred to as a "daemon". Daemon comes from ancient Greek mythology and it means a "guardian angel". Usually a daemon starts when the system boots up. The program runs in the background on the host server. Typically, a daemon process is not continually running on the server. It is triggered by some sort of event, such as a client request. The Process/Application layer has a set of standardized protocols to provide terminal emulation, file transfer, electronic mail, and other applications such as:

1) FTP (File Transfer Protocol)—you can use FTP to transfer files between a PC and a remote host. In addition, you may use FTP to access directories and files on the remote system and list, copy, and manage directories and files on the remote system. Files can be transferred in ASCII or binary, depending on whether you want to transfer text or programs. When you use FTP, you will need an account login ID and a password.

2) TFTP (Trivial File Transfer Protocol)—This protocol is similar to FTP. TFTP does not support an account name or password and takes fewer overheads than FTP because FTP uses TCP, while TFTP uses UDP. (TCP and UDP protocols are discussed in the next section.) TFTP may be used to download, transfer, or copy files between two systems without specifying an account or a password. However, you may not use TFTP to list files or directories. Since TFTP does not use accounts and passwords, most TFTP implementations restrict the types of files a workstation can access and deny access to a file unless every user on the host can access the file.

3) TELNET (Virtual Terminal Emulation)—This protocol provides access to a computer connected to the network. The connection is in the form of a terminal session that appears to users to be hard-wired directly to the host. The interface looks the same as it would if you were using the console on the host itself. A TELNET application lets you emulate a terminal connected to a remote host. Once you log into the remote host, you can execute commands and perform any operations the remote host supports.

4) SMTP (Simple Mail Transfer Protocol)—This protocol is used to communicate with other network users. You may use SMTP to send and receive electronic mail (e-mail). SMTP is the engine that delivers mail on the TCP/IP host. Novell has a similar product for IntranetWare called MHS (Messaging Handling Services).

5) NFS (Network File System)—This protocol lets your file server provide services as a distributed file system for TCP/IP hosts.

6) Broadcasts—This protocol is a packet delivery system that delivers a copy of a given packet to all attached hosts.

7) LPD (Line Printer Daemon)—This protocol is designed for printer sharing. It allows print jobs to be spooled and sent to network printers.

8) RPR (Remote Printing)—This protocol is designed for remote printing.

9) SNMP (Simple Network Management protocol)—This protocol is designed for network management.

10) X Windows—This protocol is used for application sharing and is designed for client-server operations. It defines a protocol for the writing of graphical user interfaces based on client-server applications.

Layer 3: Host-to-Host Protocols:

This layer is responsible for creating and maintaining connections between communicating hosts. It is responsible for the following:

a) The integrity of data transfer.
b) Setting up reliable, end-to-end communications between systems.
c) Providing error-free delivery of data units, in proper sequence and with no loss or duplication.
d) Providing reliable, sequenced delivery of messages.

There are two protocols that function at this layer:

1) TCP (Transmission Control Protocol)—This protocol provides a reliable connection between communicating hosts. It also sequences and acknowledges packets. It establishes a virtual circuit for communications. Upper-level protocols that use TCP protocol include FTP, SMTP, and TELNET. There is more overhead because of the tracking that must be done to ensure that the packet is transferred smoothly with no error.

TCP is like a polite telephone conversation. Before you can speak with someone on the phone, you dial his or her number and establish connection with the other person. This is like a virtual circuit with the TCP protocol. During the conversation, you may periodically ask, "Did you get that?" This is like TCP acknowledgement. You may also ask during your conversation "Are you still there?" to verify that the phone connection still exists. At the end, you may end the conversation and hang up the phone.

TCP connection begins with a client requesting a virtual connection from a remote host. No communication is possible until the remote host responds. Whenever a message is sent to a host, an acknowledgement packet is returned. Periodically, the packets may be exchanged just to make sure the connection has not been lost. Each host will notify the other when the connection is to be closed.

2) UDP (User Datagram Protocol)—This protocol provides connectionless, but unreliable delivery services. It assumes that the upper-layer protocol will take the responsibility for ensuring that packets are acknowledged. It lets upper-level applications send sections of messages, or datagrams, without extra overhead. UDP does not acknowledge the packets or the virtual connection, nor does it check to make sure that the data was received. You may use UDP to broadcast messages to all other hosts on the network. If a host needs to be notified that its

message reached its destination, the application will acknowledge it. Upper-level protocols that use UDP protocol include TFTP, NFS, and Broadcasts.

UDP is like sending a postcard in mail. To send a postcard, you do not need to contact the other party first. You simply write your message, address it, and mail it. This is similar to UDP. To send data to a remote host, the data is simply transmitted. No acknowledgement is expected. The UDP protocol is faster than TCP, but at the expense of reliable delivery.

<u>Layer 2: Internet Protocols:</u>

This layer is responsible for routing data between hosts. It is also responsible for finding the "best" router. (Best router sometimes means the fastest.) Internet layer protocols are responsible for correctly routing packets across the internetwork. Connecting different local area networks together may create a complicated maze. Therefore, the hosts may be located on different networks separated by several routers. Here is a list of the Internet layer protocols.

1) IP (Internet Protocol)—This protocol is primarily responsible for the addressing of computers and the fragmentation of packets. It provides datagram service between communicating hosts. It also performs routing, fragmentation, and reassembly of datagrams.

2) ARP (Address Resolution Protocol)—This protocol translates a software address provided by IP into a hardware (MAC) address that is used by the Network Access layer. ARP functions as follows:

    a) IP presents a datagram to the network access layer, which searches a temporary table for a physical address to match up with the IP address for the destination host. If an entry exists, the packet is sent to that physical address.
    b) If no entry exists, an ARP broadcast is sent out on the network requesting the physical address of the intended host.
    c) All PCs on the network receive the ARP broadcast and determine whether the requested address is the same as its own. The host with the same IP address as the one requested replies to the originator with its physical address.
    d) The originator host updates its table and sends the initial datagram to the receiver with the proper physical address.

3) RARP (Reverse Address Resolution Protocol)—This protocol functions in the reverse order as ARP. It translates a hardware address to a software address. RARP is used when a diskless workstation, which already knows its own hardware address, needs to acquire an IP address.

4) BootP—This protocol is used by diskless workstations to discover the IP address, discover the address of the server host, and discover the name of a file that is to be loaded into memory and executed at boot up.

5) ICMP (Internet Control Message Protocol)—This protocol is responsible for transporting error and diagnostic information for IP. It lets routers or hosts send error or control messages to other routers or hosts. ICMP allows a router with a full buffer to tell other routers to use another route. It allows a host to determine if another host is reachable.

Layer 1: Network Access Protocols:

This layer is responsible for the physical connection between hosts. It defines the specifications related to the physical, or hardware, medium for data transmission, such as network interface boards, cabling, and network topology. The main functions of this layer are as follows:

a) Receiving an IP datagram and framing it into a stream of bits for physical transmission.
b) Specifying the hardware (MAC) address.
c) Making sure that the stream of bits composing the frame has been accurately received.
d) Specifying the access methods to the physical network, such as contention-based for Ethernet and token-passing for token ring networks.
e) Specifying the physical media, the connectors, electrical signaling, etc.

The IEEE Project 802 established standards that define interface and protocol specifications for various network topologies. For LAN-oriented protocols, you have Ethernet (10Base5, 10Base2, and 10BaseT), token ring, and ARCnet. For WAN-oriented protocols, you have PPP (Point to Point Protocol), X.25, ATM, and frame relay. All of the above protocols are covered in chapter 1. On the IntranetWare server, you may bind TCP/IP to the LAN and WAN ODI (Open Data-link Interface) drivers.

As data is passed down from a client application, it must pass down through the four layers of the DoD model on the local system. It is then passed up the protocol suite on the remote host to reach the daemon process. Each layer adds a header and passes the data to the lower layer as shown below:

- Process/application layer—An application, such as SMTP, passes its data to the host-to-host layer.

- Host-to-host layer—TCP or UDP adds a TCP header to the data unit. TCP header contains the source and destination ports identifying the upper layer protocol. It contains sequence, acknowledgement numbers, the header size, and flags that establish, control, or terminate the connection. The TCP header also contains the maximum amount of data that the host is willing to accept and it uses checksum to guarantee data integrity. The message is then passed down to the Internet layer.

- Internet layer—The internet layer adds an IP header to the message. The IP header contains information used to route the packet across the internetwork to the remote host. The IP header includes information, such as the software addresses of the source and destination hosts, the host-to-host (TCP or UDP) that is to receive the message, and flags controlling the fragmentation and reassembly of the packet. In addition, it contains segmented packets with an ID number, the size of the packet, a header checksum, and TTL (Time-To-Live) to limit the life of the packet. The packet is then passed to the network access layer.

- Network access layer—The network access layer adds a MAC (Media Access Control) header to the packet. On Ethernet networks, a frame includes information, such as the MAC header containing the source and destination hardware addresses, IP header, and frame sequence containing CRC (Cyclic Redundancy Check) of the MAC header. CRC is designed to ensure data integrity.

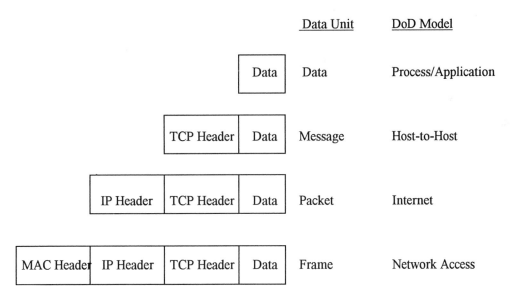

Figure 10.1 Passing Data through the DoD model protocol stack.

The four layers of the DoD model reside on the client and the server systems. Each TCP/IP protocol on the client side communicates directly with a corresponding TCP/IP protocol on the server side. When the frame reaches its destination, data passes up through the same four layers. Each layer strips off the appropriate header, processes the data, and passes the remaining data to the next layer until it reaches the application.

10.2 USING TCP/IP WITH INTRANETWARE

Integrating TCP/IP instead of the default SPX/IPX on an IntranetWare server has the following advantages:

1) Efficient routing using the capability of IP. Especially in WAN environment.

2) Remote access of IntranetWare servers that use the IP protocol.

3) Simplified administration by reducing the number of protocols supported.

4) Efficient management of the IntranetWare servers. Since the IntranetWare servers are using IP protocol, they can be managed from a single server.

5) An international standard, such as TCP/IP.

TCP/IP also provides advanced services, such as SNMP (Simple Network Management Protocol), SLIP (Serial Line Interface Protocol), and PPP (Point-to-Point Protocol). Integrating Intranetware and UNIX resources becomes a high priority since nearly half of all NetWare LANs also support the TCP/IP suite, and almost all major corporations use both UNIX and PC LANs. The TCP/IP protocol suite is supported on UnixWare products. It is a standard part of the UnixWare Application server and is an add-on option to the UnixWare Personal Edition. In order to give a UNIX or IntranetWare user full access to resources on the network, Novell offers the following products on the platforms:

DOS and Windows Clients:

1) LAN Workplace for DOS—This allows DOS or MS Windows users to access a UNIX host directly through the TCP/IP protocol suite. It provides fast, direct access to enterprise-wide TCP/IP resources, including the internetwork from a variety of workstations. It includes both DOS and MS Windows TCP/IP applications, as well as new native language versions in French, German, Spanish, Portuguese, and Japanese. LAN Workplace products are also available for users of Macintosh and OS/2 clients. LAN Workplace runs on the client's machine and uses TCP/IP as its communication protocol instead of SPX/IPX. It has many of the TCP/IP application protocols, such as FTP and Telnet, built in.

NetWare server:

1) LAN Workgroup for DOS—This product is similar to LAN Workplace for DOS, except that it runs on the IntranetWare server. It has the following additional features and benefits:

   a) Centralized installation, administration, and maintenance from the server.
   b) Ability to monitor application use.
   c) Automatic configuration and assignment of Internet addresses.
   d) The TCP/IP protocol stack does not have to be loaded on client machines.

2) NetWare NFS—This product is a server-based software that allows the integration of a NetWare file system and a UNIX files. NetWare NFS allows UNIX clients to share files and other network resources with NetWare clients, such as DOS, Macintosh, and OS/2 computers from their native OS environment. This product is designed for NetWare 3.11 and later releases.

3) NetWare NFS Gateway—This also a server-based product that allows clients to store and access files on another NFS server, such as a UNIX NFS host. It transparently integrates NetWare clients into NFS servers. It allows DOS and MS Windows clients access to the files on the local and remote NFS servers. It enables the use of NetWare commands to access files that reside on NFS servers.

4) NetWare NFS Services-NetWare 4 Edition—This is the NDS version of the NetWare NFS and NetWare NFS Gateway products combined. This product will not work with any NetWare released before NetWare 4.02. It features and supports the following:

   a) FTP (File Transfer Protocol)
   b) Berkeley UNIX LPD (Line Printer Daemon) protocol (RFC 1179)
   c) MIT, X Windows System X11/R4 (RFC 854)
   d) Lockd and Statd DARPA (RFC 959)
   e) VT100/220 terminal emulation accesses to XCONSOLE (RFC 854)
   f) DNS (Domain Name System)
   g) NIS (Network Information Services)
   h) Password synchronization between NetWare and UNIX
   i) Full NDS support
   j) PC NFS daemon

5) NetWare FLEX/IP—This is a collection of NLMs that allows TCP/IP-based file transfers and printer sharing. It enables UNIX network supervisors to manage NetWare servers from within the X Windows environment. NetWare FLEX/IP features and benefits are as follows:

    a) FTP (File Transfer Protocol)

    b) Berkeley UNIX LPD (Line Printer Daemon) protocol (RFC 1179)

    c) MIT, X Windows System X11/R4 (RFC 854)

    d) VT100/220 terminal emulation accesses to XCONSOLE (RFC 854)

6) NetWare/IP—This allows NetWare clients to access NetWare server services through TCP/IP instead of SPX/IPX. It provides the following features and benefits:

    a) It runs on the server and provides efficient scaling and routing over WANS.

    b) It allows clients to access servers from workstations on remote TCP/IP networks.

    c) It allows a single server to manage all the NetWare/IP servers.

    d) It simplifies administration by reducing the number of protocols supported and managed.

UnixWare Client:

1) UnixWare Application Server—This integrates desktop computers into a client/server network. You may use UnixWare Application Server to integrate desktop computers into client/server networks to server mainstream business needs. It also provides multi-user support, thus offering considerable flexibility in configuring an optimum workplace computing environment. UnixWare Application Server supports both NetWare SPX/IPX and TCP/IP protocols. It is designed for implementation in both NetWare and native UNIX environments. It gives users simultaneous access to a range of heterogeneous computing resources. SPX/IPX gives users access to NetWare services. TCP/IP gives users access to UNIX services and Internet services.

2) UnixWare Personal Edition—This type of client can use the TCP/IP protocol suite to connect and run numerous applications on a UNIX host. It is an economical front end for large client-server networks. UnixWare Personal Edition has the following features:

    a) A 32-bit multitasking client operating system.

    b) It is based on the industry standard UNIX SRV4.2.

    c) It is a Graphical User Interface.

    d) It provides the standard TCP/IP application protocols, such as FTP, remote login, and Telnet.

    e) It uses the VESRITAS journaling file system for additional reliability.

    f) It supports both TCP/IP and SPX/IPX.

    g) It provides access to NetWare file and print services.

h) It provides connectivity to enterprise-wide computing services through NetWare and ONC (Open Network Computing) protocols.

A TCP/IP network consists of a group of computers that can communicate using TCP/IP protocols. A TCP/IP network might be a LAN composed of a small number of computers, or it might be a corporate network made up of thousands of computers or hosts. TCP/IP provides a variety of network-based applications that can provide access to information on local networks, or on remote networks on the other side of the world. TCP/IP applications may include terminal sessions, file transfer, electronic mail, network administration, and distributed file system support.

As mentioned before, LAN Workplace for DOS allows DOS or Windows clients to access UNIX hosts. The LAN Workplace product from Novell offers Telnet applications, FTP applications, and a unique Windows interface to networking applications. The following is a list of the LAN Workplace Windows icons and LAN Workplace for DOS commands used to launch applications:

TCP/IP Application	DOS Command	MS Windows Icon
Telnet	TNVT220	Host Presenter
FTP	FTP	Rapid Filer
Remote Shell	RSH	Remote Shell
PING	PING	IP Resolver

You may establish a Telnet session to a remote host from a workstation running LAN Workplace for DOS by entering the DOS command TNVT220 hostname. Replace "hostname" with the name of the remote host you wish to log in. TCP/IP hosts are identified by a hostname within the network. You may also use the LAN Workplace icon Host Presenter to start a Telnet session. The Telnet application allows the workstation to emulate a terminal and connect to a remote host on the network. The Telnet application permits multiple concurrent sessions with one or more remote hosts. You may log in to the remote host as if you were using a terminal directly connected, or hard-wired, to the remote host. Once logged on to the remote host, you may execute any of the following commands and perform any operations the remote host supports:

Telnet Command	Description
(Carriage Return)	Exits the Telnet command mode and returns to the Telnet session with the remote host.
close	Ends the current session, disconnecting from the remote host.
display	Shows the operating parameters for the current session.
open hostname	Establishes a connection with the remote host named in the command.
quit	Exits the Telnet application.
set	Allows you to set Telnet parameters.

Another application protocol in LAN Workplace for DOS is FTP. You may initiate an FTP login from the DOS command prompt by executing the command, FTP hostname. Replace "hostname" with the name of the remote host. TCP/IP hosts are identified by a hostname unique within the network. You may also use the LAN Workplace Windows icon Rapid Filer to start an FTP session. After entering your current account and password, you may enter commands to transfer files or perform simple file management on the remote host. The FTP application allows you to transfer files between a workstation and a remote host, or between two TCP/IP remote hosts on the network. FTP supports the transfer of ASCII or binary files. ASCII files are converted to the format of the destination host.

The FTP application also allows you to access directories and files on the remote system and perform the usual directory and file operations, such as changing working directories, and listing and renaming files and directories. The following are common FTP commands that are supported by most versions of FTP:

Command	Description
ascii	This is the default mode. It establishes transfer mode to ASCII. This is the faster mode to transfer.
binary	Establishes transfer mode to binary. Executable files must be transferred in binary. Executable files transferred in ascii mode do not run.
bye	Exits back to the operating system prompt.
cd	Changes the directory on the remote host.
lcd	Changes the directory of the local host.
close	Ends an FTP session, but remains at the FTP prompt.
delete	Deletes a file on the remote host.
mdelete	Deletes multiple files on the remote host.
dir	Lists the contents of a directory on the remote host in a UNIX long format.
ldir	Lists the contents of a directory on the local machine in a UNIX long format.
exec	Executes a command on the remote host.
get	Enables you to take a file from the remote host and place it onto the local host.
mget	Copies multiple remote files to the local machine.
help	Displays the help information.
mkdir	Makes a directory on the remote host.
open	Opens a host session.
put	Transfers or copies a file from the local system to the remote host.
mput	Transfers or copies multiple files from the local system to the remote host.
prompt	Toggles interactive prompting for multiple file transfers.
rename	Renames a file.

When you are using UNIX through terminal emulation, Telnet or the equivalent, you have access to normal UNIX commands. The commands in the following list are the most popular commands used in UNIX:

Command	DOS equivalent	Description
cat	TYPE, APPEND	Displays the contents of a file.
cd	CD	Changes to a new directory.
cp	COPY	Copies a file.
date	DATE, TIME	Displays date and time.
exit	LOGOUT (IntranetWare)	Logs off the system.
finger	NLIST /A /B (IntranetWare)	Shows which users are logged on.
grep	FIND	Searches file contents for text strings.
ls	DIR	Lists the contents of a directory.
man	HELP	Displays help commands.
mkdir	MD	Creates a new directory.
mv	RENAME	Renames or relocates a file.
pwd	CD	Finds the name of the current directory.
rm	DEL	Deletes a file or multiple files.
rmdir	RMDIR, RD	Deletes an empty directory.

10.3 IP ADDRESSING

One of the most important topics in any discussion of TCP/IP is IP addressing. An IP address is a numeric identifier assigned to each workstation on an IP network. This is a software address, and not a hardware address, that designates where the workstation resides. The most important duty of the network administrator on an IP network is to assign and maintain IP addresses for the hosts (workstations, or nodes) on the network.

IP addressing is the most complex part of TCP/IP. For example, an Ethernet hardware (MAC) address is 48 bits. An IP address is 32 bits. As a result there is no direct connection between the two numbers. That is why ARP is needed to match the numbers in a cached table. The computer needs the MAC address and TCP/IP needs the IP address. It is not easy to remember a 48-bit MAC address or even a 32-bit IP address. By convention, the IP address is usually represented in a dotted decimal notation, such as the IP address 204.78.135.15. Each segment of the network on the internetwork is also assigned a network address, which is represented by a portion of the IP address of each host on the network. From the user's point of view, it is convenient to associate a name to each host or network.

To make this practical, so that you do not have to remember IP addresses, the following three methods are commonly used to map host names (ASCII names that you can recognize) to IP addresses.

1) Host tables—A host table is a text file that maps the commonly used host name to that host's IP address. It translates the host name of a machine to its IP address, or software address. On a UNIX system, the host file hosts is located in the /etc directory. On the IntranetWare server, the file HOSTS will be in the directory SYS: ETC\. Below is an example of a host table:

# Internet Address	Host Name	Aliases	Comment
127.0.0.1	localhost	lb	# loopback
192.67.67.20	NIC.DDN.MIL		# DoD domain
255.255.255.255	broadcast		

For each host, there should be one line in the host file with a format such that each host file entry provides information about one host on the Internet. In addition, any number of blanks and/or TAB characters separate items. The format of the host table of SYS: ETC\HOSTS is equivalent to the host table in UNIX systems /etc/hosts. From the above host table the format is as follows:

[IP Address]   [Host Name]   [Alias] [Comments]

a) IP Address—The IP address is a 4-byte address in standard dotted decimal notation. Each byte is a decimal or hexadecimal value separated by a period. Hexadecimal numbers must start with the character pair "0x" or "0X". This address is assigned to the host. On the IntranetWare server, this assignment is made when you bind the protocol to the network board. On the workstation, the IP address is assigned in the NET.CFG file.

b) Host Name—The host name is the name of the system with the given address. Each host name should be unique and can contain any printable character other than a tab, space, new line, or a number sign "#". This name is arbitrary and is chosen by the system administrator. The host name for a NetWare server should be the same as the server name.

c) Alias—The alias is another name for the host. A host may have many aliases. A space is required between each name.

d) Comments—A "#" indicates the beginning of a comment. You may place a comment at the end of a host name or on a line by itself. Routines that search files do not read characters following a "#".

Another file that is similar to a host table is a network table. A network table contains names and network addresses of known networks. On UNIX systems, the network file is the file etc/networks; and on the IntranetWare server, the host file will be SYS: ETC/NETWORKS. Below is an example of a network table:

# Network Name	Network Address	Aliases	Comment
loopback	127		# loopback network number
Novell	130.57		# Novell's network number

For each network, one line should be represented in the network file with the format that each network file entry provides information about one network on the

Internet. In addition, any number of blanks and/or TAB characters may separate items. From the above network table the format is as follows:

[Network Name]   [Network Address]   [Alias] [Comments]

a) Network Name—The network name is the network name assigned to this network number. Each host name should be unique and can contain any printable character other than a tab, space, new line, or a number sign "#".
b) Network Address—The Network Address is the number of the network. It is the network portion of the IP address for all hosts on that network. Hexadecimal numbers must start with the character pair "0x" or "0X".
c) Alias—The alias is another name for the network. A network may have many aliases. A space is required between each name.
d) Comments—A "#" indicates the beginning of a comment.

2) DNS (Domain Name System)—DNS is widely used on the Internet to translate host names to IP addresses. It is a mechanism that helps users to locate the name of a machine and to map a name to an IP address. Because the Internet contains thousands of systems, it is possible for two different computers to have the same host name. To avoid confusion, the Internet has a number of domains. Machines throughout the Internet called name servers keep a database of large numbers of host names. The database is arranged in a hierarchical manner, starting with the root and moving down to the domain, subdomain, and finally to the host name. The Domain Name System hierarchy is shown in figure 10.2.

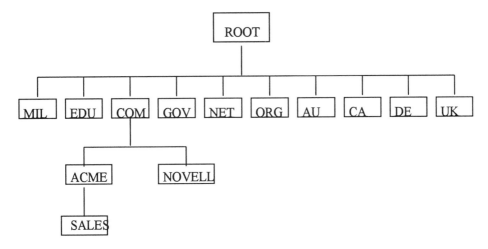

Figure 10.2 Domain Name System (DNS) hierarchy.

From figure 10.2:

Domain	Acronym	Description
MIL	Military	Used by the Department of Defense (USA only).
EDU	Education	Used by colleges and universities.
COM	Commercial	Used by corporations or businesses.
GOV	Government	Used by government organizations (USA only).
NET	Network	Used by an administrative organization for a gateway or a network.
ORG	Organization	Used by other organizations.
AU	Australia	
CA	Canada	
DE	Germany	
UK	United Kingdom	
IT	Italy	
NZ	New Zealand	

As shown in figure 10.2, DNS is structured as an inverted tree, much like the directory structure on an IntranetWare volume. Each node on the tree represents a domain. Each domain has subdomains, which can have further divisions as necessary. Name servers are set up to maintain host addresses for each subdomain or zone within the name space as well as the addresses of the root name servers. Using recursive queries or referring clients to other servers, a DNS server is capable of resolving the IP address for any host on the Internet. The domain name for a host consists of a set of domains separated by periods. The format is HostName.Subdomains.Domain. In figure 10.2, you have the domain SALES.ACME.COM.

3) NIS (Network Information Services)—NIS is another type of name service commonly used on IP internetworks. You may use NIS servers to provide host-to-address translation within domains. Domains are groups of computers. NIS servers contain databases, called maps. In addition to host names and addresses, maps may contain user and group information. Maps are shared by a group of computers.

When you connect two systems together using TCP/IP, each protocol layer on one host communicates directly with the corresponding layer on the other host. For example, the network access layer on one host communicates directly with the network access layer on another host. Each DoD layer identifies a host using one of the following addressing schemes.

DoD Layer	Addressing Method
Process/Application	Host name
Internet	IP Address
Network Access	Hardware address

An IP address is made up of 32 bits of information. These bits are divided into four bytes (octets). There are two methods of representing an IP address:

1) Dotted-decimal, as in 204.65.156.25
2) Binary, as 11001100.01000001.10011100.00011001

Both of these examples represent the same IP address. Each TCP/IP host must have an IP address. All hosts must have a software address at the Internet layer. The IP address (Internet address) is a software address for a host in a TCP/IP network and it identifies the network to which the host is attached. Routers use the IP address to forward messages to the correct destination. For each host the IP address is divided into two parts—a network address and a node (host) address. The network portion of the IP address must match the network address of every other host on the same network. The Host (node) portion of the IP address must be unique.

For example, an IP network has been assigned the network address of 140.56. Its network address uniquely distinguishes it from all other networks on the internetwork. Each host or node on this network must have an IP address of the form 140.56.x.x where the last two octets of the address must be unique on the network. A node assigned the last two octets of 25.150 is uniquely identified on the internetwork by using 140.56.25.150 as its address.

There are five classes of IP addresses. The chart below sets the groundwork for understanding IP addresses:

Class	First byte address range	Left-most bit pattern	Network/host designation
A	0 to 127	0	N H H H
B	128 to 191	10	N N H H
C	192 to 223	110	N N N H
D	224 to 239	1110	Multi-cast addresses
E	240 to 255	1111	Internet Experimentation

From the above chart, the leftmost column shows the class type. Column two shows the number range for the first byte that defines the range. Column three shows the binary bit pattern that is the beginning of the range byte; this pattern is helpful if you forget which class an address belongs to. Column four shows which bytes are for a network (N) address and which are for a host (H) address. Now we will describe each class in a little more detail:

- Class A—The first byte is the network address. The first bit must be zero. The next three bytes are for the node (host) address. On the Internet, all class A addresses are already assigned. There are 127 class A networks. Each class A network may have up to $2^{24} = 16,777,216$ hosts per network.

- Class B—The first two bytes identify the network address. There are $2^{14} = 16,384$ class B networks and $2^{16} = 65,534$ hosts per network.

- Class C—The first three bytes define the network address. There are $2^{21} = 2,097,152$ class C networks and 254 hosts per network.

- Class D—The range is between 224.0.0.0 to 239.255.255.255. the addresses are used for multicast packets. Multicast packets are used by many protocols to reach a group of hosts. ICMP router discovery is a protocol that uses multicast packets. A host can determine the addresses of routers on its segment by transmitting a packet addressed to 224.0.0.2, which is received by all routers on the network.

- Class E—The range is between 240.0.0.0 to 255.255.255.255. Class E addresses are reserved for future addressing modes.

Class D and E addresses are not assigned to individual hosts on the internetwork. In addition, there are some reserved IP addresses for special purposes as shown below:

Address	Description
Network address of all 0s	Refers to "this network".
Node address of all 0s	Refers to "this node".
Network address of all 1s	Refers to "all networks".
Node address of all 1s	Refers to "all nodes" on a specified network.
The entire IP address is set to 0	Refers to the default route. This route is used to simplify routing tables used by RIP protocols.
The entire IP address is set to 1	Refers to broadcast to all nodes on the network.
127.0.0.0	Reserved for loopback. The address 127.0.0.1 is often used to denote or refer to a local host. Using this address, applications can address a local host as if it were a remote host without relying on any configuration information.

NIC (Network Information Center) is responsible for assigning network addresses to all the computers on the Internet. For further information contact:

Network Solutions
InterNIC Registration Services
505 Huntmar Park Drive
Herndon, VA 22070

You may also obtain help by e-mail at hostmaster@internic.net. Once the network address is assigned, you may assign addresses to individual hosts on the network by using the same network address and a unique host address for each node. For example, if you have a class B network address of 140.67.0.0, you may assign any of the following addresses to the hosts within the network:

140.67.59.32
140.67.0.19
140.67.125.234

If your network is not connected to the Internet, you are free to assign any network address you wish. If your organization has a relatively large number of computers, you may want to divide the network into smaller networks. You may use routers to filter traffic to reduce the amount of networking activity seen by any host. However, dividing the network and using several network addresses may cause problems on a large Internet that requires the site be seen as a single network. You may use subnetting to break up the network into smaller networks and provide the following benefits:

1) Reduced network traffic.
2) Optimized performance.
3) Simplified management.
4) Effective span of a large geographic area.

Subnetting is a TCP/IP software feature that permits a single IP network to be divided into smaller, logical subnetworks. This is done by using the host portion of an IP address to create what is called a subnet address. Subnetting is implemented by assigning a subnet address to each system on a given physical network as shown in figure 10.3. The subnet mask is a 32-bit number that is applied to an IP address to identify the network and node address of a host. Any bit that is part of the network address is assigned a value of 1. Any bit that is part of the node address is assigned a value of 0.

The default masks used by class A, B, and C networks are as follows:

Class	Default
Class A	255.0.0.0
Class B	255.255.0.0
Class C	255.255.255.0

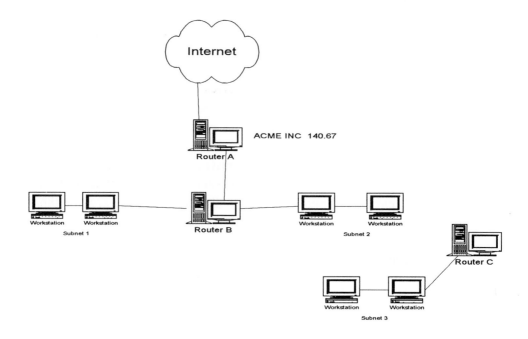

Figure 10.3 A network with subnets.

As shown in figure 10.3, the internetwork of ACME Inc. consists of the following:

1) Several networks linked together with routers.
2) A T1 leased line connected to the Internet.
3) A class B network address of 140.67 assigned by the NIC.

To assign a unique network address to each network within the company, you may use subnet masking to redefine how each IP address within the corporation is partitioned. You may configure each host and router with a subnet mask of 255.255.0.0 decimal. Each IP address now has three parts:

1) A network portion found in the first two octets.
2) A subnet portion contained in the third octet.
3) A node portion contained in the fourth octet.

This is how you assign IP addresses within the network:

1) Every host is assigned the value 140.67 for the network.
2) Each segment or subnet is assigned a unique value for the third octet.
3) Within each subnet, each host is assigned a unique node value.

The Internet protocol and subnetting specifications state that subnets whose bits consist of all zeros or ones should be reserved for local network or broadcast messages. Hence, making a full octet for a subnet creates 254 possible subnets. Using zero as a subnet permits up to 255 subnets. Novell's implementation of TCP/IP on the IntranetWare server and Novell's MPR recognize zero as a valid subnet address. You should not use zero as a subnet unless all routers recognize zero as a subnet value. Using a subnet of 0, the number of possible subnets shown below is increased by one. You may use fewer bits to define the subnet if you have a class C address or have more than 254 hosts in any subnet. Let us say that you use four bits to define a subnet for a class B with a network address of 140.67. The subnet mask in binary would be 11111111.11111111.11110000.00000000, which is 255.255.240.0 in decimal.

The following is a table that shows a list of commonly used subnet masks for a class B network, their bit patterns, and the theoretical number of subnets and hosts per subnet.

Subnet Mask	Bit patterns	Subnets	Hosts
255.255.192.0	11111111.11111111.11000000.00000000	2	16,382
255.255.224.0	11111111.11111111.11100000.00000000	6	8,190
255.255.240.0	11111111.11111111.11110000.00000000	14	4,094
255.255.248.0	11111111.11111111.11111000.00000000	30	2,046
255.255.252.0	11111111.11111111.11111100.00000000	62	1,022
255.255.254.0	11111111.11111111.11111110.00000000	126	510
255.255.255.0	11111111.11111111.11111111.00000000	254	254

Notice that fewer hosts and subnets exist than you might calculate. The addresses of 0 and 255 are not allowed. In general, you can use the following formulas to compute the number of possible subnets and possible hosts per subnet using a given network and mask:

$$\text{Possible subnets} = 2^{(\text{number of masked bits})} - 2$$
$$\text{Possible hosts} = 2^{(\text{number of unmasked bits})} - 2$$

For example, if you have a network address of 140.67 and a mask of 255.255.240.0, the equivalent binary notation of the mask number is 11111111.11111111.11110000.00000000. From the mask number, we have 16 network bits, 4 subnet bits, and 12 host bits. Therefore:

$$\text{Possible subnets} = 2^{(\text{number of masked bits})} - 2 = 2^4 - 2 = 14$$
$$\text{Possible hosts} = 2^{(\text{number of unmasked bits})} - 2 = 2^{12} - 2 = 4094$$

Once you have selected a mask number for the network, you may list the possible subnet number as shown below for a network address of 140.67 and a mask number of 255.255.224.0, then assign a subnet number to each LAN:

Mask number	Subnet	Node	
11111111 . 11111111	. 11100000	. 0000000	(255.255.224.0)

The possible subnet numbers are:

Mask number	Subnet	Node	
11111111 . 11111111	. 00100000	. 0000000	(255.255.32.0)
11111111 . 11111111	. 01000000	. 0000000	(255.255.64.0)
11111111 . 11111111	. 01100000	. 0000000	(255.255.96.0)
11111111 . 11111111	. 10000000	. 0000000	(255.255.128.0)
11111111 . 11111111	. 10100000	. 0000000	(255.255.160.0)
11111111 . 11111111	. 11000000	. 0000000	(255.255.192.0)

Once the subnet value has been assigned to a network, you may use the following rules to assign IP addresses to each host:

1) Each host address must be unique.
2) The network numbers must be the same for all hosts.
3) The subnet numbers must be the same for all hosts on the same segment.
4) The node portion of the address must not be set to all ones or zeros.

When first setting up the internetwork, it is difficult to predict how many subnets or hosts you may be supporting in the future. You may modify the way you subnet your network without having to reassign any IP addresses. RFC 1219 suggests a strategy for assigning IP addresses. You should assign subnets by placing ones (1s) only in the leftmost portion of the masked address and assign host addresses by placing ones (1s) in the rightmost bits of the IP address. For the example above with the network address of 140.67 and a mask number of 255.255.224.0, the list below is how you should assign the IP addresses:

Mask number	Subnet	Node	IP Address
11111111 . 11111111	. 10000000	. 0000001	(255.255.128.1)
11111111 . 11111111	. 01000000	. 0000010	(255.255.64.2)
11111111 . 11111111	. 11000000	. 0000011	(255.255.192.3)
11111111 . 11111111	. 00100000	. 0000100	(255.255.32.4)
11111111 . 11111111	. 10100000	. 0000101	(255.255.160.5)
11111111 . 11111111	. 01100000	. 0000110	(255.255.96.6)

Using the strategy suggested in RFC 1219, you should assign subnets in the order of 128, 64, 192, 32, 160, 96, 224, etc., and assign host addresses in each subnet in the order of 1, 2, 3, 4, 5, 6, etc. Using this strategy, there is a buffer of bits bordering the division of subnet and host that are all set to zero. If at a later date it becomes necessary to change the mask to permit more hosts or networks, adding additional bits to the mask should not require reconfiguring the IP address on any host.

Let us look at two examples to try to grasp the concept a little bit better.

Example 1:

A company has received a class B address of 155.160.0.0. The administrator will assign the last two bytes of this address. The administrator has two cables on his/her network. Therefore subnetting is required. The administrator assigns the number 155.160.55.1 to the first board of the file server. The mask chosen is 255.255.240.0, where the portion 255.255 is for the network, the portion 240 is for the subnet, and the portion 0 is for the host. Compute what the subnet number is.

Solution:

You must use the bit pattern of the subnet number in the subnet mask to figure out the subnet number. Remember, class A addresses use the second octet, class B addresses use the third octet, and class C addresses use the fourth octet of the subnet position. For this example the binary equivalent of 240 is 11110000 and the binary equivalent of 55 is 00110111. The pattern then is:

	Subnet		Host	
	1111		0000	(240)
	0011		0111	(55)
Result =	0011		0111	
In decimal =	48	+	7	= 55

As long as all the nodes connected to the network board with the address of 155.160.55.1 have a bit pattern in the third byte that begins with 0011, they are on the same subnet. If the bit pattern changes for the first four bits, the subnet changes.

Since the network has two boards, another address needs to be chosen. This new number should have a bit pattern in the third byte (octet) that is different than 0011. A bit pattern of 0010 can be arbitrarily chosen. This choice makes the subnet number 32. The last 4 bits still remain, and just to make it easy, the pattern 0111 is chosen, which matches the host bit pattern of the previous address. The address assigned to the second board is 155.160.39.1. Figure 10.4 shows the graphic depiction of what was assigned.

	Subnet		Host	
	1111		0000	(240)
	0010		0111	(39)
Result =	0010		0111	
In decimal =	62	+	7	= 39

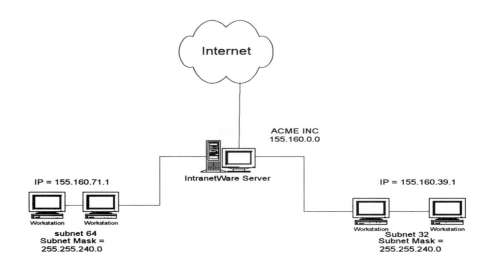

Figure 10.4 A subnetted network from Example 1.

Example 2:

Which IP address is located on the same subnet as 162.67.175.6 if the submask number is 255.255.240.0?

a) 162.67.200.3
b) 162.67.170.16
c) 162.67.150.3
d) 162.67.120.16

Solution:

This is a class B IP address, because 162 lies between 128 and 191.

	Subnet		Host	
	1111		0000	(240)
	1010		1111	(175)
Result =	1010		0000 to 1111	(the host number can range between 0000 and 1111)
In decimal =	150	+	0 to 15 =	160 to 175 is the subnet number

The right choice should have a subnet number that starts with 1010 (160 to 175). Therefore the answer is b (162.67.170.16).

10.4 CONFIGURING AND MANAGING TCP/IP ON AN INTRANETWARE SERVER

The ODI (Open Data-link Interface) is used on IntranetWare servers to support multiple network boards as well as multiple protocol stacks, such as TCP/IP, IPX/SPX, or AppleTalk. All of these communication protocols could use Ethernet LAN board drivers. ODI provides a standard interface for transport protocol to share a NIC. ODI directs the flow of packets between the protocol stacks and the LAN drivers. ODI allows more than one protocol stack to share multiple LAN drivers. LAN ODI drivers can be written for Ethernet (10Base2, 10Base5, 10BaseT), Token Ring, and ARCnet. WAN drivers can be written for PPP (Point-to-Point), X.25, and Frame Relay. You may configure TCP/IP over any LAN driver to the ODI specification.

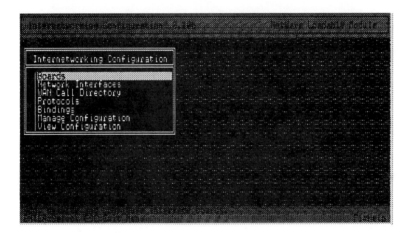

Figure 10.5 INETCFG.NLM main menu.

With ODI, the TCP/IP stack can use the same LAN drivers as the IntranetWare SPX/IPX, AppleTalk, or other supported protocols. Configuring TCP/IP on an IntranetWare server requires you to load and configure the network driver, load and configure the TCP/IP protocol stack, and finally bind the TCP/IP protocol stack to the network interface.

You may load INETCFG.NLM from the server console to configure and manage MPR, to set routing and bridging configuration, or to configure the TCP/IP protocol stack on the server. The main menu of INETCFG.NLM is shown in figure 10.5. INETCFG will build the correct LOAD and BIND commands in the AUTOEXEC.NCF file. You must reboot the server to activate the changes made to the AUTOEXEC.NCF file. You may select "Boards" from the main menu of INETCFG.NLM to configure a network driver. A list of configured network interface boards will be displayed. You may press the <Insert> key to add additional boards. You may press the <Tab> key to enable or disable an interface that is highlighted. The program may prompt you for information about the interface, such as a memory address or an interrupt, before the driver can be loaded. After you have configured a new board, you must exit from INETCFG.NLM and execute the command REINITIALIZE SYSTEM to load and activate the driver. You must select "Network Interfaces" from the main menu of INETCFG.NLM to configure individual interfaces on WAN boards. This procedure is not required for LAN boards.

You may enable and configure the TCP/IP protocol stack on the InternetWare server by selecting "Protocols" from the main menu. If you select TCP/IP from the list, the current configuration will be displayed as shown in figure 10.6.

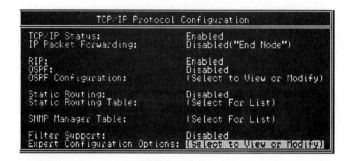

Figure 10.6 TCP/IP current configuration.

From the above figure:

- TCP/IP Status—This is set to "Enabled" if the IntranetWare server is an IP host.

- IP Packet Forwarding—This is set to "Enabled" if multiple boards are installed on the server and the server is an IP router between different networks. Set it to "Disable" if the server is only attached to one network.

- RIP—This is set to "Enabled" to send or receive RIP routing information.

- OSPF—This is set to "Enabled" to send or receive OSPF packets.

- Static Routing—This is set to "Enabled" to create static routes whenever the server boots up or is reinitialized.

- SNMP Manager Table—This is used to enter the destination addresses for SNMP traps that are transmitted from the server.

- Filter Support—This is set to "Enabled" to activate filters configured from FILTCFG.NLM. TCP/IP supports packet forwarding filters and routing information filters. You may load FILTCFG.NLM to configure these filters.

- Expert Configuration Options—If you have enabled the "IP packet Forwarding" option, then you may set the "Expert Configuration Options" because the server is now an IP router. Figure 10.7 shows the TCP/IP Expert Configuration options.

Figure 10.7 TCP/IP Expert Configuration options.

From the above figure:

- Directed Broadcast Forwarding—This is set to "Enabled" to forward directed broadcasts to a subnet.

- BootP Forwarding Configuration—This is set to "Enabled" to forward BootP requests. Enter addresses of BootP servers on the internetwork.

- EGP—This is set to "Enabled" to enable the Exterior Gateway Protocol.

After configuring the TCP/IP protocol parameters, you may select "Bindings" from the INETCFG.NLM main menu to bind TCP/IP to the network interface. After your selection, a list of bound interfaces will be displayed. You may bind the TCP/IP interface by pressing the <Insert> key and selecting TCP/IP from the list. You may then select the interface from the list of the loaded network interfaces. Finally, you must enter the IP address and subnet mask for the interface. In the "Binding TCP/OP to a LAN Interface" window you may select "Expert TCP/IP LAN Options". In this window you may select "Frame Type" to change the frame type to Ethernet_II or Ethernet_SNAP for Ethernet drivers. You can validate the current configuration of all protocol stacks on the IntranetWare server by executing the command CONFIG. If IP has not been successfully loaded on the server, you should reboot the server, examine the warning and error messages that appear on the console, and determine the cause and correct it.

RFC 1908, which is SNMP (Simple Network Management Protocol), enables you to monitor an IP network from an SNMP manager. SNMP manager is an IntranetWare server with TCPCON.NLM loaded. You may monitor the status and configuration of hosts and routers on an IP internetwork. You may also use SNMP for managing and troubleshooting an IP internetwork. From an SNMP manager, you may make inquiries to another network device called the SNMP agent. The SNMP agent could be a TCP/IP host, router, terminal server, or another SNMP manager. SNMP agents use a community name to authenticate requests from an SNMP manager.

An SNMP manager includes a community name with each request to an agent. On IntranetWare servers, a SNMP manager provides the monitor community name, which allows read access to the MIB (Management Information Base). In addition, it provides the control community name, which permits to modify objects within the MIB. You may configure SNMP community names from INETCFG.NLM. You may load TCPCON.NLM to access SNMP MIB on any SNMP agent. MIB contains information you may request from an SNMP agent.

Internet-Standard MIB (RFC 1066) defines the object types that can be in the MIB of an SNMP agent The objects within the MIB may include network and hardware addresses, counters, and statistics, as well as routing and ARP tables. Different vendors may not support all data types within their MIB or may include other information not defined within the RFC. An SNMP manager can inspect or alter the variables contained within the agent's MIB. You can examine the ARP table for another host and delete or change an incorrect entry.

The SNMP protocol offers limited security. The agent's MIB contains a number of variables representing its information base. Each variable includes a flag that determines the type of access that will be granted for a request coming from a specified community. If an agent does not want its routing table changed by a manager in the "public" community, you may configure the variable for its routing table, or ROUT-TABLE, for "read-only" access for any request originating from "public". Because of this limited security mechanism, many vendors are reluctant to support requests to alter variables in their agent's MIB.

An SNMP agent sends a notification or an SNMP "trap" to the SNMP manager when it senses a special event, such as:

1) When an agent reinitializes its configuration tables. This may happen when a cold or a warm start occurs.

2) When a network interface either fails or comes back to life, or when IP protocol is bound or unbound from a network interface. This is called link up or link down.

3) When an unrecognized community name has an SNMP request. IntranetWare server does not issue authentication failure traps when an unauthorized community name is used to access the server.

4) When an agent can longer communicate with its EGP (Exterior Gateway Protocol) peer. EGP is a protocol router used on the Internet.

5) When a specific event occurs. These traps depend upon the vendor's implementation of the protocol. IntranetWare servers running NetWare UNIX

services, for example, can generate a trap whenever the CPU utilization reaches a set level.

You may configure the network so that every host will send its trap messages to an IntranetWare server. For example, you may configure a router to send a message to an IntranetWare server when one of its interfaces comes up or goes down or when its routing table is reset. While the RFC specifications for the SNMP protocol define several types of events that can trigger a trap message, trap messages can be transmitted for any reason. For example, you may configure an IntranetWare server running NetWare UNIX services to send a trap message whenever CPU activity exceeds a preset level.

An IntranetWare TCP/IP server can act as either a SNMP agent or a manager on a TCP/IP network. Whenever you load TCP/IP on a NetWare server, the SNMP agent is also automatically loaded. IntranetWare TCP/IP includes two modules that provide support for SNMP—SNMP.NLM and SNMPLOG.NLM. SNMP.NLM converts the server to an SNMP agent. It provides Simple Network Management agent services, and maintains the MIB on the IntranetWare TCP/IP system. SNMP.NLM grants SNMP managers access to the MIB of an SNMP agent. TCPIP.NLM requires the services of the SNMP.NLM module. Hence, TCPIP.NLM will automatically load SNMP.NLM. SNMPLOG.NLM is an SNMP trap logger.

You may use the following commands to load SNMP.NLM:

Sample Command	Description
LOAD SNMP <options>	Loading SNMP.NLM on a server makes the server an SNMP agent. <options> are community names.
LOAD SNMP M = SECRET	SNMP managers using the "SECRET" community name will have read only access to the MIB of this server.
LOAD SNMP C	No SNMP manager can write to the MIB of this server.
LOAD SNMP C =	All SNMP managers can read or write to the MIB of this server.
LOAD SNMP T= NOVELL	Trap messages from this server will be sent to the address
LOAD TCPIP Trap=155.16.89.123	155.16.89.123 with community name "NOVELL".

An SNMP manager sends a community name with each request to the SNMP agent. An SNMP agent may use the following SNMP community names to authenticate the requests from the SNMP manager.

Community type/ Default	Description
MonitorCommunity [= <name>]	Any SNMP manager that provides this community name is granted read access to the SNMP information base, or MIB. By default, the monitor community is set to "public".
ControlCommunity [= <name>]	Any SNMP manager that provides this community is granted full read and write access to the MIB, but only a limited number of MIB objects can be modified. It can

| | modify the routing table, enable or disable an interface, or enable a server. An SNMP manager cannot modify counters indicating the number of packets that have been processed. By default, the control community name is disabled. |
| TrapCommunity [= <name>] | Send this along with all trap messages to the SNMP manager. We may use the TRAP option while loading TCPIP.NLM to specify which SNMP manager is to receive our trap messages. The SNMP manager receiving the trap messages must also be configured to accept traps from the trap community. By default, the trap community name is set to "public". |

You can enter only the first few characters of the name to specify the option parameters, such as M or MON or MONITOR for MONITORCOMMUNITY; C for ControlCommunity; or T for TrapCommunity. Community names are ASCII text strings of up to 32 characters. They are case sensitive. You may include any characters except space, tab, opening square bracket ([ ), equal sign, colon, semicolon, or number sign (#) in community names. If an equal sign with no community name is appended to a community parameter, any community name is a match for the community parameter specified. By default, the monitor and trap community names are "public". By default, the control community is disabled.

SNMP traps can be sent to our IntranetWare server from any SNMP agent on the network. Before an IntranetWare server can accept SNMP and read trap messages you must load the SNMP trap logger, SNMPLOG.NLM, on the server, then open the SNMPLOG file from TCPCON. SNMP trap messages report the significant TCP/IP events that occurred on the agent. Once SNMPLOG.NLM is loaded, SNMPLOG processes trap messages sent to the NetWare TCP/IP server, then SNMPLOG writes trap messages to the binary files SYS: ETC\SNMP$LOG.BIN on disk. You may load SNMPLOG.NLM after loading TCPIP using the command LOAD SNMPLOG to load the SNMP trap logger. This command may be included in the AUTOEXEC.NFC file to auto-enable the trap logger.

The SNMP manager saves the SNMP traps received in the SYS: ETC\SNMP$LOG.BIN file. The trap log file is in binary format. You may select "Display Local Traps" from the main menu of TCPCON to view trap messages. Trap messages appear in reverse chronological order with the most recent entry first. You may press the <Esc> key to return to the main menu of TCPCON. Before returning to the main menu, we will be asked if we wish to delete the trap file. It is always a good idea to delete the file frequently because it can become quite large.

You may load INETCFG.NLM to carry out tasks, such as defining community names, or targeting managers for SNMP traps.

- Defining community names—You may select "Configure SNMP Parameters" from the "Manage Configuration" menu of INETCFG.NLM to configure the community names on the IntranetWare server. The control and monitor communities can be configured in one of the following ways:

a) Any community may access the information base.
b) No community may access the information base.
c) Only a specified community can access the information base.
d) The currently configured communities can continue to access the MIB.

• Targeting SNMP traps—You must specify where the trap messages should be sent if you have configured your server to transmit trap messages. By default, the traps are sent to 127.0.0.1, your local system. You may select "TCP/IP" from the "Protocol Configuration" menu of INETCFG.NLM to specify the SNMP managers that are targeted for SNMP traps. You may select "SNMP Managers Table" to declare the target SNMP managers. The IntranetWare server, or SNMP agent, will send SNMP traps to the specified SNMP managers when the IP protocol is bound to a network interface, the IP Protocol is unbound from a network interface, or the loss of an Exterior Gateway Protocol (EGP) neighbor is detected.

You may use the SNMP manager to perform tasks such as loading TCPCON.NLM, the SNMP manager implementation on NetWare server; configuring SNMP access; accessing MIB objects; or accessing MIB trap objects. You may modify some of the IntranetWare server configuration by loading TCPCON.NLM or INETCFG.NLM on your NetWare server. Changes made from INETCFG do not take effect until the server is restarted. Changes made from TCPCON take effect immediately, but do not affect the default configuration of our server when it is restarted.

You may load TCPCON.NLM on our NetWare server to query the MIB of any SNMP agent or TCP/IP host that supports the SNMP protocol. You may also use TCPCON to examine the contents of the trap log maintained by SNMPLOG. You may load TCPCON.NLM after TCPIP.NLM to monitor TCP/IP operations. TCPCON allows an IntranetWare TCP/IP server to function as an SNMP manager. You may use the command Load TCPCON [target][options...], where [options] are community names, or the command Load TCPCON sales community = secret.

You may load TCPCON.NLM with options that include the target host and the community name that accompany each request to the SNMP agent. The option "Target" with the default of "Loopback" specifies the target SNMP agent by its symbolic name or IP address. The option "Community=" with the default of "public" specifies the community name to be included with each SNMP request.

The interface to TCPCON.NLM is similar to the interface to INETCFG.NLM. The TCPCON main menu displays information about the target host and offers a menu for further actions. The main screen summarizes the information about the target host, such as target host name or IP address, target host uptime, target host system descriptions, IP transmit and receive counts, IP packets forwarded, and TCP transmit and receive counts.

Additional information can be displayed by selecting the following menu selections:

Available Options	Description
SNMP Access Configuration	Specifies the name or IP address of the remote SNMP agent, the transport protocol, and the community name that accompanies each query to the agent.
Protocol Information	Allows you to view and change the parameters controlling TCP/IP protocols.
IP Routing Table	Allows you to view and modify the system's routines.
Statistics	Allows you to view the statistics relating to the TCP/IP protocols.
Interfaces	Allows you to view the information about the network interfaces configured on the server.
Display Local Traps	Displays traps.

By default, you may access the MIB on the local server after TCPCON is loaded. You may use TCPCON to access the MIB on any SNMP agent. After selecting the "SNMP Access Configuration" option from the main menu of TCPCON, you may modify the following SNMP access parameters:

Parameter	Description
Transport protocol:	This is the transport protocol used to reach the remote host. Select IPX to access any remote NetWare server, or TCP/IP to access any TCP/IP system.
Host:	This is the name or address of the remote host. Press <Insert> to display a host table or a list of servers on the internetwork.
Community Name:	This is the community name. The remote agent uses this name to authenticate the request.
Timeout:	This specifies how long TCPCON should wait for a reply from the agent.
Poll Interval:	This specifies how often to query the agent for updating the TCPCON screen. Enter 0 to access the system as frequently as possible.

Before we can modify a MIB object on an SNMP agent, the MIB object must be configured as read-write on the remote agent. You may configure write access for SNMP agents running on Novell products as follows:

Product	Procedure
NetWare 4 Servers	Set the Monitor and Control community names within INETCFG.NLM.
Lan WorkPlace	Load SNMP.EXE to provide read access to the MIB
Lan WorkGroup	Set community names in the NET.CFG file following the PROTOCOL SNMP statement.
UnixWare	Configure read-write access by editing the /etc/netmgt/snmpd.comm.file. Display the contents of the file for more information.

TCP/IP has a menu offering a choice of the following tables:

TCP/IP Tables	Description
Address Translation Table	Contains IP addresses and associated hardware addresses of the hosts. TCP/IP uses ARP to map an IP address to the hardware, or MAC, address.
Interface Table	Lists the interface type, interface number, hardware address, and the statistics for each LAN driver installed on the target host.
Local IP Address Table	Lists the local IP addresses of the selected hosts.
Routing Table	Lists routes known to the selected TCP/IP host.
TCP Connection Table	Lists TCP connections maintained by the selected TCP/IP host. Each TCP connection entry consists of a local host, source port, remote host, destination port, and connection state.

Following are keys commonly used in manipulating TCP/IP tables:

Command	Description
Up arrow	Moves the cursor up.
Down arrow	Moves the cursor down.
Enter	Selects or modifies the highlighted field.
F1	Help
INS	Adds an entry field.
DEL	Removes the highlighted entry from the table.
TAB	Toggles display of hosts between symbolic name and dotted decimal notion.

From TCPCON, you may select table entries for detailed information. A colon (:) following an object name identifies that object as read only; a colon/period (:.) combination following the object indicates that the object may be modified. Modifying a field also requires the appropriate SNMP community name.

Some of the tables, such as the routing table or ARP table, reference an interface number. You can determine which interface on the server is being referenced by selecting Interfaces from the main menu of TCPCON. In IntranetWare servers, separate entries in the interface table are displayed for each frame type that is supported on the network board.

You may use an SNMP manager, or TCPCON, to diagnose and correct some common IP internetwork problems on an SNMP agent, such as enabling or disabling a network interface, resetting a TCP connection, enabling or disabling routing, or modifying a MIB table object such as the contents of the routing or ARP table.

Suppose that several users are complaining that their workstations hang whenever they attempt to access one of the NFS servers on a remote network. You suspect that there is a problem with one of the interfaces on a router and want to bring the interface down until the interface can be checked or the phone company can repair the line. To accomplish this, we may work through the following steps:

a) Check the error count for the interface on the router. Select each interface from the interface table of TCPCON to view the statistics.
b) Bring the interface down. After determining which of the interfaces is reporting the error messages, we may select the "Administrative Status" option to bring the interface down.
c) Bring the interface up. After the line is repaired, we may select the "Administrative Status" option to bring the interface back up.

Suppose that an unknown host has established an FTP connection with a server on your network. You must determine the IP address of the intruder, then disable the corporate router until an appropriate filter can be applied to incoming traffic. To accomplish this, we may work through the following steps:

a) Use TCPCON to query the FTP server. Select "TCP Connections" from the TCP protocol information screen to display the connections. Press <Delete> to reset the connection.
b) Terminate the connection. The connection table shows the IP address of the intruder, Pluto. You may then write down the IP address of the intruder. Select the intruder connection, then press <Delete> to reset the connection.
c) Disable the router. To prevent the intruder from reestablishing contact with the server, we may use TCPCON to query the router to the outside world. You may set "IP Packet Forwarding" to " End Node" in the IP Protocol Information screen to disable the router. This does not affect any other services offered.
d) Enable the router. After configuring the IP packet filtering on the router, we may set "IP Packet Forwarding" to "Router" in the IP Protocol Information screen to enable the router.

Suppose that a user is no longer able to maintain a Telnet connection with a UNIX host on the network, but the other workstations are able to establish Telnet sessions to the host. You may have a duplicate IP address for two workstations. To eliminate this problem, you may work through the following steps:

a) Using TCPCON to examine the ARP table of the Telnet server, you may select the "IP Address Translations" option from the IP Protocol Information screen to display the ARP table.
b) Correct the ARP entry. After verifying that the ARP entry is incorrect, you may edit the entry by entering the correct hardware address and specifying the entry as static.
c) Remove the entry. You may remove the entry later after locating the incorrectly configured machine.

10.5 CONFIGURING AND MANAGING IP INTERNETWORKS

There are four types of devices for connecting network segments and/or subnetworks.

No	OSI Layer	Device	Responsible Task
7	Application	Gateway	Used to connect networks that use different protocols above the network layer. They can be standalone, box-level products. Gateways are complex, very capable, and relatively slow. A gateway translatesbetween two separate protocols. You need to use a gateway if you need to transfer a file from a host that understands only TCP/IP to a host that understands only IPX/SPX. Like a router, a gateway supports only specific protocols. You must configure a gateway for each protocol that it supports. In addition, gateways may not be able to translate all upper-level protocols but only a limited number, such as a terminal emulation, file transfer, or electronic mail.
6	Presentation	Gateway	
5	Session	Gateway	
4	Transport	Gateway	
3	Network	Router	Used to connect two subnets at the network layer. A router can bridge at the data link layer also. Routers work at the network layer of the OSI model. Routers have multiple network boards, each connected to a separate network. Each network interface must be configured with an IP address and subject mask. Routers can connect networks of different topologies, e.g., Ethernet-to-token-ring. Routers filter internetwork traffic based on the logical address or software address. A router processes only those packets addressed specifically to it. When a router receives a packet from a network interface that is intended for a remote network, it forwards the message to the intended recipient or to another router. Gateways support all transport protocols, such as TCP/IP, DECnet, AppleTalk, NetWare, etc. But, routers are protocol specific.You must configure a router for each protocol that it supports. Packets may pass through a router only if the protocol is supported on the router. Routers have access to information from the following three lower OSI layers: the physical layer; the data link layer with the physical address, or hardware address information; and the network layer with the logical network address, or software address information. Routers can calculate the best path through an internetwork based on the least number of hops on the

way to the destination and the least amount of transmit time. Routers require greater intelligence than bridges to direct a packet to its correct destination. Hence, routers tend to have a lower throughput than bridges. The most efficient routers can process up to 100,000 packets/second.

| 2 | Data link | Bridge | Bridges can filter network traffic by station hardware address. Hence, you may use bridges to divide a busy network into segments, or to connect two segments at the data link layer. There are two kinds of bridges: transparent or spanning tree bridges; and source routing bridges, found mostly in IBM networks. Bridges work at the data link layer of the OSI model. Bridges can connect different segments of the same network but can connect segments with the same topology only, i.e., Ethernet to Ethernet. They support all transport protocols, such as TCP/IP, DECnet, AppleTalk, NetWare, etc. Bridges can filter network traffic to a new segment based on the hardware address. A bridge contains a table of hardware addresses for each segment of the network. They have no software address and are invisible to the network. Bridges effectively isolate traffic and increase network performance by: |

a) Receiving all data on segment A.
b) Dropping all packets addressed to nodes on segment A.
c) Retransmitting all the other packets out to the appropriate line.
d) Doing the same functions for data on other connected segments.

Bridges generally have a high throughput: they may process up to 1 Mega packet/second.

| 1 | Physical | Repeater | You may use repeaters to extend the network cable length. The repeater reproduces and retransmits the signal by stripping out and saving the received digital data, then reconstructing and retransmitting the signal. Repeaters work at the physical layer of the OSI model. They connect different segments of the same network. Repeaters can connect segments with the same topology only, i.e., Ethernet to Ethernet. As electrical signals travel across a medium, they begin to fade or attenuate. A repeater picks up a signal on one segment and retransmits it to another. Repeaters are protocol independent and are not aware of the upper-level protocols. Repeaters require no software configuration |

You may use the following simple case to understand how routing is performed on a IP network:

Process	Description
Request to send message	A local host, A, wants to send a message to a remote host, B.
Get IP address of the destination	The IP address of the destination host, B, is obtained using DNS, NIS, or the local host.
Add IP header to the message	The IP protocol attaches an IP header to the message. The source and destination fields of the IP header contain the IP address of the local host, Spain, as the source address, and the IP address of the remote host, B, as the destination address.
Decide which router to use	The network address of the local host is compared with the destination to determine whether the remote host is on the local LAN segment. IntranetWare decides that the destination is on a remote network. Hence, the request must be sent to a router to reach its destination. To determine the router to be used IntranetWare then checks the router table. The router table contains a list of remote networks and/or hosts and the appropriate router to use for that destination. Every host must have a routing table that contains, at the very least, the address of a default router.
Get MAC address of the router	At the host access layer, the frame must be addressed to a host on the local segment. The ARP (Address Resolution Protocol) is used on broadcast networks to translate an IP address to a MAC address. It uses ARP to broadcast a packet over the LAN segment requesting the MAC address associated with the IP address of the router. The router replies by sending its MAC address back to the requestor.
Send frame to the router	The local host creates a MAC frame to be forwarded to the router. The hardware address of a local host is the source address. The hardware address of the router is the destination address. The frame is then sent directly to the router and passed to the IP.
Router examines the frame	The router receives the packet from the source and examines the IP header of the frame to determine the packet's final destination. The router compares the destination IP address with the addresses of its interfaces and notes that the final destination is on a directly connected network.
Router creates a new frame	The hardware address of B is obtained from the ARP protocol. The router creates a new MAC frame to be forwarded to B. The hardware address of the router is the source address, and the hardware address of B is the destination address. The source and destination fields of the IP header contain the IP address of the local host, A, as the source address and the IP address of the remote host, B, as the destination address.
Send frame to the destination	The packet is transmitted to its final destination by the router.

B may use the same processes to send acknowledgement to A.

As the network expands, we will need to access resources on remote networks. All IP hosts maintain a routing table to enable communication with remote networks. You may load TCPCON.NLM to add, remove, or modify IP routes on your NetWare server. The routing table plays an important function in connecting your system to a remote network. IntranetWare uses the routing table to determine where to send packets. A routing table must be maintained on every host and router on the internetwork. On most IP machines, the routing table is maintained in RAM. The optimal route between any two given hosts can change frequently due to network loads, routers that go off-line, or other changes in the internetwork.

The server must be able to adjust its routing table to reflect these changes. Routes can be entered manually into the routing table or entered automatically by IP routing protocols. You may load TCPCON.NLM on the IntranetWare server to view the routing table of any SNMP agent. The routing table contains entries to remote networks specifying the routers for reaching those networks. Each router table entry contains:

Field	Description
Destination	Host or network displayed as either a name or IP address. The destination 0.0.0.0. denotes the default router
Next Hop	The host name or IP address of the router to be used to reach the destination host or network.
Type	Direct or remote. The local segment to which the host is attached is a direct connection. Destinations that require forwarding through a router appear as remote.
Cost	Metric defining the cost of sending a packet to a destination. Normally, the cost represents the number of routes, or hop count, for a packet to reach its final destination. You may assign a higher cost to an interface to discourage its use.
Interface	Which NIC on the local host must be used to reach the destination. You may use TCPCON to find the number in the interface table.

The MIB II specifications offer additional information for a routing table entry. This MIB II information can be seen on the IP Route Information form. The additional information in the IP Route information form is described as follows:

Parameter	Description
Mask	A subnet can be associated with a destination. This parameter allows for variable length subnet masks within your network.
Protocol	Indicates how the host learned of this route. The "netmgmt" in this field indicates that this entry was entered using TCPCON or any other SNMP manager. Routes can also be learned from ICMP, RIP, or EGP on a NetWare server.
Age	Time since this route was last updated or verified.

Metric 2	Some routing protocols use secondary metrics to select the shortest path
Metric 3	among multiple routers advertising the same destination and cost.
Metric 4	This parameter should be set to −1 if it is not used.

IP routes can be entered into the routing table in either static routing or dynamic routing.

a) Static routing—You may configure a routing table manually if your network has a limited number of routers. Static routes do not change and should only be used when remote destinations can only be reached through a single router. Remember that static routing does not keep up with dynamic changes to the internetwork.

b) Dynamic routing— Dynamic routes are entered into a routing table automatically using information obtained from one or more routing protocols. Routing protocols are designed to adjust quickly to changing network conditions to maintain the shortest route to any destination. IntranetWare servers support protocols such as ICMP (Internet Control Message Protocol), RIP and RIP II (Routing Information Protocol), OSPF (Open Shortest Path First), and EGP(Exterior Gateway Protocol).

You may load INETCFG.NLM to enter static routes into the routing table of your NetWare server. To configure a static route, we may first select "Protocol" then "TCP/IP" from the main menu of INETCFG.NLM.

a) Set Static Routing to Enabled. You may then enter the static routes.
b) Display the Static Routing table.
c) Insert or select a static route to configure. Select an existing route or press <Insert> to display the static route configuration form.
d) Configure the static route. Enter the name or IP addresses of the destination and associated router. Modify other parameters as necessary.
e) Escape from the static routing table to update the database.
f) Load the database. Enter the command LOAD IPCONFIG at the system console to load the database into the system.

It is not necessary to create a separate routing table entry for every remote network. If there is a default routing entry in the routing table, then packets destined for networks not specifically listed in the routing table are forwarded to the default router. You may configure a default router by creating a routing entry using 0.0.0.0 as a destination.

Before a host can send packets beyond the local network, it must learn the address of at least one router on the network. IP routing has been designed to provide a means to communicate routing information among routers and hosts within the internetwork. IP routing protocols maintain routing tables by discovering routes to remote destinations, and they advertise routes and their costs to other routers and hosts.

The IntranetWare server supports dynamic IP routing protocols, such as, RIP, Routing Information Protocol Versions I and II, OSPF, and EGP. The IntranetWare server may enter routes dynamically using protocols such as ICMP (Internet Control Message Protocol), distance vector routing protocols, or link state routing protocols.

Routes may be automatically added to the routing table by ICMP. The IntranetWare TCP/IP transport supports ICMP and no configuration is necessary. Routers often use ICMP to communicate error messages to other hosts and routes. The IntranetWare TCP/IP sends an ICMP message when:

a) A packet cannot reach its destination.
b) A packet's TTL (time to live) has expired.
c) There is a problem with a parameter within the IP header.
d) A router does not have enough buffer space to store the packet or cannot keep up with the packets.
e) The router advises a host of a shorter route to a destination.
f) A host sends an echo packet to determine if another host is alive.
g) A host needs to determine to which network it is attached.

Hence, ICMP messages provide a dynamic means to keep a routing table up to date.

- Using ICMP router discovery—ICMP implementation on NetWare supports router advertisements and solicitations. An IntranetWare server can transmit a multicast packet (244.0.0.2) over the network asking neighboring routers to identify themselves when it first starts up. All routers supporting OSPF router discovery read the packet. Routers attached to the network respond by sending their addresses to the server. Router discovery is not a router. Router discovery only allows the host to discover neighboring routers. Router discovery does not provide information about the best router to use to reach a particular destination. If a host chooses the incorrect router to reach a destination, it receives an ICMP redirect from that router identifying a better one.

- Configuring ICMP router discovery on an IntranetWare server—You may configure an IntranetWare server to use ICMP router discovery packets when we bind the TCP/IP stack to a network interface using INETCFG.NLM. Select "Router Discovery Option" from the list of expert TCP/IP LAN options. You should enable ICMP router discovery only if the routers on the segment support it. You must enable ICMP router discovery separately for each network interface.

By using distance vector routing, routers keep each other informed of known destinations. When a router starts, it requests the contents of other routing tables on the network. This information includes a destination and a metric for each route. The metric indicates the cost of the route. The router determines the shortest path to each destination by selecting the route with the smallest metric and fills its routing table accordingly. The router then periodically (every 30 seconds) informs other hosts of all the destinations it knows and how many hops it will take to get to each one. For example, routers A, B, and C connect LAN 1, LAN 2, and LAN 3. Router B broadcasts over LAN 2 that it is one hop from LAN 1. Router C, hearing this, then broadcasts to LAN 3 that it is two hops from LAN 2. Hosts on LAN 3 also hear router A advertise that it is two hops from LAN 1, and they route all packets to LAN 1 through router A because it advertises the route with a lower metric. While the metric usually represents a hop count, routers can advertise higher metrics to discourage other routers from using an expensive phone line or a slow asynchronous link.

On the IP networks, the RIP and RIP II protocols perform vector distance routing. RIP is an acronym for Routing Information Protocol. The cost associated with each route is a metric between 1 and 16. A route with a cost of 16 is considered to be unreachable or infinite. The original RIP specifications were minimal. The protocol has been updated to RIP II to provide additional support for the following:

Parameter	Description
Authentication	A password can be used for authentication.
Subnet masks	A subnet mask can be associated with each destination to allow variable-length subnet masks within an internet. This increases the number of hosts or subnets that are possible on Internet.
Next Hop Addresses	The IP address of the router that should be used to reach each destination. This prevents packets from being forwarded through extra routers on the system.
Multicast Packets	Used to reduce the load on the host not listening to RIP II packets. The IP multicast address for RIP II packets is 224.0.0.9.

To configure RIP on a NetWare server, you must do the following:

a) Enable the TCP/IP stacks to send and receive RIP packets. Load INETCFG.NLM on the server to enable the TCP/IP protocol stacks.
b) Configure RIP options for each interface that TCP/IP has been bound to.
c) Configure TCP/IP to send and receive RIP packets. RIP is enabled from the TCP/IP protocol configuration form within INETCFG.NLM. We must set RIP to "Enabled" to allow the protocol stack to send and receive RIP packets.
d) Configuring RIP options for each interface. Once RIP has been enabled for the TCP/IP protocol stack, we need to configure the options for each network interface on the server. The RIP options for each interface are configured from INETCFG.NLM. Selecting Expert TCP/IP Bind Options from a bound interface accesses the RIP Bind Options menu. We must set "Status" to "Enabled" to allow the interface to send and receive RIP packets.

The following two options are commonly used to handle the convergence process on internetworks using RIP:

Options	Description
Poison Reverse	Poison Reverse enabled. Destinations will be advertised with a cost of 16 (infinity or unreachable) from the interface from which they were learned. Reduces the time required for convergence on RIP internetworks. This increases the amount of RIP traffic on the network.
Split Horizon	Poison Reverse disabled. Destinations will not be advertised from the interface from which they were learned.

We may use "RIP Mode" to configure an interface for the following modes:

Option	Description
RIP I	RIP I is the standard that is supported on most routers and end nodes.
RIP II	RIP II is an enhanced version of RIP that includes the subnet mask in the routing information and supports variable-length subnets.
RIP I and RIP II	
Send Only	Causes routers to broadcast RIP packets describing the routing table. Incoming RIP information, however, is discarded. This mode is useful if the routers are using OSPF routing throughout the internetwork and you want to distribute routing information to end nodes on your network that do not support OSPF.

You must make sure that the mode you configure is compatible with all implementations of RIP on your network. You may use "Neighbor List" to enter IP addresses of the routers to receive routing information from your server on networks that do not support broadcast messages, such as an X.25 Public Data Network (PDN), or a network using frame relay. The neighbors must be on the network connected to this interface.

Link-state routers build their own route tables on "first-hand" information. Instead of broadcasting a packet containing an entire routing table, a link-state router only distributes information about its directly connected interfaces and their costs. Each router constructs a database representing a map of the internetwork based on the link-state information it obtains from other routers. When it is detected that the state of a router's interface has changed, the information is distributed to all the other routers through a process called flooding and each router's database is updated. OSPF protocol is a link-state protocol most commonly used on IP internetworks. Each OSPF router maintains a topological database of the internetwork. This database is constructed from the link-state information distributed by each router. From the database, each router constructs a shortest path tree to each internetwork destination.

OSPF is considered to be a superior routing protocol to RIP for the following reasons:

a) Support for large internetworks. OSPF can support larger internetworks than the RIP protocol. RIP cannot route a packet through more than 15 routers. An OSPF metric can be as great as 65,535.

b) Variable-length subnetting. LSAs (Link-State Advertisements) include subnet mask information about networks. You may then use a different subnet mask for each segment of the network. This increases the number of subnets and hosts that are possible for a single network address.

c) Rapid convergence. OSPF networks may detect internetwork changes and calculate new routes quickly. The period of convergence is brief and involves a minimum of routing traffic. The count to infinity problem does not occur on an OSPF internetwork.

d) Reduced internetwork traffic. Less internetwork traffic is generated by OSPF. RIP requires that each router broadcast its entire database every 30 seconds. OSPF routers, on the other hand, resynchronize their database every 30 minutes. When a change to the network occurs, such as a router failure or a new network link, the information is sent quickly to every router in the internetwork using LSAs. The packets containing the LSAs are small. Flooding is the process of distributing the information through the internetwork.

Before configuring the IntranetWare server as an OSPF router, it is important to understand the following terms relating to OSPF:

Term	Description
AS	An AS, Autonomous System, is a group of routers exchanging routing information using a common routing protocol, such as the OSPF protocol.
Area	An area is a contiguous network within a large enterprise internetwork. For small or medium size networks, distributing LSAs throughout the internetwork and maintaining topological databases at each router is not a problem. When the internetwork grows to a size that includes hundreds of routers, maintaining the topological database can require several megabytes of RAM for storage. With a large database, additional time is also required to recompute new routers each time a router interface goes up or down. Large internetworks are logically divided into smaller contiguous networks, called areas. An area usually corresponds to an administrative domain such as a department, a building, or a geographic site. OSPF routers within an area are not required to maintain a link-state database that includes routers and networks of other areas. When an interface is added to the area, LSAs only flood the local area. This reduces the number of LSAs that must be sent throughout the internetwork, the size of the topological database on each router, and the amount of time required to recompute routes when changes are made to the internetwork.
Backbone	OSPF areas are connected in a hierarchical manner. A backbone is a special area that is directly connected to all other areas.
ASBR	An ASBR, Autonomous System Border Router, is a router that connects a corporate network to the Internet, and it exchanges routing information with routers belonging to other ASs. The ASBR has access to corporate network and

	Internet routing information using the EGP, Exterior Gateway Protocol. ASBRs distribute external destinations routing data to the AS using external link.
ABR	An ABR, Area Boundary Router, is a router that attaches an area to the backbone, exchanges information about the area with the backbone, and provides routing data about the rest of the network to the area routers.
Stub area	A stub area contains only one ABR. There cannot be an ASBR within a stub area. The ABR advertises itself as the default router to all external destinations. All routes to destinations outside of the area must pass through this ABR. This reduces the bandwidth and the size of area topological databases.
Transit area	Areas containing more than one ABR are transit areas.

To configure on the NetWare server, we must load INETCFG.NLM to do the following:

a) Enabling OSPF. You must enable "OSPF" from the TCP/IP Protocol Configuration menu of INETCFG. By default, OSPF is disabled. You should also enable IP packet forwarding.

b) Configuring ASBRs. Select "OSPF Configuration" from the TCP/IP Protocol Configuration menu to do this. You must enable the "Autonomous System Boundary Router" option to have the router add routes learned from sources, such as RIP, EGP, or static routes to the OSPF database. An ASBR router can be any router on the backbone or within a transmit area.

c) Configuring areas within the AS. You must assign a unique four-byte address to each area within the AS. The address, while in the same format as a host IP address, does not need to correspond within any IP address used on your network. If the AS is divided into areas based upon a network address, it would be logical to use the network address as the address of the area. The backbone of the AS must use the 0.0.0.0 address. You must configure all the OSPF areas that are connected directly to the router by selecting "OSPF Configuration" – "Area Configuration" from the TCP/IP configuration form. When defining an area, enter the following information for the area:

Parameter	Description
Area ID	Enter the unique four-byte ID for the area.
Authentication	If enabled, routing exchanges are authenticated within the area. We must specify an authentication key when we bind OSPF to the interface.
Area Type	
Normal	Specify "normal" if the area is a transmit area. A transit area has more than one router connected to the backbone.
Stub	Specify "stub" if the area is a stub area. A stub area has only one router connected to the backbone and no ASBRs. In stub areas, the border router notifies the other routers within the area that it is the default router to the backbone and we must specify a cost for all packets routed from the backbone to the area.

d) Making sure the backbone is contiguous. When dividing the network into areas, all areas must be attached to the backbone with a router, and all areas, including the backbone, must be contiguous. You may partition the backbone if an internetwork extends to remote geographical regions. When this happens, it is necessary to create a virtual link from the backbone to the area. A virtual link is not a physical connection between the areas, and a configured link between a backbone router and a router on the remote areas. The ABRs at each end of the link treat the path as a point-to-point link. With the virtual link, the partitioned link is reunited. You may configure the virtual link from the routers at both ends of the link by selecting the OSPF Configuration option from the TCP/IP Protocol Configuration menu.

e) Binding OSPF to each interface within the AS. To configure OSPF options for a network interface, you must bind IP to the LAN or WAN board from INETCFG. View the "Expert TCP/IP Bind Options" for the interface, and select "OSPF Bind Options" to display the configuration settings for the board. You may then enter data for the following:

Parameter	Description
Status	The PSPF protocol enabled for the interface.
Cost of interface	The cost of routing a packet over the interface. Enter a higher cost to discourage the use of this interface.
Area ID	The Area ID for the area where this interface is connected.
Priority	This is a value for the priority of this router. The "Hello" protocol uses a priority value to select the designated router. The designated router for the network is responsible for advertising the network link advertisement on behalf of the network. This parameter coordinates the synchronization and dissemination of advertisements.
Authentication key	When authentication is enabled, we may enter an eight-byte text string authentication key here for the area where the interface belongs.
Hello Interval	The length of time, in seconds, between transmission of hello packets on this network interface. All routers on the network must be set to the same value.
Router Dead Interval	The length of time, in seconds, for a router to wait for a Hello packet before declaring to the internetwork that a router is down. All routers on the network or virtual link must be set to the same value.
Neighbor List	A neighbor list is required for non-broadcast networks such as frame relay, X.25, and PPP networks.

You may view SNMP MIB objects for OSPF by loading TCPCON.NLM on an IntranetWare server and then selecting "OSPF" from the "Protocol Information" menu. A brief description is displayed at the bottom of the screen when a field is highlighted. With the exception of the Autonomous System Border Protocol field, all objects are read-only. You should use INETCFG.NLM to modify the parameters for the OSPF protocol.

You may select "Link-state Database Advertisements" from the "OSPF Protocol Information" menu to view the link-state database. The database is shown in hex and is different to interpret, but you may use the 32-bit checksum to determine whether the database is identical to another router's database.

Following are the design recommendations for planning PSPF within an internetwork:

a) Large internetworks should be divided into areas. Routers only exchange link state information with other routers within the same area, with border routers providing links to other areas. If an internetwork of 250 routers is divided into 5 areas of 50 routers each, then routers can recalculate routes much more quickly since they have smaller databases to work from.

b) Select border routers carefully. Area border routers must devote additional memory and CPU cycles to maintain multiple topological databases for each area. Bottlenecks can result if a NetWare server, already burdened with a heavy demand for file and print services, is assigned the role of a border router, autonomous system boundary router, or even the role of designated router within a network.

c) Assign the proper cost to each interface. You may assign higher-cost routes based upon throughput, bandwidth, and reliability. Ultimately, OSPF selects its routes based on cost. This may assist OSPF in selecting the route that is truly the shortest path.

10.6 TUNNELING IPX OVER IP AND TCP/IP TROUBLESHOOTING

Tunneling is the process of encapsulating a packet of a different protocol. Normally, NetWare IPX packets cannot travel across an IP internetwork since IP routers do not support the IPX protocol. The IntranetWare TCP/IP server can route only IP packets and IntranetWare server can route only IPX packets. You may have two IntranetWare servers connected together at the physical layer using T1 or X.25 lines, but they will be unable to communicate with each other because they support only IP packets.

IPTUNNEL allows two or more IPX networks to exchange packets through an IP network. In an IPTUNNEL, PX packets are encapsulated within a UDP datagram. In an IPTUNNEL, RIP and SAP broadcasts are replaced by unicast packets delivered to other IPTUNNEL servers on a peer list. You may use IPTUNNEL to route IPX packets from NetWare workstations and servers over an IP internetwork by encapsulating IPX packets within IP packets. By simply adding an IP header to an IPX packet, our NetWare TCP/IP server can then send the packet to another NetWare server over an IP network. IPX uses the Open Data-link Interface (ODI) to pass packets through the IP tunnel. The IP tunnel sends each IPX packet across the IP internetwork by encapsulating it in a User Datagram Protocol, or UDP, packet.

To ensure data integrity, the IP tunnel includes a UDP checksum in each packet. The UDP checksum protects packets from damage while traveling through the internetwork. By default, the IP tunnel uses the UDP port 213 as the endpoint of communication between both ends of the tunnel. The tunneling LAN driver at the destination removes the UDP header from each arriving packet and passes it through the ODI to IPX. The IPX packet is then routed to its final destination on a NetWare LAN.IP

IP tunneling requires at least two hosts. Both hosts must be capable of encapsulating or unencapsulating IPX packets. The NetWare IP tunnel LAN driver transports IPX packets across an IP internetwork connecting two or more IntranetWare networks. The IP Tunnel LAN driver performs the same functions as any other NetWare LAN driver. The IP Tunnel internetwork is represented within the configuration as an IPX network with a logical network number, passing packets among the IPX nodes connected to it. The IP tunnel LAN on the NetWare server can work with Novell's NetWare 3.x and 4.x servers with the TCP/IP NLMs, LAN WorkPlace for DOS, Schneider & Koch's SK-IPX/IP Gateway, and Schneider & Koch's SK-IPX/IP DOS client. You may load INETCFG.NLM to configure IPTUNNEL on a NetWare 4.x server. You may edit the NET.CFG file to configure IPTUNNEL on a DOS workstation.

IntranetWare servers typically distribute routing and service information to servers by frequently broadcasting SAP and RIP information over each interface. Because of the limited broadcast facilities on the IP internetworks, the IP tunnel handles SAP and RIP broadcasts differently. When starting the IP tunnel, a list of IP addresses representing the other IP tunnels on the server reads the internetwork. These other IP tunnels are known as peers. Whenever IPX broadcasts a packet, the IP tunnel duplicates the packet and sends one copy directly to each peer.

In order for the IP tunnel to function correctly, the same group of computers should be entered into the peer list of each IP tunnel on the internetwork. Also, because of the overhead involved with using multiple unicast packets instead of a single broadcast packet, we should try to keep the size of the peer list to a minimum. You should not include LAN WorkPlace for DOS and SK-IPX/IP Gateway PCs in the peer list, since they do not need to see broadcast RIP and SAP information.

IPRELAY is a WAN driver that stimulates a collection of point-to-point PVCs, or Permanent Virtual Connections, between routers. You may use the IPRELAY driver to tunnel IPX packets over a WAN link. Please see the NetWare MultiProtocol Router 3.1 Advanced Configuration and Management Guide for information on the IPRELAY WAN driver.

NetWare/IP uses Domain SAP/RIP Servers (DSS) to maintain up-to-date routing service information for the internetwork. You may use NetWare/IP products to transport IPX packets over an IP internetwork if you need to configure several nodes as IPTUNNEL servers.

You may configure the IP tunnel LAN driver just like any typical NetWare LAN driver. You may configure IPTUNNEL on an IntranetWare server by configuring and loading the TCP/IP stack, configuring and loading the IPTUNNEL LAN driver, binding the IPX protocol stack to the IP tunnel LAN driver, and adding remote IPTNNEL servers to the peer list.

You may load and configure IPTUNNEL LAN and bind the IPX protocol stack to the driver from the INETCFG configuration module. Once INETCFG is loaded, select "Boards" from the main menu to display a list of configured boards. Press <Insert> and select IPTUNNEL from the list of available drivers. Configure IPTUNNEL and enter values in the board configuration.

The configuration parameters for the IPTUNNEL LAN driver are:

Parameter	Description
Board Name	Required. Enter the name associated with the LAN driver.
Peer IP Address	This is the IP address of the other end of the IP tunnel. Only one address can be entered here. You may add additional peers by using the command LOAD IPTUNNEL PEER = peer_address.
Local IP Address:	Enter the IP address of the local tunnel end point. This address should also be in the peer list of peer servers.
UDP Checksum:	A checksum is in the UDP header to ensure the integrity of the data. Set to "YES" to enable checksums on transmitted packets. If we want to disable this, set CHKSUM to "NO"
UDP Port:	You may specify which UDP port the IP tunnel should use. Each end of the IP tunnel should use a UDP port. By default, IntranetWare server uses port 213 IPX packets. SK-IPX/IP products use UDP port 59139 for IPX packets. Older versions (before version 3.1) of Schneider & Koch SK-IPX/IP gateways use UDP port 59139.
Comment	Enter a comment of up to 50 characters to describe the driver.

Selecting Bindings from the main menu of INETCFG.NLM performs protocol bindings. Bind IPX to IPTUNNEL as you bind IPX to any LAN interface. You must provide a logical network number for the IP internetwork connecting all the IPTUNNEL servers. The same network number must be used for all IPTUNNEL servers. After binding IPX to the IPTUNNEL driver, restart the server.

To add additional addresses to the peer list for your server, enter the command LOAD IPTUNNEL PEER=Remote_IP_address from the system console of your server. (Replace "Remote_IP_address" with the address of the remote IPTUNNEL server.) You must reenter the command for each IPTUNNEL server's SYS: SYSTEM\AUTOEXEC.NCF file to ensure that the peer list is properly configured whenever the system boots. You should make every effort to keep the peer list as short as possible. Every time an IPX packet is broadcast, the IPTUNNEL server transmits a separate packet to each host in its peer list. It is recommended that you should have no more than 10 peers for any server.

After configuring IPTUNNEL for the first time, or when troubleshooting the network, we may use system console commands to verify the configuration of the IPTUNNEL driver and binding of the IPX protocol stack.

a) To verify the configuration of IPTUNNEL on the NetWare server, we may enter the command LOAD IPTUNNEL SHOW=YES at the server console. Make sure that the remote IPTUNNEL server is configured with this local address.

b) To verify that IPX has been correctly bound to the IPTUNNEL driver, we may enter the command CONFIG.

You must configure both server and workstation so that the server can service DOS clients who can reach it only over an IP internetwork. The AUTOEXEC.NCF file for the IntranetWare TCP/IP server should contain the lines:

```
:LOAD TCPIP
:BIND IP TO NE2000 ADDR=146.57.235.78
:LOAD IPTUNNEL
:BIND IPX TO IPTUNNEL NET = 6001
```

Since there is no other IP tunnel, there is no need for the PEER parameter while loading the IPTUNNEL. LAN Workplace for DOS includes an IP tunnel driver for DOS ODI clients. The LAN Workplace for DOS IP Tunnel utility is in the directory \XLN\BIN40. To use the IPTUNNEL from a DOS workstation, you must configure the IPTUNNEL in NET.CFG and load, or execute the IPTUNNEL utility.

The LAN Workplace IP tunnel has the NET.CFG parameters Gateway, Port, and Checksum. The IPTUNNEL utility for DOS ODI workstation has the same parameters you may use for loading the IPTUNNEL driver on your IntranetWare TCP/IP server.

You must execute the DOS ODI workstation files in the order shown below to load DOS IP tunnel, and log in to the NetWare server:

Sample Command	Description
LSL	Loads the link support layer interface.
NE2000	Loads the appropriate mild, or LAN, driver.
TCPIP	Loads TCP/IP.
IPTUNNEL	Executes the IP tunnel.
IPXODI	Loads IPX.
VLM	Loads the DOS requestor.

If IPTUNNEL fails to load properly, check the configuration parameters that are displayed when the IPTUNNEL and IPXODI drivers are loaded. Make sure that IPXODI binds to the IPTUNNEL driver and not to the same Multiple Link interface Driver (MLID) that is used by the TCP/IP stack. You may use SNMP and LWPCON to list the drivers on the workstation. Make sure that the interface number for the IPTUNNEL driver is entered in the Bind IPX section of the NET.CFG file.

It is impossible to describe all the possible problems that can arise on an internetwork made up of several different applications or implementations of TCP/IP.

But, you may use the IntranetWare server as a tool to diagnose and correct the common problems occurring as the of DoD model layers The host-to-host, Internet, and physical access

You may need resources, such as network analyzers, to troubleshoot a large corporate network. But the IntranetWare server also provides you with tools such as TCPCON.NLM, which is used to view or modify MIB objects on remote IP hosts. The PING.NLM and TPING.NLM are used to send ICMP echo packets to remote hosts. You may load the two NLMs PING.NLM and TPING.NLM on an IntranetWare TCP/IP server to determine whether a physical connection exists between our server and a remote host.

If you are having trouble accessing a remote host, you should verify that the host is online. TPING.NLM sends ICMP, or Internet Control Message Protocol, echo packets to remote host. Whenever an IP host receives an ICMP echo packet, it returns the packet to the sender. It verifies that the host is online and that a physical route exists to the host. You may load TCPING to send an ICMP echo packet to a remote host by using the command LOAD TPING Host[packetsize[retrycount]], where "Host" is the host name or IP address, "packetsize" is the size of the ICMP packets, and "retrycount" is the number of ICMP packets.

PING.NLM sends ICMP echo packets continuously to the remote host. In addition to verifying that the remote host is online, PING.NLM tracks the amount of time it takes for a packet to make a round trip between the server and the remote host. PING.NLM also allows you to track several hosts concurrently. You may load PING to send ICMP echo packets continuously to a remote host by using the command LOAD PING Host, where "Host" is the host name or IP address.

You may also load TCPCON.NLM and PING.NLM to diagnose error messages such as "Network is unreachable", "Host XXX is unknown", "Connection refused", or "Request timed out". The "Network is unreachable" message appears when we are trying to connect to a host on a remote network and there is no known route to the network. Possible causes for the "Network is unreachable" problem can include an improperly configured host or host table, an improperly configured routing table on the client host, or an improperly configured or inoperable router on the internetwork.

a) Improperly configured host or host table. If both hosts are on the same LAN segment, then either the host address or subnet mask has been improperly configured on one of the machines. You should check the configuration of each host or reconfigure each host as necessary. You may then try to connect to the remote host using an IP address instead of a host name. If you are successful using an IP address, then the host table or DNS server has been incorrectly configured. We may then edit the host file or contact the administrator of the DNS server. For example, suppose there are two computers on the same LAN segment configured with different subnet masks.

NY

IP Address:155.137.223.51

Netmask:225.225.225.0

CA

IP Address:155.137.25.15

Netmask:225.225.0.0

When NY compares the IP address of CA with its subnet mask of 225.225.225.0, it determines that CA must be located on a remote network and it searches for a possible router. It finds no such router, and so it returns the "Network is unreachable" error message

b) Improperly configured routing table on the client. You may use TCPCON to examine the contents of the routing table of the client. You should add the route to the routing table if no entry exists for either the remote network or for a default router.

c) Improperly configured or inoperable router on the internetwork. It is possible that a router has gone down and a new route has not yet been computed, or that there is simply no route to the destination at the present time. You may use TCPCON to determine how a router has been configured. You may use TPING or PING to see if a router is online.

The "Host XXX is unknown" message appears as a result of entering a host name whose address cannot be found. The host you specified is not in your host table or in the DNS server. To correct the problem, you may check the spelling of the host name you entered, enter the host name in your host table, or use the IP address to connect to the remote host.

The "Connection refused" message indicates that the remote host is up but cannot service the request for a connection. Possible causes for the "Connection refused" problem can include the daemon process on the remote host is not running, or the remote server does not have the resources needed to service the request at this time. You may use TCPCON to examine the TCP connections table on the remote host.

Each daemon process is assigned a port. Common protocols and their sockets are listed in the SYS: ETC\SERVICES file. If no port is shown for the requested service, contact the remote host system administrator. If the maximum number of concurrent connections has been reached on the remote host, you must wait until another user logs off from the remote host. If several hosts are already connected to a server, a "Connection refused " message probably means the server is too busy at this time.

Possible causes for the "Request timed out" problem can include the target host is offline, or there is no route to the remote host. You may use TPING.NLM or PING.NLM to determine whether the target host is offline. If the host is running, contact the system manager of the target host.

Questions

1) List all the popular services available on the Internet.
2) List all the layers of the OSI model, and what data is called at each layer.
3) Describe the function of each layer of the OSI mode.
4) Where do the following devices operate in the OSI model? Describe the function of each.

   Gateway, repeater, bridge, router

5) List all the layers of the DoD model.
6) How does the DoD model compare to the OSI model?
7) List all the protocols in each layer of the DoD model.
8) Write down what the acronym of each protocol stands for and describe what each one is used for.
9) Given an IP address = 209.35.67.35

   a) What is the host address? _____
   b) What is the network address? _____
   c) What is its class? _____
   d) What is the default mask?_____

10) How many network and host (node) addresses can classes A, B, and C have?
11) You need a patch from Novell. What is the command to enter to get Novell's domain?
12) What is the DoD layer that routes packets between different hosts or networks?
13) Name three protocols that provide file transfer functions.
14) What TCP/IP protocol provides terminal emulation?
15) What TCP/IP protocol uses the equivalent of the transport layer of the OSI model?
16) What protocol provides connectionless delivery service of datagrams between hosts?
17) What protocol is responsible for guaranteed delivery?
18) What is the Internet layer protocol that translates IP addresses into MAC addresses?
19) What is the Internet layer protocol that translates MAC addresses to software addresses?
20) What is the DOS command on a LAN WorkPlace for DOS workstation that initiates terminal emulation session?

21) What is the correct syntax to copy a file from a remote host to the local system?
22) What contains host names, addresses, and maps, and may contain user and group information?
23) What is the address reserved for loopback?
24) What address is used to denote the local host?
25) What must you do if you were assigned one network address by the NIC?
26) You have 18 internetworks. What is the subnet mask number to allow the maximum amount of hosts per segment?
27) What two things define SNMP?
28) What is the command to use to provide read/write access to the MIB in SNMP? To provide read access?
29) What is the command used to load a static routing table into the database?
30) What is meant by cost (hops) = 16?
31) What is an OSPF containing one ABR? Containing multiple ABRs?
32) If you have a congested LAN and only one router, how would you configure it using OSPF so that Internet traffic is not routed through your site?
33) In IP tunneling, what is the command used to add additional peers?
34) Name a valid reason for the "Host XXX is unknown" problem.
35) What are the two possible causes for the "Connection refused" problem?
36) What are the two possible causes for the "Request timed out" problem?
37) What are the possible subnet values within a subnet mask that has an IP address of 130 and three masked bits (11100000) in the network address?
38) What must you do to disable a router?
39) What is the command used to set the static routing to Enabled?
40) What must you do after you configure a new board and exit INETCFG.NLM?

Index

W

WAN, 3
Wireless communication, 16
WMAIL.EXE, 222
Workstation, 1, 44, 241
WWW 354

X

X.25, 396

Z

Zero encoding, 10